"*Woman with Guitar* is not simply a carefully researched biography of Memphis Minnie, compiled from the memories of her relatives, friends, and fellow performers: it is a vivid portrait of a talented singer and guitarist. But it is much more than this. By an imaginative application of Freudian analysis, Paul and Beth Garon unpeel the layers of meaning in the themes and motifs of her lyrics. They reveal the complex personality of an assertive black woman who established her supremacy in the male-dominated field of city blues, but whose artistry was deeply rooted in African-American lore. The authors have added a new dimension to blues scholarship."

—Paul Oliver, author of *Blues Off the Record*

"*Woman with Guitar* is a delight. The book is both thorough and brilliant, a rare combination these days. It is wide ranging and supported by astonishingly diverse and wise readings into psychoanalysis, feminism, and Black studies. A fanatic interest in Minnie underpins and energizes this wonderful biography."

—David Roediger, author of *The Wages of Whiteness*

"Most impressive is the scholarship on Memphis Minnie's life and career. Captures the elusive essence of Memphis Minnie as a woman and an artist."

—Daphne Duvall Harrison, author of *Black Pearls*

Books by Paul Garon

THE DEVIL'S SON-IN-LAW: THE STORY OF
PEETIE WHEATSTRAW AND HIS SONGS

RANA MOZELLE

BLUES AND THE POETIC SPIRIT

WOMAN WITH GUITAR

Memphis Minnie's Blues

Paul and Beth Garon

DA CAPO PRESS • 1992

Library of Congress Cataloging in Publication Data

Garon, Paul.
  Woman with guitar: Memphis Minnie's blues / Paul and Beth Garon.
    p.   cm.
  Includes bibliographical references and index.
  Discography: p.
  ISBN 0-306-80460-3
  1. Memphis Minnie, 1896-1973. 2. Blues musiciansUnited StatesBiography. 3.
Memphis Minnie, 1896-1973Criticism and interpretation. 4. Blues (Music)History
and criticism. I. Garon, Beth. II. Title.
ML420.M376G4   1992
782.42'1643'092dc2092-312
[B]CIP

Photo Credits

George Adins: 31, 32, 33
Blues Unlimited: 9
Dennis Bonner: 1
Larry Cohn: 45, 46, 47, 48
Ethel Douglas: 8
Beth Garon: 36, 37, 38
Paul Garon: 6, 10, 11, 18, 26
Harry Godwin Collection: 34, 35
Daisy Johnson: 16
Daisy Johnson, Amie D'evereaux, Jim O'Neal: 15, 17, 22, 23, 24, 25, 42, 43, 44, 50
Juke Blues: 27
Don Kent and Shanachie Records: 2
Mississippi River Museum, Mud Island, Memphis: 49
Harvey Newland: 7
Paul Oliver: 5

Published by Da Capo Press, Inc.
A Subsidiary of Plenum Publishing Corporation
233 Spring Street, New York, N.Y. 10013

To Daisy Douglas Johnson and Ethel Douglas

*"I must tell the tales, sing the songs,
do the dances and repeat the raucous
sayings and doings of the Negro farthest down."*

—Zora Neale Hurston

ACKNOWLEDGMENTS

Without the help of the Pace Trust—and our friends, the trustees Laura Orr and David Orr—this book would not have been able to appear in its present form. To them we owe our greatest thanks.

The information supplied by Daisy Douglas Johnson and Ethel Douglas was crucial to our ability to sketch such a solid version of Minnie, as was that supplied by Brewer Phillips, Homesick James, Jimmy Rogers, Johnny Shines, Sunnyland Slim, Big Lucky Carter, Bill Dicey, Champion Jack Dupree, Joe Duskin, Mose Vinson and Wade Walton. What secrets would have remained hidden without the extraordinary interviewing talents of Jim O'Neal (Homesick James, Jimmy Rogers) and Steve Cushing (Brewer Phillips), we'll never know! To Jim O'Neal we owe an extra debt of thanks for combing through his numerous interview tapes and unearthing diverse and wonderful reminiscences by Blind John Davis, Memphis Slim, Sunnyland Slim, James Watt and more.

Critical assistance and advice was supplied by Georges Adins, David Evans, Don Kent, David Orr, Pam Raitz, David Roediger, Franklin Rosemont, Penelope Rosemont, Adena Siegel and Bev Zeldin. Photographs were kindly made available to us by Georges Adins, *Blues Unlimited*, Dennis Bonner, The Center for Southern Folklore, Ami D'evereaux, The Harry Godwin Collection, *Juke Blues*, Jo Ann Kelly, Harvey Newland, Nick Perls, Shanachie Records and John Summaria. Composer credits from 78 rpm issues came from our own collection and from Howard Berg, Joe Bussard, Don Kent, Mike Rowe, Russ Shor, Darryl Stolper, Sherman Tolen, Pete Whelan, Clint Wilson and Terry Zwigoff.

Various documents that appear throughout the book were supplied by the Blues Archive at the University of Mississippi, the staff at the Chicago Federation of Musicians (Local 10-208 of the American Federation of Musicians), Larry Cohn, Joel Silver and William Cagle of The Lilly Library, Paul Oliver, The Rodgers and Hammerstein Sound Archives of the New York Public Library, Sharon Howard at The Schomburg Center for Research in Black Culture, and Dick Shurman.

Indeed, we have even more to be grateful for, and we extend our heartfelt thanks to the following individuals and institutions: the Catfish Institute; Michel Chaigne; Columbia College Library; James Craddock; David R. Crippen, Curator of Automotive History, Henry Ford Museum and Greenfield Village; Norman Darwen; F. Wentworth Ford; Hugh Ford; M. Forshage; Gérard Herzhaft; Terry House; Robert G. Koester; Sam Lehman, MD; Sandra Lieb; *Living Blues*; Thomas Magee; Memphis Shelby County Public Library and Information Center, History Department, and Memphis Room; Memphis and Shelby County Film, Tape and Music Commission; Brian Myers; Hal Rammel; Mike Rowe; Neil Slaven; *Soul Bag*; Richard Spottswood; Christopher Starr; Chris Strachwitz; Charles Sweningsen; Tom Tsotsi; Ernest Virgo; John Waldrop; and Ted Watts.

Part of the chapter on "Dirt Dauber Blues" appeared earlier in *Arsenal: Surrealist Subversion 4.* (Chicago: Black Swan Press, 1989).

Technical Note

Minnie's rushed and compressed delivery presents a number of problems, not the least of which is the number of words that exist somewhere short of articulation, in the vicinity of the implicit and the suggested. Often a word like "you" is only broached with a barely detectable "y" sound, and we are faced with the choice of rendering it "you" or "y' ", or ignoring it entirely. This difficulty leads to another. Rather than print lyrics in pseudo-dialect, we have chosen not to attempt to render every aspect of Minnie's (or any singer's) accent. But this decision puts even more strain on the question of the words whose first syllable is barely articulated, if that. There is no ideal solution to this problem, but we feel our quoted texts accurately represent the songs.

We use the standard method of transcribing verses where the first two lines are alike or similar by adding a (2x) at the end of the first line, and following it with the third line thus:

I found my rooster this morning by looking at his comb. (2x)
You can look out now, pullets, it won't be long.

This method ignores the idiosyncrasies that occur between Minnie's various renderings of the same line, where line two is of the form, "awwwwww, by looking at his comb," but it is othewise textually faithful. Further, the (2x) system became an economic necessity for a book of this size. All songs appearing in the text without an author credit are by Memphis Minnie.

In all cases, "harp" refers to harmonica.

CONTENTS

Part I: THE LIFE

1. THE HEROINE 3
2. WOMAN WITH GUITAR: THE RISE OF
   MEMPHIS MINNIE 7
3. SOUTHERN NIGHTS 13
4. CHICAGO DAYS 33
5. ME AND MY CHAUFFEUR 47
6. "I DRINK ANYWHERE I PLEASE" 65
7. "THE BEST THING GOIN' " 83

Part II: THE SONGS

8. TO MAKE HEARD THE INTERIOR VOICE 91
9. BUMBLE BEE 103
10. CRIME 115
11. DIRT DAUBER BLUES 133
12. DOCTORS AND DISEASE 143
13. DOORS 163
14. DIRTY DOZENS 169
15. DUETS 177
16. FOOD AND COOKING 191
17. HORSES 199
18. TRAINS AND TRAVEL 207
19. MAD LOVE 229
20. WORK.. 239

A DISCOGRAPHY OF MEMPHIS MINNIE 257
NOTES 283
INDEX 319

Part: I
THE LIFE

1. THE HEROINE

*If women remain passive, I think there is
little hope for survival of life on this earth.*
—Leonora Carrington

Who was Memphis Minnie? She may be relatively unknown to
the general public, but among blues fans, her feats are legendary:

Memphis Minnie was one of the greatest blues singers
of all time,

said *Living Blues* magazine.[1]

In a 1973 obituary, one critic called her "the most popular female country blues singer . . . ,"[2] while *Blues Who's Who* quotes another commentator who stated,

Memphis Minnie was without doubt the greatest of all
female singers to record.[3]

She was among the first twenty performers elected to the Hall
of Fame in the inaugural W. C. Handy awards in 1980,[4] and she
won the top female vocalist award in the first *Blues Unlimited*
Readers' Poll in 1973, finishing ahead of Bessie Smith and
Ma Rainey.[5] And this wouldn't be the only time Minnie was
compared to such greats. Helen Oakley Dance ranked T-Bone
Walker "at the top . . . with ladies like Bessie Smith, Ma Rainey, Memphis Minnie. . . ."[6]

Many blues artists date an entire era in their lives by referring
to her. As Koko Taylor said, "the first blues record I ever heard

was *Me and My Chauffeur Blues,* by Memphis Minnie."[7] Hound
Dog Taylor, speaking of his early days in Chicago in 1943-1944,
noted that "47th Street was jumping on the South Side. When I
first come up Memphis Minnie was playing at the old 708 Club
with her first husband."[8] When Baby Boy Warren looked back on
the singers who influenced him the most and for whom he had
the most respect, he commented, "The other musician I admired
[besides Little Buddy Doyle] was a woman—Memphis Minnie."[9]
And Bukka White reminisced, "Memphis Minnie, Washboard Sam,
Tampa Red, Big Bill, they were my favorite 'cause they really
would knock the cover off a house. They play in the nightclubs,
would play house parties through the day. Otherwise they were
rehearsing; people would be there, as many as they would be at
the nightclub sometimes."[10]

Many people who have heard of Big Bill Broonzy or Tampa
Red still don't know much about Minnie. But her songs have been
recorded by performers as diverse as Bob Wills and His Texas Playboys, Mance Lipscomb, Muddy Waters, Clifton Chenier, and dozens of others, both obscure and well known. It would be no
exaggeration to say that Memphis Minnie was one of the most influential blues singers ever to record.[11] Few today realize how extremely popular she was, with a string of hits and nearly 100
records to her credit.[12]

Countless performers were influenced by her. Johnny Shines,
Eddie Boyd, Calvin Frazier, J. B. Hutto, Lowell Fulson and J. B.
Lenoir all testified that they derived some aspects of their style
from Memphis Minnie.[13] Of course, a list of blues artists who
played with Minnie in Chicago, not to mention those who frequently heard her and were influenced by her, would read like a
Chicago Blues Who's Who, with Big Bill, St. Louis Jimmy, Washboard Sam, Memphis Slim, Tampa Red, Black Bob, Jimmy Gordon, Blind John Davis, Charlie McCoy and Sunnyland Slim near
the top of the list and dozens more below.

The breadth of Minnie's influence is striking. When Chuck
Berry arrived in Chicago, Minnie was recording for Leonard
Chess's Checker label. Berry would soon become a Chess star, and
Minnie was an important influence on his musical development.

There are even rumors of a mysterious tape of an extended jam session involving Chuck Berry and Memphis Minnie, but Berry has kept silent about its details, refusing even to reveal when it was made or what songs it contains.[14]

Because Minnie began her recording career in 1929 and kept going for three decades, her presence was written large across the whole history of the recorded blues. Year after year, her style evolved, and by the time illness forced her to retire, she had recorded the country blues, the urban blues, the Melrose sound, the Chicago blues and the postwar blues. Nonetheless, surprisingly little documentation exists for so extensive a career. Fortunately we have the testimony of Minnie's youngest sister, Daisy Douglas Johnson. Mrs. Johnson has remarked, however, that while her information has come directly from Minnie herself, most of it was transmitted *after* Minnie had her first stroke.[15]

Many of the details of Minnie's life story that came from early reports by pioneer blues researchers Georges Adins and Mike Leadbitter remain unsubstantiated, but we do not reject them out of hand.[16] Indeed, in the absence of standard printed sources that usually provide the foundation of historical and biographical studies—in the absence, for example, of birth certificates and marriage licenses for Minnie, Joe McCoy and Ernest Lawlars (Son Joe)—and in the presence of four different dates of birth established for Minnie in various works of blues criticism,[17] our tale will be, by necessity, unorthodox and anecdotal. Nonetheless, we do provide documents rarely seen in blues biographies, e.g., union records and recording contracts.

We hope the organization of this book will present Minnie and her work in an enjoyable and readable form. Chapter 2 contains a historical overview of the development of blues during Minnie's lifetime, and how Minnie seemed to stretch the boundaries of its forms. Such a perspective is of crucial importance in understanding the unique aspects of Minnie's role and function. Chapters 3 through 7 provide a chronology of Memphis Minnie, from her birth to her death, in the words of her friends and relatives. Wherever possible, this information is supplemented by material from printed sources. Chapters 8 through 20, the *raison d'etre* of the book, attempt to view Minnie's songs as specific products of a specific cultural moment, acted upon by conflicting forces of gender, race and class. In twelve chapters, each devoted to a group of songs that bear upon a specific idea or theme, we analyze the cultural forces through which the blues, and Minnie's blues, in particular, come into being. This twelve chapters are introduced by a brief discussion of the principles of interpretation that we use throughout the analysis. Finally, we provide a thorough discography of Memphis Minnie's work, complete with Library of Congress copyright information and, where possible, composer credits taken from the labels of the records themselves.

While our main purpose is to celebrate and delineate Memphis Minnie's life and songs, we will also examine Minnie's songs as exceptional examples of the blues genre, stunning pieces that reveal not only Minnie's magnificence, but the grandeur of the blues as well. The hundreds of sides Minnie recorded are the perfect material to teach us about the blues. For the blues are at once general, and particular, speaking for millions but in a highly singular, individual voice. That is part of their magic, their art. Listening to Minnie's songs, we will hear her fantasies, her dreams, her desires, but we will hear them as if they were our own.

2. WOMAN WITH GUITAR: THE RISE OF MEMPHIS MINNIE

Knock hard. Life is deaf.
—Mimi Parent

The first blues was recorded in 1920,[1] but in the ensuing years blues performance styles on record underwent numerous modifications as they reflected the subtle changes in tastes, economic pressures, and trends in the entertainment industry. The first blues to be recorded were the "Classic" blues, and we use the terms "Classic" blues, or "vaudeville" blues, to describe that style of blues usually sung by women like Bessie Smith or Ida Cox, from a stage, and accompanied only by a male pianist or band. The songs themselves were often composed by black male songwriters, although a few of the Classic women singers, e.g. Ma Rainey, wrote a number of their own songs. Their heyday on record began in 1920 and ended with the Depression. The label "Classic" has been assailed for its unsuitability, but its detractors have not been convincing.[2] For some, there may be a reluctance to grant Classic status to a period of blues dominated by women, especially when they can point to a subsequent period that seemed to be dominated by men, but the priority on record of Classic blues, and the women who sang them, speaks for itself.[3]

Classic blues dominated the blues recording industry for five or six years, beginning in 1920, but by the mid-1920s, country blues began to appear more and more frequently in the record company catalogs. Country blues continued to be widely recorded until the Depression brought the recording industry to a near standstill in 1932-1933. By 1934, when the recording industry began to stir again, a new combo style of blues was in the air. Throughout the thirties and into the forties and fifties, blues singers on record tended to be accompanied by a piano and drums, a bass, one or two guitars, and occasional horns or harmonicas. Amplifiers for guitars became a common sight by the 1940s. While this combo style dominated the blues scene of the 1930s and 1940s, neither "urban blues," "city blues," "Chicago blues," or half a dozen other nominees, has ever become the standard term to describe the music played by these small blues groups of the thirties and forties. "Urban blues" may be the most apt and the least confusing. By the late 1940s and early 1950s, this urban style had crystalized in the hands of Muddy Waters, Howlin' Wolf and many others to produce the well-known electric sound of what came to be called the the postwar blues, or Chicago blues.

These demarcations are neither as linear nor as finely drawn as our sketch suggests, however, and last night's Classic blues queen could easily be the morning's country blues artist. Singers like Lottie Kimbrough (nee Beaman), for example, performed in both styles, with either Classic or downhome accompaniment, and many 1930s as well as postwar performances also refuse to fit the molds we've created for them. But it is important to understand these structures in order to understand how Minnie cracked them.

While the Classic blues singers were relatively sophisticated women singers who performed on the stage, the country blues artists tended to be unsophisticated males who accompanied themselves on acoustic guitars.[4] These downhome musicians played for family and friends, at home or at parties, in juke joints or at picnics and suppers. Country blues performers tended to be semi-professionals who also farmed or performed other seasonal labor in the logging industry, levee camps, turpentine camps and similar places, but the most famous performers were often able to get by on their musical skills alone.

In many ways the ascendancy of country blues seemed progressive, and a new and younger audience was quick to respond to these highly rhythmic songs. The self-accompanied country blues performer embodied a new autonomy, and for many rural record buyers, country blues on record, as well as in person, was a fascinating step into the future. This was an exciting dance music, and the couple and individual dances that listeners did to blues accompaniment represented greater individualism for blacks than the square dances which were done to pre-blues forms.[5]

That most of the guitar-playing country blues artists on record were male is of critical importance, however, for such "progress" often contains a secret: the oppression and exploitation of women. If we are inspired by Fourier's notion that the general index of emancipation is the level of the emancipation of women, we are confronted with the fact that just such moments as the "ascendancy" of country blues needs re-evaluation. Have we not already seen that there is major resistance to calling the period of female-dominated blues recording Classic, even though Classic satisfies the requirements of many defininitions of the term, and is used to describe the period that was, in fact, the blues' first heyday? In contrast, the vintage years of recorded (male) country blues, 1927-1933, are usually considered the "prime" years of blues recording. For example, in 1965 one critic gloated that country blues 78s were finally being recognized as valuable, while the previously highly-esteemed Classic blues of the vaudeville-influenced blueswomen were now being devalued.[6]

From one perspective, then, what had happened to the Classic blueswomen was not at all unusual. To hire black men to fill jobs once held by black women was consistent with sexist practices of the day and upheld the mainstream cultural notions that a woman's place was in the home, that men were better than women at most jobs, and that it was man's role to work for a living for the rest of "his" family. Further, it was a pact between males—songwriter/bandleader Perry Bradford and Okeh's Fred Hager—that allowed Mamie Smith to make her first record. While this view should not be allowed to obscure the fact that Bradford and Smith were a black team that achieved an important victory for black culture, the very fact that Smith's recording sessions had to be negotiated by Bradford supports the thesis of the pact between two males with a woman as its object.

Add to this the fact that the Classic blueswomen were being paid far more than the country blues men, and the former's disappearance from record is more easily understood. For example, at the beginning of her career with Columbia, Bessie Smith was paid $125 per usable side, the same amount she was paid during her last year with Columbia; but at her peak, she was receiving $200 per usable side. Meanwhile, Columbia's male country blues "stars" like Peg Leg Howell or Barbecue Bob received only $15 per side. Minnie and Joe were probably paid at this latter rate for their first Columbia sides, and it's doubly ironic that Minnie, who was so often said to "play like a man" was also *paid like a man* in this atypical case where women were paid more than men.[7]

But it would be a mistake to think that the men "replaced" the women, or that country blues "replaced" the Classic blues. The Depression not only ended many Classic blues careers, but it put the same final stamp on the livelihood of countless male country blues artists as well. When the economic situation began to improve, and blues singers began to return to the studios, neither Classic blues singers nor country blues artists would last very long. The artists who survived would be those of both sexes who had sufficiently urbanized their styles, or who could demonstrate the greatest affinity for the new swing-influenced rhythms.[8]

Minnie was a pioneer at precisely the time and place that all of these forces coalesced. Before attempting to understand how she survived the Depression, we must first understand how she faced it, as a self-accompanied guitarist playing country blues. Almost by default, "women's blues" has come to denote Classic, vaudeville-style blues. Minnie's fame thus fell into the gap created by the prominence of the Classic blues singers on one side and the progressive aspects of the male country blues stylists on the other. A number of women refused the Classic designation by virtue of their having seized some of the privileges customarily reserved for men. To "play as good as any man" also meant to be doing what men were supposed to be doing and what women were not supposed to be doing, for such a music style was largely confined to men, or so it has been thought. But guitar-playing women like Minnie (yes, there were others) constituted an effective link that served to give female blues singing a continuity in its leanest years. Even their number is impressive.

Many of these singers are known to us through their phonograph records: The rough-voiced Mattie Delaney; Minnie's niece, Ethel McCoy; Rose Lee Hill—all of these women accompanied themselves on guitar, as did the obscure Elvie Thomas and Geeshie Wiley, and as does Jessie Mae Hemphill today. Other female instrumentalists never recorded, and it was all too easy to read a hint or two about their existence without its ever registering in one's consciousness. For example, one writer noted that Teddy Darby had "fooled around with his mother's [guitar] . . . but had made slight progress on it at that time."[9] Nothing more is known about the guitar talents of Darby's mother, and this isn't the only enticing reference of this kind. McKinley James, Robert Shaw, Louis Myers, J. B. Lenoir, and Tommie Lee Russell all had guitar-playing mothers![10] In sum, while dozens of female performers gained a reputation as blues singers on the vaudeville stage in the early twenties, the later twenties saw the rise in popularity of the self-accompanied, downhome male blues singer. Hidden by this schematic, however, were a number of women who performed in a rural style, and accompanied themselves on guitar. How well hidden they were can be seen from this comment by bluesman James Watt, when asked about Minnie's same-sex competitors. "There was only Memphis Minnie. There wasn't too many girl blues singers out."[11]

Thus there was a significant current of women country blues performers, hidden from us through the traditional manipulation of "opposing" categories like male/female, urban/rural, downhome/city.[12] What was also hidden was the degree to which this performance style embodied, for the blueswoman, a real gain in autonomy and independence, usually reserved for male artists. Even the most pragmatic assessment reveals considerable personal benefit.

For example, much glamour was attached to the role of blues singer, regardless of how and where it was fulfilled. The wages of even the lower paying music jobs were considerably in excess of the pitiful amounts paid to women in agriculture and domestic service or the lowest level factory work open to poor and under-educated black women. And blues singing was far easier than back breaking work like picking cotton.[13] We will see that it was this latter task that Minnie would do anything to avoid. What made her so unusual was that she *could* do something.

Performance at picnics, suppers and juke joints also enabled her to establish an intimacy with her audience that the stage-bound vaudvillians never had. Further, Minnie wrote much of her own material. This not only enabled her to avoid the pressure and management of the often exploitative male songwriters, but it reinforced her own imaginative committment to her songs. She was also her own manager, a gratifying role for such an obviously independent woman. Finally, Minnie played the lead guitar of her partnerships and performed more lead and solo vocals than did her partners. She also released more single records than her partner(s) or husbands. All of these factors combined to make it possible for Minnie to assume a musical identity that before her time had been achieved mostly by males. And there is considerable evidence that Minnie was acutely aware of the unusual aspects of the life she chose to live.

3. SOUTHERN NIGHTS

I want to be the opening act
between this planet and the sun.
—Jayne Cortez

In 1904, Memphis Minnie's family moved from Algiers, Louisiana, located right across the Mississippi River from New Orleans, to Walls, Mississippi, just outside Memphis, Tennessee. Nearly a century later, you could stand on the railroad tracks in Walls, and with your face turned to the west, look out over dusty farmlands that had changed little in the last hundred years. That the view to the east was dissimilar and a bit more modern gave you the eerie feeling that for just the moment of your standing there, you actually *embodied,* in a symbolic way to be sure, part of the history of Memphis Minnie. For the drama that began there and unfolded in Chicago and Memphis and all points in between, and that finally played itself out in Memphis, never freed itself from the critical crossing of the modern with the old, the city with the country, the urban with the rural. Within the nexus of these contradictory and opposing forces, and probably rarely at peace, Memphis Minnie sang her blues.

It is tempting to believe that Minnie had one idea in mind almost from the day she was born: To leave the farm and go to town, to leave the site of backbreaking labor and meager wages for the land of good times and loud music: Memphis, Tennessee. Decades later, after Memphis seemed no longer misty and far away, Chicago became the far-off land, and she soon conquered it as well. Indeed, the tension between her distaste for farm work and her desire for a active musician's career may have been the prime source of energy that carried her through life. We would not be surprised to learn that the unconscious vicissitudes of these forces drew her back to Memphis from the North, again and again, just as it sent her North at the start, and just as it set her out on the road, time after time. But before we begin to follow the way-ward path of these currents, let us go back to the beginning, in southern Louisiana.

Minnie was born in Algiers (Orleans parish), Louisiana, on June 3, 1897.[1] She was the oldest of the thirteen Douglas children. Daisy Douglas Johnson, Minnie's only surviving sister and an important informant for this work, was the youngest.[2] Minnie's father was Abe Douglas and her mother was Gertrude Wells Douglas. Abe was a sharecropper all his life, and his level of education, as well as that of his wife, is unknown. There were nine children who grew to adulthood and four who died young. The brothers Willie, Leo, Miller and Jack all did factory work, while Edward worked for the city of Memphis and Hun was a minister. A sister, Dovie, died in 1941. Minnie's given name was Lizzie Douglas, although the family always called her "Kid," and "Kid" Douglas is how she was first known in the music world. "She never liked 'Lizzie' ," Daisy said, "she never would use that name." Ultimately, "Kid" Douglas be-came known to the world as "Memphis Minnie," the name she used on nearly all of her records and in her personal and profes-sional life as well. At home, she was still called "Kid," but everyone in the world outside called her "Minnie" or "Memphis Minnie." A few of her colleagues even referred to her as "Memphis."

The family moved to Walls around 1904. No one knows exactly how far Minnie got in school, but she was just able to read and write.[3] At the time, this hardly seemed to be a handicap; Minnie was a wild youngster who never took to the farming life and she ran away from home at an early age. Her first guitar had been a Christmas present given to her in 1905, a significant event for a talented musician like Minnie. Indeed, such individuals frequently report that in their childhoods, they had "music in their head all the time," and it is for precisely these people that the "first instru-ment" has such totemic significance.[4] For Minnie, musical instruments only intensified her desire to leave home. She began to run away to Memphis' Beale Street with some regularity. When times were tough and nickels and dimes were hard to find, she returned to the farm to live, but rarely to work.[5]

Traveling with a show was one way to gain experience, and Minnie toured the South in the war years with a Ringling Brothers show she joined in Clarksdale, Mississippi.[6] "She was a showman," said James Watt, "a showman all the way. She'd stand up out of that chair, she'd take that guitar and put it all 'cross her head and everywhere, you know."[7] Minnie was to become an expert and professional entertainer, but the lessons were not easily learned. A young girl in a traveling show needed more than psychic defenses, and this rugged way of life gave her valuable experience not only as a polished professional, but as a woman who could take care of herself. Johnny Shines recalled, "Any men fool with her she'd go for them right away. She didn't take no foolishness off them. Guitar, pocket-knife, pistol, anything she get her hand on she'd use it; y'know Memphis Minnie used to be a hell-cat. . . . I never had no problem with her. I know others that did."[8]

Echoes of this rugged life appear throughout Minnie's songs, but her repertoire also presents a nearly opposite face. In spite of her aversion to farm life, many farm and rural images are also distributed liberally through her early pieces, and songs like *Frankie Jean (That Trottin' Fool)*, *Sylvester and His Mule Blues*, and *Plymouth Rock Blues* are steeped in the lore of the farm and farm life. The Douglas farm had Plymouth Rocks—chickens of all kinds, in fact—as well as hogs, cows, and a mule. In Walls, "we raised sugarcane, cotton, corn and 'garden,' you know, like peas, beans. We used to raise something you call sorghum. It's sugarcane; you strip it, and then you carry it to the mill, and they grind it up, get the juice, and they cook it," said Daisy. Minnie's nephew (Daisy's son) Lee added. "When I was a kid, that was my job, to walk behind the mule with a switch. They had a machine that would grind the cane, run by a mule to turn the wheel, and I was a little kid with a switch, walking behind the mule."[9] Needless to say, Minnie had songs about that, too, and her *Good Soppin'* uses the imagery of cane and cane stripping, while *What's the Matter with the Mill?* uses the imagery of the grinding mill.

The Douglas farm was like thousands of farms all over the south, with a small town address but miles from the nearest gas station. Indeed, while Minnie is buried in a Walls cemetery, the church and its graveyard are at least ten miles from the center of Walls, even though Walls is only what Lee called a wide spot in the road. It had a cotton gin, but Daisy's comments showed how the importance of rural areas like Walls had shifted with the passing years. "The IC train used to run right through there, the Illinois Central, and it stopped in Walls. It went on through Tunica, Lakeview, Robinsonville, Clarksdale, below there—Mound Bayou. Right through the Delta. But they don't have no train run down there now. They stopped that train fifteen years ago or more."[10]

Daisy Johnson had rattled off the stops as if they came straight from the Illinois Central timetable. The Memphis-to-Vicksburg route was covered by the IC's "Delta Express" and "The Planter," with stops at Lake Cormorant, Robinsonville, Hollywood, Tunica, Clayton, Dundee, Lula, Coahoma, Clarksdale, Alligator, Mound Bayou, Merigold, Cleveland and smaller stops in between. Hollywood, Mississippi, would soon become a stop-on-request-only station, as Walls had been for a number of years. But the train traveled North and South just east of the Mississippi River, through Delta towns that were rich in blues history: Lake Cormorant hosted Willie Brown and Memphis Minnie, and decades later, it was the site of the famous Library of Congress session where Son House, Fiddlin' Joe Martin, and Willie Brown were recorded. Muddy Waters sang of Dundee for the Library of Congress in his Burr Clover Blues, and Gus Cannon and his Jug Stompers recorded *Hollywood Rag.* Clarksdale was the site of the Afro-American Hospital where the dying Bessie Smith was taken after her grisly road accident. The hospital is now the Riverside Hotel where many a blues singer has passed the night. Robert Johnson was a regular in the Robinsonville area, and Charlie Patton sang of Lula in his *Dry Well Blues.* Patton, Johnson, Son House and countless others traveled through Merigold, Tunica, and so many similar towns that anyone familiar with Delta blues repertoires hears the same towns mentioned a hundred times in the songs. Our dreams are full of the rich textures of the names' magical ferment. Every wide spot in the road was a mile post of the blues' evolution.

But Minnie didn't care much for the wide spot on Highway 61, not when Beale Street was so close. What was it about Beale Street that drew so many rural dwellers to this famous city? Blacks were leaving the rural South in droves, and many were migrating out of the South entirely, some to Chicago, some to Detroit and other large cities of the North. But many rural blacks traveled shorter migratory routes and landed in the large cities of the South: Birmingham, Atlanta, New Orleans or Memphis. While one of the chief motivations for rural blacks to move to the urban areas was greater economic opportunity, discriminatory activities still held sway in these cities of the deep South. For example, while the Negro Urban Leagues in Kansas City, Baltimore and Louisville helped Negro mechanics organize for the first time, they ran into trouble in Memphis. The American Federation of Labor (AFL) denounced the Memphis mechanics' association as "communistic," and the league was forced to abandon its labor activities, lest they be cut off from community-chest funding.[11]

Other racist practices guaranteed that black children would receive a poor education. Schools for blacks opened and closed in synchrony with planting and harvesting, and when all was said and done, many black children went to school only three months a year.[12] No aspect of everyday life was free of racist taint. For example, Lena Horne's scenes were cut out of *Stormy Weather* and *Until the Clouds Roll By,* and *Annie Get Your Gun* was banned in 1947 because the part of a railroad conductor was played by a black.[13] It was amid this atmosphere that the black citizens of Memphis carried on their affairs.

Memphis had always had a large black population, and its history has been a colorful one. Indeed, the violence along the infamous black thoroughfare of Beale Street led to Memphis being called "the murder capitol of the world."[14] As Will Shade of the Memphis Jug Band recalled,

> You could walk down the street in days of 1900 and like that and you could find a man wit' throat cut from y'ear to y'ear. Also you could find people layin' dead wit' not their throat cut, money took and everything in their pockets, everything took out of their pockets and

thrown outside the house. Sometimes you find them
with no clothes on and all such as that. Sometimes you
could find them throwed out of winders and so forth,
here on Beale Street. Sportin' class o' women runnin'
up and down the street all night long . . . git knocked
in the head with bricks and hatchets and ham-
mers—pocket knives, razors and so forth like
that. . . .[15]

Such accounts illuminate one aspect of black Memphis life
among the lower classes, but there is another side to the story.
Diurnal Beale Street was also the focus for the most mundane activities of everyday living, and not simply gambling, drugs and prostitution; thus, in among the clubs and dives were the doctors'
offices, grocery stores and insurance companies one finds in every
neighborhood.

But Memphis', and Beale Street's, main claim to fame was its
music, and the most famous name in Memphis music was com-
poser/bandleader W. C. Handy. Handy was born in Alabama, but
his path to fame began in Memphis in 1909 on the eve of Boss
Crump's election. Club-owner/politico Jim Mulcahy hired Handy
to play for Crump. Mulcahy was the most recent proprietor of the
Panama Club at Fourth and Beale—its first three owners had all
died violent deaths—and he would be warmly regarded for his be-
neficent treatment of Memphis blacks during the Depression.
"They spent money with me when they had it—how could I not
feed them now?" he remarked. If these words have a familiar ring,
we should remember that when Mulcahy did time in Atlanta on
liquor charges, he became friends with radical labor leader Eugene
Debs, and became a staunch supporter of Debsian ideals.[16]
Handy's enticing *Mr. Crump* helped carry Boss Crump to victory.
*St. Louis Blues, Beale Street Blues, Make Me One Pallet on the Floor,
Yellow Dog Blues, Hesitating Blues,* these, too, were all Handy numbers, but these carefully and formally composed pieces had only a
little to do with the downhome blues, or country blues of our subject, Memphis Minnie. Nonetheless, Handy's existence as a Memphis figure is an important aspect of the city's musical history. As

for his pieces, many people will recognize *Mr. Crump,* in its most popular guise, as *Mama Don't Allow No Easy Riders Here.*

Memphis was also the site of the founding of the Theatre Owner's Booking Association in 1909. The TOBA gave many black musicians and entertainers an opportunity to play in dozens of locations throughout the Eastern US. Of course, blues artists on the TOBA circuit tended to be Classic blues singers like Ma Rainey or Bessie Smith, and their more vaudevillian counterparts. Blues guitarists like Minnie didn't work the TOBA, although they did appear in various theatres, like the Indiana Theatre in Chicago. As these remarks make clear, much of Memphis' blues fame derives from the more sophisticated blues of W. C. Handy and the vaudeville-oriented blues sung from the TOBA stage. Even pianist Memphis Slim was at pains to separate the classier sort of bluesmen, like himself, from the more raggedy guitarists who played in Church's Park.[17] And yet the Church's Park singers pointed to the existence of a mighty blues current flowing rapidly along beneath the veneer established by W. C. Handy and the TOBA, a current not so much subterranean as unheralded, a current at home in the dives and joints along Beale.

Guitarists Frank Stokes and Furry Lewis, two participants in that current, both provided advice and inspiration to Minnie in her early days in Memphis. Minnie's duets with Kansas Joe drew as much inspiration from the guitar teamwork of Frank Stokes and Dan Sane,[18] who recorded as the Beale Street Sheiks, as from her own early "partnership" with Willie Brown. Jim Jackson was already popular by that time, and he could be seen playing in Church's Park along with other musicians like the guitarist Robert Wilkins. Wilkins remembered that Minnie "was beginning to learn guitar and he was able to teach her a few things,"[19] but before long, Minnie herself was the reigning blues queen of Memphis, and there was little she could learn from the competition.[20] The proximity of Memphis, Walls and Lake Cormorant to the Mississippi Delta blurred any distinctions that might be invoked to separate the Memphis singers from the Mississippi ones, and comparisons of the Memphis blues with the Mississippi blues may not accomplish much. For example, Minnie played at a roadhouse with Frank Stokes and Memphis Willie B, all Memphis artists, but across the street at another club, were Mississippians Son House and Willie Brown (ex-partner of the legendary Charlie Patton).[21] And as we shall see, Minnie and Willie Brown were partners for a number of years.

Like many blues singers, Minnie was, in her own words, a "downhome girl," and while she would come to play in finer clubs, she was still willing to play for friends at home, or at a picnic, or even on the street. "She'd play *anywhere*," Memphis Slim recalled. "I'm tellin' you. She came in there from Mississippi playin' around in the streets and different places and people's houses and house parties and things, until she made *Bumble Bee Blues*, and then she [got famous and] came to Chicago."[22]

Minnie baby-sat for future bluesman Eddie Taylor, with whose mother she had gone to school,[23] but she wasn't home enough to do much baby-sitting. She traveled through Texas with the circus, and she worked in Greenville, Mississippi, with trombonist Pee Wee Whittaker.[24] When she wasn't traveling, she was hanging out on Beale Street playing with various local musicians, from Joe Mc-Coy or the Jed Davenport jug band, to the Memphis Jug Band or the band led by Jack Kelly. It was in these years when Minnie was still in her teens or twenties that she is said to have married Will Weldon, AKA Casey Bill.

While little is known of Weldon, he is said to have been born in Pinebluff, Arkansas, in 1909, and to have recorded with the Memphis Jug Band during their halcyon years of the mid- to late 1920s.[25] Ultimately, he emerged as a solo artist, billed on record as "Casey Bill, the Hawaiian Guitar Wizard." "Casey" was an expanded variation of "KC," for Kansas City, and on his first slide guitar outing in 1935, he was indeed billed as "Kansas City Bill Weldon." The 1927 *Turpentine Blues* and *Hitch Me To Your Buggy, and Drive Me Like a Mule* was recorded as by Will Weldon,[26] and it has always been assumed that the two were the same singer. Stylistically, however, there is nothing to link the 1927 Victor session with the bulk of Casey Bill's recorded output from the 1930s; this, and his probable Kansas City origin, suggest that the two Weldons were not even the same person.

Minnie's liaison with Casey Bill has come under increasing attack in recent years, until now many critics doubt whether the relationship even existed. Indeed, it may be that he and Minnie not only never married, but never even met until their recording session together in 1935.[27] This may seem an extreme view, but a close inspection of the facts at our disposal suggests it is correct. The only historical *evidence* linking Minnie and Weldon is Weldon's certain presence on Minnie's Bluebird session of October 31, 1935—his "Hawaiian" style is so unusual that his presence is instantly recognizable. The only other links between Minnie and Casey Bill are Leadbitter's early report and Big Bill Broonzy's autobiography. But Leadbitter may have used Broonzy's book to ask leading questions, and Broonzy's book has led many researchers down the wrong path. It is noteworthy that in Georges Adins' pioneering interview with Minnie and her family, the name Casey Bill Weldon was never mentioned. Logically speaking, a Minnie/Weldon liaison in the mid-thirties makes much more sense than one in the mid- or early twenties,[28] but there is no evidence for the "logical" 1930s relationship either. Weldon's name is not recognized by either Daisy Johnson or Ethel Douglas, Minnie's sister-in-law, both of whom remembered Joe McCoy, and both of whom were intimate with Minnie's last husband, Ernest Lawlars. Ethel was especially close to Minnie in her early years, and she'd never heard of Casey Bill Weldon. Casey Bill was at least a part-time participant in the Chicago music scene, but none of our informants knew him or linked him with Minnie. He remains a shadowy figure about whom little is known. According to at least one source, Minnie lived with a man called Squirrel in the mid- to late 1930s, and this may or may not have been Joe McCoy. It could also have been Casey Bill.[29]

If the image of Minnie's relationship with Weldon has melted away, a new and different image has come to replace it. Shortly after World War I, Minnie followed the Mississippi River, and Highway 61, a few miles south of Walls to the Bedford plantation, just west of Lake Cormorant. This was where Willie Brown had lived since 1916,[30] and it was with Brown that Minnie formed one of her earlier liaisons. When bluesman Willie Moore first saw Minnie, "her and a boy was playin' mandolin and a guitar together. . . . All of us called her 'Kid' Douglas."[31] Moore was already impressed with how superbly she played the guitar, even as a young girl: "She could make a guitar 'talk', say: 'Fare thee well.'"[32]

Along with Willie Brown and Willie Moore, Minnie often played for white parties, either when W. C. Handy couldn't make it down from Memphis, or when the party was too small to warrant his august presence. Minnie, like Brown, played popular material when she played for whites, and one of her favorite pieces was *What Makes You Do Me Like You Do Do Do,*[33] a piece also prized by Leadbelly. Minnie, Brown and Moore also played for local storekeepers who used their talents to attract black customers. Minnie always played lead when playing with Willie Brown, or with the three-guitar trio of Brown, Moore and herself. She also handled the vocal chores, although occasionally Brown sang, too. Minnie was clearly Brown's superior when it came to guitar skill, and Moore commented, "Wasn't nothing he *could* teach her. . . . Everything Willie Brown could play, she could play, and then she could play some things he *couldn't* play." Minnie played with Brown around five or six years, during the time she lived in Bedford, but even in those days she was well known as a traveler—"she'd skip around every which a-way," and by the late twenties, she had left the Bedford area to make her fortune elsewhere.[34]

This is our first view of Minnie as an exceptional performer, and it won't be our last. Critics agree that her guitar skills were remarkable, and her guitar playing on the early *When the Levee Breaks* has been called *the* most rhythmically varied accompaniment in 'Spanish' tuning. "Though fingerpicking, she plays with the speed and finesse of a flatpicker. The variety of her performance is all the more remarkable in view of the fact that it is basically confined to the first three frets."[35] Her recorded performances reveal the same sort of *verbal* creativity and agility, as well. For example, for a Bumble Bee Slim song which became a blues standard, *Sail On, Little Girl, Sail On,* Minnie took the word "sailor" and made it a sexual figure in an innovative way, not used by other purveyors of the song, or indeed, by any other blues artist at all. The first and last verse were present in the original:

KEEP ON SAILING

Sail on, sail on, aww baby, sail on. (2x)
I don't mind you sailing,
but please don't sail so long.

Ooh, boy(s),
   now don't you want to ride with me. (2x)
I'm got the best sailor in this world
you ever seen.

Going away,
   going away but I ain't gonna stay. (2x)
'Cause that sailor you got,
I sees it each and every day.

Sail on, sail on, aww baby, sail on. (2x)
You gonna keep a-sailing
till you find your mama gone.

We shall see many more examples of Minnie's songs, but for the moment, let us return to her early years. Soon she teamed up with Joe McCoy in Memphis, and it was with McCoy that Minnie made many of her most exciting records. Joe McCoy was born in 1905, in Raymond, Mississippi, located in the southwestern part of the state, just west of Jackson and a bit north of Crystal Springs. His younger brother Charlie was born in Jackson five years later, and he, too, recorded with Minnie. The McCoys were close to the Chatmons who hailed from nearby Bolton, and who became the widely recorded and influential Mississippi Sheiks, a recording unit consisting of Walter Vinson (also from Bolton) and various members of the Chatman clan, fiddler Lonnie or guitarists Bo (Carter) or Sam. The McCoys and Chatmans often played together, and like many Jackson-area musicians, they were influenced in varying degrees by Tommy Johnson. As one would expect, Joe and Minnie often played in the Jackson area. McCoy was a talented and versatile musician who recorded under many pseudonyms. While his

records with Minnie are marked by his sharply articulated bass runs
that were the perfect foil for Minnie's treble leads, his solo outings
show him to be a more skilled guitarist than the duets suggest. His
heavily accented voice had power and control, if not subtlety, and
he sang in various groups, from the Jed Davenport jug band in
Memphis to the Harlem Hamfats, a jazz group fronted by trum-
peter Herb Morand.[36] Even with the Hamfats, Joe sounded
right at home, another mark of his versatility.

Minnie and Joe met sometime in the 1920s, and they played on
the Memphis streets until the pair was discovered by a Columbia
scout, playing in a Beale Street barber shop for dimes.[37] Their first
recording session was arranged, and in the summer of 1929, they
traveled to New York to record for Columbia. They were married
this same year,[38] although no marriage license has been found for
this or any of Minnie's marriages. The marriage to Joe McCoy as
well as the later one to Ernest Lawlars may have been by common
law.[39] Minnie also had numerous informal liaisons. Fiddlin' Joe
Martin, Willie Brown, perhaps Blind John Davis, possibly Homesick James, and even Peter Chatman, Sr. (father of Peter Chatman,
also known as Memphis Slim) have all been linked with Minnie.
About the latter, Sunnyland Slim commented, "I met her, I met
Minnie ... around '25, '27 in there. . . . Memphis Slim's daddy was
really in love with her, see he was running through the country
trying to do everything he could, trying to keep her, you know,"
and according to Memphis Slim, his father had been instrumental
in bringing Minnie to Chicago.[40]

When Johnny Shines came upon Minnie in Memphis, she was
already with Joe McCoy. "I met Minnie the first time in 1928 or
1929. She and Joe and [his brother] Charlie was all in Memphis.
They knew this fellow that kind of ran something like an open
house, and they were just there playing and people buying booze
and stuff like that for 'em. It was in North Memphis. . . ." For
Shines this was ultimately a crucial meeting. "It was an influence
because I liked what I heard, and I'd never heard anything like it
before. I played a couple of her songs myself. *Bumble Bee Blues,*
and something else I used to play, *Black Rat.*"[41]

One of the songs that Shines remembered—*Bumble Bee*—was
recorded at Minnie and Joe's first session. They cut six sides for

Columbia in 1929, accompanying themselves on guitar and performing vocals in various combinations. The first coupling to be released, *That Will Be Alright* and *When the Levee Breaks,* had vocals by Joe alone. It was scheduled for release in early August and first appeared in the Columbia Supplement catalog for late September. Two months later, *'Frisco Town* and *Goin' Back to Texas* were released, marking Minnie's first vocal appearance on a record. She soloed on *'Frisco Town* and shared vocals with Joe on *Goin' Back to Texas.* Columbia waited until mid August of 1930 to release the final two numbers, *Bumble Bee* and *I Want That.* The latter song was sung by Joe, while *Bumble Bee,* sung by Minnie, became one of the best known songs of the period.

Regardless of who performed the vocal, all of the Columbia sides were labeled as by "Kansas Joe and Memphis Minnie;" Minnie would keep her *nom de disque* throughout her life, both on record and off, but Joe stopped recording as Kansas Joe at the end of 1935. From what Daisy and Ethel knew, a Columbia A and R man had named Minnie and Joe "Memphis Minnie" and "Kansas Joe."[42] It would not be the only time white record company personnel gave blues singers their pseudonyms, and Sunnyland Slim recalled that he met Minnie back in the late 1920s, back before a white man gave him the name "Sunnyland."[43]

It has also been suggested that Minnie's name derived from Cab Calloway's famous piece, *Minnie the Moocher,* but Cab's tune dates from 1931. In his autobiography, Calloway notes that his composition was inspired by the melody of *St. James Infirmary* and by two torch songs, *Willie the Weeper* and *Minnie the Mermaid,*[44] but the latter song was from 1930, again too late to have inspired Minnie's pseudonym. Others have suggested that the popularity of Walt Disney's Minnie Mouse was at the root of Minnie's pseudonym,[45] but there is no evidence to support this idea, either. But the very existence of *Minnie the Mermaid,* Minnie Mouse and *Minnie the Moocher* all suggest that between the mouse and the mermaid, the name "Minnie" was sufficiently in vogue in 1929 to strike the fancy of either "Kid" Douglas or a Columbia A and R man.

When the Levee Breaks, cut at their first session, reveals the breadth of experience from which Minnie and Joe drew their songs.

The devastating effects of the 1927 flood were still more than a memory for many of Minnie and Joe's listeners, and Minnie's sister-in-law Ethel Douglas vividly remembers the flood:

> When we lived on the levee, right near Walls, [Minnie] and her oldest brother lived with us then. The levee *did* break, and we left from there. I'm sure that's what she was singing about "when the levee broke" 'cause we were scared to death when it broke, 1927. The levee broke and the water come over. Me and my two little children left and went to Walls, up on the hill there. 'Kid' and them, they come on to town. When the water went down, we went back.[46]

The flood waters left scars upon the land and upon the heart, but the blues is a technique of psychic mastery. *When the Levee Breaks* was not so much a cry of pain as an announcement of a new beginning, even in its sadness.

Minnie and Joe returned to the Columbia studio a second day to record two pieces, both of which featured Joe's vocals, but neither was released. They eventually remade the same songs, and they were issued by Vocalion in 1930. This pattern would be repeated throughout Minnie and Joe's partnership: Nearly every piece that was rejected by the record company was eventually accepted and issued, although some pieces required three takes, done at three separate studio sessions, before an acceptable master was cut. Only a few songs remained permanently unissued, like Minnie's *Midnight Special,* recorded for Victor with "Bessie McCoy," or Joe's *Rowdy Old Soul,* cut as by "The Hillbilly Plowboy".[47]

With some justice, one could think of the Columbia sessions as mere appetizers to the luscious feast that would soon follow on Vocalion. The relationship with Vocalion began in February of 1930, and for Minnie, it was an affiliation that lasted for nearly a decade, in spite of interruptions to record for Okeh, Decca and Bluebird in the early to mid-1930s. Vocalion's own history, however, was just as complicated and just as full of interruptions. The label had been purchased by Brunswick-Balke-Collender in the summer of 1925, and by 1929, under the direction of J. Mayo Williams, it was regularly recording race items in the field, instead of in Chicago. Ultimately the field unit visited Chicago, Atlanta, Dallas, San Antonio, Fort Worth, Los Angeles, New Orleans, Knoxville, Hot Springs, Birmingham and, most important from our perspective, Memphis.

Vocalion had inaugurated its 1000 series of race records in March of 1926, and it ran for 746 records in six years. Most of the great blues hits of the day were on Vocalion: Jim Jackson's *Jim Jackson's Kansas City Blues,* Tampa Red and Georgia Tom's *It's Tight Like That,* and Leroy Carr's *How Long—How Long Blues.*[48] Nearly all of Minnie and Joe's vintage material was issued in this race series. Vocalion was absorbed into the American Record Corporation (ARC) stable of labels at the end of 1931, and a new race series began at 25001 in September 1933. Minnie never appeared on the 25000 series, which was changed at number 25021 to 2522. Race and country items were then prefixed with a zero, like Minnie's *Stinging Snake Blues,* issued on Vocalion 02711 in 1934. The race series items were dropped in price from 75 cents to 35 cents.

Minnie's 1930s sides were usually issued only on Vocalion, while the more popular Big Bill had many of his records issued on ARC's dime-store labels as well. The ARC labels controlled a large segment of the market by virtue of their having Tampa Red, Big Bill, Memphis Minnie, and for awhile, Peetie Wheatstraw, but this was not to last. Tampa Red soon became a Bluebird artist, and Wheatstraw decided to stick with Decca for whom he had begun to record in mid-1934; even Minnie didn't settle down with Vocalion until late 1935.

Minnie and Joe first recorded for Vocalion's Memphis field unit in February, 1930. After that they traveled regularly to Chicago to record, finally moving there themselves in the early 1930s. While we don't know precisely when they moved north, Sunnyland Slim recalled Minnie and Joe traveling to Chicago to record, and then returning to Memphis where they still lived,[49] and his recollection is supported by Big Bill.[50] This was a common pattern, as Arthur "Big Boy" Crudup has testified: "I had to record, I had a big family. And I'd go to Chicago to record and go back South and work."[51]

Minnie's family had not yet moved to Memphis, although they did move to Brunswick, Tennessee, a few miles northeast of the city. Other members of the family lived closer to Cordova, a few miles to the South. "It was a little town, right out from Cordova, called Leno,[52] Tennessee. And that's where I went to school," said Daisy, reminiscing about the 1920s. "We went to school at Brunswick for awhile and we went at this little school they call Morning Grove School, that was between Leno and Cordova...."[53] Shortly after Gertrude died in 1922, Abe Douglas moved back to Walls. He had been dissatisfied with the farming in the hills around Brunswick, and he farmed the richer Delta land in Walls until he died in 1935.

Ethel commented, "You know, it was up in Brunswick where my house caught fire...around 1925, 1926, before the flood. When the house burned, I moved in with [Daisy's] Papa. And by there being no fire department and no water, the house burned to the ground. No water around! The next year we all moved back to Walls."[54] Fire was a significant agency that wound its way through Minnie's repertoire—another brother's house burned to the ground a year later—and Ethel's very words are uncannily similar to the lyrics of Minnie's *Call the Fire Wagon*.

Minnie and Joe cut their first two double-sided duets during their second Vocalion session: *What Fault You Find of Me, Part 1 and 2,* and *Can I Do it for You?, Part 1 and 2.* Almost unnoticed was Minnie's lilting harmony on Joe's *She Wouldn't Give Me None,* a lovely contribution, in a role she never played again. But the two-sided duets established a pattern for the teasing, please-give-it-to-me, you-can't-have-it, songs with which Minnie and Joe punctuated their repertoire. While these duets shared much with the vaudeville tradition—Minnie probably got her feet wet playing pieces like these in traveling shows—the former's musical qualities often set them above and apart from their vaudeville counterparts. When the period of the duets ended, Minnie's lyrics often still sounded as if the replying male was only a few feet off-mike. Jed Davenport and His Beale Street Jug Band also cut six sides for Vocalion on that same February day. Kansas Joe is obviously the vocalist on two of the numbers, *You Ought to Move Out of Town* and *Save Me Some,* and both he and Minnie may share guitar honors. Minnie may even play mandolin on one cut, as she does on her own *After While Blues,* cut two years later.[55] Minnie is said to have learned banjo even before she learned guitar,[56] but none of her associates has ever mentioned her playing banjo, and her banjo playing has gone unrecorded. She may have even been able to play piano, having learned from a fellow-musician from Walls, Kid Crackintine.[57]

Minnie and Joe's last Memphis session was for Victor in May of 1930. Many of the details surrounding the Victor session remain obscure. Minnie's name appeared on the Victor label as Minnie McCoy, while Joe appeared as either "Joe Johnson" or as one-half of "McCoy and Johnson". It's possible that Joe McCoy had signed an exclusive contract with Vocalion and Minnie had not, for many blues pseudonyms functioned as a means of avoiding the typically exploitative contractual obligations of the major record labels. Nonetheless, for years many listeners thought "Joe Johnson" was a cousin, even though he sounded surprisingly like Joe McCoy.[58]

After Minnie and Joe cut a remake of their duet *Goin' Back to Texas,* as *I'm Going Back Home,* Minnie recorded a (third) version of her hit *Bumble Bee,* and the first of two versions of *Memphis Minnie-Jitis Blues,* here called simply *Meningitis Blues.* For *Bumble Bee Blues* and *Meningitis Blues,* she was accompanied by the popular Memphis Jug Band, all colleagues and friends, who were recording that day for Victor. It's worth noting, however, that the careers of the Memphis Jug Band, like ninety percent of the other blues stars of the twenties, were winding down; they had a few more sessions with Victor, and a session or two in the thirties, but after that, their recording opportunities were almost non-existent. Minnie and Joe's careers were just *beginning.*

Also in the Victor studio was Washington White, a fiercely powerful Delta bluesman who recorded later as Bukka White and who eventually became popular among young whites in the years of the blues revival. This was Bukka's first session, and in the background of *I Am in the Heavenly Way* and *Promise True and Grand,* singing above the popped strings of White's steel-bodied National, is a woman's voice, the singer identified only as "Miss Minnie", but probably Minnie McCoy.

After White's sides, the Victor engineers recorded four sermons with singing, and then closed up shop for the day. The next two days were devoted to recording old time music for Victor's several hillbilly series, and on May 29, Joe and Minnie returned to the studio. They were joined by Bessie McCoy, who played no instrument and who sang on only one number, the unissued *Midnight Special*. Other than the appearance of her name in the files, we know nothing else about her. No test pressing or master of *Midnight Special* has been made available. Minnie and Joe's titles were eventually released, but less than a thousand copies were pressed of *Don't Want No Woman* and *I Never Told a Lie*, and less than 200 were pressed of *Georgia Skin* and *I'm Going Back Home*.[59]

Joe and Minnie's next recording session, June 5, resulted in Minnie's humorous *Plymouth Rock Blues*, and five unissued pieces that were all eventually remade and issued: Joe's *Cherry Ball Blues* and *Botherin' That Thing*, Minnie's *Bumble Bee No. 2* and *Georgia Skin*, and the traded-verse duet, *I Don't Want No Woman I Have to Give My Money To*. The guitar interplay on Joe's *Botherin' That Thing* was superb, with Joe's aggressively high-timbred bass-string runs playing hop-scotch over Minnie's treble teasings. Critics of guitar music, even outside the field of blues, were impressed with Minnie and Joe's skills.[60] Sometimes the ear is deceived as to precisely what type of guitar each is playing. A picture from the Victor files of this period shows a young Minnie standing by a seated Joe, both holding wooden guitars, yet we know from their records that by then, both also played steel-bodied National guitars.

Joe Calicott remembered Minnie recording for Vocalion while he was also at the studio recording. "She and Tampa Red had the first steel boxes we ever saw."[61] Early pictures of Tampa Red do indeed show him with a National steel, but Minnie and Joe were as significant as Tampa in this regard, and one critic notes that these Nationals "were first brought to Jackson by Memphis Minnie and Joe McCoy in either late 1929 or early 1930 when the pair came from Chicago to play a club date."[62] Johnny Shines also remembers Minnie and Joe's guitars, from the first time he saw them play in 1929. He hadn't yet begun to play himself, but he vividly recalls the performance by Minnie, Joe, Charlie McCoy and a fourth musician. "And they all had the first steel guitars I had ever

seen, they all had National steels. They was such *pretty* things."[63]
Who actually brought the first National to the region is obviously
a matter for speculation—Walter Vinson of the Mississippi Sheiks
was known to play a steel-bodied National guitar, and he was from
the Jackson area and acquainted with Joe and Charlie McCoy—but
the testimony we do have suggests that Minnie and Joe were
among the first to use them, and that those who saw them were
much taken with them.

Each new trip to the Vocalion studio brought new successes for
Joe and Minnie and more listening treats for their audience, occasionally including "new" versions of Minnie's "old" standards like
Bumble Bee and *I'm Talking About You. New Dirty Dozen,* however,
may have derived the designation "new" from its having been recorded by Minnie in her role as guitarist for the Jed Davenport
version five months earlier;[64] if this is so, it provides a backhanded
confirmation of the presence of Minnie's guitar on the Davenport
sides. By this time, Minnie was not only producing more solo records than Joe—she was producing the *hits.* Another ominous sign
from Joe's point of view was the legend running beneath the "Kansas Joe" artist credit on his solo vocal (with two guitars), *Botherin'
That Thing:* "Guitar by Memphis Minnie". This notation was to
appear with increasing frequency on his records.

In spite of this, *all* of their duets for Vocalion were labeled as
by "Kansas Joe and Memphis Minnie." They were never labeled
as by "Memphis Minnie and Kansas Joe," although it was clearer
each day that Minnie was the more popular and the more appealing artist of the duo. No doubt this was just another sign of how
male-dominated country blues recording was at the time. "If a male
sang on a record, he was probably the star," may have been their
motto, and Kansas Joe was treated as such, even on those duets
where his part was relatively minor: *What's the Matter with the Mill?*
and *You Stole My Cake.*

Every two or three months, Minnie and Joe would return to
the Vocalion studio to record. Some sessions would result in two
Kansas Joe vocal sides, issued under Joe's name, and one vocal by
Minnie, but the latter might be labeled as by "Kansas Joe and
Memphis Minnie". Others would result in two songs under Min-
nie's name, and no others; but often as not, they'd be back in the

studio a few days later to record a few other pieces that would be issued under their various combinations of names. Thus, on October 9, 1930, Minnie sang *You Dirty Mistreater* and the haunting *Dirt Dauber Blues,* the former to the tune of the Mississippi Sheiks' hit, *Sitting on Top of the World.*[65] They returned two days later and cut Joe's *That's Your Yas Yas Yas* and *I'm Fixed for You,* Minnie's *North Memphis Blues,* and the rousing duet masterpiece, *What's the Matter with the Mill?*

This was a typical recording pattern for many blues artists on many labels, and the session of January 30, 1931, not only resulted in no rejects, but it generated several magnificent sides. Joe's *Shake Mattie* and especially *My Washwoman's Gone* featured biting slide guitar work, probably by Joe himself, while Minnie cut the startling *Crazy Crying Blues* and Lucille Bogan's famous *Tricks Ain't Walking No More,* one of the few songs Minnie sang that was identified with and written by another singer. Four classics in one day wasn't a bad day's work! A rich legacy was being created for their many followers, and this period fittingly culminated with the February 4, 1932, session—back in New York for the first time since their debut in 1929—where they waxed the final, *quartet* version of Minnie's hit, this time titled, *Minnie Minnie Bumble Bee,* featuring Vocalion all-stars Memphis Minnie, Georgia Tom, Tampa Red and Kansas Joe!

4. CHICAGO DAYS

I believe I'm at the crossroads of the wind.
—Alice Rahon

By this time, nearly 240,000 blacks had moved to Chicago.[1] In fact, the growth of Chicago's black population, most of whom had come from the South, had been phenomenal. In 1850 Chicago had a black population of just over 300.[2] By 1900, one hundred times that number of blacks called Chicago their home, and this number was to increase again by more than tenfold over the next five decades. By 1950—around the time of Minnie's session for Regal— there were 492,000 blacks in Chicago; by 1960, the number had reached 813,000. Most of these new residents had come from the South, and many were potential purchasers of blues records. Ninety percent of US blacks lived in the South in 1900, but by 1960, only sixty percent still lived there. This move from South to North was accompanied by a simultaneous move from rural areas to cities. In 1900, approximately seventy-five percent of Southern blacks lived in rural areas, but by 1960, only twenty-five percent lived in rural areas.[3] One of the most typical migration paths was from New Orleans through the Mississippi Delta to Memphis and then on to Chicago, precisely the path that Minnie followed from her birthplace in Algiers. Some Minnie followed, while some followed Minnie.

Chicago was by no means "the land of the free," however. In 1917, after the East St. Louis riot, a number of black Chicagoans armed themselves against the possibility of a similar event taking place in Chicago, and a race riot did occur two years later. While the spark that set it off was an incident at a beach, the riot actually developed amidst a series of home bombings aimed at blacks who had moved into the ever-expanding ghetto between 35th and 63rd, Lake Michigan and State Street. Thirty-eight lives were lost during the riot itself.[4]

Economically, conditions were also far from ideal. By 1930, when the depression was making life tough on the white masses as well as the black, blacks held only nine percent of the manual labor jobs and two percent of what sociologists Drake and Cayton, in their classic study of Chicago's black community, called "good" jobs: professional, managerial, clerical.[5] In Northern cities like Chicago, white workers often protested the hiring of blacks in their plants, but the situation was never as hopeless as in the South. For example, it was in Chicago that the garment workers union was able to organize the same black women who had been used as strikebreakers against them in a 1917 labor action.[6]

Thus, if the Chicago *Defender* never tired of exhorting Southern blacks to flee the South and come North, it was because the possiblility of just such hopeful actions was far higher in the North. In spite of the level of discrimination in Chicago, compared to the the rural South, it was an economic oasis: In Chicago the black median wage in 1949 was $1919; in Mississippi it was $439.[7] While men usually led the migratory way to industrial cities like Pittsburgh and Detroit, "Chicago, with its more diversified female occupational structure, [also] attracted single women and wives. . . ."[8] Drawing blacks to Chicago were jobs for males in the stockyards, the meat packing plants, the steel mills, and the foundries. Jobs for women—and men—could be found in the hundreds of lighter industrial occupations, the large mail-order businesses, Chicago's countless warehouses, and domestic work. At the time of the Depression, blacks were doing thirty four percent of the servant work in Chicago.[9]

With economic opportunities so constricted during the Depression, the fact that Minnie and Joe's recording careers were nearly curtailed is no surprise. Minnie was always able to support herself with her music, and the vicissitudes of the Chicago industrial and service-oriented job market never affected her directly. On the one session that Minnie had amidst the bleakness of 1933, however, Joe was nowhere to be seen.[10] The first stylistic phase of Minnie's career was coming to an end. In 1934 and 1935, she began to experiment with the new sounds that would carry her through the thirties and forties. But before renewing her contract with Vocalion (now under new management), she recorded nearly 20 sides for Decca, and eight sides for Victor's Bluebird subsidiary. Thus Minnie recorded for all three of the major race series labels of the 1930s. When the Depression began to ease in 1934, only Victor/Bluebird and the American Record Corporation (ARC) remained as powerful race contenders, but they were soon challenged by Decca, which began its race series in 1934. Blues and jazz were issued in the 7000 series, for which Decca charged a competitive 35 cents.[11] Bluebird was a dime-store label that Victor introduced to compete with the other 35-cent labels.[12]

The Decca sides retained the flavor of Minnie's rural-sounding duets, but they were slightly less intricate. As a soloist, her need to support her treble runs with her own bass line may have made complex passages more difficult, e.g., in *Chickasaw Train Blues (Low Down Dirty Thing)* or *Keep It to Yourself,* but the truth is that even with Joe— *You Got to Move (You Ain't Got to Move)* or *Hole in the Wall*— the complicated interplay of the two guitars, so common in 1930-1932, was no longer in evidence. Yet the Decca sides especially, as well as the sides cut at the first Bluebird session of July 27, 1935, retained a downhome flavor that was absent from much of her 1930s recorded repertoire. It's also worth noting that it was in the Decca days that "Memphis Minnie and Kansas Joe" finally appeared on a record as an artist credit, instead of Vocalion's insistent "Kansas Joe and Memphis Minnie."

The ribald Decca session of January 10, 1935, was one of her most interesting, not only for the songs recorded—*Dirty Mother for You, You Can't Give It Away* and the topical *Sylvester and His Mule Blues*—but for the accompaniment, as well: This was the first outing in which Minnie was seriously accompanied by a piano. The pianist is yet to be agreed upon, although discographers Dixon and Godrich cite Jimmy Gordon, who was in the Decca studio the *next* day. As Minnie clearly says to the piano player, "Play it, Dennis," and as the composer credits on the Gospel Minnie sides—made five days later in the same studio—are to "Dennis-McCoy" we suggest the piano player is not Jimmy Gordon, but rather a still unidentified pianist named "Dennis."

The Gospel Minnie sides are engaging, but Minnie never got religion before, during, or after recording them. Indeed, Minnie never went to church, and according to Brewer Phillips, the only time she was in a church was to hear a gospel group perform in Hughes, Arkansas.[13] Daisy had never heard about the Gospel Minnie sides, although she was thrilled at their existence when we played them for her, saying, "She never told me about those!" Perhaps Minnie thought Daisy wouldn't approve of such hypocritical treatment of gospel music, although there is a long and established history of blues singers doing a few gospel numbers, with or without "the feeling."

Perhaps Minnie was simply going along with Joe who recorded four sermons with singing that day (as Hallelujah Joe), but if that's what she was doing, it's the last time she did it. Minnie's September 10, 1934, *Squat It* and *Moaning the Blues,* released on Decca 7146 and 7037, both issued as by "Memphis Minnie," mark the last time she and Joe recorded together. The last record issued as by "Memphis Minnie and Kansas Joe" was Decca 7038, the two-part *You Got To Move (You Ain't Got To Move),* part 2 of which was cut on August 31, 1934. Joe's reputed jealousy at Minnie's fame and success is often given as the reason for their breakup. For example, Leadbitter has noted, "Joe had a hard time with such a popular wife, and they split up in 1935 or so."[14] However, no corroborating evidence has come to light to support this idea. Other sources confirm that he actually did become a preacher,[15] and unlike Minnie, he returned to the studio a second time to record four more Halleluhah Joe sermons. But in early 1937 Joe and the Harlem Hamfats cut a number called *Hallelujah Joe Ain't Preachin' No More;* presumably his preaching career had ended.[16]

Joe seemed to do better for himself at Decca, where his output was not overshadowed by Minnie's like it was at Vocalion. He not only recorded solo pieces before and after the gospel sides, but he continued to record with the jazz group, the Harlem Hamfats through the rest of the decade.[17] His stint with the Hamfats ended a few years later, and by 1940 we find him leading various washboard bands, recording as either Big Joe and His Rhythm or as Big Joe and His Washboard Band. The records from these sessions are all quite interesting and feature Robert Lee McCoy (later known as Robert Nighthawk) on harp or guitar, Amanda Sortier or Washboard Sam on washboard, Charlie McCoy on mandolin, and Joe on guitar. Most of the vocals were done by Joe, but Sortier sang one duet with him, and Harmon "Peetie Wheatstraw's Buddy" Ray sang on several numbers.[18] But Joe didn't seem to be a regular part of the Chicago milieu in which most of the singers participated, and neither Jimmy Rogers or Johnny Shines ever met him. Even Ethel Douglas, who married Leo Douglas in 1921, couldn't remember much about the quiet and retiring Joe McCoy, although he and Minnie had lived with Leo and Ethel in Walls.

Joe McCoy died on January 28, 1950, of "spontaneous cerebral apoplexy due to hypertension heart disease" and was buried in Rest Vale Cemetary in Alsip, Illinois. His death certificate gave his occupation as "laborer," although he'd been a professional musician for at least twenty-five years. The informant on the death certificate was Virginia McCoy, possibly his second wife who is said to have had two children by Joe. Her address is different than his, however, which was 4216 Calumet at the time of his death. Thus, Virginia McCoy may have been separated from Joe by 1950, or she may not have been his wife at all. Big Bill wrote that not even Minnie or his friends from the Harlem Hamfats attended the funeral,[19] and for Memphis Slim, the funeral was an especially bitter occasion.

"Joe wrote this song, *Why Don't You Do Right?,* and Irving Berlin presented this song at the Chicago Theater, with Peggy Lee and all that thing. And at this particular time, Joe McCoy was laying in state at the Metropolitan Funeral Home, and we had to beg money to bury him. Boy, I'll never forget that. I thought that was a damn shame. They had the *headlines* of the Chicago Theatre. 'Peggy Lee and Irving Berlin.' And here's the man that wrote it, and he told me he never get no money. That Lester Melrose. The *'great'* Lester Melrose. He stole *all* our money. And then went and had a accident and got paralyzed from the waist down. [Smirks] He had to go around in a wheelchair until he died, which wasn't long, I don't think, after that. But, you know, he took *everybody's* money."[20]

Was Joe McCoy the man named Squirrel who Jimmy Rogers remembered as Minnie's companion in the mid- to late 1930s? Rogers knew that Squirrel played guitar and recorded with Minnie, but he could take us no closer to Squirrel's true identity. No other informant recognized the name. "They say she was kind of rough with him," Rogers recalled.[21]

As we're coming to see, the image of Minnie as a rough customer rings true. "She chewed tobacco," said Homesick James. "She kept it in her mouth all the time. Even when she was singing, she kept that tobacco in her mouth. She had a coffee cup, be singing, spit right in there, the spit-cup right over there. Hee, hee, hee. She did that seriously, man, and when she got through, she'd just pick it up and spit, man, she didn't care!"[22] Brewer Phillips used to pick up Minnie's tobacco and snuff for her at the store, along with Wild Irish Rose and food for the evening meal. "She didn't only chew tobacco, she dipped snuff. Her brand of snuff was this Copenhagen and her tobacco was Brown Mule. She didn't smoke, though. She would get her a little twig and she would get the ends off, and dip it down in the snuff bottle and dip it down in her jaw. And the chewing tobacco, she'd put that in her jaw, and you know a lot of times, she'd be singing, she'd have that chewing tobacco in her jaw."[23] By the time she came to Daisy's house to stay, Minnie had given up tobacco.

On May 27, 1935, Minnie cut her last session with Decca, producing four splendid, downhome sides: the *Milk Cow Blues*-influenced *Jockey Man Blues, Weary Woman's Blues, Reachin' Pete* and *Down in New Orleans,* with the latter's enticing implications of voodoo and conjure. Two months later she cut four sides for Bluebird, three of which were issued under the name "Texas Tessie." *Good Mornin'* was a spin-off of Kokomo Arnold's wildly successful *Milk Cow Blues,* but it was rejected by Bluebird, and it only reached the public in mid-1936 when Minnie re-recorded it for Vocalion. The Bluebird session had several highlights, though, not the least of which was Big Bill's guitar solo on the pop song,[24] *I'm Waiting on You,* and Minnie's dynamic vocal on *You Wrecked My Happy Home.*

By 1937, the Texas Tessie sides were no longer listed as being available in the current Bluebird race lists, although the "Memphis Minnie" Bluebird sides from the October 1935 session were still in the catalog. A Vocalion catalog from September, 1934, when Minnie had just started recording for Decca, showed virtually all of her vintage pieces, solo or with Joe, as being still available at the new price of 35 cents or three for $1. Minnie's Decca records from 1934-1935 were still available in 1944, but Decca had kept virtually their entire 7000 series in print.

In August of 1935, she recorded her two tributes to the black national hero, boxing champion Joe Louis: *He's in the Ring (Doing That Same Old Thing)* and *Joe Louis Strut.* Pianist Black Bob (Ed Hudson), with whom Minnie was to have a lengthy working relationship, made his first appearance as Minnie's accompanist on this session.[25] On the last Bluebird session, October 31, 1935, she was accompanied by Casey Bill Weldon for the first time. Casey Bill accompanied her on two sides, *When the Sun Goes Down, Part 2,*[26] and the prostitution song, *Hustlin' Woman Blues,* but he dropped out for *Selling My Pork Chops* and *Doctor, Doctor Blues.*

While tracking singers through the recording studio provides insight into a major aspect of their lives, even the stars spent only a small part of their working careers in the studio. What was Minnie doing when she wasn't recording? Like so many blues artists, Minnie traveled considerably, and she frequently returned to the South to play. Like Johnny Littlejohn, Homesick James and countless others, she continually renewed her music at its source. As James himself declared. "Chicago, then back down South, Chicago, then back down there; Mississippi, all the way through. That woman she used to *go. . . .* She'd play at those Saturday night fish fries! They would have a big hall, it was just a big room or house, they would take all the beds down, and the kitchen wood stove back there, that's where they be frying the fish. . . ."[27]

Sunnyland Slim emphasized how Chicago was just an anchor point for the various travelers who passed through, stayed awhile, but always kept traveling. "Me and her, she's just like me, when she come here, she didn't stay, wouldn't stay. I'll go back to Cairo, or like other places in the South."[28] Bobo Jenkins remembered seeing Minnie during the mid-thirties playing at a Mr. Towels' store in Walls, and thirty-five years later, he still remembered Minnie's beads and fancy clothes.[29]

Memphis pianist Mose Vinson played with Minnie frequently throughout the thirties and later as well, while Fiddlin' Joe Martin played with her on 8th Street in Memphis for Big Lewis, and worked the Jackson jukes with her during the later thirties. Minnie and Martin also worked the Robinsonville area, and he was fond of recalling that he had learned the guitar part for *Good Morning, School Girl* (also known later as *Me and My Chauffeur Blues*) from Minnie personally. Martin also remembered that Willie Brown could play the same guitar part. Martin played with Minnie on and off over the years, meeting her early on in Shelby, Mississippi, and ultimately traveling with her to Chicago where he was thrown over, probably in favor of Blind John Davis, with whom Minnie began to record.[30]

Davis himself preserved a priceless anecdote from those years when he accompanied Minnie. "Minnie paid $200 for a wig. At that time women wasn't wearing wigs, you know, unless they just *had* to. She paid $200 for a wig, she got drunk and went home that night, leave that wig on a chair. And somebody done give her a little old puppy. She woke up the next morning looking for her wig, her wig was [scattered] all over the house! Minnie hit [the puppy] with her guitar and broke the neck off of it, and Son Joe let him out, and he said that dog didn't even look back! That puppy didn't come back there at all! Oh, god, they had me laughing! I had to get up and go in another room. 'Cause, man, she was cursing, 'I'll kill that so-and-so if I catch him.' That puppy figured that, too."[31]

By late 1935 Minnie had settled into a relaxed groove under the supervision of Lester Melrose. Many blues artists were not able to make the transition from rural-sounding downhome blues to the more sophisticated sounds Melrose's artists turned out, and it is a remarkable sign of Minnie's resiliency[32] that she adjusted so well, becoming a major figure in the blues world of the next two decades, and continuing to have a new record issued every few weeks until the beginning of the war. One critic described Minnie as a "female Big Bill,"[33] pointing not only to the crucial role Big Bill and Memphis Minnie played in the consolidation of the Melrose sound, but to the ease with which they tailored their music to the new style. Bill's remarkable popularity can too easily obscure the fact that stylistically Minnie was as much if not more of an innovator than Bill was.

To appreciate the evolution of Minnie's style, we must look more closely at the Melrose phenomenon. According to Melrose, it was in early 1934, when taverns were reappearing in the wake of the repeal of prohibition, and when every bar had a juke-box, that he sent a letter to Columbia and Victor saying that he could provide unlimited blues talent to meet their recording needs. Their response was enthusiastic, and "from March, 1934, to February, 1951, I recorded at least 90 percent of all rhythm-and-blues talent for RCA Victor [which included their Bluebird subsidiary] and Columbia Records."[34] Among the majors, only Decca went forward without Melrose's assistance.

Melrose recruited his artists by traveling throughout the country, from city to city, and from bar to bar, looking for blues singers. He also used bluesmen like Big Bill, Big Joe Williams and Walter Davis as talent scouts to bring him new artists. During Minnie's heyday of the 1930s and 1940s, Melrose was the single most powerful and most influential man in the blues recording field, and one glance at his "stable" shows why: Big Bill, Washboard Sam, Merline Johnson (Yas Yas Girl), Arthur Crudup, Tampa Red, Lil Green, St. Louis Jimmy, Roosevelt Sykes, Memphis Minnie, Curtis Jones, Big Joe Williams, Walter Davis, Sonny Boy Williamson, Doctor Clayton, Lonnie Johnson, Tommy McClennan, Big Maceo, Bumble Bee Slim, and many others were all Melrose artists. No one has ever accused him of exaggerating when he said "90%"!

Melrose's artists often gathered at Tampa Red's house at 35th and State, and blues bassist and impresario Willie Dixon first met Melrose there in the mid- 1940s. He saw Minnie and Son Joe there, along with Big Maceo, Sonny Boy Williamson (John Lee Williamson), Blind John Davis and others who used to "hang out" and practice at Tampa's. Playing on Melrose sessions with Minnie and Son, as well as with Sonny Boy Williamson, Lil Green and others, influenced his own later work as a producer.[35] Muddy Waters remarked that one had to go through Tampa to be welcome at the rehearsal hall and there was the implication that Tampa Red was also the route to Melrose's good graces or managership.

Some critics think Melrose "ruined" the blues by imposing, on so many records, a uniform house style, obtained by repeatedly using the same musicians, on their own and on each others' records. Thus, phrases like "The Bluebird Beat," the "Melrose Mess" or the "Melrose machine"[36] emphasize the monotonous regularity imposed by the Melrose regime. Big Bill was sharply critical of Melrose's financial dealings, too.[37] Brewer Phillips' remarks seem pertinent here. "She *always* would tell me that she'd been messed around in the music. So I'd say, 'How can they mess you around'? She say, 'They'll take your money.' And she'd always say,' You can learn to play, but don't let them take your money.'"[38]

Other critics like Delmark Records' Bob Koester point to the New Orleans jazz backgrounds of Melrose sidemen and emphasize the positive aspects of Melrose's productions, like their danceable rhythm and their popularity. Further, unique and unusual artists like Arthur "Big Boy" Crudup were as much a part of the full Melrose picture as the "regularized" Big Bill or Washboard Sam were. Koester also notes that "Melrose is remembered with unusual fondness by the artists he recorded. There are noticeably fewer complaints of sharp practices and frequent praise of his musical perceptions and social attitudes."[39]

In evaluating Melrose's role in the changes that seemed to sweep through the blues recording world in the New Deal years, two rarely-considered perspectives should be emphasized. The reputedly monotonous combo sound of the 1930s may be less a Melrosian artifact than the result of a change in styles already in effect by the late 1920s. The sound was solidified with the rise of the piano inaugurated by Leroy Carr, who, with Scrapper Blackwell, recorded the instant hit, *How Long—How Long Blues* on June 19, 1928.[40] Peetie Wheatstraw began recording in 1930, and his post-1933 records were influential in consolidating the sound that had begun with Carr and Blackwell, well before the Melrose empire was in place. Blues record impresario Nick Perls was only half joking when he commented, "Peetie Wheatstraw ruined the blues almost single-handedly," for Wheatstraw's smooth style of the 1930s seemed to typify the forces that spelled doom for so many rural-sounding, country blues artists.[41]

One should also assess the role of the Melrose musicians from a *post*-World War II perspective, i.e. from the other end of their period of dominance, to see the vitally important role played by the expressive harp and vocal style of Melrose headliner Sonny Boy Williamson in providing inspiration for the new electric Chicago sound of Little Walter, Snooky Pryor and other newcomers. Sonny Boy had begun recording in 1937, and his records were among the most popular of any blues artist's ever.

From these alternating perspectives, Melrose becomes a sign of regularity caught in the midst of two innovations: Carr, Wheatstraw and the rise of the piano, and Sonny Boy, Little Walter and the rise of the harp. Melrose had little *personally* to do with Carr or Little Walter, but his presence during the critical period of 1934-1951 was strongly felt. At the very least, Melrose's *refractive* powers affected the music that passed from Carr to Little Walter, but all concerned would agree that his regime was more than simply catalytic.[42] And if we query the evidence and not the critics we find that these extremely popular and danceable records are "monotonous" only for those commentators who so ardently and exclusively crave vintage Delta blues or the piercing electric guitars and harps of the 1950s.

Minnie's last intricately picked guitar duet was recorded in 1932, and the presence of a piano on her January 10, 1935, Decca session was the strongest sign of what the future held. Henceforth, Minnie's guitar began to play a more supporting role, and even on the two-guitar sessions that lacked a piano, Minnie seldom brought an elaborate picking technique to the recording studio. If a piano wasn't on a session, it might as well have been. This was a music styled for the tough joints on Chicago's South Side, and not for the country suppers and fish fries Minnie played for in the South.

But did her city guitar style evolve out of the notion that her more dexterous rural style was old fashioned and dated, or was it merely the socioeconomic requirements of tavern music? Were her more frequent spoken asides in the later records a way of covering over silences emanating from the gaps in her new style of playing, or did she think she was being urbane and cosmopolitan? While some of her mid- to late 1930s Vocalions might suggest she was a typical Melrose musician, her vocals nonetheless injected a rougher, grittier and more vital feel into many of her songs, and the absence of a piano on her sessions between 1938 and 1947 kept her output from being overly smooth and monotonous. Yet this is only half the story, the part that can be told from Minnie's childhood through early 1934.

From a modern perspective, i.e., viewed from Chicago instead of from the South, Minnie's seizure of modern guitar styles was as much innovation as it was adaptation. While other blues artists also sought techniques that would bring their performances up to date, Minnie *immediately* grasped the lyric quality of the single string picking that had been pioneered by Lonnie Johnson a decade earlier.[43] This same style would eventually emerge victorious in the hands of T-Bone Walker and B. B. King, after passing through the hands of electric guitar pioneers George Barnes and Willie Lacey, in the thirties and forties respectively, and even Django Reinhardt could be said to have blossomed from the same tree. Yet Minnie was one of the first blues artists to use the electric guitar.[44]

She frequently played at the 708 Club with Big Bill, and she played at the Tramor Hotel and Cafe at 740 E. 47th St, accompanied by Black Bob on piano and Arnett Nelson on clarinet.[45] Broonzy wrote that he and Minnie had "played in night clubs all over the States together,"[46] and Minnie and Black Bob traveled together as well, probably in the mid-1930s.[47] Moody Jones talked about what a perfectionist Black Bob was and how he was likely to stop the band right in the middle of a number, even in front of a big crowd to say, "You didn't do that right!"[48] Much like Minnie, as we shall see. Often when she returned from her travels, she had no home to come back to, and on those occasions she stayed with friends and colleagues like Sunnyland Slim and his wife, Bessie. Sunnyland recalled, "When Memphis Minnie come here . . . she stayed with Tampa like one night sometimes, or she'd stay with me and Bessie. And then she moved to Milton [Rector's] daddy's.[49] And she stayed there for a little and she got that job at the 708 Club. Well, me and Sykes had been playing there, and I got her that job at that 708 Club. She stayed there. And then I got her another job out in Argo [a Chicago suburb]."[50]

Minnie had had seven recording sessions in 1935, for three different recording companies! On her first session of 1936, she cut four lyrically interesting songs, one of which was *I'm a Gambling Woman*. "Yeaaah, Minnie shot craps like a man," said Homesick James, "playing those cards, man, raising all kind of hell, heh, heh. All of them women who'd sing the blues, would curse, be drunk, just sit up and talk a lot of shit, man. What foul language!"[51] Johnny Shines confirmed Homesick's observation, "yeah, Minnie gambled like a dog!"[52]

Minnie's sidemen are not always easy to identify, especially during this period of her career, where the personnel suggested by Dixon and Godrich can't easily be confirmed. A number of authorities have challenged the notion that Blind John Davis plays piano on these sessions, and it does seem more likely that the pianist is Black Bob for several sessions that previously were thought to include Davis.[53]

Sometimes even a mistake will help to verify the personnel on a recording session. Alfred Bell's trumpet flubs suggest his presence on the November 12, 1936, session as well as the June 9, 1937 session, although Dixon and Godrich note his presence on the second session only.[54] Whether trumpets were never more than Melrose "experiments" in the first place,[55] or whether a too-close look at Bell's sour notes ultimately soured Melrose on brass, we'll never know, but Minnie was never to record again with trumpets or even saxes.

She did, however, record an entire session on June 23, 1938, accompanied by Charlie McCoy on mandolin, while in the preceding session, many sides of which exist only as test pressings, Arnett Nelson again accompanies her on clarinet. She herself may have taken up the mandolin again for several sides. Close listening is required to hear the mandolin on many of these—and often it cannot be said with any certainty that a mandolin is present—but it can be clearly heard on take -2 of *Running and Dodging Blues*.[56]

The most important event of this period was the beginning of her assocation with Ernest Lawlars, otherwise known as "Little Son Joe," soon to be her second husband.[57] Son Joe was a talented guitarist, and he and Minnie were very close. Minnie even gave up one of her later show tours because she couldn't be accompanied by Son Joe. "She never did do anything that her husband couldn't follow her about. . . . She was very faithful to him, you know she never did get carried away, 'bout her husbands," said Brewer Phillips.[58]

L-A-W-L-A-R-S is the correct spelling of Ernest and Minnie's last name, but misspellings, of the type of which they were certainly aware, continued to plague them even beyond their deaths. Ernest's death certificate cites his wife's name as "Winnie," and on Minnie's death certificate, her last name is given as "Lawlers." While the Arkansas Department of Health, Division of Vital Records, has no record of Ernest Lawlars' birth, the death certificate shows Hughes, Arkansas as his place of birth, and the date as May 18, 1900. The information was supplied by Daisy, who never knew Son's parents' names. Son Joe was "Little Son Joe" in the music world, but he was called "Son" by Minnie and her family.

Son Joe's first recording session, for ARC in Jackson, Mississippi, on October 10, 1935, produced one unissued side, *Sin and a Shame Blues*. In those days, before he met Minnie, he lived with a woman named Ferdella at 227 12 Mulberry, in Memphis, and a year later, they moved to 124 W. Illinois, rear. Son was a laborer at the time, and Della worked as a domestic. Beyond 1937, however, we lose official track of Son Joe until he reappears as Minnie's husband in 1939. Various sources give Minnie and Son's place of meeting as Memphis, but our first substantial glimpse of them as a couple is the February 3, 1939, recording session in Chicago. Shortly before, Minnie had moved from 230 E. Garfield Blvd., where she had lived since the early thirties, to 5300 S. Prairie. Both addresses were in the heart of Chicago's South Side.

But for the abortive attempt in Jackson, this was Son's first recording session, and all six of his pieces were issued, as were all four of Minnie's. Son Joe's *Key To the World* was even a tribute to the "woman I got now" who was "the key to the world," Memphis Minnie. The decade closed with another Vocalion session three days later, where for reasons we'll never know, Minnie reverted to her 1930 picking style and cut the downhome, rural-flavored *Call the Fire Wagon*. But the decade of her greatest popularity was yet to come.

5. ME AND MY CHAUFFEUR

Everything I touch becomes blue.
—Kajsa Bergh

We was all around playing the blues in Chicago.
—Jimmy Rogers

Many factors combined to make the 1940s the years of Minnie's most fruitful reign. Minnie and Son's first two sessions of the forties, June 27, 1940, and May 21, 1941, were recorded without piano, as had been the case with their last two sessions in 1939. These 1939 sessions had been supported by Fred Williams' drumming, but the first session of the new decade featured Minnie and Son alone, and in May of 1941, they were accompanied solely by an unknown bassist. Son Joe not only provided Minnie with solid backing, but did so imaginatively and with skill. As Moody Jones commented, "Her husband Son he was the onliest fella . . . that knew more about them chords than I did."[1] Son Joe had joined the Barber Parker band in the mid-forties, traveling throughout the Delta with Parker, Willie Love, and G. P. Jackson, and Jackson remembers Son Joe as not only an excellent guitarist, but as a washboard player as well,[2] a memory consistent with the fact that Son played drums on his and Minnie's last session in 1959.[3]

The first session of the decade had produced *Ma Rainey,* Minnie's tribute to the Classic blues star who had died just before

47

Christmas. It was a compelling song, and Minnie sang it well, carrying on the blues tradition of such memorials as *Wasn't It Sad About Lemon,* by Walter and Byrd, *The Death of Leroy Carr,* by Bumble Bee Slim, and *Death of Blind Boy Fuller,*[4] by Brownie McGhee, to name only a few. The same session produced the well-known *Nothing in Rambling,* but Minnie and Son's star rose to its zenith in the next two sessions, in 1941.

In May of that year, Minnie recorded her biggest hit of all, *Me and My Chauffeur Blues,* an updated, elaborated meditation on the *Garage Fire Blues* kernel, sung to the tune of Sonny Boy Williamson's influential *Good Morning, School Girl.*[5] It was so popular that Minnie cut it eleven years later for the Chess brothers' Checker label. *Chauffeur* was a favorite among Zydeco performers, too, with Rockin' Dopsie and Clifton Chenier both turning in their own versions, and at least two other blues artists, Lightnin' Hopkins and Eddie "One String" Jones, recorded "reply" songs.[6] The same session produced the well-received *Can't Afford to Lose My Man,* cut later by Minnie's friend, Homesick James, who backed it with another Minnie hit, *Please Set a Date.*[7]

It was the December studio visit that yielded two other Chicago blues standards, *Looking the World Over* (later recorded by Whispering Smith and Big Mama Thornton, at least) and Son's *Black Rat Swing* (also known as *You Is One Black Rat),* a tremendously influential blues hit. Versions of *Black Rat Swing* have been recorded by Big Mama Thornton, Lightnin' Hopkins, Muddy Waters, and many others.[8] While Son takes the vocal on *Black Rat Swing,* he sounds so much like Minnie that virtually every blues artist who remembers the song remembers it as Minnie's. Minnie performed the song frequently, however, so that her colleagues who remember the song from club dates have good reason to think of it as hers. To make the identification with Minnie complete, however, Okeh issued *Black Rat Swing* as by "Mr. Memphis Minnie!"[9]

"Minnie Lawlars" first appears in the records of the black local 208 of the Chicago Federation of Musicians (American Federation of Musicians) in 1939, but the date is less a function of when she joined as it is of how far back the records go. She may have joined earlier as Minnie McCoy or Minnie Douglas, but the records don't show it, nor do they show a Joe McCoy as a member of the union, although he almost certainly was. By the time the merger between local 208 and local 10 (the white local) was finalized in 1966, the records of local 208 were already incomplete, deteriorating and in disarray, compared to their more recent records or to the earlier records of local 10.

The records show that in 1941, Minnie was fined several times for "non-attendance of union meeting," such fines having been a common means by which small unions supplemented their small treasuries.[10] During the war years, Minnie paid between $3.50 and $4.25 in dues per quarter. In 1943, however, she failed to pay her second quarter dues ($3.50) on time, and she had to pay a $5 reinstatement fee, along with her second and third quarter dues ($7.50) in August, when the third quarter was due. For the last year of the war, as well as when the war was over, the dues stabilized at a slightly lower level, and for the next seven years, 1945 through 1951, Minnie paid only $4 per quarter. Dues were increased to $4.25 in 1952 and by the mid 1950s, Minnie was paying $6.25 per quarter in dues, although her regular jobs were becoming few and far between. This figure remained the same until April 2, 1958, the last date a payment is recorded. The union records represent another case of confusion in the spelling of Minnie's and Son Joe's name. While the first available ledger page is headed "Minnie (McCoy changed July 10)" and below that, "Minnie Lawlars", the third and fourth page are headed "Minnie Lawlers". All pages agree that her "business" is "guitar."

Minnie may have paid her dues through the duration of the war, but her recording career was to be curtailed nonetheless, not so much from shellac rationing as from a total ban on recording imposed by the American Federation of Musicians.[11] On August 1, 1942 the AFM's James Petrillo proclaimed a ban on new recordings in an attempt to stifle the competition that juke boxes represented for working musicians, and in order to collect royalties from the major labels. Few recordings were made throughout the period of the ban. In September, 1943, Decca agreed to the AFM's demand for royalties on new recordings, and Capitol agreed in October. Finally, Victor and Columbia, who had held out until November, 1944, also gave in. But as one historian notes, the collection of 1% of retail price that the AFM demanded was ultimately declared illegal and a violation of the Taft-Hartley act of 1947. This led to another ban running from late December 1947 to December 1948, although this one was less successful.[12]

Minnie may not have realized it, but the 1940s were to become significant in blues history in a way that neither she nor Petrillo had yet to dream of. For the period also marked the first hesitant stirrings of a new kind of record company, the small, independent labels which often paid less than union scale, and who understood the signs long before the majors. As they were, in fact, "independent," they had the flexibility of vision necessary to record a new and unusual, fiercely electric sound, a music before which Lester Melrose could only move out of the way. Like any record company, these small labels were affected by rationing, too, but restrictions were relaxed as the war neared an end. When shellac was scarce, record producers like Gold Star's Bill Quinn recycled thousands of old 78s (and no doubt many treasures among them) to provide the raw material for their new releases, giving a bizarre literalism to the notion of one style developing out of another. Many of Lightnin' Hopkins' early records were literally *made* out of melted down Minnie's and Big Bill's!

There were signs enough for Minnie and her colleagues to see which way the stylistic winds were blowing. By 1945, Melrose artists like Sonny Boy, Big Bill and Minnie found that many of their regular gigs were going to jump blues and R & B bands. The smaller clubs were starting to hire younger—and cheaper—artists.[13] If this wasn't always the case by 1945, it would be by 1949. Was it jeopardy itself that was audible in Minnie's late 1940s repertoire, her weakest period, in terms of composition?[14] *I'm So Glad, Killer Diller* and *Three Times Seven* were appealing, evocative numbers, still prized by her fans, but *Tears on My Pillow, Tonight I Smile on You, Jump Little Rabbit,* and the overdramatized *Night Watchman Blues* lack excitement. True, these are the most vulnerable spots in her broad repertoire, but the fact remains that Columbia soon dropped their blues artists, Minnie among them.

The lyrics of Minnie's songs had always been exceptional—she was a composer of outstanding talent—and while her late repertoire displays a gradual diminishing in both lyric and musical qualities, her fame as a songwriter is nonetheless well established. From the highly original *Frankie Jean* to the no less remarkable *I'm Gonna Bake My Biscuits,* Minnie created one exceptional piece after another. But did she write them all?[15] The determining of who wrote what songs is never simple. Composer credits on the record labels themselves may or may not show the true state of affairs. Library of Congress records do give a composer of the piece, if the song was registered there, but most of Minnie's songs were not. Sifting through the available evidence is nonetheless revealing.

First let us turn to the actual 78s. Virtually all of Minnie's records, if they bear composer credits at all, have label copy giving composer credits to "McCoy" or some variant of "Lawlars;" some bear the name "Minnie McCoy."[16] The label copy shifts from "McCoy" to "Lawlars" in 1940-1941, shortly after Minnie met Ernest.[17] Thus the early and late records are divided by composer credit between "McCoy" (early) or "Lawlars" (late). Copyright records reveal that while most of Minnie's songs are not registered, those early songs that were registered and bear a composer credit "McCoy" (as well as those bearing a composer credit "Minnie McCoy") were composed by Minnie herself and not Joe McCoy. Those late records that were registered and which bear a composer credit "Lawlars" were composed by Ernest Lawlars, and not Minnie.

What this means, *if we take the copyright records at face value,* is that Minnie wrote *all* of her early material, from the vintage period beginning in 1929 through the entire decade of the 1930s, but after meeting Ernest Lawlars and playing with him for a year, she never again recorded material she herself wrote, but only material that Son Joe wrote. Minnie's longtime fans may find this difficult to believe, as do we.

Me and My Chauffeur Blues, In My Girlish Days and Minnie's other popular songs of the 1940s were, therefore, written by Son. Is this possible? Is she less talented than we thought? We say her "talent" is amply demonstrated by the history of her first forty years. If, for whatever reason, she stopped songwriting in 1940, what does it matter? Perhaps she found it an odious chore she was glad to unload. Blues artists who recorded prolifically were under continual pressure to produce enough original material to please the record company's A and R personnel as well as their listeners, thus assuring the continuation of their recording careers, and it was difficult to always meet this demand.

Further, if Ernest Lawlars wrote Minnie's 1940s hits, he must also have written her 1940s flops as well, not to mention *Shout the Boogie* or *Tonight I Smile on You,* and other sentimental songs. One could theorize that if Son was the composer of most of the late pieces, that would explain the "untypical" aspects of some of the songs: the pseudo-sophisticated verbiage and the passive sentimentality. That Minnie felt uncomfortable when singing in such a tender and maudlin mode is demonstrated mid-way through *When My Man Comes Home,* where she says, "Anybody's man, don't make me no difference." Indeed, this statement almost directly insists that this Lil Green-like number is none of her own.

On the other hand, Library of Congress registrations may not be redeemable at face value, for Minnie and Son, or Lester Melrose, may have had their own reasons for specifying Ernest Lawlars as the composer of Minnie's post-1940 pieces. Composer credits were often given to non-composers as a way of distributing royalties and even session fees, and they were often used as a means for paying the scouts who brought the singers out of obscurity and into the studios. Further, not a single informant or source suggests that Son ever wrote *any* songs, while the same sources agree almost unanimously that Minnie did write most, if not all, of her material. She not only continued to write songs in her later years, but she gave them away to younger artists in need of material. According to Brewer Phillips, Minnie not only wrote songs for Willie Love, but she wrote a number of songs for Robert Nighthawk, as well.[18] Sunnyland Slim remembers Minnie writing songs for Baby Face Leroy, at least as late as 1940.[19] Brewer's and Sunnyland's remarks are more than suggestive, we think, and they should be considered in conjunction with the facts already mentioned: that we've *never* come upon anecdotal evidence that Son was a songwriter, or that Minnie ever stopped composing. It is most likely, then, that Minnie continued to write her own material, as she always had, and Son may have written *some* of the later songs.

If this is so, why were the songs credited to Son Joe as composer? We can only speculate: If it was true that Joe McCoy's envy of Minnie's "stardom" broke up their marriage, Minnie may have decided to prevent a re-occurrence of this trauma. Treating Son Joe as the composer of her songs may have been one step she took in this direction. Another step may have been her frequent asides to him on record: "All right, Son Joe, I'm looking at you," etc, giving him a more substantial *presence* on her records. A third step may have been her attempt to make him co-host of her Blue Monday parties by including the phrase in *Daybreak Blues,* "*This man* pitches a party every first of the week. . . ."

If Minnie's compositional talents occasionally come under scrutiny, so do her skills as an instrumentalist. While generally considered an extremely accomplished guitarist on the basis of her early work,[20] some of her later work sounds lazy in comparison. Minnie never became a sophisticated, modern instrumentalist, nor may this have ever been her desire, although her favorite guitarist was the polished stylist, Robert Jr. Lockwood. Some of Minnie's colleagues have disclosed their real feelings about her "limitations" as an artist, and doubtless these shortcomings may have ultimately worked to handicap her. Homesick James commented somewhat harshly, and incorrectly, that she could only play a D chord, and Moody Jones used to tease her, saying that she only played on one string, adding "but what she was doing, she could do it."[21]

She certainly could! At the dawn of the new decade, Minnie's popularity was hardly on the wane. Minnie, now with Son Joe, continued to work at the 708 Club at 708 E. 47th St., where they were often joined by Big Bill, Sunnyland Slim, or Snooky Pryor. The 708 was a favored hangout, recalled fondly by Pryor, who remembered that "it used to be right side of Montgomery Ward. Memphis Slim, he used to play there," and Pryor's partner, Moody Jones, remembered seeing Minnie at the 708 Club, too.[22] The 708 was Minnie and Son's "home club," to the extent that they had one, and it was the tavern most frequently mentioned by Minnie and Son's compatriots.

But Minnie played at dozens of the better known (and better paying) nightclubs, from the Music Box and Club DeLisa to Martin's Corner, Gatewood's Tavern, and the White Elephant (Don's Den). Minnie and Memphis Slim played together at Gatewood's, especially when Big Bill was out of town,[23] and she often played across the street from the White Elephant.[24] As likely as not, she was joined by local musicians like Homer Harris or James "Beale Street" Clark;[25] (the latter's home became the new rehearsal hall when Tampa Red "went nutty" after his wife died).[26] Minnie was a regular participant in Chicago's blues milieu, a hard drinker who played just as hard. One night, she, Son Joe, and Sunnyland got drunk together, and in the wee hours of the morning, Sunnyland staggered home. The next day, and after a good, recuperative slumber, he went over to Little Brother Montgomery's. Lee Collins was there, and so were Minnie and Son, still partying! They hadn't been to bed since Sunnyland left them.[27]

Son Joe, Minnie and Roosevelt Sykes occasionally played the midnight show at the Indiana Theatre,[28] just as they played at the Square Deal and The Flame. While most singers had regular gigs at certain clubs—for Minnie, the 708 and Sylvio's, like most blues artists, she played at dozens of clubs with scores of colleagues. As Jimmy Rogers put it, after patiently explaining that he had seen Minnie playing in the basement at 31st and Indiana, as well as on the North side, "we was *all around* playing the blues in Chicago."[29]

Poet Langston Hughes saw Minnie play at the 230 Club, and he was impressed enough to devote his entire *Chicago Defender* "Here to Yonder" column for January 9, 1943 to the occasion:

"... Memphis Minnie sits on top of the icebox at the 230 Club in Chicago and beats out blues on an electric guitar. . . . She grabs the microphone and yells, 'Hey, now!' Then she hits a few deep chords at random, leans forward ever so slightly over her guitar, bows her head and begins to beat out a good old steady down-home rhythm on the strings—a rhythm so contagious that often it makes the crowd holler out loud.

"Then, through the smoke and racket of the noisy Chicago bar float Louisiana bayous, muddy old swamps, Mississippi dust and sun, cotton fields, lonesome roads, train whistles in the night, mosquitoes at dawn and the Rural Free Delivery that never brings the right letter. All these things cry through the strings on Memphis Minnie's electric guitar, amplified to machine proportions—a musical version of electric welders plus a rolling mill. . . ."

Interestingly enough, drummer Jump Jackson was convinced that Langston Hughes got his report secondhand, even though his

own report tallies with Hughes'. "What would he know? He would-
n't probably go in that joint. Yeah, he wouldn't rub shoulders with
them." [laughs] But Jackson *was* with Minnie on the same job. "I
worked with Memphis Minnie. I remember we was on, the little
club at 51st and Prairie, way up on top of a icebox. Just drum and
guitar. She had that place packed. You know those walk-in cool-
ers? I said, 'Minnie, gee, I'm gonna work this week out, but I can't
take this! I'm gonna fall and break my neck here.' They had a
banister up there but if you'd fall against it, you'd go right through
that thing. Fall right down on the people."[30]

Disc jockey Big Bill Hill used to host a "cocktail party" that
moved from club to club on Sundays: From the 708 Club to the
Du Drop Lounge to Sylvio's to the Blue Flame. But there were
other, more famous, parties for Chicago blues singers, and these
were hosted by Memphis Minnie. These Blue Monday parties often
took place at Ruby Lee Gatewood's, Big Bill's Lake Street home
base.[31] The parties were well attended and recalled with great
pleasure, and Minnie herself memorialized them in her *Daybreak
Blues*.[32]

DAYBREAK BLUES

Come daybreak in the morning,
I'm gonna take the dirt road home.
Wooo, soon daybreak in the morning,
I'm gonna take the dirt road home.
'Cause these Blue Monday blues
is 'bout to kill me, sure as your born.

Well, this man pitches a party,
every first of the week,
I can't cross the floor
for other people's feet.
Come daybreak in the morning, etc.

Well, I went to my kitchen,
intendin' to eat a bite.
The table was crowded

from morning till night.
Come daybreak in the morning, etc.

Spoken: All right, Little Son Joe.
Yes, I know. Keep on playing.
I'll come home.

Hey, now I turned around,
aimed to go to bed,
There's four at the foot
and six at the head.
Come daybreak in the morning, etc.

As Brother John Sellers recalled, "Memphis Minnie . . . really those Blue Monday parties in those days were too much . . . ! With all her greatness and her songs and her Blue Monday parties that she gave, she was . . . a singer to be remembered."[33] Said J. B. Lenoir, "[Minnie] used to give cocktail parties, you know—those Blue Monday parties at the Gate, you know, and I actually found she would ask *me* to play a number for *her*."[34] Lenoir's experience was not unusual, for Minnie could be very generous, and she often turned the spotlight on unknown or younger performers, both at her parties and when she was on stage.[35] Billy Boy Arnold was another young performer that Minnie encouraged. "I had the privilege to go on a gig with Memphis Minnie. I was at Blind John's house when Lee came by and he said, 'I'm going out in Robbins with Memphis Minnie, you wanna go with me? Got your harmonica?' I said, 'Yeah.' So I went to Robbins with him and I sat in with Memphis Minnie and Son Joe. . . . Then I got to know them pretty well and everywhere they play I'd come around and they'd let me sing and play one."[36]

When Daisy visited Minnie in Chicago, Minnie was living at 5943 S. Indiana. Daisy hadn't known where Minnie was, but when a friend passed on the news that Minnie was living in Chicago, Daisy went there and found her. Minnie was living in a two-room apartment, although Lee and Daisy both also remember an apartment consisting of one large room that Minnie had in the later 1940s. They enjoyed being shown around the big city by Minnie, where Daisy was even mistaken for Minnie's daughter.[37] She also was able to see Minnie perform at the Club De Lisa, an unusual experience for Daisy who was more used to seeing her at home in Memphis, or in Walls, playing for friends or for the crowds that would gather to hear Minnie every time she came home for a visit. "She carried us to a club. She was pretty free with her money and I remember she bought everyone a drink. She set up the whole club. It was during the war, 'cause a lot of soldiers was at the club that night . . . and when she would hit the guitar, to start to playing, they would go to screaming and hollering."[38]

Minnie and Son both played guitar, accompanied by a piano and perhaps a drum. Daisy enjoyed herself, but she was not present for what became, among collectors and later fans, Minnie's most "famous" appearance, the legendary blues contest between Memphis Minnie and Big Bill Broonzy. As we show, such contests were by no means a figment of Broonzy's imagination, and as his version is the pioneer version, and the one with which most readers are familiar, it's worth discussing on its own. The story was first reported by Broonzy, in his autobiography, *Big Bill Blues,*[39] a body of work that has lost much of its credibility over the decades. The alignment of the forces of criticism, whereby both amateur collectors of anecdotes as well as professional folklorists and historians have come to emphasize fact-based research and decry all else as "romanticism," even as they welcome or tolerate "oral history," has resulted in a tarnished image for works like Broonzy's, one of the very few works that has the actual power of evocation so missing from academic and non-academic studies alike. We suggest that Broonzy's tales contain more truth than fiction, and that the commentary on it provided by Jimmy Rogers and James Watt shows precisely the poetic longitude one must occupy to grasp the lesson of the tale.

Big Bill faced Minnie in the "first contest between blues singers that was ever given in the USA, in 1933, on my birthday, June 26." The judges of the contest were bluesmen Sleepy John Estes and Tampa Red, and songwriter/band-leader Richard M. Jones, composer of the famous *Trouble in Mind.* The contest took place on the first floor of a hall crowded with blacks and whites alike, while the citizens on the sidewalk outside jammed each window for a view of the proceedings. Bill would play and sing *Just a Dream* and *Make My Getaway,* while Minnie would perform *Me and My Chauffeur Blues* and *Looking the World Over.* By the time the contest started at 1:30 a.m., Bill and Minnie were both quite high. Many onlookers thought that a male vs. female guitar contest was loaded from the start, and one white man approached Big Bill, saying, "'You know you can beat that woman playing and anybody in here knows that you're the best blues player around and anywhere else.'" But, wrote Bill, "they had never heard her play or sing because when she would come to Chicago and make records her husband would take her back to Memphis."

The white man was ultimately convinced the contest would be a fair one, what with Minnie a qualified contender and three expert judges. The prizes were a bottle of whiskey and a bottle of gin. When Bill was called to the stage, the crowd went wild, and minutes passed before they were quiet enough for him to play his songs. Then Minnie was called to the stand, and the crowd went quiet. She played *Me and My Chauffeur Blues* and "the house rocked for twenty minutes." After she sang *Looking the World Over,* Estes and Jones went to the stand, picked Minnie up and carried her around the hall to proclaim her the winner, until her jealous husband said, "'Put her down, she can walk.'" Minnie won the two bottles, but Bill grabbed the whiskey and ran away and drank it while Minnie called him dirty names.

Bill's story does have a few inconsistencies, but they are probably a result of combining memories of many contests into one single one. For example, Minnie's pieces date from the 1940s and were probably not in her repertoire as early as 1933, the year Bill assigns to the contest. Nor were Bill's tunes likely to have been in his own repertoire that early. Further, none of our informants has ever suggested that Son Joe was an unusually jealous man; quite the contrary. But Joe McCoy may have been. These latter facts, and Bill's remark that "when she would come to Chicago and make records her husband would take her back to Memphis," are the only pieces of testimony that make it sound as if the contest was held in the early thirties.

While Bill may be the only known eye-witness to the particular contest he described, there were many other contests, and we now have fresher descriptions and intepretations, sometimes from the participants themselves. Jimmy Rogers participated in many such contests. "Minnie would come around and jam with us and we'd have a thing in Chicago you call 'contests' you know, like Sunday matinee or Sunday evening. It would be cocktail hour on Sunday, from one club to the other in the afternoon. And she would come sit in. And sometimes they'd win maybe $25 and a fifth of whiskey, or something like that you know. Big Bill would be there with us; we were having fun. Really, it was more fun than money at the time. About her being a lady guitar player, quite naturally, you know, we'd, they'd give her the benefit of the doubt. You see, we was the roughest out there, man, and she couldn't really compete with our unit. Just two people there, [but] we had a band [Muddy Waters' band], and we were pumping pretty heavy."[40]

James Watt, vocalist with the Blues Rockers,[41] has vivid memories that do not tally with Rogers'. "Playing that guitar, her and Muddy. They used to have these contests, the one who win the contest, they would get the fifth of whiskey. And Memphis Minnie would tell Muddy, 'I'm getting this fifth of whiskey.' She'd get it every time, though. She would get it *every time*. Muddy just couldn't do nothing with Memphis, no, uh uh, not back then. [This was] over at Du Drop, Du Drop Lounge, 3609 S. Wentworth." Who were the judges? How was it decided who won? "Oh, the customers. The customers. By applaudin'. Uh huh. And they would always give Memphis Minnie, every time. She would actually win it. I saw her beat ten different artists one night."[42]

Was Minnie simply a local favorite? And what does "local" mean? For we are not suggesting that the Chicago taverns were, in any sense, Minnie's "real" locus of performance, any more than was the vaudeville troupe she organized and traveled with through the South or was Mr. Towels' store in Walls. In fact most blues singers' existence could only be grasped through an understanding of the dialectical relationship that existed between the various sites and sounds of their travels.

Champion Jack Dupree never saw Minnie inside a Chicago club, but he did see her playing on the street in Memphis. "I met her—not in Chicago. I met her in Memphis. She used to play outside . . . on Beale Street. That's where I met her. She was younger then, and she never had a husband that couldn't play guitar. . . ."[43]

Blue Smitty was living in Memphis after he was discharged from the service in 1946: "I was on Beale Street listenin' to a lot of guys up and down there during that time. I heard Sonny Boy Williamson, Little Son Joe, all them guys . . . they used to be up and down Beale Street sittin' out playin', you know."[44] But a phrase like "playing on the street," or "playing on Beale Street in Memphis" can be subject to many interpretations, or misinterpretations. Memphis Slim commented on a specific facet of the Beale Street phenomenon, the number of blues singers who claimed to have played at the Midway on Beale Street. In a few short words, Slim demonstrates that within the black, working-class blues world itself, there is an upper and lower class; pianists belong to the former, self-accompanied guitarists to the latter. "Most all of them people say, 'Yeah, I played at the Midway on Beale Street.' They didn't play here—they didn't play no Midway on Beale. The only two blues singers known that played the Midway on Beale Street was Roosevelt Sykes and myself. And the only people that ever played there were piano players, because guitar players couldn't play nowhere in those days but in the park or in the street somewhere. Piano, that was *it*. 'Cause the guitarists couldn't play unless they were playin' out in the park. Even Memphis Minnie."[45]

We will discuss the street and the alley at greater length in the section on crime, but we will emphasize here that street-singing gives the blues artist a special accessibility. Having conquered the alienating distance between vaudeville stage and audience seating (or standing), the tavern or club entertainer (like Memphis Slim) nonetheless played on makeshift platforms or within circumscribed areas reserved for the performers. And even this distance was relinquished by the streetcorner entertainer of Smitty's reminiscence.[46] Part of the sense of community the blues audience feels between itself and its representative, the blues artist, is kindled by the very availability of the street singer, often the same performer who held forth from a tavern stage only a few hours earlier.

Memphis wasn't the only town on Minnie's southern route, although dozens of performers saw Minnie playing there, just as Joe Duskin did before he went into the army around 1940.[47] Brewer Phillips saw Minnie and Son Joe playing at a club in Senatobia, Mississippi on Highway 51 ten years after Duskin saw them in

Memphis. Bill Dicey saw Minnie at a black beach resort in Maryland, near Annapolis, at the end of the 1940s.[48] What makes these reports of great interest is that they all refer to periods during which Minnie was reportedly "in Chicago." But it would be closer to the truth to say that while Minnie used Chicago as her home base, she spent much of her time traveling. Some blues artists were more sedentary than others, but Minnie occupies a place on the other end of the continuum, an unusual spot for a woman. But then Minnie was an unusual woman. She is said to have owned and operated a blues club with St. Louis Jimmy in Indianapolis, but this has yet to be confirmed,[49] although poet Ted Joans saw Minnie perform in Indianapolis in the 1940s, where she was the headliner on a dance bill.[50] Minnie and Son may also have spent as long as three years in Detroit in the late 1940s, playing at the Koppin Theatre, and at various clubs and bars in the area.[51]

We are beginning to see the dimensions of her popularity and appeal, but there is one aspect of this appeal that deserves amplification: her visual allure and attractiveness. This dimension of her personal life is rarely mentioned in her songs, and Minnie may have had a great antipathy for becoming a visual commodity.[52] The fact that Minnie did not refer to her own visual appeal sets her apart from so many other blueswomen who, in their songs, often referred to their own looks. One early female critic wrote, "The prowess of the female blues singer lies largely in her ability to attract men and to entice them away from other women. . . . Some women boast of attributes of their appearance; others claim attractiveness despite physical drawbacks."[53] We are not proposing that Minnie was ignorant of her appeal, however, and two anecdotes illustrate this fact. Brother John Sellers remembered Minnie playing at the Blue Note in Chicago's loop, and he remarked, "Studs Terkel said one time, 'The only thing about Memphis Minnie, she pulls her dress so high when she come in and set up.'"[54] This seemingly odd anecdote received an unexpected confirmation from a listener to Steve Cushing's blues radio show. When Cushing asked for anyone with memories of Minnie to call the station, a listener called who saw Minnie playing at the Mona Lisa in East Chicago Heights in the 1950s. Minnie was soloing on acoustic guitar and played for several hours. This informant volunteered the information that Minnie "liked for men to look up under her dress, and she had on nice underclothes." Another fan, Robert Little, had seen Minnie playing on the West Side in a club on Madison Street. She was playing solo electric guitar. She came and sat in the lap of Mr. Little's cousin who accompanied him to the gig. This was in the late forties to early fifties, probably the latter. Minnie was "very friendly," said Little.[55]

In his 1970 article, Mike Leadbitter noted that Minnie's "looks and singing became a real attraction. . . ." when she was traveling with Ringling Brothers in the World War I years,[56] and certainly every photo of Minnie bears witness to her beauty. She wore a ring showing the face of a die, and all of her friends and relatives remember the beautiful clothes and jewelry she wore. Daisy searched everywhere for a silver dollar minted in the year of Minnie's birth. She eventually found one, and Minnie had the 1897 dollar made into a bracelet. In the photo of Minnie wearing a white gown and holding her guitar—a photo that Daisy has conspicuously on display in her home—the silver dollar bracelet is quite prominent. Minnie wore glasses from time to time and she had sparkling gold teeth all across the front of her mouth.

Daisy describes Minnie as tall and slim, but with the first part of this description, all other sources disagree. The consensus is, rather, that Minnie was slender and somewhat short, and a superbly dressed woman.[57] "And the mens, you know," said Brewer Phillips, "they had to fight the mens away from her. She was, pretty hair, soft hair, black, she could fix it any way she want to; and boy, she used to look good! She kept herself up, she's always neat, and the mens, she's signing autographs at the time, [1958] yeah, you know, the young kids, and the older mens, they was standing back and they admired her. She showed me some pictures from when she was twenty-one, twenty-two years old, oh yeah, you talk about airplanes full, man. . . . I just wonder how in the hell could *he* [Son Joe] hold onto *her*, a beautiful woman like she was, and all the mens and things pulling at her; but she loved him."[58]

Minnie had the talent in the family, but she wasn't the only glamorous one, as pictures of Daisy and Dovie make clear. Dovie died young, however, and Daisy's life has been devoted to raising children and taking care of other members of the family. But Minnie was different. "She wouldn't have her frilly things on every day, but she really got up and dressed, fixed her face, everyday; her hair was in place, she just *dressed*. And stayed dressed most all the time. She didn't be around in a duster or housedress," said Daisy. "Cause she was expecting somebody to come in," Ethel said, "and mostly somebody *did* come in."[59]

"Well, she would dress . . . nice," Jimmy Rogers laughed. "She would wear nice dresses, suits, eh, ladies suits, high heel shoes, and she had bracelets, she wore a bracelet around each wrist, made out of silver dollars, and then she had a set of earrings with two silver dimes on the earrings. That was her trademark, there: Money! Yeah, she was all right."[60] Was Minnie's trademark really money? As Minnie herself sang in *Don't Turn the Card*, "Money, you know, is my lovestone." Further, as Johnny Shines recalled. "Now a woman who knew her from childhood said that when Minnie got broke, she'd get out in her boots and walk down through the fields, go to people houses, telling fortunes, anything. Anything to get money, you know. And this woman that spoke of her, she was old enough to have known her all of her life. And she said Minnie even bluffed her for a few dollars. In other words, Minnie had a pretty smooth head on her."[61] Here was an early example of Minnie's willingness to do anything to avoid farm work.

Minnie occasionally sang songs in which other women were treated in a comradely fashion, and she sang of them as competitors, as well, as in *Good Biscuits* or *Biting Bug Blues*. Minnie could be very competitive, and one example, occurring toward the end of her life, is particularly telling. Richard Spottswood visited Minnie when he was traveling through the South recording. He had just taped Fred McDowell, whose guitar work and vocals would soon become the rage among collectors and fans. This was in 1962 and by then, Minnie was half paralyzed, bed-ridden and barely able to speak. They chatted a bit, and then Spottswood played her the Fred McDowell tape. As he later wrote, she "was contemptuous of it, saying she hadn't played that way since she was first learning guitar."[62] In actuality, few guitarists, male or female, and few women posed a threat to Minnie. In the late 1920s, when Minnie left the Lake Cormorant, Mississippi, area, her "removal came as a welcome departure to Lake Cormorant's female citizenry, which viewed her as a threat: 'They didn't like her....' "[63]

This toughness, this audacity, operating through many signs and with, no doubt, many roots, nonetheless came to be a characterological principle in Minnie's development. It gave her a strength and a will she would not have otherwise had, and with it she was able to conquer decade after decade as a magnificent entertainer.

6. "I DRINK ANYWHERE I PLEASE"

> *The universe is at root a magical illusion, a strange,*
> *mysterious, fabulous game, and that is how [we] play it.*
> —Eileen Agar

Among the items left behind after Minnie's and Son's deaths were a number of song lists, dating from the 1940s (see illustrations). The list headed "Songs to be Maid" includes the only piece on these lists that we know Minnie recorded, *Oh Believe Me (Believe Me)*, but what is most interesting about the lists is the hidden side of Minnie and Son Joe that they reveal.

Nearly all of the pieces are popular songs or rhythm and blues hits from the 1940s, and hardly a one could be considered a blues. We know from personal testimony and a glance at the discography that such material was not foreign to her repertoire. Witness *How Come You Do Me Like You Do Do Do, As Long As I Can See You Smile, I'm Waiting On You,* and more. Yet, both Brewer Phillips and Big Lucky Carter testified that they had never heard her perform a non-blues![1]

This seeming contradiction needn't puzzle us long, however. Many rural blues performers played frequently for white audiences, and their repertoires usually reflected this fact. By the 1940s, in Chicago, playing for "white parties" was probably a thing of the past, but to hold down a steady gig at the 708 Club would have required a reasonable amount of musical urbanity. The 47th Street clubs were relatively sophisticated, compared to the many neighborhood taverns that were home to so many singers, and fielding requests for songs by Louis Jordan *(Caldonia, Don't Worry About That Mule)* and Billy Ekstine *(Prisoner of Love, Jelly Jelly)* would have been par for the course. Indeed, the roots of many of the listed songs are quite fascinating: *Soft Winds* had been recorded by Benny Goodman and Lionel Hampton, *I Love You for Sentimental Reasons* by Nat King Cole, *Into Each Life* by the Ink Spots and Ella Fitzgerald, *Jersey Bounce* by Les Hite, Benny Goodman, and Red Norvo, and *How High the Moon* by Lionel Hampton and dozens of others. Many of the songs, like *When My Dreamboat Comes Home* and *On the Sunny Side of the Street,* were pop songs, pure and simple. Minnie's command of this diverse repertoire is simply another sign of her remarkable skills and adaptability. This talent would be stretched to the breaking point at the dawn of the new decade.

Certainly Minnie must have realized that her close colleagues like Big Bill and Washboard Sam were no longer the real competition, and that a new and different sound was necessary to compete against Muddy Waters and Howlin' Wolf, not to mention the countless new rhythm and blues bands. By the 1950s, she had made the leap to postwar blues, and several of her last pieces were excellent examples of powerful, 1950s Chicago-style blues. Minnie's voice was still strong and vibrant, and she might have become a fine, post-war (style) performer. Indeed, she was even under the management of Monroe Passis and race record impresario J. Mayo Williams, the same team that was guiding the careers of Muddy Waters, Jimmy Rogers, Sunnyland Slim, and Little Walter.

This period of Minnie's life properly begins with her 1949 Regal session. In spite of her command of more modern chords, her asides and forced laughter during these songs betrayed considerable discomfort. If anybody wondered where Minnie's roots had gone, the answer wasn't far to seek: *Kidman Blues* sounded like Minnie had reached back twenty years for *Mr. Tango Blues,* and brought it out again in a new suit. This anxious and troubled melange of the old and the new must have struck a somewhat welcome chord for Regal's Fred Mendelssohn who had come to town looking for old-timers to record, but the record had only a limited commercial success. Nonetheless *Billboard* for May, 1950, noted it thus: "The hard-shouting Southern blues thrush pipes a potent torchy blues, selling strong all the way."

Minnie's next session was for the Chess subsidiary label, Checker, on July 11, 1952, when the label was barely two months old. One side even sported Little Walter's harmonica, and the unissued *Lake Michigan* bore witness to a certain restrained intensity. The instrumental break in her Checker remake of her Okeh hit, *Me and My Chauffeur Blues,* had a compellingly danceable pulse, but she still didn't sound completely at home with the new sound. This may indeed have been "a futile attempt to bring [Minnie and Son Joe] up to date,"[2] as one critic has remarked, but Checker's 1960 catalog still listed Minnie's release, Checker 771, amid the Little Walter's, the Bo Diddley's and new releases by The Flamingos. Minnie's session had also produced *Broken Heart.* A year later Jimmy Rogers recorded it as *Left Me With a Broken Heart,* and his version became a blues hit.

Minnie's most exciting session of the fifties, however, was her 1953 outing for Joe Brown's JOB label. Brown started out in 1949 in partnership with St. Louis Jimmy Oden, and he captured much of the cream of the crop in postwar Chicago blues. While Eddie Boyd's *Five Long Years* was his only national hit, Brown ultimately recorded Baby Face Leroy, Snooky Pryor, Grace and John Brim, J. B. Lenoir, Johnny Shines, Floyd Jones and Sunnyland Slim. In *World of Trouble,* one hears the raw power of the era, with each component at last firmly and fully integrated, and with Minnie's strong and forceful vocal evocative in the extreme. One could even say that *World of Trouble* alone finally articulates the precise defects of the Chess and Regal sessions. It is noteworthy, also, that this fairly seamless post-war effort finally comes together with pianist Little Brother Montgomery, not only one of the most versatile pianists, but one with the deepest roots; and, one would have thought, the one most alien to the new post-war sound!

Jimmy Rogers recorded with Minnie during these years, and while there is still some uncertainty as to precisely which sessions and which sides he appeared on, it does seem fairly clear that he did record with Minnie. He remembers playing on *Me and My*

Chauffeur at 14th and Michigan at a Joe Brown session, but this memory seems to combine several. In spite of Minnie's hard reputation, she and Son treated Rogers and Walter almost like sons, giving them pointers on session work and helping them to become fully competent blues artists.[3] Many younger bluesmen looked up to Minnie as their teacher and mentor. But others saw her differently. Rogers may have enjoyed working with Minnie, but many did not. Indeed, we most often heard that Minnie was tough and hard and ready to fight at a moment's notice, an habitual drinker who didn't take any lip from anyone. And of course, there are stories to prove it. Joe Callicott remembered Minnie recording *Bumble Bee* for Vocalion while he was at the studio to record, but the only things he remembered were Minnie's National guitar and her drinking.[4] Johnny Shines, too, thought that Minnie's drinking was worth mentioning—"When I knew her in Chicago she was drinking a lot of gin".[5] Considering that Minnie's crowd was a hard drinking crowd, these memories are striking. Underneath them all, however, may be the simple fact that Minnie was a tough, hard drinking *woman* in a crowd of tough, hard drinking men.

Joe Duskin remembered her as a "good little girl" who "cussed like a sailor." We came to realize that this was a not unusual characterization, for James Watt and Blue Smitty both described her in an almost identical fashion.[6] Indeed, Minnie's personality can only be understood when it is acknowledged how freely these seemingly opposite traits were mingled within her. Many of these traits may even have coexisted in desperate longing for a mitigation that never appeared, but that was Minnie, precisely. Even Muddy Waters had an opinion on the matter, although it may have been tempered by the fact that Minnie used to tease him when he first came to Chicago.[7] In a lengthy interview, he recalled that his *Can't Get No Grinding* came from Minnie and Joe's *What's the Matter With the Mill?*, "a thousand years ago," and he continued, "She was a great girl, but she was a woman. You know, in this business, I don't know how you is in your business, you can be a little evil when—when—(laughs). Yeah, you know, when a woman's out there doing the job, you're doing the job she's doing, it could get a little evil sometimes. She don't have the strong mind like the man because she can get flustrated [sic] and can fly off the handle and that's the only thing that's wrong with her—she would get a little evil sometimes."[8]

Jimmy Rogers acknowledged that his getting along so well with Minnie was only one side of the coin, a coin he had often seen flipped. "Oh, man, that she was real bitchy, you know. I've seen her be real bitchy now, uh, even to Son Joe. I remember one night we was over at the 708 Club, we was playing, on Monday nights, Muddy and Walter and I played Monday nights there, and she came in from someplace she had been playing. She got off early, before we got off. She came in and had a few drinks. And we'd talk with the people 'cause we carried a pretty decent crowd all the time. Son Joe was over in the booth where we were, talking and drinking. And there was a few ladies sitting around there. And Minnie was, uh, flying all over the place. So she came over where we was sitting at, and he had a glass, and she picked his glass up. I thought she was gonna drink it. She picked the glass up and dashed the whiskey in his face, man. Uh, that was rough. He didn't do a thing. There wasn't too much he could do at that time but take his pocket handkerchief and try to get it out. Oh, man, that was burning whiskey, that alcohol burn real bad. So, uh, they was leading him around, somebody had a car and taken him home and I didn't see Son Joe for, oh, a couple of weeks. He was wearing shades, his eyes was red. He finally got over it. That's the roughest I've seen her, but they say she could get rougher than that. She always treat me nice, though. I don't know how Son Joe get into something like that, man. He knowed her reputation, and he went in. I guess it was because he could understand her type of music and they could team together and so they just went from there."[9]

"Y'know her and Son Joe, Roosevelt Sykes used to work together . . . boy!" declared Johnny Shines. "They'd have some of the terriblest rows but Memphis Minnie be the winner every time—she'd have it her way or else."[10] Later he remarked, "Especially with Son Joe. She didn't have no trouble with him. She just worked him over when she felt like it. I heard a lot of [other] things about her. I didn't know these things from personal acquaintance, but I heard a lot of things about her. They tell me she shot one old man's arms off, down in Mississippi. Shot his arm off, or cut it off with a hatchet, something. Some say shot, some say cut.

Minnie was a hellraiser, I know that! A lot of things they say she did in the past, I believe it! She'd work Son Joe over right on the bandstand, right in front of the whole audience. Bang, bop, boom, bop! Ha, ha. And Roosevelt [Sykes] too. She'd work both of them over. You know, Roosevelt wasn't never no fighter. When he was young, he was too little and too slow, and after he got older, he was too big and too slow!"[11]

Said Homesick James, "She was real hard to get along with. I mean, she be arguing all the time. 'You ain't made that change right, you didn't do this, you didn't do that...' She would always get pissed off about it, the way I played. That woman was tougher than a man. No man was strong enough to mess around with her. Minnie couldn't get along with nobody. She was a fighter."[12]

In the end, these vignettes are not so much history as versions of history, and for every version, there seems to be at least one counter-version. For example, Big Bill, Minnie's ex-partner and a man reputedly beloved by all, had seriously slipped in Minnie's eyes by the late 1950s. "Oh, she talked about Big Bill," said Brewer Phillips. "She say he's a crook, she said he always was a sneak. You know, he wanted all the money. You never could pay *him*. I don't want to speak, to speak bad about him, but she always say, 'Don't be like him.' He wasn't like Robert Junior and Sunnyland Slim and Joe Hill Louis and Roosevelt Sykes."[13] Yet Brother John Sellers remarked, "Big Bill would never do anything unless'n he called Minnie. 'Let me call Minnie on the phone and see what she say about it', he'd say. And she'd say, 'aww ... well, all right, Bill ... I'll come over ... I'll see....' in her gruff way. But she would come because she was big in her heart, even though she could be rough. You know, blues singers on the South Side work in small spots and they can be very tough."[14]

Sonny Boy Williamson (John Lee Williamson) is as much the subject of conflicting reports as Big Bill. Homesick James felt that Minnie and Sonny Boy were professional enemies but his view is not supported by Brewer Phillips' observations. "[Sonny Boy Williamson] came up back in the thirties, that's John Lee Williamson, and Memphis Minnie was in her prime then. And she used to tell me about what a nice guy he was. Now they never did record together, but they was on a lot of tours together. And them little tours was in that '38 Ford, it was brand new, then. And she owned it. And she run it till it just quit. She never was able to buy nary another."[15]

One of the most famous of the Minnie tales is the one provided by post-war harmonicist Billy Boy Arnold in his marathon interview with *Blues Unlimited*'s Mike Rowe. "Memphis Minnie was playing down the street. So I walked down the street, me, Blind John and Big Bill—those were the beautiful moments. I was walking with the great Big Bill. So we went down the corner where Memphis Minnie was playing. And Memphis Minnie was talking to somebody and I was trying to talk to her. . . . I was, y'know, I wanted to meet her and I said, 'Memphis Minnie, Memphis Minnie.' She kept talking, the joint was loud, y'know, the juke-box was playing—it was on intermission and she turned round and said, 'Man will you get out of my ass!' She was rough!"[16]

On the other hand, and Arnold is no exception, nearly every blues artist who testified to Minnie's rough behavior also loved and respected her. Many spoke of her generosity as well. Thus Jimmy Rogers' depiction of Minnie's ferocity ends with "She always treat me nice, though," and Arnold was, ultimately, thrilled that he was eventually able to go on gigs with Minnie and Son, and was often called to the stage to play a song or two when Minnie saw him in the audience. It doesn't take too much imagination to understand the whole episode as an initiation rite. Soon Arnold became a Chicago blues singer himself and was no longer simply a young hopeful. Soon, *he* would call younger singers to the bandstand.

Brother John Sellers had already passed through the gauntlet by the time he spoke to Paul Oliver in the 1960s, and his memory of Minnie is more balanced. "Memphis Minnie. . . . She was a very funny woman and she always wore those great big ear-rings . . . and she was a very fine guitarist. But she was so stern sometimes and Memphis Minnie would always say, 'I drink anywhere I please!' Cause Minnie was used to a rough life. She had a rough life and she lived rough. You know they don't talk about Memphis Minnie like they do Bessie Smith, but she was a great artist and she knew the guitar and played it well and she used to be the tops."[17]

Minnie and Son Joe often took separate jobs to make more money, although most of our witnesses speak of Minnie and Son Joe as an active team. Most likely, when times were toughest, separate jobs would have been gratifying, if they could be found. But tough times are almost synonymous with times of no work. When times were better, teamwork seemed to be the rule. And that is how their colleagues remember them. "Just the two of 'em, Minnie and Son Joe. That was enough. She didn't need anybody else."[18]

While Minnie and Son teamed up for many of their gigs, the requirements of the record companies often dictated a different arrangement in the studio. "She didn't usually have a band," said Jimmy Rogers. "She mostly just play, she and a guitar player would be together, that's the way. She had a couple of her husbands were guitar players, and they'd team together most all the time. But on records you'd have to take more pieces when you go to the studio, so that's why I got a chance to record with her. And on gigs we'd play here, local in the city of Chicago, she would come and be on our set and we introduced her on the stage, she and Son Joe. And they'd come up and do numbers like that. I guess that's how she heard me and was interested in my guitar enough to want to put it on records with her. So I was proud of that."[19]

Much of the time, however, Minnie did perform with others, like Big Bill or Sunnyland Slim, or Roosevelt Sykes. Indeed, Minnie led a scalding, dynamic trio consisting of her, Son Joe and piano/vocalist Sykes. Sykes was born in Arkansas in 1906, and he lived and worked in Saint Louis and Northern Arkansas before settling in Chicago. His boisterous charm and sensitive piano technique made him a respected and cherished figure in the blues world, and his prolific recording career spanned the decades from the 1920s through the 1970s. While he accompanied numerous blues singers on their own records, he never recorded with Minnie and Son, but they worked together for a number of years during the 1950s.[20]

"I knew she'd teamed up with Roosevelt Sykes, and they had been around," Brewer Phillips reminisced. "She and Roosevelt Sykes was the main thing! They'd been in Missouri and things. . . . She would talk about how much money they made, you know, about how much they was getting for a gig. And how many gigs, and they couldn't get around to them all." Some years later, Phillips tagged along. "We was out 41 Highway almost to Georgia, and Rufus Thomas, James Walker, I, Memphis Minnie and her husband, and Roosevelt Sykes, we all drove out there. . . . Minnie was a traveler, you know. She lived in Alabama for awhile, I think out there where the vocational college is, in Tuscaloosa, she lived in Kentucky for awhile. 'Child,' she'd say, 'I been all over the world, New York, Chicago, California.' "[21]

Minnie even participated in an East Coast folk festival like the ones that were held at Fort Valley State College in Georgia. At least, we know that Minnie, Brownie McGhee and Sonny Terry were at what Brewer Phillips called a "hillbilly concert" in the Washington, DC, area, sometime in the 1940s. They had to sleep in a field since they were barred from the hotel, and they were not permitted to eat at the same table as the other, white, entertainers.[22]

But after any of these tours, Minnie and Son would always return to Chicago. Minnie's union records provide documentation of her employment at various Chicago clubs, but while we have union records for as early as 1939, they do not begin to show the club dates and the clubs themselves until 1952, when she held down gigs at Sylvio's, Joe's Rendezvous and the Indiana Theatre, all in the early part of the year. In early 1953, she worked the 2200 Club (possibly the same as the H & T at 22nd and State), and by the summer, she was due to play at the 640 Club, but this job was apparently canceled. Throughout 1954, Minnie, or Minnie and Son, appeared at Little Eddie's, Joe's L. A. Bar and Tiny Davis' Lounge, and in 1955, she played at the Painted Doll. The club names are significant, for in among the well-known names like Sylvio's and the Indiana Theatre, are a few names rarely mentioned by historians: The 2200 Club, Tiny Davis' Lounge, Little Eddie's, and the Painted Doll. Perhaps these were smaller clubs, but it is interesting to note how easily the fact of their existence has eluded our grasp, for until now, no singer has ever mentioned their names.

As jobs became harder to find, Minnie wandered farther afield to find work. Jazz aficionado Charles Sweningsen saw Minnie perform at a small strip joint on Milwaukee Avenue just over the Chicago line in Niles in the mid-1950s. She played and sang blues with an occasional pop tune thrown in, as intermission music and between the acts. She was applauded by this difficult audience and presented a very uncompromising performance: She told no jokes and made no song announcements, and she never indulged in small talk with the spectators. Minnie stood and sang and played guitar and was occasionally accompanied by a male guitar or bass. "She was an impressive performer," Sweningsen reported.[23]

His report is interesting from another perspective, for it highlights one characteristic of the new style that swept through the Chicago blues in the 1950s, but which has gone nearly unmentioned in the literature. Because it played a great role in the evolution of his own style, Buddy Guy remarked on it when he discussed his first days in Chicago, in the mid 1950s: "See most guitar players were sitting in chairs in those days—Muddy, Dee Lewis, Dave Mayes [sic] and all them were sitting down—and I was standing straight up, had this guitar hanging down like Guitar Slim. . . . And so the people were saying, 'What is *this*?' ".[24]

Minnie's playing standing up at the strip club in Niles may help to date the gig, since it would have been unusual for her to play standing up prior to 1955. Even so, Homesick had never heard of Minnie playing like that. "Always sitting down! Lord, I never seen her stand up in my whole life, and I don't think nobody else did, either. You know, this standing up thing's just started happening. You know, in the '50s, nobody stand up and play."[25] "Mostly she sat down all the time when she played," said Brewer Philips. "I seen her do a good show, at the Royal Theatre on Beale Street, in Memphis, and that's the first time I seen her stand up and play."[26] As we noted earlier, a fan named Robert Little had seen Minnie playing solo electric guitar in a club on the West Side on Madison Street. Little remembered that she played standing up.[27]

Standing up was one of the more silent "sounds of the city," but its implication of assertion and resistance was another sign of the times. Let us pause for a moment and examine the period during which these changes in performance style were taking place. The vibrant sound of the new postwar blues, as dispensed by Muddy Waters, J. B. Hutto or Jimmy Rogers was piercingly electric and stunningly modern. For at its heart, it embodied not only the necessity of a new sound to match the fresh conditions of the work site—loud instruments for noisy clubs, a cause-and-effect relation-ship too often emphasized—but a new poetic need felt by singer and audience alike, to respond to the social climate of the black ghetto and black working-class life. Certainly the new younger sing-ers were rebelling against the older blues tradition and the way of life that fostered it, but they spat out their lines with an urgency that was wholly unfamiliar.

The blues styles that rose to prominence in the era of the Brown desegregation decision (1954), could no more separate themselves from the powerful forces that inspired the black com-munity, than could civic beautification (pacification) measures prevent the outbreaks of rioting in Watts, Detroit, Chicago and dozens of other cities in the coming decade. For Brown, the blues and Watts were all driven by an impulse to freedom that could not be stifled, an impulse that insisted that poetic needs will manifest themselves, even when their articulation is con-fined and restrained, just as will physical and aggressive impulses under the same confinement.

Those critics who think that *Take This Hammer* is a protest song, while Floyd Jones' *Stockyard Blues* is not, are holding valentines to their ears, listening for their heartbeat. Yet the proof that they are themselves alive—that we are all alive—must be sought else-where, by a psyche that is always learning to hear, learning what to listen to, and what to listen for. The poetic vein of the blues is so rich, and yet so objectionable to the self-righteous, that the whole notion of the "sound of the city" can too easily be used to obscure the vital configuration of forces that beats at the heart of the blues. The many appeals in blues criticism to understand the blues in terms of the sociology of the "work site" or of "leisure-time activities" are too often only white projections of the "non-political" onto black lives, in a misguided attempt to quell the critics' own fears and hesitations about the role of racism, segre-gation and discriminatory practices in the struggles of everyday life in the ghetto. Often it is as simple as the fact that white critics and fans cannot bear the thought that the blues singers often de-spise them, and see them, correctly, as the architects or at least the accomplices of so much of the squalor in which they are forced to live. But the "sounds of the city" are as much the sounds of

riot and looting, crime and its victims, and black against white, as
they are the whirring belts of the factories and the piercing sounds
wrung from the new electric instruments. Together they created
an atmosphere that Minnie responded to swiftly. Decades later,
we are still learning to respond ourselves.

Let us return now to Minnie's last years in Chicago. One of her
last "jobs" in Chicago was playing at Studs Terkel's memorial concert for Big Bill Broonzy, who had died in August 1958. The concert was held at the Clark Street jazz emporium, the Blue Note,
in downtown Chicago, shortly after Broonzy died.[28] Minnie and
Son may have moved to Memphis that year, or they may have com-
muted between Memphis and their apartment at 4518 S. Wood-
lawn, in Chicago. Chicago had been her home for twenty-plus
years, but Memphis had been, too, for she had never stopped vis-
iting her relatives there, and she never stopped touring. Often the
troupe would come to Walls in a bus before playing at the Palace
on Beale Street in Memphis. The audience would throw money
on the stage and Minnie had several people there to pick it up.
Sometime Minnie would come home without a troupe, and on
these occasions she would play mostly for audiences of blacks from
the area around Walls. "When 'Kid' was in town, folks from miles
around came to our house in Walls to hear her sing and play.
Sometimes she would stay four or five months or sometimes a few
days; then sometimes we wouldn't hear from her for two or three
years."[29]

It was Ethel and Minnie's brother Leo that she most often visited. "This house would always be her stopping place," Daisy said
of Ethel's house at 1701 Kansas Street. "She was very devoted to
my sister-in-law and my brother.... She would come to their house
when she didn't go to nobody's house. That was right here or
Walls. We moved here from Walls in 1948."[30] As Ethel herself
remarked, "I knowed her since 1921. See, when I married, she was
away from home. Of course, she did come back. She was playing
music then. She'd bring her guitar when she came back. She could
play, too. This was in the twenties, thirties. I never heard her play
anywhere but in my house. People would just *come* in when they
heard tell of her being down to Walls, folks down there she used

to play with and all. They would just come in to hear her play. It was amazing."[31]

When Minnie and Son left Chicago for good, in 1958, they moved in with Leo and Ethel. "They came here to Kansas Street first, before they were out on their own, on Linden. Her trunk was sitting on the porch when I come from work," Ethel remembered.[32] They stayed there for a while, but eventually took up residence on Third and Beale (a corner memorialized by Sleepy John Estes),[33] and it took no time at all for them to be back in the thick of things.

William "Boogie Man" Hubbard who plays organ with the Hollywood All Stars in Memphis, used to play with Minnie in a band in the late 1950s. They had a regular Saturday night gig at the Red Light in Millington, just north of Memphis. The band consisted of Minnie and Son Joe, guitars, Boogie Man on piano, Sam Coleman on harp, and Sam's brother ("Beale Street") on drums.[34] While Minnie usually worked as a team with Son, they also had occasional three-guitar extravaganzas, and Big Lucky (Carter) was often the third guitarist. A friend would hold a fish fry, and the guitar trio would be the entertainment. The crowd would be drinking, as would the trio, and everyone would have a great time in the country. Homesick, too, occasionally played third guitar with Minnie and Son, and as always, Minnie would play the lead.[35]

Besides the country fish fries, Minnie and Son also played the rougher juke joints. "She did tell me how juke joints and things, they have to run at night when they start cutting and shooting, but she'd always take her guitar with her. You know, she'd tell me 'Stay out of places like that!'" At more placid moments, James Walker would invite Minnie and Son to his place for supper and they would play for Walker's family and their guests. Minnie would be drinking corn whiskey, and she'd be in good humor.[36] On another occasion Minnie accompanied Brewer Phillips to a job in Hughes, Arkansas, because he was too nervous to go by himself. Ultimately, Brewer was too shy to play at all, and Minnie had to play the job for him![37]

The Memphis musicians with whom Minnie congregated had their own rehearsal hall, just as the Chicago artists of the thirties and forties met at Tampa Red's for socializing, practicing or hang-

ing out. The St. Louis singers like Charlie Jordan, Peetie Wheatstraw, Roosevelt Sykes and Big Joe Williams kept alive a similar
hall at 17th and O'Fallon in St. Louis,[38] and nearly every major
city with a sizable black population had a similar gathering place.
The Memphis blues artists had a friend with a wire recorder, and
he'd bring it to the rehearsal hall where Brewer, Walter Davis,
James Walker, Minnie and Son Joe were playing. They usually
played without electricity and without drums; just guitars, harmonicas and an out-of-tune piano that only worked in one or two keys.
"Anyway, they'd say, 'You is one black rat, some day I'm gonna
find your trail.' We'd be a bunch of us dancing, and you oughta
heard them working in person. Boy, it was the most beautiful music
I ever heard!"[39]

During these later days in Memphis, Minnie even did a segment
or two with Sonny Boy Williamson No. 2 (Rice Miller) and Joe
Willie Wilkins for King Biscuit Time. In the 15 minutes they were
alloted, she played two numbers and Sonny Boy did two, or at
other times they would alternate between Sonny Boy, Robert Jr.
Lockwood, Minnie and Willie Love. They would go to KFFA in
Helena, Arkansas, to pre-record the program, but it wouldn't be
aired for a month. Minnie also appeared on WDIA in Memphis.[40]
Minnie managed to have one more recording session, in Memphis,
in 1959, but the record was never issued. She was accompanied by
a small Memphis group, with Son Joe on drums, and she sang superbly.[41] One thing was certain: Memphis in the 1950s still bore
the marks of Memphis Minnie.[42]

Minnie's effect on younger blues artists had always been mag-
netic, and Eddie Kirkland's recollection is revealing in its nearly
mesmerized mood. "I went by another house party a guy told me
'Memphis Minnie's over there playin'.' I say, 'I'm goin' over there
and see her' 'cause as a kid I used to sing her record *You One
Black Rat* so I want to see her. She was a coal-black woman—
pretty white teeth that had gold in her mouth. She had long,
black curly hair—she was a *beautiful* woman. Right then she was
an age—that was the first and last time I see her—I sit there
all night and watch her play that guitar, her and Son Joe. Sat
there all night long in the corner, Eddie Burns on one side, me
on the other."[43]

We are fortunate to have the testimony of other singers who came under Minnie's tutelage. Homesick James saw Minnie as his principal mentor. "Memphis Minnie was . . . about five years older than me [actually 13 or 14 years]. She's where I learned my lessons and my behavior and learned the lines, how to sing, the pronunciation. About my beat, about my timing. . . ."[44] Brewer Phillips also saw Minnie as a great influence and teacher. To Brewer, Minnie was "just downhome people and she never had an attitude because of her success." How else to explain the fact that everyone in Memphis in those days called her "Aunt Minnie!" Displaced rural-sounding pieces like *Call the Fire Wagon* may reflect this side of Minnie, but Phillips himself offered a surprising comparison. "She's something like Aretha Franklin. Just as country, just like Aretha. She wasn't a fancy woman, no lipstick, no perfume, and she already had pretty hair. I'm telling you, she didn't know too much, and never tried to know anything."[45]

Indeed, Minnie never even learned how to drive, and although Son could drive, they didn't own a car. The last car they owned had been Minnie's old 1938 V-8 Ford, the one she toured in during the late thirties and forties. By the time they moved back to Memphis, cars were out of the picture for good. Whether it was Joe Hill Louis, James Walker or Brewer himself who organized the gig, they would drive over to Minnie and Son's and take them out to the job. Brewer had moved to Memphis in the early 1950s, and his greatest ambition had been to meet Memphis Minnie. Thanks to James Walker who also helped get him a truck-driving job, meeting Minnie and Son was pretty easy. Soon Phillips began stopping off at Minnie's every night after work. He'd try to bring food, and Minnie would give him guitar lessons. Brewer saw Minnie and Son Joe almost every day for the next two years. She always encouraged Brewer to find his own voice, and not simply to play like her, but to play what he felt. While she showed him basics, timing, and the neck of the guitar, she left him to pick out tunes by himself. Sometimes, when he thought she wasn't listening, he'd go off into another room to practice and he'd hear her say "you about to git it" or "you gonna make it." And that was how he learned guitar.[46]

Minnie and Son had returned to Memphis because of Son Joe's health. Son had a serious heart condition that was only aggravated by their lifestyle, and their life in Memphis was lived at a slower pace that bought him a few more years. But his health did not improve, and their financial problems seemed to worsen each day. Minnie's guitars were constantly in and out of the pawnshop. We already know that Minnie was one of the first blues stars to use a steel-bodied National guitar, and later photos from the forties show her still playing a National. But in the later photographs, it has become an archtop f-hole model, not at all common among blues singers, but nonetheless a sign of Minnie's pioneer modernizing. By the time Brewer met Minnie, she had changed guitars again, as she had probably done many times. "It was an old make of Gibson, a good guitar at the time, but the older makes didn't have the cut in the neck, you know down at the little recording [the pickup], it was just the plain neck. Like an acoustic. But it was good, and it was a Gibson, but it was a hollow box. And then the next one she bought had the cut in it. That was an expensive guitar at the time. So, she could get more money for that at the pawning shop. You could get fifteen or twenty bucks on it if it was at least a $250, $300 guitar at that time. When I'd get paid, I'd have a few bucks left and I'd get her guitar out of the pawning shop on the weekends."[47]

Minnie and Son had neither a television nor record player, but they did have an old radio that worked off of a battery that they kept outside the window. They occasionally listened to serials, but they rarely listened to music. However, every now and then she'd tune in to Rufus Thomas on WLOK and listen to the blues. As Brewer remarked, "She was in bad shape finance-wise, didn't have *anything*. And they was on the welfare at that time." Minnie cooked for her husband and Brewer, too, even when beans was all they had. Occasionally, when Brewer fell asleep on the couch and got up the next morning to go to work, Minnie would ask what he wanted for supper that night, and he'd leave $3 or $4 and Minnie would do the shopping and then cook supper for the three of them that evening.[48] Brewer remembered, "On the weekend when I got paid, I'd buy her some wine, you know, give her a few dollars. Son and I would go to the store or something. She drank Wild Irish Rose. She drink corn whiskey, too. But anything like bourbon, or Canadian whiskey, well, we didn't know anything about that.

[laughs] You know, and home brew, they'd make it out of yeast cakes and potatoes and things like that, she drink that; and wine. And as I heard she wasn't getting any bookings or anything."[49] The last thing Brewer had heard, Bonnie Raitt was trying to reach Minnie to pass on some royalties to her. "Cause this girl Bonnie Raitt became a star, and she looked up Memphis Minnie."[50] Minnie would never be forgotten. And she never laid her guitar down until she could literally no longer pick it up.

7. *"THE BEST THING GOIN' "*

The last word has golden rays.
—Méret Oppenheim

But that time was to come soon. Minnie was taking care of Son in their duplex apartment on Linden when Daisy received a call from Minnie's next door neighbor. Minnie had had a stroke. Daisy and her husband rushed to the apartment, where they immediately realized that Minnie and Son could no longer live by themselves. They sent for two ambulances and had Minnie and Son brought to the house on Adelaide, which they remodeled for the afflicted couple. Henceforth, if Minnie or Son had to go to the doctor or the hospital, Daisy would take them, and Ethel would come over and stay with the one who had been left behind, for they could not really care for themselves anymore. Son's heart condition had worsened to the point where he could just barely get around, and Minnie was confined to a wheelchair, as she would be until she died thirteen years later.[1] As if this weren't enough, Minnie had been treated for asthma in Chicago and was told by the doctor to move to the South, but in the South, she found little relief. "It seems like I had asthma here bad as I did there," she told Georges Adins.[2]

Her condition continued to deteriorate, especially after Son's death in the fall of 1961, which provoked another stroke, and she soon needed full-time custodial care. Still Minnie did not go into the nursing home, even after two strokes. Many blues fans are familiar with the photographs of Minnie in a wheelchair, sitting on the front porch at 1355 Adelaide. "That's where she liked to stay!" said Daisy. "I dressed her every day and put her on the porch when the weather was nice, so she could watch things."[3] Daisy continued to provide full-time nursing care to Minnie until she herself became exhausted and ill, and the doctor told her that she couldn't continue. Minnie was sent to the Jell Nursing Home, where her brothers and sisters were able to visit her frequently. When possible, Ethel would cook fish for Minnie and then ride the bus to the nursing home so Minnie could have one of her favorite meals.[4]

Daisy kept Minnie clean and well-dressed, so she would be presentable to her fans and other visitors, but Minnie was still acutely embarrassed in front of visitors because of her impaired speech. "People would go out there to see her that I didn't even know would go," Daisy has said, and Minnie was indeed visited by old friends and fans. The visits were regular, if not frequent. Wade Walton met Minnie when he was on the way to New Jersey to record for Bluesville, in 1962. "I met her after she had her stroke. I told her we always loved her records, about 'be my chauffeur' and she started to cry. Yes, she started to cry. But back when I was still boyish, she was *very* popular. Yes, she was something."[5] Bukka White called on Minnie from time to time, and his report was not heartening. "I see Memphis Minnie sometimes, too. She's in a nursing home now, and I went with a white boy from Washington to see her not so long ago. You know, she got fat as a butterball, that woman did, and all she do is sit in her wheelchair and cry and cry. But in her time, she was really something. She was about the best thing goin' in the woman line. . . ."[6]

Minnie's tiny social security income was hardly enough to get by on, and many fans responded promptly when they heard of Minnie's needs. Guitarist Jo Ann Kelly, together with her brother who ran a blues club in London held a benefit for Minnie. Minnie had been a fundamental inspiration for Kelly, and she was especially eager to help. Harry Godwin, Memphis blues and jazz buff, located Minnie at the Jell Nursing Home, and arranged a more formal presentation of the money from the Kellys' benefit. On May 24, 1968, Harry Godwin presented the money to Minnie at the nursing home while Daisy and brother Edward Douglas looked on. Pianist Joe Dobbins gave up his supper hour to come over and play blues for the attending guests. The money purchased considerable comfort for the ailing Minnie.[7] In addition, Chris Strachwitz of Arhoolie Records, as well as *Living Blues* and *Blues Unlimited,* all made public appeals to Minnie's many fans to send money to Daisy for Minnie's care.

And the fans responded. In 1971 *Blues Unlimited* printed a letter they received from Daisy Johnson (and Minnie):

> Thank you for the magazine *Blues Unlimited* you sent to my sister Minnie and I. I think the story you wrote was just great. I'm sorry I could not be more help to you than I was, but being the youngest in the family, I know no more.
>
> We have received letters, cards, and money! I wish there was some way that we could thank all of Minnie's fans and friends for their help and good wishes. My sister Minnie was so happy and rejoiced over the write-up.
>
>
> (signed)
> Memphis Minnie and Daisy Johnson[8]

Minnie's parents had been church-attending Baptists (as Daisy still is), but Minnie was "too sick to go to Church" when she returned to Memphis. How eager Minnie was to go to Church remains to be seen, however, even granting the reputed frequency with which blues singers "repent" in their later years.[9] Minnie's remarks suggest her "faith" existed more to please her sister than out of any concern for her own soul. Daisy told it like this: "She always told me, after she came here, she said that she was very religious, [but] every time she would get ready to be baptized, said it was, she couldn't resist going to play for a nightclub! And she never got baptized. . . . But now, later on, she did get baptized . . . in the 1960s," Daisy said. The preacher who presided at the funeral was the same one who baptized Minnie, "right here, in the wheel chair."[10]

Minnie died on August 6, 1973, and she was buried in New Hope Cemetery. There is no grave stone or marker. Her death was announced in the Memphis *Commercial-Appeal* for August 7, 1973, as well as in *Billboard* and *The Black Perspective in Music.* *Living Blues* carried an obituary and a tribute.[11] *Blues Unlimited* and the *River City Review* both carried the Steve LaVere obituary that appeared in *Living Blues,* and these were by no means the only publications to notice Minnie's death.

Thomas Millroth, writing in the Swedish blues magazine *Jefferson*,[12] compared Minnie to Bessie Smith and Ma Rainey, finding Minnie superior in spite of the fact that Bessie and Minnie performed in somewhat different fields. He noted further that the rock group Jefferson Airplane, who recorded *Chauffeur Blues,* paid no royalties to Minnie. Critics were often in awe of her talent. Studs Terkel, reminiscing about earlier days in Chicago, evoked an era by invoking Minnie's name, along with the names of her colleagues. "Dude and I had been buying all kinds of 'race records:' Vocalion, Okeh, Bluebird. We were hooked on Big Bill, Tampa Red, Memphis Minnie, Big Maceo, Peetie Wheatstraw, the High Sheriff of Hell, Rosetta Howard and the Harlem Hamfats."[13] Jeff Titon wrote that Minnie "had few equals on guitar,"[14] while blues authority Paul Oliver described her as "the greatest of the women singers outside the 'Classic' vein."[15] Dean and Nancy Tudor called Minnie the best female vocalist in the country blues tradition, and they noted, "All of her work was of exceptional quality, and there is not a clinker in any of her over 200 sides."[16]

Minnie recorded over 180 issued sides, and much unissued material has now been released, as well. Such a total does not even include those pieces on which she played but did not sing, and on which her name did not appear. Her career was longer and more successful than many other blues artists. Her records were constantly and consistently on the market from 1930 to 1960, and as late as the mid-1960s, record shops like Derk's in the Maxwell Street market area of Chicago still had boxes of Minnie's red label Columbia 78s, and a few pink Okehs, along with similar records by Big Bill, Blind Boy Fuller and other popular blues artists.

One measure of Minnie's immortality is her wide-ranging influence, and we will cite only a few, recent examples. A few years ago, Joyce Cobb, a polished Memphis singer, performed Minnie's *In My Girlish Days* at the Greenville, Mississippi, nightspot CJ's.[17]

Poet Eunice Davis has issued an album containing songs by Minnie and Victoria Spivey, as well as her own material.[18] It is not surprising, of course, to find that so many women have done Minnie's songs, for she has been a role model for many performers. As we noted above, Jo Ann Kelly claimed Minnie as her first inspiration to sing blues.[19] And the appearance of three Memphis Minnie songs on one Big Mama Thornton album is a significant fact in itself.[20]

Besides winning best female singer award in *Blues Unlimited's* first readers' poll,[21] albums containing her work are regularly mentioned in other award ceremonies.[22] UK critic Peter Moody issued a small booklet on Minnie in 1967. It contains a brief biography and discography, as well as the transcriptions to eight of Minnie's songs, and it's a pioneering work of Minnie appreciation.[23] She has not been ignored, however, in the standard sources: She is listed in Eileen Southern's *Biographical Dictionary of Afro-American and African Musicians*,[24] as well as in Roger D. Kinkle's *The Complete Encyclopedia of Popular Music and Jazz, 1900-1950.*[25]

As Bukka White said, "She was about the best thing goin' in the woman line."

Memphis Minnie

1. Memphis Minnie, from a 1930 Vocalion flyer.

"She Wouldn't Give Me None"

1576—SHE WOULDN'T GIVE ME NONE & MY MARY BLUES
Vocal Duet with Guitar Acc.
Memphis Minnie-Kansas Joe 75c

2. Minnie and Joe, from a 1931 dealer's flyer. Note that the record highlighted is by no means their newest.

3. Memphis Minnie and Kansas Joe, 1930.

Here's a sweet one
by Kansas Joe and
Memphis Minnie

"THAT WILL BE ALRIGHT"

Kansas Joe sure gets right down to his croonin' in this number—and Memphis Minnie mixes in a mean and melodious guitar. It's great! This record with double guitar accompaniment is just too good to let your ears miss! Hear it today—at your Columbia dealer's!

Record No. 14439-D, 10-inch, 75c

That Will Be Alright
When the Levee Breaks } Vocals - Kansas Joe and Memphis Minnie

4. The public's first view of Minnie and Joe, a 1929 Columbia advertisement. Both vocals were by Joe.

5. Vocalion advertisement, 1930.

6. A Vocalion catalog from 1934 lists nearly all of Memphis Minnie and Kansas Joe's vintage recordings as still available.

MEMPHIS MINNIE (MINNIE McCOY)—Vocal (Race)

1658	After While Blues
1476	Bumble Bee
1556	Bumble Bee No. 2
1678	Crazy Cryin' Blues
1638	Dirt Dauber Blues
1673	Don't Bother It
02711	Drunken Barrel House Blues
1711	Fishin' Blues
1588	Frankie Jean
1603	Georgia Skin Blues

(28)

MEMPHIS MINNIE (Minnie McCoy)—Vocal (Race)—Con't

1603	Good Girl Blues
1665	Hard Down Lie
1678	I Don't Want That That Junk Outta You
1512	I'm Gonna Bake My Biscuits
1476	I'm Talking About You
1556	I'm Talking About You—No. 2
1718	Jailhouse Trouble Blues
1711	Kind Treatment Blues
1665	Lay My Money Down
1588	Memphis Minnie—Jitis Blues
1512	Mister Tango Blues
1618	New Bumble Bee
1618	New Dirty Dozen
1698	Outdoor Blues
1631	Plymouth Rock Blues
1688	Socket Blues
1658	Soo Cow Soo
02711	Stinging Snake Blues
1673	Today Today Blues
1653	Tricks Ain't Walking no More
1698	Where Is My Good Man?
1638	You Dirty Mistreater

MEMPHIS MINNIE AND HER JUG BAND—(Race)

1601	Garage Fire Blues
1601	Grandpa and Grandma Blues

MEMPHIS MINNIE, GEORGIA TOM, TAMPA RED AND KANSAS JOE—(Race)

1682	If You Want Me to Love

1588 Memphis Minnie-Jitis Blues—Guitar and Talking Memphis Minnie (Frankie)

7. Memphis Minnie, from a 1939 Vocalion Catalog.

8. Publicity photo of Minnie displayed in Ethel Douglas's family group of pictures.

9. Memphis Minnie in a 1930s publicity photograph.

10. A 1939 Vocalion catalog.

11. This numerical listing of Decca's race series shows nearly every title as still available in the 1940s.

12, 13, 14. Memphis Minnie in 1940 Columbia publicity photographs.

15. Ernest Lawlars, better known as Little Son Joe.

16. Daisy Johnson in the 1940s, when she went to Chicago to search for Minnie.

17. Big Bill Broonzy inscribed this picture to Minnie and Son Joe.

18. A page from an Okeh catalog for 1941-1942, only a few years after the label was resumed.

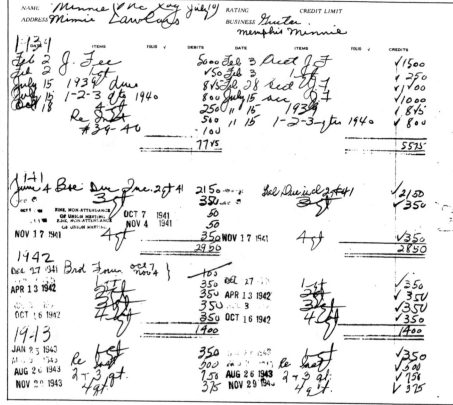

RECORDS *OKeh*

06007 Back Door Stranger	03318 We Want To Have A Talk With Jesus
06056 Be Good To Me	04394 What Are They Doing In Heaven
06056 Born For Bad Luck	03074 What Kinda Shoes Do The Angels Wear
06007 I'm Callin' Daisy	
05812 Let Me Tell You 'Bout My Baby	03015 What More Can Jesus Do
05923 Me And My Dog Blues	04472 While He's Passing By
05812 My Barkin' Bulldog Blues	03015 Who Was John
05881 Not Guilty Blues	04783 Won't I Be Glad
05785 Picking My Tomatoes	04964 You Got To Stand Judgment
05881 Poison Woman Blues	

MEMPHIS MINNIE
(Vocal Blues with Inst. Acc.)

04797 Bad Outside Friends	
05670 Boy Friend Blues	
05728 It's Hard To Please My Man	
05728 Lonesome Shark Blues	
04797 Low Down Man Blues	
05670 Nothing In Gambling	

MONKEY JOE
and his MUSIC GRINDERS
(Vocal Blues with Inst. Acc.)

05685 Bad Luck Man Blues	
06153 McComb City Blues	
06153 Old Man Blues	
05685 We Can't Get Along	

19. Minnie's union records for 1939-1943, showing the change in her name from McCoy to Lawlars.

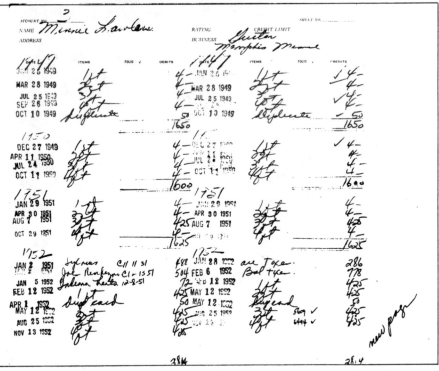

20. Minnie's union records for the years 1944-1948.

21. Minnie's union records for 1949-1952 establish her playing at Sylvio's, the Indiana Theatre, and Joe's Rendezvous.

22. Memphis Minnie wearing her silver dollar bracelet, 1950s.

23. Little Son Joe, unknown, Memphis Minnie, unknown, at the Big Apple, 1957.

24. Minnie and Son Joe, 1957, at the Big Apple.

25. Son Joe, unknown, unknown, Memphis Minnie, at the 708 Club, 1940s.

CHECKER RECORDS

758 -- JUKE
Can't Hold On Much Longer
(Little Walter)

762 -- Every Day I Have The Blues
They Didn't Believe Me
(Joe Williams)

764 -- MEAN OLD WORLD
Sad Hours
(Little Walter)

765 -- BAMBALAYA
Dinah
(The Bayou Boys)

768 -- TRAIN, TRAIN, TRAIN
I'll Wait
(Danny Overbea)

770 -- OFF THE WALL
Tell Me Mama
(Little Walter)

771 -- BROKEN HEART
Me And My Chauffeur
(Memphis Minnie)

774 -- FORTY CUPS OF COFFEE
I'll Follow You
(Danny Overbea)

776 -- TAKE IT TO THE LORD
Twelve Years Old
(Silver Stars)

777 -- COUNTRY BOOGIE
Muddy Shoes
(Elmore James)

780 -- BLUES WITH A FEELING
Quarter To Twelve
(Little Walter)

781 -- CAN'T GET ALONG
Plumb Get It
(Morris Pejoe)

—2—

26. Checker catalog from 1960 showing Minnie's *Broken Heart* and *Me and My Chauffer* as still available eight years after their release.

27. *Cash Box*, May 22, 1954.

ST. LOUIS—MEMPHIS—NEW ORLEANS

15-3 The Chickasaw	205-+5 Panama Limited	201-1 City of New Orleans		Table I		+6 Panama Limited	16 The Chickasaw	2-202 City of New Orleans
			All Pullman.		All Pullman.			
10.35PM	6.45PM	9.22AM		Lv ... ST. LOUIS, MO ... Ar		7.45AM		9.55PM
1.50AM	9.41PM	12.36PM		Lv .. CARBONDALE, ILL .. Ar		3.30AM	4.25AM	6.58PM
7.05AM	2.12AM	4.57PM		Ar } MEMPHIS, TENN. { Lv		11.00PM	11.05PM	2.38PM
9.10AM	2.22AM	5.07PM		Lv		10.50PM		2.28PM
7.15PM	9.30AM	11.55PM		Ar .. NEW ORLEANS, LA .. Lv		4.15PM		8.00AM

SOUTHBOUND
No. 15—THE CHICKASAW
Sleeper:
St. Louis to Memphis, 8-Sec.-1-D.R.-3 Dble. Bedrooms.—Car 151. (Occupancy 9.30 P.M. to 8.00 A.M.)
Cincinnati to Memphis, 10 Sec.-Comp -D. R. —Car 1031. (B. & O. No. 63 Cincinnati to Louisville). No. 103 Louisville to Fulton.
Coaches. St. Louis to Memphis.
Fulton to Memphis (No. 103 from Louisville).

No. 201—THE CITY OF NEW ORLEANS
Streamlined Coaches. Deluxe Reclining Seats.
St. Louis to Carbondale
St. Louis to New Orleans. (No. 1 from Carbondale.)

No. 205—THE PANAMA LIMITED
Sleeper:
St. Louis to New Orleans, 6-Sec.-6 Roomette-4 Double Bedrooms—Car 505. (No. 5 Carbondale to New Orleans.)
Parlor-Lounge Car. Radio. Sandwiches—Refreshments. St. Louis to Carbondale—Car 2051 (Illinois Central Parlor Car). I. C. Tickets. (Diner No. 5 Carbondale to New Orleans.)
Coaches. St. Louis to Carbondale.

NORTHBOUND
No. 16—THE CHICKASAW
Sleepers:
Memphis to St. Louis, 8-Sec.-1-D.R.—3 Dble. Bedrooms—Car 162. (Open 9.30 P.M.)
Carbondale to St. Louis, 6-Sec.-6 Roomette-4 Double Bedrooms—Car 604. (No. 6 New Orleans to Carbondale.)
Parlor Lounge. Radio. Refreshments. Carbondale to St. Louis. Car 164. (Illinois Central Parlor Car) I. C. Tickets.
Coaches. Memphis to St. Louis.

No. 202—THE CITY OF NEW ORLEANS
Streamlined Coaches. Deluxe Reclining Seats. New Orleans to St. Louis. (No. 2 to Carbondale.)
Carbondale to St. Louis.

No. 226
Coaches. Carbondale to St. Louis.

28. An Illinois Central timetable from April 30, 1950, showing the route of the Chickasaw train, that "low down dirty thing."

29. Minnie's union records for 1953-1955 show her playing at the 2200 Club, Little Eddie's, Joe's L. A. Bar, Tiny Davis' Lounge and the Painted Doll.

30. In the records for 1956-1958, Minnie's name has deteriorated from Lawlars to Lawlers, as it had on the preceding page.

31. David Collins, Joseph Washington, Daisy Johnson, Minnie Lawlars in the house on Adelaide, December, 1962.

32. Daisy Johnson and Memphis Minnie, Memphis, 1962.

33. Memphis Minnie on the porch at 1355 Adelaide in Memphis.

34. Memphis Minnie, late 1960s.

35. Harry Godwin, Memphis Minnie, and Joe Dobbins at the piano, Jell Nursing Home, Memphis, May 24, 1968.

36. Ethel Douglas, Minnie's sister-in-law, at her house at 1701 Kansas Street, where Minnie and Son often stayed on their Memphis visits.

37. Daisy Johnson, on her porch at 1355 Adelaide in Memphis, 1987.

38. House, Walls, Mississippi, 1987.

CERTIFICATE OF DEATH
TENNESSEE DEPARTMENT OF PUBLIC HEALTH FILE NO. **5109**
DIVISION OF VITAL STATISTICS

BIRTH NO.				
DECEASED — NAME FIRST	MIDDLE	LAST	**DATE OF DEATH** (MONTH, DAY, YEAR)	
1. Minnie		Lawlers	2. 8-6-73	
RACE WHITE, NEGRO, AMERICAN INDIAN, ETC. (SPECIFY)	4. SEX	**AGE — LAST** BIRTHDAY (YEARS)	UNDER 1 YEAR / UNDER 1 DAY	**DATE OF BIRTH** (MONTH, DAY, YEAR)
3. Negro	4. Female	5a. 76	5b. / 5c.	6. 6-3-97

COUNTY OF DEATH 7a. SHELBY **CITY, TOWN, OR LOCATION OF DEATH** 7b. MEMPHIS **INSIDE CITY LIMITS (SPECIFY YES OR NO)** 7c. YES **HOSPITAL OR OTHER INSTITUTION — NAME** (IF NOT IN EITHER, GIVE STREET AND NUMBER) 7d. 1355 ADELAIDE ST.

STATE OF BIRTH (IF NOT IN U.S.A., NAME COUNTRY) 8. LOUISIANA **CITIZEN OF WHAT COUNTRY** 9. USA **MARRIED, NEVER MARRIED, WIDOWED, DIVORCED** (SPE. (FY) 10. WIDOWED **SURVIVING SPOUSE** (IF WIFE, GIVE MAIDEN NAME) 11.

SOCIAL SECURITY NUMBER 12a. 335-16-7910 **SERVICE IN ARMED FORCES (SPECIFY YES OR DATES OF SERVICE)** 12b. NO **USUAL OCCUPATION** (GIVE KIND OF WORK DONE DURING MOST OF WORKING LIFE, EVEN IF RETIRED) 13a. HOUSEKEEPER **KIND OF BUSINESS OR INDUSTRY** 13b. OWN HOME

RESIDENCE — STATE 14a. TENNESSEE **COUNTY** 14b. SHELBY **CITY, TOWN, OR LOCATION** 14c. MEMPHIS **INSIDE CITY LIMITS (SPECIFY YES OR NO)** 14d. YES **STREET AND NUMBER** 14e. 1355 ADELAIDE ST.

FATHER — NAME 15. ABE DOUGLAS **MOTHER — MAIDEN NAME** 16. GERTRUDE WELLS **INFORMANT — NAME** 17. DAISY JOHNSON- SAME **MAILING ADDRESS**

18. PART I. DEATH WAS CAUSED BY: [ENTER ONLY ONE CAUSE PER LINE FOR (a), (b), and (c)] **APPROXIMATE INTERVAL BETWEEN ONSET AND DEATH**

IMMEDIATE CAUSE (a) Cerebral Vascular Disease

CONDITIONS, IF ANY, WHICH GAVE RISE TO IMMEDIATE CAUSE (a), STATING THE UNDERLYING CAUSE LAST DUE TO, OR AS A CONSEQUENCE OF: (b)

DUE TO, OR AS A CONSEQUENCE OF: (c)

PART II. OTHER SIGNIFICANT CONDITIONS: CONDITIONS CONTRIBUTING TO DEATH BUT NOT RELATED TO CAUSE GIVEN IN PART I (a) **AUTOPSY (YES OR NO)** 19a. No **IF YES WERE FINDINGS CONSIDERED IN DETERMINING CAUSE OF DEATH** 19b.

ACCIDENT, SUICIDE, HOMICIDE, OR UNDETERMINED (SPECIFY) 20a. Natural **DATE OF INJURY (MONTH, DAY, YEAR)** 20b. **HOUR** 20c. M. **HOW INJURY OCCURRED** (ENTER NATURE OF INJURY IN PART I OR PART II, ITEM 18) 20d.

INJURY AT WORK (SPECIFY YES OR NO) 20e. **PLACE OF INJURY** AT HOME, FARM, STREET, FACTORY, OFFICE BLDG., ETC. (SPECIFY) 20f. **LOCATION** (STREET OR R.F.D. NO., CITY OR TOWN, STATE) 20g.

PHYSICIAN — CERTIFICATION I ATTENDED THE DECEASED AND DEATH OCCURRED AT THE PLACE, ON THE DATE, AND, TO THE BEST OF MY KNOWLEDGE, DUE TO THE CAUSE(S) STATED. **SIGNATURE** 21a. **DEGREE** 21b. **DATE SIGNED** (MONTH, DAY, YEAR) 21c.

MEDICAL EXAMINER — CERTIFICATION ON THE BASIS OF THE EXAMINATION OF THE BODY AND/OR ON THE INVESTIGATION, IN MY OPINION, DEATH OCCURRED ON THE DATE AND DUE TO THE CAUSE(S) STATED. **SIGNATURE** 22a. James Spencer Bell M.D. **TITLE** 22b. **DATE SIGNED** (MONTH, DAY, YEAR) 22c. 8-7-73

CERTIFIER — NAME (TYPE OR PRINT) 23a. James Spencer Bell, M.D. **MAILING ADDRESS** STREET OR R.F.D. NO. 23b. 858 Madison Ave. **CITY OR TOWN** Memphis, **STATE** Tenn. **ZIP** 38103

BURIAL, CREMATION, REMOVAL (SPECIFY) 24a. BURIAL **DATE** 24b. 8-10-73 **CEMETERY OR CREMATORY — NAME** 24c. NEW HOPE **LOCATION** 24d. WALLS, MISSISSIPPI

FUNERAL HOME — NAME AND ADDRESS (STREET OR R.F.D. NO., CITY OR TOWN, STATE, ZIP) 25. SOUTHERN FUNERAL HOME-440 VANCE-38126 **REGISTRAR — SIGNATURE** 26a. Wilma Diethoza Deputy **DATE RECEIVED BY LOCAL REGISTRAR** 26b. AUG 1 0 197

39. Death certificate for Memphis Minnie.

40. Death certificate for "Kansas Joe" McCoy.

41. Death certificate for Ernest Lawlars.

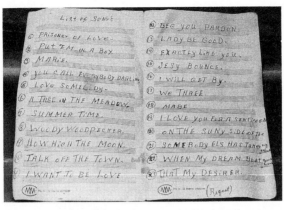

42. This "Request" list suggests how diverse and adaptable Minnie's repertoire was.

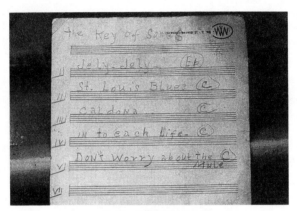

43. The Key of Songs.

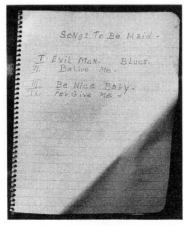

44. Songs to Be Maid.

Contract M-223 SIVE ARTIST	DATE MADE	MATRIX NO.	TITLE	PUB.	DATE O.K'D	DATE PAID	AM'T PAID	LISTED
	1938							
MEMPHIS MINNIE	6-23		C 2280 to C 2287 inclusive				100.00	
DEPT. (Minnie Mc Coy)	2-3		C 2452 to C 2453 inc.				25.00	
LANG.								
CLASS.	2-6		C 2454 to C 2460 inc.				87.50	
CODE Vocalion - Race								
DATED Jan. 7, 1938								
TERM 1 year								
COMMENCING Jan. 7, 1938								
ENDING Jan. 7, 1939								
RECORDINGS 16 selections								
ROYALTY								
ADV.-ON-ACCT.								
FLAT PAYM'T $12.50 per sel.								
GUARANTEE								
OPTION 1 year								
NOTICE 30 days								
REMARKS:								

45. Minnie's contract with Columbia for 1938-1939 shows her earning $12.50 per selection.

Contract EXCLUSIVE ARTIST	DATE MADE	MATRIX NO.	TITLE	PUB.	DATE O.K'D	DATE PAID	AM'T PAID	MONTH LISTED
MEMPHIS MINNIE	5/21/41	C 3764	IN MY GIRLISH DAYS	218				October
		5	ME AND MY CHAUFFEUR BLUES	208	'			July
DEPT. Race		6	DOWN BY THE RIVERSIDE	Pub Wabash				
LANG.		7	I GOT TO MAKE A CHANGE BLUES	Wabash				Dec
CLASS.		8	PIG MEAT ON THE LINE	218	'			October
CODE		9	MY GAGE IS GOING UP	218				Dec
DATED Letter agreement		70	THIS IS YOUR LAST CHANCE	228	'			
	12/12/41	C 4090	CAN'T AFFORD TO LOSE MY MAN	208				July
TERM (see new contract) 9/1/43		1	YOU GOT TO GET OUT OF HERE	Wabash	90134			Infra 4. 8-16-48
COMMENCING		2	DON'T TURN THE CARD	"				
		3	LOOKING THE WORLD OVER	*6707				Feb 1963
ENDING		4	IT WAS YOU BABY	262				Mar 42
		5	YOU NEED A FRIEND	Wabash				
RECORDINGS		6	I AM SAILIN'	Wabash				
		7	REMEMBER ME BLUES	Wabash				
ROYALTY		8	BLACK RAT SWING	*6707				Feb 1963
		9	JUST HAD TO HOLLER	Wabash				
ADV.-ON-ACCT.	New Contract							
	12/19/44	C 4302	FASHION PLATE DADDY					
FLAT PAYM'T		C 4303	WHEN YOU LOVE ME	2f	*6783			2-5-45
GUARANTEE		C 4304	PLEASE SET A DATE	Rel.50	36895			12-17-45
		C 4305	MEAN MISTREATER BLUES		37295			3-24-47
OPTION		C 4306	LOVE COME AND GO	2f	*6783			2-5-45
		C 4307	TRUE LOVE	Rel.50	36895			12-17-45
NOTICE		C 4308	WHEN MY MAN COMES HOME					
REMARKS:	2/26/46	CCO-4504	I'M SO GLAD					
		CCO-4505	HOLD ME BLUES					
		CCO-4506	FILLER DILLER					
		CCO-4507	MOANING BLUES					
		CCO-4508	GOT TO LEAVE YOU					
		CCO-4509	THE MAN I LOVE					
			See new Contract 7-19-45					

46. Minnie's contract with Columbia 1941-1944.

Contract EXCLUSIVE ARTIST	DATE MADE	MATRIX NO.	TITLE	PUB.	DATE O.K'D	DATE PAID	AM'T PAID	MONTH LISTED
	2/26/46	CCO-4504	I'M SO GLAD	Wabash	37295			3-24-47
		CCO-4505	HOLD ME BLUES	"	7co			
MEMPHIS MINNIE		CCO-4506	KILLER-DILLER REJECT	"	"			
DEPT. c/o Lester Melrose		CCO-4507	MOANING BLUES "	?	"			7
LANG.		CCO-4508	GOT TO LEAVE YOU "	"	"			
CLASS. Race		CCO-4509	THE MAN I LOVE	"	"			
CODE	9/30/46	CCO-4625	GOT TO LEAVE YOU Remake	"	"			
DATED July 19, 1945		CCO-4626	KILLER DILLER Remake	"	37977			11-17-47
		CCO-4627	MOANING BLUES Remake	"	7co			
TERM Two Years		CCO-4628	HOLD ME BLUES Remake		37977			11-17-47
		CCO-4629	FISHMAN BLUES		37579			7-21-47
COMMENCING September 1, 1946		CCO-4630	WESTERN UNION		30134			8-16-47
		CCO-4631	MY MAN IS GONE		7co			7-21-47
ENDING September 1, 1947 ✓		CCO-4632	LEAN MEAT WON'T FRY		37679			
	12/27/47	CCO-4968	THREE TIMES SEVEN BLUES	Wabash	38099			2-16-48
RECORDINGS 8 per year		CCO-4969	DAYBREAK BLUES "	"	30178			5-17-48
		CCO-4970	MILLION DOLLAR BLUES	"	30128			5-17-48
ROYALTY none	✓	CCO-4971	SHOUT THE BOOGIE	"	38099	good - 1st		2-16-48
ADV.-ON-ACCT.								
FLAT PAYM'T $35.00 per recording payable to Melrose								
GUARANTEE We pay for accomp.								
OPTION One year								
NOTICE								
REMARKS:								

47. Minnie's contract with Columbia for 1945-1947 shows her earnings have increased to $35 per side, payable, however, to Lester Melrose.

Contract EXCLUSIVE ARTIST	DATE MADE	MATRIX NO.	TITLE	PUB.	DATE RELEASED	DATE PAID	AM'T PAID	RECORDED
	4-23-49	CCO-5043	TEARS ON MY PILLOW	Wabash	11-16-49		30176	
MEMPHIS MINNIE		CCO-5044	SWEET MAN	Wabash	11-18-49		30176	
(Mrs. Minnie Lawlar)		CCO-5045	LUCK WILL CHANGE SOME DAY	Wabash	7co			
DEPT. c/o Lester Melrose		CCO-5046	BELIEVE ME	Wabash	7co			
8922 S. Hoyne Ave.		CCO-5047	TONIGHT I SMILE WITH YOU	Wabash	7-4-49		30164	
Chicago 20, Illinois		CCO-5048	JUMP LITTLE RABBIT	Wabash	7-4-49		30164	
DATED July 19, 1948								
TERM One year								
COMMENCING September 1, 1948								
ENDING August 31, 1949								
RECORDINGS 8 sides per year								
ROYALTY Will pay Lester Melrose $45.00								
ADV.-ON-ACCT. for each satisfactory recording.								
FLAT PAYM'T								
GUARANTEE								
OPTION 2 one year ops.								
NOTICE								
REMARKS We will pay for accompaniment								

48. Minnie's 1948-1949 contract. Note record numbers in AMT PAID column. Her session fees were higher than ever, but her contract would not be renewed.

49. *Boogie Train* sheet music.

50. A list of songs and song ideas to be added to Minnie and Son's repertoire.

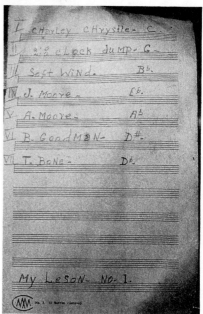

Part II:
THE SONGS

8. TO MAKE HEARD THE INTERIOR VOICE
A Note on Method

*That's how I talk to myself when I'm alone, I tell myself
all kinds of stories. And not only silly stories;
actually I live this way altogether.*
—Nadja, quoted by André Breton.

*Music is prophecy. Its styles and economic organization are ahead
of the rest of society because it explores, much faster than material
reality can, the entire range of possibilities in a given code. It
makes audible the new world that will gradually become visible. . . .
It is not only the image of things, but the transcending of the everyday, the herald of the future. For this reason musicians, even
when officially recognized, are dangerous, disturbing, and subversive; for this reason it is impossible to separate their history from
that of repression and surveillance.*[1]
—Jacques Attali

In our discussion of Minnie's songs, we have arranged the songs
by analogic propensity, or to borrow an expression of Goethe's,
"elective affinities," an arrangement whereby hidden sympathies
orchestrate the structure and content of an organizational method
and thus bring to the surface new and often wonderful relationships. An important aspect of this type of organization is that in

its search for new and possible connections, lost and hidden ones are also re-established, and the most significant aspect of the blues to be revealed by such an arrangement is its subversive character. The blues itself sabotages "bourgeois discourse" by its advocacy of non-repressive values; similarly, Minnie undermines the male standard of the country blues by the subversion and opposition inhererent in her role. One technique for accomplishing such a subversion is by singing supposedly "conventional" lyrics from her own non-traditional position, i.e., she challenged and weakened the patriarchal notion that blues women should sing on stage, with male orchestral accompaniment. Her guitar proficiency as well as her adaptation to stage, platform and ground-level performance so completely upset the patriarchal apple-cart that her admirers continually described her, with awe, as playing "as good as any man."

The form and structure of her songs also carry the potential for subversion, and we reveal how interruptions, for example, subvert more traditional structures of meaning. We will also search for the difference in a woman's blues, even while it appears to be the same as a man's. Since blues, moreover, is a cultural expression of the black working class, it is necessary to consider factors of class and race, together with that of gender, before we can truly appreciate the historic breadth, scope and uniqueness of the blueswoman's contributions. Our discussion of crime, for example, highlights all of these issues.

Throughout these pages we pursue poetic categories, as well as psychological and social ones, because of their *necessary*—i.e. desirable—character, because without them, our ability to relate the blues to our own deepest needs grows ever more desperate and ever more difficult. Our aim is to reveal the unheard side of Minnie's entire realm so that we might recover the power of her achievement in a way that addresses the urgent needs of humankind today. Indeed, the specific perspective of this study is its emphasis on society's *present needs* as envisioned through a contemporary surrealist lens, focused on the past, for it is the ceaseless re-evaluation of the past that enables us to step more confidently into a provocative future.

What is required is a particular instance of daring, a willingness to venture into the truly unknown where no guiding hand is available, where one can meet the imaginative poetics of the blues *head on*, with a critical imagination equal to the task. "The imagination is not . . . the faculty for forming images of reality; it is the faculty for forming images which go beyond reality, which *sing* reality. It is a superhuman faculty." We shall be defined by the sum of those tendencies which drive us to surpass the *human condition*.[2]

As listeners, then, we must go armed primarily with imagination, the true source of psychic production, for it is the imagination that creates us as listeners by determining the reaches of the mind that will be available to song. Instead of simply giving new meanings to blues lyrics, we are trying to show ways in which we, and every listener, can be, or have been, *changed* by the blues. Simultaneously, we hope to demonstrate ways in which blues *criticism* can be changed by the blues, for we must learn to bring a poet's attention to our task.

Critics are listeners who are not dissimilar in kind to any other listeners. And they, like the singers, engage in acts of interpretation. For us the product of the artist and critic is not only the work of criticism but the work of art itself, which grows out of the relationship between the listener and the singer. The blues singers are interpreters, just as voodoo doctors are often called *interpreters*, because of the process of transmutation that they work upon the raw materials of life experience in the making of a blues into an imaginative (and interpretive) product. The singer constantly and continually engages in interpretive performance, reshaping the final work, which by its continual reshaping can never really be final. Yet we have used the term transmutation in its alchemical sense of changing base metal into gold, for that evokes the degree to which the singers' accomplishments exceed mere transformation.

The meaning of the work is shaped and reshaped again by the listener, each of whom makes his or her own interpretation while doing so. All listeners are interpreters, just as all listeners can become listener/poets. Further, the work of poetic criticism of the blues must occupy the same position in relationship to its readers as the the blues singers occupy in relationship to their listeners. The readers of blues criticism must themselves become interpreters willing to confront imagination with an imagination of their own.

But what of this imagination of the poet/critic? What can it do for us beyond the realm of history and biography, within the boundaries of imagination? Besides the obvious goals of leading listeners to certain songs and certain aspects of the singer's life, the listener/poet will hear each song within a special context. Such listeners will emphasize the relationship of the songs to other songs in the blues, while attempting to cast light on references that may seem arcane. Further, with eyes on the social fabric through which the blues is filtered, such a listener will be in an excellent position to elucidate the many ways the imagination is affected by the movement of society itself. Further, the meaning in a work always exceeds the author's intent, for to be received by a society of other imaginations, in a world held together by a multiplicity of forces, only a few of which are clear to us, it could have no other effect. While the realm of shared experience provides a common ground on which the singer and listener meet, the bond between them, symbolized by the work of art, but hardly limited to it, lies deeper still. Scholarship may discover hidden patterns within the songs, or historical forces that helped to shape the blues, but then it must go forward, into a realm often dismissed by scholars as "mere poetry," but a realm nonetheless that locates the source of the interchange that constitutes the heart of the blues.

We view the blues as a totally authentic medium, presided over by artists who are the guardians of an important secret.[3] The blues singer's role as seer, as visionary, allows us to see the fertile ground in which such imaginative possibilities grow, and it is in this sense that the listener or the critic must accept the responsibility of the *initiate*, to be a seer as Rimbaud demanded of his fellow poets, and to continually threaten the established order, as any real poet must. The blues junction is one of the crucial crossings of poet and musician, and there are a number of vehicles that will convey us to this site: The paranoiac-critical method—the imposing of a systematically deranged "delusion" on to a hostile, "realistic" frame; black humor (apparent in Minnie's *Plymouth Rock Blues* or *New Dirty Dozen*), and analogy as a revolutionary/poetic principle are among these vehicles. The paranoiac-critical method, like the dream and like delirious/paranoiac interpretations, will often seize on a single "exterior" manifestation to "explain" or interpret aspects of life commonly thought to be separate from (or internal to) the manifestation itself.[4] The confusion between internal and external is itself the clarity of the explanation. A number of the ideas introduced throughout the rest of the book can be considered exercises in the paranoiac-critical method.

As for analogy:

> . . . the only evidence in the world is commanded by the spontaneous, extralucid, insolent rapport which establishes itself, under certain conditions, between one thing and another, and which common sense hesitates to confront. . . . I say only analogical tools reach fleetingly towards their re-establishment. Whence the importance assumed at long intervals, by these brief flashes from a lost mirror.
>
> Poetic analogy . . . transgresses the deductive laws in order to make the mind apprehend the interdependence of two objects of thought situated on different planes, between which the logical functioning of the mind is unlikely to throw a bridge, in fact opposes *a priori* any bridge which might be thrown. . . . *Only the analogical switch arouses our passion, only by it can we start the world's motor.*[5]

We will use the current generated by such an analogical switch to understand Minnie's work. But if her unusual role as a woman guitarist who "played like a man" suggests the potential for alienation, we would note that such fragmented identities and the unstable categories that surround them are themselves important functions of the opposition to rigid, "scientific" thinking. The morbid preoccupation with "objectivity" and "neutrality" is not only alien to the human spirit and the quest for liberation, but is opposed to desire itself.[6] Indeed, the very question of "desire" is difficult to raise in such an atmosphere, where one must rely on the destabilization of thought[7] to achieve a poetic stance of resistance.

It is only the poetic act that can offer a *poetic reality* as a viable alternative to the belief in religious illusion or scientific (positivist) "fact."[8] "Scientific knowledge of nature would be valuable only if *contact* with nature were re-established by poetic—I dare say mythical—methods. It must remain understood that all scientific progress completed in the framework of a defective social structure works only against man, helping to aggravate his condition."[9]

The affinity that surrealists have with so-called "primitive" or aboriginal arts and rituals, the people and their culture is embodied in a special claim, based on "the specific origins of surrealism in the practices of poetry, mediumistic experiment, dream exploration and other avenues of 'under-determined' thought." If these aspects of life existed in primitive or ancient cultures in an inseparable network of forces governing everyday life, rather than as separate entities, as many researchers believe to be the case, then surrealism is an historically unexpected resynthesis of our oldest traditions.[10]

This idea has been elaborated by Senegalese surrealist Cheikh Tidiane Sylla:

> If blues and jazz, more than other kinds of music, have been acclaimed by surrealists for their genuinely surrealist approach, and their capacity for provoking inspiration, their African origin is surely a determining factor.
>
> In the ecologically balanced tribal cultures of Africa, the surrealist spirit is deeply embedded in social tradition. [African philosophy presupposes] a highly charged psychic world in which every individual agrees to forget himself or herself in order to concentrate on the least known instances of the mind's movement—a thoroughly *emancipatory* experience. This psychical world . . . is a superior transcendance of the "real functioning of thought" over ordinary reality, something that vulgar materialists can never perceive. . . .

Arguing that black Africans enjoyed the practice of poetry "throughout the totality of their traditional social life," Sylla calls the latter "the *living experience of surreality*" and concludes that "Surrealism and black African art remain irreducible examples in the development of the complete unfettering of the mind."[11]

Although surrealism's affinity for the blues has been elaborated most extensively in recent years, its links to black music were insisted upon years ago by many surrealists as well as by noted Belgian jazz critic Robert Goffin in his article, "Hot Jazz," in Nancy Cunard's *Negro: An Anthology*. Emphasizing the improvisational aspects of certain forms of black music, Goffin drew an analogy between the poetry of André Breton and Louis Aragon, the paintings of Giorgio de Chirico and Max Ernst, and the "hot" music produced by black musicians.[12] But this analogy should not deflect our attention from the role both the listener and the singer *share* in "the living experience of surreality."

In the section on voodoo and hoodoo songs, we raise the question of blues, voodoo and women as negating principles. At the heart of this notion lies the fundamental radical principle of opposition itself, a principle that cannot be overemphasized:

> . . . more than ever before, the very principle of opposition needs to be fortified. All triumphant ideas head for disaster. Men must be convinced that once general agreement has been won on a given question, individual resistance is the only key to the prison. But this resistance must be *informed* and subtle. By instinct I would contradict a *unanimous* vote by any assembly which does not itself intend to contradict the vote of a more numerous assembly; by the same instinct I will give my vote to those who *rise*, to all programs not yet subjected to the test of fact and tending toward the greater emancipation of man.[13]

Our earliest personal history remains hidden from us by repression, but the veil hiding our analogous social history is more permeable, more vulnerable to our perception, and we must begin by attempting to utter what was there in hopes of what might be. The blues can also be seen as a constant attempt to name the primal scenes of personal and social history, even while it can never quite succeed in this utterance. Nor can it be said that its prime function is to do so. Nonetheless, this is precisely where the liberating aspects of the blues are located. By insisting on the dismantling of the "should" and on the exteriorizing of guilt, to be located outside the subject, the blues singer tries, unsuccessfully of course, to perform a guiltless song, and to instruct us in a new stance for living beyond repression. We see Minnie's recordings as viable and substantial accounts of women's history, sung and recorded by a woman, i.e. precisely the sort of history too easily lost, misplaced or forcibly pushed toward oblivion. But they are not simply history or even simple history. They are poetic documents that only a poetics of passion can elucidate. In trying to determine the poetic dimensions of an historic period where the written record is far from complete, we feel justified in turning our attention to the folklore of the people who have had their lives obscured by the broad brush strokes of a reality depicted according to the dominant culture, in this case, the white male bourgeoisie.

Instead of the positivist "objectivity" that has dominated the social sciences for so many decades, we have preferred to follow our own very different path, letting analogy, free association, and the magnetism of hidden attractions construct the framework on which we build our study. For us, the text, like the dream, is a door standing open. If it is for the poet to recognize the open door where others see only a wall, it is for all of us to pass through.

In the sections that follow, we will take an open-ended approach to Minnie's work that we hope will suggest still other possibilities of new meanings of her songs. While we do not hesitate to make our own specific interpretations, we hope that our method itself will, by example, encourage ever newer interpretations as the contexts for interpretation evolve new and different forms. Differences in interpretation will always occur from listener to listener, for the listeners will invoke their own interpretations according to their poetic needs, and it is clear that women hear the blues in ways that men do not. A single example only hints at the possibilities, and for this purpose, we call on a verse from Tommy Johnson's *Maggie Campbell Blues*:

> Crying, who's that yonder,
> coming down the road? coming down the road?
> Ummmm, who's that yonder
> coming down the road?

> Well, it looks like Maggie, baby,
> but she walks too slow.[14]

The male author of this work always assumed that the woman referred to in the song was not Maggie but looked very much like her, a woman who walked like her, except for the too-slow pace. The female author assumed the woman *was* Maggie, but a Maggie who was hesitant to come, a slower Maggie without her usual confidant stride.

These differences are at last being investigated, and one promising sign has been the feminist turn in blues criticism: Women listening to the blues, raising the question: How do we hear it? From the constant issue of women's blues LPs by Rosetta Records to the well-crafted and pioneer biography of Ma Rainey by Sandra Lieb, and Daphne Duval Harrison's *Black Pearls*, more and more women are focusing on women's blues. As one critic wrote of these women's blues, "They are the expression of a particular social process by which poor Black women have commented on all the major theoretical, practical, and political questions facing us and have created a mass audience who listens to what we say, in that form."[15]

The same critic emphasized the "rendering of . . . high art" in the works and lives of Bessie Smith, Lucille Bogan, Billie Holiday, Nina Simone and Esther Phillips ("Little Esther"), supplying an evolutionary schematic with a radical analysis. She suggests that with Bessie Smith, "Black women in American culture could no longer just be regarded as sexual objects. She made us sexual subjects, the first steps in taking control."[16] Yet as another feminist critic mentions, it is too easy to perpetuate stereotypes by highlighting the stars like Bessie Smith.[17] It is interesting to note that the Classic female singers like Bessie Smith, Ma Rainey and Alberta Hunter have received nearly all of the attention of recent feminist blues scholarship. Nonetheless, a view that most of these critics share is the notion that blues singing itself is "critical to defining the spectrum of possibilities for black women beyond servility and self-abnegation."[18]

The difference in meanings that listeners generate are not always only gendered differences, however, and many times, the place, the mood, and the time of day is sufficient to give the same song multiple interpretations. As soon as a record like *Me and My Chauffeur Blues*[19] begins to turn, listeners begin to generate meaning for themselves and Minnie, as when a listener says, "Hey, Minnie, play that one about the V-8s and their chauffeurs." Still, the record continues to turn, Minnie is still up on the icebox, out of the way of the turning drinkers and dancers: "Hey, Minnie, play that one about where your man drives you *everywhere!*"

Do the unlimited playings and hearings *defer* meaning, as Derrida would have it, or isn't it simply a question of realizing that there is no singular, original truth that can be, or should be, *restored* to the song?[20] "Hey, Minnie, play that dirty dog song where he's driving *other girls* around." Thus *Me and My Chauffeur Blues* may be heard as a song about 1) cars and chauffeurs, 2) a man who'll take you everywhere or 3) a cheating song! And this is to say the least.

Many meanings can be attached to blues lyrics, but is a particular lyric always the same? Audiences may expect the musicians to perform their records accurately at live performances. But when bluesman Son House was asked to listen to his early records and "decipher" unintelligible phrases, he insisted that it didn't matter what he sang on the record, since the record was only a brief moment in a song that was always in the process of continual change. "Just because those words were the ones that got to be on the record don't mean that it was the only ones that could fit there. We changed them songs around all the time. It don't matter what you want me to listen to right now. I probably never done it again that way anyhow!"[21]

Nor is a simple realistic depiction the face value or "real meaning" of a poem or song. Were that the case, poetry would have been abolished long ago, its place and function taken over by prose. For precisely this reason, the revolutionary political content of the blues cannot be found in narrowly "political" images. Throughout this book we will be discussing the politics of blues as well as its poetics, and we will distinguish the imagery of politics from the politics of imagery. But the foundation for understanding such a distinction is the realization that the politics of the blues does not necessarily lie in traditional images of politics and protest. Far from it!

> Every 'poem' which willfully exalts an indefinite 'free-dom', even when it is not embellished with religious or nationalist attributes, ceases first of all to be a poem and ultimately becòmes an obstacle to the total liberation of man, for it deceives by indicating a 'free-dom' concealing new chains. On the other hand, from every authentic poem escapes a breath of complete and stirring freedom (even if this freedom is not evoked in its political aspect), and thus it contributes to the effective liberation of man.[22]

Even the question of what Minnie's "politics" were is something of a stumbling block for those who would abuse the connection between poetics and politics in the blues. The conscious political position of any artist is secondary to the way the artist's work treats the social forces of the time, and in fact, her views may even be different than those expressed in her art. But if her work embodies the contradictory aspects of social currents while objectively de-picting those same forces, and at the same time, evokes inspiration in her listeners, the requirements of a radical political definition are easily met.[23] Moreover, as Penelope Rosemont has written, "dream, chance, imagination and desire . . . always have been enemies of God and the State."[24]

Meanings that are unconscious, in the psychoanalytic sense, will also be relevant to our inquiry. Not only do listeners and singers give multiple meanings to songs and song elements, but they do so on both conscious and unconscious levels, and there is little doubt that much of the gratification we experience in hearing the blues has unconscious sources.

The realization of certain potentials for meaning will also be determined by the milieu from which they are generated. It is clear that the foundation in experience at the source and heart of Min-nie's songs is the entire range of life experiences of working-class black women and the working-class black community as a whole.

It is the autobiography of black women as well as the story of the black community.

Blues songs, like other poetic works, may be wrapped in layers of meaning, each layer hidden by conflicts generated by the layer above it and closer to the surface, but each also continually subverting the reality to which it has access. The potential for meaning within the blues is indeed complex, and these remarks are meant to serve as an introduction to the specific meanings we will array as we move from song to song and from subject to subject. A final surrealist admonishment will send us forth on our endeavors in the proper spirit:

> A monstrous aberration leads men to believe that language was born to facilitate their mutual relations. To this utilitarian end they compile dictionaries, where words are catalogued, endowed with a well-defined meaning (so they think) based on custom and etymology. But etymology is a perfectly vain science, giving no information at all about the real meaning of a word, that is, its particular, personal signification, that everyone must assign to it according to the convenience of his mind. As for custom, it is superfluous to mention that it is the lowest criterion to which we may refer.[25]

9. BUMBLE BEE

Remember: the flower comes implicit in the bud.
                                                    —Mary Low

Memphis Minnie and Kansas Joe made their first record in the Columbia studio in New York; it was on a Tuesday, June 18, 1929, just four months before the stock market crash that was to rock the record industry, putting some labels out of business and sending others into receivership. One of the songs Minnie and Joe recorded was the soon-to-be-famous *Bumble Bee.* Eight months later, February 20 and 21, 1930, Minnie and Joe recorded 12 sides for Vocalion, for whom Minnie was to record until the label was phased out in 1940.[1] It was on this session that she again recorded *Bumble Bee,* the song that made her famous. It remains to be seen whether Columbia would have ever released their version if Minnie had not already had a hit with it on Vocalion, for whom she performed the song at a slower pace with a more confident and polished delivery. By the time Columbia did issue their *Bumble Bee*, the first version Minnie *recorded,* Vocalion had already issued *their* versions of *Bumble Bee*, *Bumble Bee No. 2* and *New Bumble Bee*!

Ultimately, Memphis Minnie recorded five different versions of *Bumble Bee* and it became a widely copied song. Among the singers who recorded versions or derivatives of *Bumble Bee* are Johnny Shines, Bertha Lee [Patton] *(Yellow Bee),* Bo Carter, John Lee Hooker *(Queen Bee),* Muddy Waters, Slim Harpo, and even the Rolling Stones. Big Bill may have been addressing Minnie when he sang,

She's long and tall, mama,
and half as sweet as she can be.
To satisfy that woman
takes more than a bumble bee.[2]

Certainly blueswoman Mae Glover hitched her wagon to Minnie's when she recorded her *Skeeter Blues* in February, 1931:

Lord, I believe to my soul,
    mosquito and a bumble bee must be kin. (2x)
Come tipping through my keyhole,
try to sting me again.

Bumble Bee Slim (Amos Easton) may even have derived his pseudonym from Minnie's song.[3]

Let's look more closely at the lyrics of the original Columbia version and Minnie's first Vocalion version, the latter of which was the first version to be released. A singer's first recording session is likely to contain her most popular songs, as judged by her previous live audiences, and it's therefore likely that *Bumble Bee* was already a "success" before Minnie and Joe entered the studio. It is noteworthy that Minnie sounds flustered on the first version of what must have been one of her most practiced pieces, but she might have been nervous precisely because she was recording for the first time.[4] Her delivery is inconsistent and the guitars are amazingly hesitant.

BUMBLE BEE
(Columbia version)

Bumble bee, bumble bee,
    please come back to me. (2x)
He got the best old stinger
any bumble bee that I ever seen.

He stung me this morning,
    I been looking for him all day long. (2x)

Lord, it got me to the place,
hate to see my bumble bee leave home.

Bumble bee, bumble bee,
    don't be gone so long. (2x)
You's my bumble bee
and you're needed here at home.

I can't stand to hear him,
buzz, buzz, buzz.
Come in, bumble bee,
want you to stop your fuss.
You're my bumble bee
and you know your stuff.
Oh, sting me, bumble bee,
until I get enough.

Bumble bee, bumble bee,
    don't be gone so long. (2x)
You's my bumble bee
and you're needed here at home.

I don't mind you going ain't
(going to stay so long).
Don't mind you going,
don't be gone so long.
You's my bumble bee,
and you're needed here at home.

I can't stand to hear him, buzz, buzz, buzz.
Come in, bumble bee,
I want you to stop your fuss.
You's my bumble bee
and you know your stuff.
Oh, sting me bumble bee, until I get enough.

BUMBLE BEE
(Vocalion version)

Bumble bee, bumble bee,
    won't you please come back to me. (2x)

He got the best ol' stinger
any bumble bee I ever seen.

He stung me this morning,
  I been looking for him all day long. (2x)
He had me to the place once,
I hate to see my bumble bee leave home.

I can't stand to hear him,
buzz, buzz, buzz,
Come in, bumble bee,
I want you to stop your fuss.
You're my bumble bee
and you know your stuff.
Oh, sting me, bumble bee,
until I get enough.

Hmmmmmmmm,
  stinger long as my right arm. (2x)
He stung me this morning,
I been looking for him all day long.

Sometimes he makes me happy,
  then sometimes he makes me cry. (2x)
He had me to the place once,
I wish to God that I could die.

Bumble Bee #2 and *New Bumble Bee* were attempts to supply new versions to the public of a song whose first version(s)
the public had eagerly purchased. This was not the case for
the first Vocalion version of *Bumble Bee*, however, and it's
more likely that it was, for Minnie, an improved version of
the Columbia side. Both songs share the same first two verses
and chorus, and Minnie may have felt that the last two verses
of the Vocalion version were simply "better" than the verse
she discarded from the Columbia version. We will see that
Minnie's next two versions are by no means similar in the way
that the first two are.

What is puzzling is the fact that Minnie and Joe gave up the
spritely, danceable rhythm of the Columbia version for the slow

grind of the Vocalion, especially considering how successful they were with upbeat, fast paced songs. One reason might be that many of their earliest recordings were uptempo, and *Bumble Bee* may have been forcibly slowed to add variety to their repertoire. Minnie falters a bit when singing the Columbia version, and she may have slowed it down to make its lyrics easier to handle. This would be somewhat surprising as Minnie was a superb handler of the language, with an amazing speed of articulation. But Minnie's faltering may be another reason why Columbia didn't issue the record until much later, when it was already famous.

As we have noted, Minnie (and Vocalion) had two more versions on the street before the summer of 1930 was over.

BUMBLE BEE NO. 2

Bumble bee, bumble bee,
　　where you been so long. (2x)
You stung me this morning,
I been restless all day long.

I met my bumble bee this morning
　　as he flying in the door. (2x)
And the way he stung me,
he made me cry for more.

Hmmmmmmm,
　　don't stay so long from me. (2x)
You is my bumble bee,
you got something that I really need.

I'm gonna build be a bungalow
　　just for me and my bumble bee. (2x)
Then I won't worry,
I will have all the honey I need.

He makes my honey,
　　even now makes my comb.(2x)
It's all I want now
my bumble bee just to stay at home.

NEW BUMBLE BEE

I got a bumble bee,
  don't sting nobody but me. (2x)
And I tell the world,
he got all the stinger I need.

And he makes better honey,
  any bumble bee I ever seen. (2x)
And when he makes it,
oh, how he makes me scream.

He gets to flying and buzzing,
  stinging everybody he meets. (2x)
Lord, I wonder why my bumble bee
want to mistreat me.

Hmmmmmm,
  where my bumble bee gone? (2x)
I been looking for him,
my bumble bee, so long, so long.

My bumble bee got ways
  just like a natural man. (2x)
He's stinging somebody,
everywhere he lands.

While each thematic section is devoted to a group of songs, it may be useful to glance at the discography from time to time to see how the songs fit in with the overall development of Minnie's and Joe's careers. For example, by the time *New Bumble Bee* was released, Minnie had recorded 24 issued sides, she was becoming a seasoned professional in the recording studio, and her voice exuded the confidence she had acquired.

In many ways, the various versions of *Bumble Bee* are prototypical blues songs: bold celebrations of eros in its inevitable conflict with the frustration inherent in the repressive dynamics of advanced capitalist society. The lyrics present an instant triangulation of pain, addiction and love, refusing the bourgeois ideology of "hearts and flowers" by insisting on images of sexuality ignited by the pain of desperation. For it isn't the fragrance of flowers but the odor of lust that attracts "the birds and the bees" in the blues, as Minnie tells us in the second verse of *'Frisco Town*.[5]

The bee is a difficult lover, to say the least. He's never at home, he's continually asked to "come back," he makes her cry, and he stings too many other women. The bee as an image of a male sex partner, then, is not only captivating with its metaphor but also with its instantaneous seizure of the contradiction of pain and pleasure. And if we don't realize how typical this is, Minnie reminds us that his ways are "just like a natural man," "stinging somebody, everywhere he lands".

But male singers also use stinging sex imagery to describe their lovers. If the "pain" in sex can be a function of male domination, how can we explain the male singers' description of their female lovers in the same terms? Is not the pain actually located within the racist and sexist structures of human relationships? It is, of course, but we do not interact with such "structures" themselves, but rather through our interactions with others. While the pain of erotic relations is embedded in the social structure, for the woman it is located and manifest in male domination, in the male demand and act. For the male singers, the pain is located in the female partner and the erotic act.[6] Lyrics like Peg Leg Howell's make this clear:

> My rider got something,
> they call it the stingaree.[7]

In the penultimate verse of the first Vocalion *Bumble Bee*, Minnie notes that her lover's stinger is "long as my right arm," a metaphor borrowed from a blues description of a bull or cow. The metaphorical flexibility that is so customary in the blues prevails here, as well, and we barely give the description a second thought, in spite of the fact that a bumble bee with a "stinger" of that size would be quite a sight. What Minnie seems to be doing here is only mimicking men's fetishization of penis size, pretending to want what the man thinks women desire in a man. Minnie's exposure of this objectivization gives us the opportunity to rethink the nature of our own response to this typical male boast. Minnie pretends to be the way men would like to think women are!

While this sort of "mimicry" is not unusual, neither is it typical. Rather, it is a form of self-objectivization which, for the most part, Minnie resisted quite actively throughout her life and career. For example, Minnie rarely refers to *how she looks* in her songs. Her use of a male partner as part of her succesful musical formula of female superiority and achievement could also be considered an indulgence of mimicry. But the term has a poetic dimension as well, and it is incumbent upon us to understand mimicry not simply as a form of "protective (self)-colorization" that can often be necessary for survival, but also as a technique of exposing patterns of domination.[8]

Minnie's choice of a bee as a representation of a stinging lover only partially plumbs the significance of the bee for Minnie's listening audience. For example, some listeners might have held the belief that because bees were the messenger of the gods and carried news of deaths to them, it was important to whisper the death to the bees whenever anyone died; otherwise, more deaths might occur and the bees themselves might leave or die. Others no doubt believed that a bee was a sign of good news. And these beliefs barely scratch the surface.[9]

Our main point is that the subject of Minnie's various *Bumble Bee* songs is hardly the "simple" bumble bee of house and garden, nor is it simply one of the many metaphors for lover that we find in the blues. Each metaphor must be judged on its own terms, and each must be sounded for depth and breadth, as well as intensity. The reduction of the representative of the male to the size of an insect can be seen as a way for the female singer to control and outmaneuver her oppression by the male, but too often in typical blues criticism, such metaphors, similes and other allusions are commented upon for their intensity alone, if they are noted at all. This practice gives the most stable forms of commentary their "dependability" as well as their monotony. Yet it is precisely such common figures as the bumble bee or the milk cow, that require our imagination. *To the suggestion that these are only conventions of representation, tacitly established within tradition and not subject to deep interpretation, we reply that it is precisely these conventions and their foundations in the material world as well as in the imagination that are so deserving of analysis and interpretation.*

The idea of comparing one's lover to a tiny insect can find illumination from many fields: psychoanalysis and psychiatry, folklore and poetry. Of course, dreams may contain the tiny or lilliputian, in a revival of the childhood wish to reduce the terrifyingly large objects of the nursery to the smallest size possible. Such "little creeping things" as insects or bugs can also represent *children* or unwanted brothers or sisters.[10] Further, flying, at least in dreams and often in folklore, can represent sexual excitement. We have already noted that male singers may refer to themselves as stinging insects,[11] just as the blueswomen refer to them. Too, there are relatively non-sexual references to insects and arachnids in the songs of male singers, like the many blues about bed-bugs, cinch bugs, and boll weevils.[12] We see at once, then, how complexly determined can be the choice of an insect as an image of a male lover in the blues! As for the notion that insects can represent undesired brothers and sisters to a young girl with many siblings, *Biting Bug Blues* seems to speak eloquently:

BITING BUG BLUES

Just a biting bug been following me
    everywhere I go. (2x)
I'm gonna kill that biting bug,
so she won't follow me no more.

Just a biting bug been following me
    from town to town. (2x)
Yes, she kept on a following me,
till my good man have done put me down.

I woke up this morning
    and that biting bug was in my bed. (2x)
Till I taken my pistol
and I shot that biting bug dead.

Spoken: Yes, yes.

Hmmmmm, I won't be worried
    with that biting bug no more. (2x)

> I done stopped that biting bug
> from following me everywhere I go.
>
> Now you girls don't have to worry,
>   because that biting bug is gone. (2x)
> I done stopped that biting bug
> from breaking up other women's homes.

The woman in the song fights to keep her man, but we may be justified in seeing something beyond the "other woman" who must be guarded against; indeed the enemy in this song is a danger to all women, women who can now rest in peace because the biting bug is dead. The notion of competition reintroduces the equation insects = children/siblings, and the listener may decide for herself whether or not the biting bug has a metaphorical meaning as broad as it is deep, ultimately representing disease or another oppressive category or institution which tends to wreak havoc on the supply of able lovers!

We must respond to the image of the bug or bee with our own imagination—where we can dream its dream as we imagine Minnie's images. For *the rational pursuit of meanings is only one of the many ways we can understand the meaning of the blues.* Even while psychoanalysis can help us to understand the role of the unconscious, and an understanding of the unconscious can illuminate the context and the content of an image, psychoanalysis itself refuses to go beyond rational and logical means of apprehension, leaving the intrinsic atmosphere and the extraordinary power of the image unexplained. Poetry itself offers us the greatest means of its own understanding.

Let's look at an example. Without any familiarity with blues—as far as we know—the French philosopher Gaston Bachelard offers us a brilliant illumination of the path to the nest of the bumble bee. He begins by quoting a few lines from Tristan Tzara:

> The market of the sun
> has come into my room
> And the room into my buzzing head.

He then explains that to properly respond to this image, one must experience "the strange whir of the sun" as it actually strikes the wall of a room, for having learned to attune oneself to that sound, the reader can then hear that every one of the sun's rays carries with it *bees*. The resulting buzzing in the head creates "the hive of the sound of the sun." Bachelard notes that he had to ignore the barriers of rationalist criticism in order to participate in the activity of the image, thereby proving its communicability. His remarks can also illuminate the blues singers' notion of the tiny insect as an image for a lover.

For us to realize how Minnie's images of the miniature can nonetheless stimulate profound values, we must go *beyond* simple logic.[13] The listener/poet must newly create the power of the image on her own, actively seeking the new associations that can carry her beyond the bounds of normal passivity, into the subliminal realm of the marvelous. Then we will understand the full course of the image, when we hear how Johnny Shines has miniaturized himself as a spider or how J. T. Smith[14] has redesigned himself as a hopping frog—but as listening poets, we will see these bluesmen not only in miniature, or in their normal stature, but especially, *larger* than life. For when the skilled blues singer wields such images successfully, the miniaturized image serves to amplify the notion of what is represented. The successful *poetic* reduction of the image increases our comprehension of its attributes. How so? While collecting work songs in Texas prisons, Bruce Jackson questioned a worksong leader about the powerful metaphor "two-barrel derringer" for shotgun. The prisoner, J. B. Smith, replied, "That's what we call 'down talkin' it, makin' it small."[15] That is to say, he spoke about the poetic method, not about images and their source.

With no difficulty one can imagine a world peopled only by bumble bees, toads, spiders, milk cows, jersey bulls, black snakes, ground-hogs, alligators, monkeys, black cats, growling dogs in short, all the animals the blues singers have used imaginatively and metaphorically to increase and quicken our grasp of their more-than-human, less-than-human and all-too-human characters. The queen-orientation of the beehive is one aspect of her metaphor that Minnie leaves unsung, and yet, it is there, within the notion of the bumble bee lover, only waiting to be seized.[16] Such a perspective was seized upon by Charlotte Perkins Gilman who, in 1911, compared the functioning of a utopian women's collective to the running of a beehive.[17] Not surprisingly, the beehive was also an important symbol of the First International.

10. CRIME

The slums take their revenge.
　　　　　　　　　—Nelson Algren

All this because I like to make love under water
. . . All this because you know I was once a thief.
　　　　　　　　　—Joyce Mansour

The blues critique of bourgeois society is especially evident in the songs dealing with crime, for crime itself serves as a critique of bourgeois society. For radical thought, evil is a necessary proposition as long as there is still the prevalent notion of some transcendental goodness to which humankind must aspire. While such an idea prevails, the "exalted representation of an innate 'evil' retains the greatest revolutionary value."[1]

The songs of the female criminal are especially evocative, combining as they do, a critique of ruling class values with a critique of racism and male domination. Our insistence that the free play of erotic desire is at the core of the blues and of all genuinely poetic and revolutionary activity becomes even more compelling when we hear it in the songs of female criminals, among whom the mere appearance of desire is often denounced as an aberration.[2]

The relationship between the blues singers and crime is not simply metaphoric. Many blues singers have spent time in prison, and their membership in the lower classes and their participation in that milieu has refined their critique of the oppressive atmosphere of bourgeois society. The bars and clubs where the blues is played

115

are permeated by a "mood of anti-authoritarianism" which makes
the police *personae non grata* in such settings.[3] In the blues, we
are not surprised to see the notion of criminality permeated with
the intimation of lust. As bluesman Bob Coleman sang,

> It takes a Cincinnati underworld woman
> to satisfy my soul.[4]

What is worthy of emphasis is that while we apply stereotypes
to our jazz and blues artists—drug addict, lazy, alcoholic, in
debt, irresponsible, immoral—identical stereotypes are applied
to musicians in other societies as well. Despite the low repute
in which these musicians are held, however, they still occupy an
important functional position in their native communities.
Throughout history, musicians were often slaves or untouch-
ables, and even in this century Islamic believers have been forbidden to eat at the same table as musicians. Music came to be
a locus of subversion, and in earlier times, these outcast participants—women, slaves and other centrifugal fugitives—often
gathered in forests, caves, and other marginal areas to engage
in forbidden rites.[5] Such outcasts also functioned as prophets.
Because they continually evoke the lost childhood of humanity
in an unauthorized attempt to bring society to a boil, such fugitives as the mad, the carnivalesque, and the blues artist, are
at onced banished and celebrated. This very location in the past
of humanity's instinctual life enables them to prepare the celebration that will herald the arrival of a non-repressed era.[6]

In America, musicians were specifically identified as criminals
by the early 18th century. In 1727, for example, one reason given
for the need to immediately construct the New Haven workhouse
was that the number of rowdy and disorderly persons had increased
so rapidly. Those to be committed included "vagabonds, and *common pipers*, [and] *fiddlers. . . .*"[7] Two hundred years later, Blind
Willie Johnson was nearly arrested for singing the spiritual, *If I
Had My Way I'd Tear This Building Down* because he was singing
it in front of a New Orleans Custom House![8] But the most ardent articulation of the notion of the street musician's subversive
potential came from the Russian anarchist, Bidbei, who asked,

"Who, if not the vagabond, can be the demon-*accoucheur* of history? From where, if not from the dismal slums, can seep the noxious poison of derision for the whole callous and cold code of shameful bourgeois morality?"[9]

Who else but the criminal, the vagabond, the street-singer, can accomplish this critique? Some blues lyrics are deliberate repudiations of law and order and even outright celebrations of crime, for in certain conditions, the working-class criminal embodies sentiments and inclinations which are primitively but fundamentally revolutionary.[10] Walter Davis sang these lines in his *Howling Wind Blues:*

> Poor people are like prisoners
>   but they just ain't got a ball and chain. (2x)
> But the way they are faring,
> I swear it's all the same.[11]

The blues critique, however, could only occasionally be this explicit, and such songs as *Jailhouse Trouble Blues, Reachin' Pete, Moonshine, Finger Print Blues* and *Remember Me,* remind us that the blues is an index of oppression as well as a clarion of liberation.

REACHIN' PETE

> Friend, you go to Helena,
>   stop on Cherry Street. (2x)
> And just ask anybody
> to show you Reachin' Pete.
>
> He's the tallest man
>   walks on Cherry Street. (2x)
> And the baddest copper
> ever walked that beat.
>
> *Spoken*: Ehh, let's go to town now.
> That's what I'm talking about.
>
> He met me one Sunday morning,
>   just about the break of day. (2x)

I was drinking my moonshine,
he made me throw my knife away.

Well, he taken my pardner
    down to the jail. (2x)
After he locked her up,
he turned and went her bail.

Reachin' Pete's all right
    but his buddy (old Buzzell?) (2x)
Everytime he meet you,
he ready for plenty hell.

Spoken: Look out, now,
here comes Reachin' Pete and Buzzell.
Don't let 'em catch you.
It'll be too bad, I'm telling you.
Aww, shake it,
that's what I'm talking about.
Boys, you tired?
Shucks, I'll go a long time. [laughs]

Moonshine is a sprightly number whose rhythm belies the negative message of its lyrics.

MOONSHINE

I'm got to leave this town,
    I'm got to go before the sun goes down. (2x)
'Cause I done got tired
of these coppers running me around.

I stayed in jail last night
    and all last night before. (2x)
I would have been there now
if my daddy hadn't sprung the do'.

I stay in so much trouble,
    that's why I've got to go. (2x)

But when I get out this time,
I won't sell moonshine no more.

I done packed my trunk
   and done shipped it on down the road. (2x)
Now I won't be bothered
with these big, bad bulls no more.

Just keep me a-moving,
   going from door to door. (2x)
I done made up in my mind
not to sell moonshine no more.

Spoken: Yeah.

These songs describe criminal activity, occasionally in detail, and then conventionally express regret or apprehension at going to jail or getting caught; there are, however, few signs of guilt, and the tempo of *Moonshine* and *Reachin'Pete,* together with Minnie's laughter during the latter piece, gives even the regrets a cardboard quality.

Gambling songs may also be grouped here, for gambling was and is illegal in most of its forms, especially in those varieties available to poor blacks. Many participants in a "friendly" game of cards or dice found themselves in jail or on a road gang for a week, a month or a year. Still, gambling retained its appeal, and for many of Minnie's audience, it was a regular activity.

GEORGIA SKIN
(Victor)

The reason I like the game,
   the game they call Georgia Skin. (2x)
Because when you fall
you can really take out again.

When you lose your money,
   please don't lose your mind. (2x)
Because each and every gambler
gets in hard luck sometime.

> I had a man,
>   he gambles all the time. (2x)
> He throw the dice so in vain
> until he like to lost his mind.
>
> Hmmmm,
>   give me Georgia Skin. (2x)
> Because the womens can play,
> well, so as the men.
>
>
> *Spoken:* Georgia Skin
> is the best game that I know.
> Georgia Skin
> is the game that I bet all of my money.

Minnie suggests that for her and other women, a primary attraction of gambling, or at least the skin game, was its "equal opportunity" nature, wherein "the women can play, well, so as the
men." And Minnie did gamble with men, just as she played guitar
with them and sang with them. Another level on which the song
can be heard would be as a message from a leader of working-
class black women to working-class black women everywhere: A
woman can play in male-dominated groups, just as she can in the
gambling group and the male-dominated field of country blues
singing.

Minnie's song about the skin game was derived partially from
Walter Beasley's *Georgia Skin*[12]—her first two verses are his
first two verses—but Beasley's song ends with only one additional verse that Minnie didn't use, and the vital "womens can
play" lines are Minnie's own. Minnie also originated the fe-
licitous phrasing, "He throw the dice so in vain," just as she
did this verse that appears only in the Vocalion version of
Georgia Skin:

> I picked up jack o' diamonds,
>   I played 'em on down to the end. (2x)
> That's why I say, I like the game they call
> Georgia Skin.

Minnie offers another perspective on gambling in her *Good Girl Blues:*

GOOD GIRL BLUES

I have been a good girl,
   going to church all of my days. (2x)
But I'm going to learn to gamble
so I can stay out late.

Crying, dice, oh, dice,
   please don't fail on me. (2x)
If you don't seven/eleven,
don't you crap and three.

Hmmmm, hmmmmmm, hmmmmmhmmm. (2x)
Hmmmmm, hmmmmm.

When your home get unhappy,
   just as well to pack up and move. (2x)
Ain't no use trying to live in confusement,
you [just like you was a fool?]

Oh Lord, oh Lord, Lord,
   what shall I do? (2x)
I done did everything, baby,
to get along with you.

Hmmmm, hmmmmmm, hmmmmhmm.(2x)
Hmmmmm, hmmmmm.

Here, becoming a gambler who "can stay out late" is a way of escaping the role of the church-going "good girl" and her family-centered, oppressive life, represented by the image of repression *par excellence*, the church. Distrust and mockery of religion, the church, and preachers is also reflected in Afro-American humor. As the obsolescence of religion became ever more apparent, jokes about preachers and the efficacy of religion itself became more commonplace.[13] The church serves the dominant social paradigm by preaching the doctrines of accomodation, repression and guilt, and its place as the *victim* of hostility and humor only confirms this notion, if it still needs confirming at this late date. The blues singer and the humorist both attempt to disarm the ruling class by "demystifying its machinery of oppression,"[14] and by dismantling the most powerful superstition of all time, the belief in God.

* * *

DOWN IN THE ALLEY

I met a man,
asked me did I want (to pally?)
"Yes, baby, let's go down in the alley."
Take me down in the alley, (3x)
I can get my business fixed all right.

I met another man,
asked me for a dollar,
Might have heard that mother fuyer holler.
Let's go down in the alley. (3x)
You can get your business fixed all right.

Spoken: Let's go.

When he got me in the alley,
he called me a name.
What I put on him was a crying shame.
Down in this alley, (3x)
Where I got my business fixed all right.

You got me in the alley,
but don't get rough.
I ain't gonna put up with that doggone stuff.
Way down in this alley, (3x)
Lord, my business fixed all right.

Spoken: Woo, it's dark.
Can't see no light.
Got to feel my way out this alley.
I'm gonna stop, boys, walking late at night.

You took me in the alley,
you knocked me down.
Now I'm gonna call
every copper in this town.
You got me down in the alley, (3x)
Now you got your business fixed all right.

Spoken: Boys, I'm sure gonna stop walking,
walking late at night.

Down In The Alley, an up-tempo number, is enticing and note-worthy for its evocation of the alley as a criminal locale. But the alley is more than that. If the town halls, bars and taverns, and other public places can be seen as the domain of the men, the private places like houses and, on a certain level, the back streets and alleys that connect them into neighborhoods, can be seen as the domain of the women.[15] This is not to suggest, of course, that men have not seized both domains for their own purposes, or that women have not reclaimed "male" territories. Thus, while the alley can function as a specific location of male criminality, it can also operate as a figure for the criminal woman because it is also a figure for the oppressed, the re-pressed, and the hidden, the place where things are put that we don't want others to see or to identify with us. For us, it operates as a highly significant representation of all that the blues can reveal, precisely because of its power and function as a symbolic hiding place.

We also suggest that the alley can be seen as the *blues equiva-lent* of "street," just as the "back door" is the blues equivalent of "front door." By "blues equivalent," we mean to suggest that the alley and the back door function in entirely different registers than white bourgeois streets and front doors. Poets have always been aware of these different registers, and for the surrealists, especially during their nocturnal wanderings through the streets of Paris, the possibility of the special functions that certain byways seemed to harbor was the promise, waiting to be fulfilled, that at any moment, the true function of the street in question might be revealed.[16]

The blues singers act as guardians of these special functions, directing inquiries down this path or the other, where desire seems to be most at home. Thus, in the blues, when "the sun's gonna shine" someday, it is usually in the "back door" and not the front door, as in the frequently heard line,

> 'Cause the sun's gonna shine, in my back door some-day.[17]

And it is out onto the alley that the back door leads. Minnie's alley song ends with a reminder that the victim of ghetto crime was usually the ghetto-dweller herself. Taken as a whole, how-ever, it can be seen to emphasize the alley as a metaphor for the ghetto, into which the white bourgeoisie has driven the lower class blacks, the alley itself the scene of the crime and the image of the unconscious in the bourgeois nightmare, constantly threatening to grow and expand, to return and penetrate the purity of the clean white streets.

* * *

Prostitutes are the protagonists in a number of Minnie's songs, of which *Tricks Ain't Walking,* originally written by Lucille Bogan, is the most well known:

TRICKS AIN'T WALKING NO MORE

> Times has done got hard,
> work done got scarce,
> Stealing and robbing is taking place,
> Because tricks ain't walking,
> tricks ain't walking no more,
> Tricks ain't walking,
> tricks ain't walking no more,
> And I'm going to grab somebody
> if I don't make me some dough.
>
> I'm going to do just like a blind man,
> stand and beg for change,

Tell these tricking policemen
change my second name,[18]
Because tricks ain't walking, etc.
And I've got to make some money,
I don't care where I go.

I'm going to learn these walking tricks
what it's all about,
I'm going to get them in my house
and ain't going to let them out.
Because tricks ain't walking, etc.
And I can't make no money,
I don't care where I go.

I got up this morning with the rising sun,
Been walking all day
and I haven't caught a one,
Because tricks ain't walking, etc.
And I can't make a dime,
I don't care where I go.

I got up this morning, feeling tough,
I got to calling my tricks
and it's rough, rough, rough.
Because tricks ain't walking, etc.
And I have to change my luck
if I have to move next door.

Hustlin' Woman Blues, a Minnie original, invokes the pimp as well as the prostitute.

HUSTLIN' WOMAN BLUES

I stood on the corner all night long,
     counting the stars one by one. (2x)
I didn't make me no money, Bob,
and I can't go back home.

Spoken: I've got a bad man.

My man sits in the window
   with his .45 in his hand. (2x)
Every now and then
he gets to hollering at me and tells me,
"You'd better not miss that man."

Spoken: I've got him, baby.

My daddy ain't got no shoes, Bob,
   now it done got cold. (2x)
I'm gonna grab me somebody
if I don't make myself some dough.

Spoken: I'm going to the Quarter Bowl,
Bob, can you gamble?
No, it's rough when you can't do nothin'.
I just want to know can you shoot dice? No?
Can't shoot no dice? I can't gamble myself.
Well, I can't do nothin', but I bet a man I can.

I'm going to the Quarter Bowl,
   see what I can find. (2x)
And if I make a hundred dollars,
I'm gonna bring my daddy ninety-nine.

    Looking at the relationship between the prostitute and the
pimp, especially at its most extreme and destructive, may reveal to
us certain hidden and more cryptic, but nonetheless damaging, aspects of "normal" relationships between women and men, especially husbands and wives. As such it becomes another example
where the crucible of disorder need only be agitated slightly in order to make manifest a startling reaction. It is this axis of desire,
as it is crossed by prostitution, that reveals why downhome blues
vocals have so often been the victims of the bourgeois jazz critic's
clean-up campaign.[19]
    The subjects of the downhome vocal blues are too lowdown, i.e.
too lower-class for middle-class jazz commentators. The more
vaudevillian performers like Bessie Smith—whose own repertoires
contained somewhat "risqué" material—are acceptable not only
because the stage itself helps distance the singer from her audience

and not only because the jazz accompaniments are more accept-able to jazz fans, but also because their material is more sophisti-cated, i.e. more middle-class. The more middle-class the listener, the more she or he wants the blues cleaned up. It is these same middle-class values in many of Minnie's fans that cause such a heated reaction to the notion that Minnie may have engaged in sex for money.

In an interview, when asked how long he'd known Minnie, Homesick James remarked, "I knowed her before she ever made [any records]. That hair-raiser! I knowed Minnie when she was just a street-walker." When asked if he meant that Minnie was *really* a street-walker, he replied "Yep!"[20] On another occasion, harpist Hammie Nixon volunteered that after a Decca session that took place over a period of days, Minnie offered to bed down with vari-ous singers (Hammie, Peetie Wheatstraw and others) for their share of the proceeds.[21]

Several factors combine to suggest that there may be at least some truth to this notion. The primary evidence is that this infor-mation comes from two entirely separate sources, without prompt-ing or without leading questions. Further, Minnie's songs of prostitution remind us that the blues is the music of that segment of culture in which prostitutes participate. And Minnie was known to be a tough participant in the same culture herself.

The real crux of the issue, if it should even be branded as one, is not so much what Minnie did as it is our reaction to what she did. When the notion of Minnie as prostitute was posed to several of her fans, one's reaction was to insist that it might be true me-taphorically, i.e., as a blues "tale," but not true in fact. Another authority wrote that we should emphasize how Minnie was a sweet, warm woman who never "really" left the country around Walls![22] Such reactions are extreme, and as we suggest, a violent antipathy to prostitutes may contain truths about our attitudes toward women in general.

At the heart of the matter is *desire*, always the first victim at these class rites, for it is perceived clearly as dripping with subjec-tivity, a drenched and humid poetics that recognizes passion in or-der to embrace it, not to tame it. It is this passion that is at the heart of the blues, a passion impossible to miss when hearing *Tricks*

Ain't Walking No More, just as it is passion at the heart of the manifesto *The Women Prostitutes Of Lyon* [France, 1975] *Speak To The People:*

> We asked the state to listen to us as women.
>
> (The Minister of the Department of the Interior) answers us with billy clubs, takes our money, puts us in prison, insults us . . . and takes our children.
>
> He refuses to see us as women.
>
> He only accepts us as sex factories.
>
> He speaks about procuring, but he takes away our money and goes free!
>
> So we say:
>   NO TO PROCURING
>   NO TO BROTHELS
>   NO TO POLICE REPRESSION
>   NO TO PRISON SENTENCES.
>   YES TO JUSTICE.
>   YES TO ALL THE ADVANTAGES AND RIGHTS
>   OF BEING WOMEN!
>
> More united than ever, in dignity, for the creation of an Estates General of women prostitutes, we come together in the struggle.
>
> Action Committee of Women Prostitutes[23]

We have quoted this manifesto as a way of suggesting and evoking an historical continuum in which Minnie's speaking and singing for the prostitutes in the 1930s ultimately enables the prostitutes to establish their own voice and speak for themselves in the 1970s. Prostitutes have organized in many areas of the United States as well, and PUMA (Prostitutes Union of Massachusetts) is only one of the many groups like ASP (Association of Seattle Prostitutes) and PONY (Prostitutes of New York).

Many people react to the notion of prostitutes' organizations with laughter, regarding the whole idea laughable and silly, but just such a reaction is the measure of how we dehumanize women. In this case, we convince ourselves that prostitutes are, in fact, sex factories, just like France's Minister of the Department of Interior said they were. It is easy to pretend that they are not *women* with desires of their own, concerns about their own children and the same cares that most of us have.

In this respect, Minnie's *You Can't Give It Away* is particularly interesting. The prostitute who is teased in the second verse of Minnie's *New Dirty Dozen*[24] is taunted much more harshly in *You Can't Give It Away:*

YOU CAN'T GIVE IT AWAY

What is that you're going around
here trying to sell?
It tain't good to eat, you know,
it ain't good to smell.
Don't nobody want it,
Don't nobody want it,
Don't nobody want it,
You can't even give it away.

First time I met you
had that meat in your hand,
Going to give it
to some woman's man.
Ah, don't nobody want it, etc.

Spoken: Play it, Dennis, tell all about it.

You got something you can't sell
and you can't give away,
You just as well to take it on back
where you stay.
Ah, don't nobody want it, etc.

And don't let me catch you
trying to give it to my man,

If you do, I'm gonna raise a pain,
I doggone can.
Don't nobody want it, etc.

Spoken: Play it Dennis,
tell all about it, boy.

Lookahere, black gal,
why don't you get off the line?
What you trying to sell,
it ain't nobody buying.
Don't nobody want it, etc.

Even this seemingly unsympathetic songs contains a different message than the one most easily heard. The blurring of the distinction between "prostitute" and "woman" by showing that the person who "can't even give it away" is the same person as the one who can't "sell it," by showing desperation, eroticism and the quest for love as motivations for the woman who also tries to "sell it," the prostitute is rescued from her static and nullifying role as something alien, and restored to herself (and to us) as a woman with her own desires.

A number of blues singers were probably prostitutes, too, singing in brothels between bouts upstairs and never making it to the theaters and finer clubs.[25] While this revelation will be shocking to some, it was undoubtedly true of a number of singers. To fail to understand this fact is to fail, again, to appreciate the true class nature of the blues.

Prostitution is only one of a number of crimes to which Minnie refers in her songs. While her recorded repertoire contains no classic "outlaw ballads" like *Railroad Bill* or *Stack O Lee,* it may be because she created nearly a dozen outlaw blues of her own. A close inspection reveals, however, that Minnie's outlaws, nearly all of them women, speak in a different voice than the more famous outlaws like Railroad Bill. The blues is an intimate language, nearly always sung in the first person, and because of this special voice, the brutality and violence in Minnie's songs are personal, too. The figure may not be a public hero, but precisely because of the "private" nature of the heroine, she is more available to the listener, and by implication insists that the listener, too, can be a heroine. This is another way Lautréamont's dictum "poetry must be made by all" can be read: Heroism is to be made by all![26]

The "hard woman" or the female criminal is the subject of not only the prostitution songs like *Tricks Ain't Walking No More* and *Hustling Woman's Blues,* but of *Jailhouse Trouble Blues, Reachin' Pete, Moonshine, Finger Print Blues, Georgia Skin, I'm A Gambling Woman* and many more. The existence of these songs, as well as their number, should suggest not that the female criminal is as uncommon as the female country blues guitarist, but mainly that the female criminal's activities are as *undocumented* as the paucity of female country blues singers would command. With too few artists to document their exploits, the existence of these activities remained a mystery, a mystery that Minnie did her part to undo. Lucille Bogan, a rough-edged, fascinating blueswoman, sang about the same subjects that Minnie did.

The clearest light in which to view Minnie and her songs's relationship to the female criminal is to see Minnie as the legitimate heir of the poet Walt Whitman and the labor leader Eugene V. Debs, for their words are her words.

In 1918 Debs addressed a Federal Court in Cleveland where he was sentenced to 10 years in prison for espionage:

> While there is a lower class I am in it; while there is a criminal element I am of it; while there is a soul in prison, I am not free.

Whitman's words were used by the writer Nelson Algren as an epigraph to his novel *Never Come Morning:*

> I feel I am one of them—
> I belong to those convicts and prostitutes myself—
> And henceforth I will not deny them—
> For how can I deny myself?

Just so.

11. DIRT DAUBER BLUES

At one time humans knew animals as their teachers.
—Gina Litherland

We might have given birth to a butterfly
With the daily news
Printed in blood on its wings
—Mina Loy

The time will come
when our silence will be more powerful
than the voices you are throttling today.
—Haymarket anarchist August Spies,
spoken on the scaffold.[1]

Dirt-daubers (mud-daubers) figure in a number of beliefs throughout the South. In Arkansas, the clay from the nests of these wasps was worn to cure sprains, while in Mississippi it was believed that when the wasps built their nests close to the ground, it was going to be a dry year. Most significant, however, are the beliefs, found in Mississippi and elsewhere, that a *tea* made from the nests will relieve or hasten labor and help expel the afterbirth, and that powdered dirt-dauber nests will cure a baby's navel that isn't healing properly.[2] Thus a constellation of these beliefs center around birth.

DIRT DAUBER BLUES

Everybody worrying me,
want to know why I'm so crazy
  about dirt dauber tea. (2x)
Because when I was young,
they built their nest on me.

Now everybody tells me I need a doctor,
I need someone to stay here with me.
But I don't need nothing
but that dirt dauber tea.
Because when I was young,
they built their nest on me.

Hmmmm, hmmmmmmm.
Hmmmm, hmmmmmmm.
Hmmmmmm, hmmmmm.

And out of all that I crave, all that I seen.
I don't want nothing but that dirt dauber tea.
Because when I was young,
they built their nest on me.

When I was down sick in my bed,
blind, couldn't hardly see.
That dirt dauber flew down in my bed and
built his nest on me.
That's why I say,
"I'm crazy about that dirt dauber tea."

Aww, dirt dauber's a builder,
Aww, dirt dauber's a builder,
Dirt dauber is a builder,
he built his nest on me.
That why I say,
"I'm crazy about the dirt dauber tea."

Dirt Dauber Blues is an excellent example of how important it is to understand black southern folk beliefs when assaying the meaning of the blues. Only a knowledge of the mud-dauber lore makes it possible to understand a critical level of meaning in Minnie's piece; otherwise, lines like "Built their nest on me" would have remained forever enigmatic. Indeed, one can hardly assert that, even now, the lyrics have given up all of their mystery. Nonetheless, the song refers to the healing properties of the powdered nests and the reference to mud-dauber tea clearly refers to its healing power. "Built their nest on me" points specifically to the navel and birth. There is a strongly voiced preference for folk medicine, and the level of detail suggests a closely modeled source, perhaps even the singer herself.

The melody of the song is quite unusual, and this eerie piece is one of Minnie's most compelling numbers, with its evocation of the image of the wasp's building a nest on someone, the nest's curative powers reverberating within our fear of the insect's sting. After the second verse, Minnie reauthenticates and makes more vivid her tale by mimicking, for an entire verse, the drone of the dirt-dauber. This buzzing moan, like humming, scat singing and nonsense sounds, serves to fasten our attention on what is really a gap in intelligibility. Where once we were hearing words, we are now hearing only inarticulate sounds and moans. Can we say that what we are not hearing acts as a metaphoric harbinger of all that is covered over or hidden in the blueswoman's song? The unconscious, serving the primacy of desire, cracks the smooth plane of conscious speech, but it is nonetheless incapable of revealing its content. And indeed, there is a level in the song, a level at which the image exists in its purest state, which should not be required to undergo further detoxification.[3]

This is not by any means the only occasion that Minnie uses humming, moaning, mumbling,[4] or related sounds in her songs, and we would be remiss if we did not notice that such sounds are also playful and humorous, as is so much of the blues. One of the first songs of Minnie's to be reissued in the early 1960s was *Where Is My Good Man?*, which contains an entire verse sung in scat-style syllables. To more fully clarify the role of moans and related sounds in the blues, we'd like to elaborate on a few ideas associated with other representations of this kind: negation and silence. By suggesting that nonsense sounds crack the facade of conscious speech, we invoke the notion of the unconscious as a power opposed to consciousness as well as to articulation. This may be seen as an elaboration of Freud's idea that word-presentations represented conscious thought while unconscious ideas could only be represented by thing-presentations; coming into language was associated with coming into consciousness.[5]

Repression could also be eluded by a change in valence, i.e. that which could not come to consciousness because of repression, could do so by becoming conscious as a negative, or with a negative sign. Thus, the common example of the revelation of the unknown woman in a dream: "I don't know who it is, but it's *not my mother.*" We know the mother was present because the dreamer mentioned her, even though she was mentioned as a negative; she came into consciousness with a minus sign attached, but she came into consciousness nonetheless. We are quite justified in concentrating on to whom the sign was attached, rather than the positive or negative aspect of the sign. +mother and -mother both evoke the signifier *mother.*[6]

Thus the unarticulated sounds may be the words themselves attempting to erupt into consciousness but *with a negative sign*, just as the negation may also be represented by silence. For silence is another sign of the unspeakable. As such, it is as significant to our understanding of the blues as the moans and cries with which we are more familiar. The meanings of silence are diverse, as we shall see. The very act of being a female country blues singer/guitarist is a significant victory over those silences "that are very nearly as Southern as manner."[7] Minnie's act of singing opposes the masculine convention of the silent woman, the ideal to which so many men feel women should aspire.

For the blues singer, silence can have not only this meaning, but more specific meanings that spring directly from the racist culture that provided such fertile ground for the blues. And the structure and content of the blues plays a part in the elucidation of this silence. Listeners and critics who came to the blues from a background of folk music and balladry have occasionally found the blues wanting in narrative continuity and plot. Of course, blues are folk lyrics, not ballads, and most listeners realize this, but the blues has always had difficulty purging itself of the notion of "something missing."[8] We suggest that while continuity of narrative is often specified as the missing element, this is merely a device that keeps us from realizing that what is really missing is racism, bigotry and murder.

This historic seizure of lyric style has given the singers an unparalleled opportunity to *not say* many things in the blues,[9] and it is through and behind these silences that a separate discourse emerges to confront the listener with the accusation of hatred and horror. We do not suggest this as a mere fill-in-the-blanks exercise in academic postmodernism, however. Rather, we insist that all blues are carefully constructed of *permissible* phrases which carry not only messages of revolt, but which *seem* to do so in the language of accomodation. In a similar manner—long accepted by the very critics who are still not willing to grant the same power of language and metaphor to the blues —early spirituals are believed to have carried veiled messages of revolt and discontent. Thus we must learn to hear blues songs as always being about one subject, even while they are also about other subjects, for the blues is truly a multi-level language. It would not seem outlandish, then, to suggest that the blues are *always* about eroticism, e.g. a "rider" as a lover, even *while* they are about repression, e.g. a "rider" as a mounted work-gang guard. The blues speak to us through many layers of meaning, multiple meanings that simultaneously shape an enriched discourse.

Let's take as an example Minnie's excellent *If You See My Rooster:*

IF YOU SEE MY ROOSTER
(PLEASE RUN HIM HOME)

If you see my rooster,
   please run him on back home. (2x)
I haven't found no eggs in my basket,
eeeehhhee, since my rooster been gone.

I heard my rooster crowing, this morning
   just about the break of day (2x)
(Crows like rooster).

I guess that was the time
he was making his getaway.

I just found out
   how come my hens won't lay. (2x)
Every time I look around
my rooster have done gone away.

Spoken: Now play it, Bob.
Tell me 'bout my rooster.

I've got too many hens
   for not to have no roosters on my yard. (2x)
And I don't know
what's the matter, eeeooo,
Something have done got 'em barred.

Now, Bob, if you see my rooster,
   please run him on back home. (2x)
I haven't found no eggs in my basket,
eeeeheeee, since my rooster been gone.

   Certainly this is a song about a missing man, a footloose lover
who may preside over his stable of women the way a rooster
guards his flock of hens, but the song can also be heard and
read, consciously and unconsciously, as a song about labor and
production, the production of pleasure as well as the production
of labor. What is in fact missing is the laborer or working man,
gone North to seek his fortune and, perhaps, to increase his
flock. But to hear the song as one about production and toil,
we need only recall that the raising of chickens has always been
a money-making and food-producing venture, and "eggs in my
basket" can refer to money, food, or sexual satisfaction. This
production can be pleasurable, sexually, or it can sound too
much like work, from which the errant rooster/lover keeps wandering.[10]
   If You See My Rooster is not Minnie's only song about chickens,
nor is it the only song whose meanings can be seen to occupy multiple levels. There is also the humorous *Plymouth Rock Blues*, one
of Minnie's finest pieces:

PLYMOUTH ROCK BLUES

I got so many chickens,
  can't tell my roosters from my hens. (2x)
I got to go back now,
and look 'em all over again.

I found my rooster this morning
  by looking at his comb. (2x)
You can look out now, pullets,
it won't be long.

My hens all cackling,
  I can't find no eggs. (2x)
You ain't got no excuse now, pullets,
ain't nothing in your way.

I'm gonna take this old hen,
  I'm got [*sic*] down to the doctor's shop. (2x)
I don't see what's the matter with 'em,
they won't bip a bop.

I done told you one time, papa,
  I don't want my chicken meat. (2x)
I don't want them banteys
mixed up with my dominiques.

Shoo, chickens, shoo,
  I don't want no banteys on my yard. (2x)
I don't want them banteys
mixed up with my Plymouth Rocks.

While many blues seem neither humorous nor funny, there is good reason to consider the thread of humor, black or otherwise, that runs through the blues as a fundamental element in the blues's assault on repressive circumstance. Indeed, a number of singers are clowns, jokesters, comedians, like Jack Dupree, Wade Walton, Charlie and Bob Hicks (hear their duets), and others. The importance of black humor is illuminating as it partly rests with the notion, carried to its extreme, that "for the great illnesses of the 'ego', great remedies . . . can come only from the 'id'."[11]

We also distinguish another form of black humor called *internal laughter*, and it is this notion that specifies the ironic blackness of much of the humor found in the blues.

> If we comprehend this latent and spontaneous burst of laughter as a *liberating* spark between reality and poetry, it is above all in the sense in which it enriches creation by certain aspects of magic, by the magic power of putting the imagination in the service of the menaced symbiosis of human and natural necessities.[12]

While traditional blues stanzas evoke many moods and emotions, the most frequently encountered one in the context of live performances is *laughter*,[13] and this is corroborated by several blues singers: Rube Lacy asserted that during the time he was a blues singer, he had all the women, whiskey and good times a man could want and "never had the blues." Like Lacy, Big Chief Ellis said "the happiest times I've ever had in my life was playin' the blues," and guitarist Etta Baker articulated similar sentiments: "I just don't find any sadness in the blues. . . . I get a happy feeling when I hear a guitar tuning up."[14] We are not suggesting that happiness, laughter and humor are identical, of course, for one is a mood, another a reaction and the last a provocateur. But they are undoubtedly related. It is entirely possible that the significance of humor in the blues, not to mention happiness and laughter, has alway been underestimated, and that it's more of a continuous, though sometimes hidden thread, rather than a special quality that makes an occasional appearance.[15]

Certainly this characterization fits the repertoire of Memphis Minnie, and her humorous presentation of the facts of life was certainly a fundamental element in her popularity. It was a key ingredient in many of the duets, especially songs like *What's The Matter With The Mill?* and *You Stole My Cake,* as well as in solo numbers like *Good Biscuits, Caught Me Wrong Again, You Can't Give It Away* and *New Dirty Dozen.*[16]

There is another aspect of Minnie's humor that deserves emphasis. Because humor is a powerful critique of repressive social standards, we may expect it to meet strong resistance, and there is considerable evidence that it has. As one writer noted, collections of humor drastically underrepresent women, not because there are so few women humorists, but because the kind of power and authority implied by the use of humor are in fact denied to women in a male dominated culture.[17]

Plymouth Rock Blues is ostensibly about the farm, its animals and the food products the latter provide, and the depiction of the farm woman shooing the wrong chickens away from the right ones, looking hard to tell the roosters from the hens, looking for eggs, wondering "What's the matter with 'em" is indeed a humorous tale that begins with the fantasy of having so many chickens that the roosters are lost in the crowd!

But Minnie's song is also about sorting and organizing her terrain and her life, the roosters, hens and pullets acting out a thinly-disguised parody of human erotic existence. Most intriguing are the hints at the importance of purity, wherein the banteys become the "dirt,"[18] contaminating the dominiques and Plymouth Rocks. We see this as a satirical reference to sexuality and racism in the South, where "crossing the line" and purity are truly matters of life and death, but are here woven into a song that could be heard without fear and "harmlessly" joked about. Interestingly enough, the bantey serves a dual existence in the blues, usually appearing as an image of strength and scrappiness. Here he is rejected as impure and probably not suitable for the kitchen, either, where he would no doubt be found too stringy and tough.

Of course, the most obvious register in which we can understand the song is the reality of the terrain itself. The yard full of chickens is such a comfortable and familiar piece of her territory that it can be used to support a multiplicity of meanings, from the most overt to the most hidden, all with an air of harmless domesticity.[19] Our notion of Minnie's yard with the chickens acting out a parody of human erotic existence and Southern race relations is also significant as a weapon against the sexist notion that a woman's territory is somehow less significant than a man's, that its location in or around home establishes it as minor compared to male territory and the latter's more important locations! Indeed, this single example suggests that the possibilities for signification of such a strategic bit of terrain may be greater than we've imagined.

It's the sheer domesticity of this territory however, that makes it so endlessly suitable as the background for a metaphoric reenactment of the gothic morbidity of Southern race relations. If the levels of meaning in the song can so wildly and continually oscillate from register to register, from unconscious to conscious, from psycho-sexual to social, it is only because the eroticized terrain of the yard itself, in all of its domestic familiarity, is instaneously and willingly capable of reabsorbing the more dangerous meaning at a moment's notice.

12. DOCTORS AND DISEASE

*Historically women were the healers, until in the modern
age when men entered this field and tried to drive women out.*
—Mary Ritter Beard

*It may be a new thing for a woman to hold a diploma, but
she has been a doctor, for ages . . . and no prospect of any
pay beyond a string of onions . . . and the reputation of a witch.*[1]

Women healers inhabit a significant location in black culture
for many reasons, some cultural, some geographic, some psychological, some poetic. Black women have always been leaders within
black culture, even if their roles have not always been officially or
sufficiently recognized. Male migration out of the South may have
helped to shape the patterns of female leadership, but there was
(and is) a direct line connecting conjure women and civil rights
pioneers. One purpose of this study is to show how the blues
woman occupies an important position on this same axis, within
the poetic dimension as well as the psychological and cultural ones.

While women healers were important throughout the South, in
cities and towns as well as in the rural areas, these women brought
their roles and abilities to the Northern cities as well. Root doctors
and folk healers continued to have active "practices" in the cities
of the North,[2] and the medicines they prescribed were often identical to the preparations they dispensed in the rural South. Just as
often the patients were Southern migrants whose ideas of doc-

tors and medicine had changed little since their coming to the North.

For Minnie's listeners, the term "doctor" referred most specifically to these conjures or root doctors, some of whom were males.[3] The alternative to the conjure doctors was the M.D., the medical doctor who could be consulted in private practice, at a hospital emergency room or at a clinic. These doctors were not always as accessible to Minnie's listeners as were the folk healers who shared not only a way of life but a place of residence with their patients, a residence situated in both the psychic and the physical geography of the black neighborhood. The assessment of "medical authority" that emerges from Minnie's songs is a mixed one, and an inquiry into the possible reasons for such an appraisal is revealing. The distrust or hostility toward medical authority is found to be mixed with the notion that doctors hold highly prestigious and financially rewarding positions that require intelligence and honesty.

Of course, doctors were no more free of racial prejudice than any other group, and if one hoped that dedication would overcome personal prejudices, this was plainly not always the case. In order to understand the most marginal reference to a "doctor" in Minnie's songs, we must grasp the *nature* of the authority that a medical doctor, especially a white one, held over a black, female patient. When blacks tried to register to vote in 1959 and 1960 in two Tennessee counties, they were denied medical care, and white doctors refused to deliver the babies of mothers blacklisted by the local White Citizens Council.[4]

The worst racist and sexist nonsense could be found in respected medical textbooks of the time. For example, in 1904, a prominent Chicago physician wrote,

> The average moralist . . . most often complains of the restrictions placed upon woman . . . but the complaint is often an innately depraved woman's cry for license. . . . I have no reason to believe that the assumption of masculine liberty on the part of women is conducive to morality.[5]

The author is G. Frank Lydston, a Professor of Genito-Urinary Surgery as well as a Professor of Criminal Anthropology and a surgeon at St. Mary's; the publisher was the highly-respected house of Lippincott. Lydston's views on Negroes were even more extreme than his views on women, and he was by no means alone in his beliefs.[6]

> The South is accursed by frequent outrages of its women by negroes, followed by swift and terrible retribution. . . . Physical and moral degeneracy and atavism is especially manifest in the direction of sexual proclivities. . . . All kinds of criminality in the Southern negro [has] increased. Considering his disproportionate sexual development, is it remarkable that with the removal of his inhibitions, sexual crimes—which were hitherto almost unknown—should result? The idea of equality with whites . . . seething in the ignorant minds of the younger generation of blacks played a powerful role in determining the sexual direction of anti-social acts.[7]

We may say that Lydston's positions are not those of the scientist but those of the "quack," so extreme do they now appear, but the sad truth is that in 1904, these remarks were not unusual in those scientific circles that concerned themselves with human behavior. In trying to determine whether scientific positions are "real" or "objective," we will not always have the luxury of passing judgment on such outlandish schemes and theories, for from the vantage point of our own time, contemporary remarks will not seem outlandish at all. How many aspects of everyday life were thus affected by the twisted teachings of a "scientist" like Lydston? The racism of a given "authority" is only part of the formula. The singer and her audience confronted that part of the medical establishment made available to poor blacks, many of whom were already victimized by the unhealthy living conditions of the Northern ghettos. For example, in the period 1923-1927, only two years before Minnie and Joe's first recording date, Harlem's death rate was 42% higher than the rest of New York. Harlem mothers died in childbirth twice as often as mothers elsewhere in New York, and the tuberculosis mortality rate in Harlem was 2½ - 3 times higher than in the rest of the city.[8] Between 1929 and 1933, Minnie and Joe's key recording years, the gap between Harlem black tuberculosis deaths and other white neighborhood tuberculosis deaths *widened* rather than narrowed, in spite of efforts by various medical agencies and groups like the Harlem Tuberculosis and Health Committee.[9]

It is against this background that *Memphis Minnie-Jitis Blues* must be heard and understood. Medical doctors appeared in Minnie's songs in a variety of contexts and fulfilling several functions, but in spite of the erotic core of the many "doctor blues" recorded by other blues singers, doctors had no special erotic function in Minnie's songs. Indeed, in the following song, the doctor is the harbinger of death and disease:

MEMPHIS MINNIE-JITIS BLUES

Mmmmm,
    the meningitis killing me. (2x)
I'm bending, I'm bending, baby,
my head is nearly down to my knee.

I come in home one Saturday night,
    pull off my clothes and I lie down. (2x)
And next morning just about day,
the meningitis begin to creep around.

My head and neck was paining me,
    seem like my back would break in two. (2x)
Lord, I had such a mood that morning,
I didn't know what in the world to do.

My companion take me to the doctor,
"Doctor, please tell me
    my wife's complaint." (2x)
The doctor looked down on me,
shook his head, said,
"I wouldn't mind telling you, son,
but I can't."

"You take her round to the city hospital,
   just as quick, quick as you possibly can. (2x)
Because the condition she's in now,
you never will get her back home 'live again."

He rode me round to the city hospital,
   the clock was striking ten. (2x)
[guitar chimes]
I hear my companion say,
"I won't see your smiling face again."

The wealth of detail, the narrative continuity and the subject matter all make this an unusual song. As an essentially accurate picture of the progress of a fatal disease, the song has a morbid quality which uses the humor of the title as an ironic weapon against the despair of the text itself: Bacterial meningitis was usually fatal in the 1920s and 1930s, it had an epidemic tendency (there had been an outbreak of one type of meningitis in Detroit in 1929, a year before Minnie recorded her song), and the lower classes in ghettos were especially vulnerable.

While spontaneous recovery, or indeed any recovery from meningitis was unlikely, it did happen and it could have happened in Minnie's case, as she often claimed it did. She used to tell with great pleasure the story behind the song, as Daisy and Brewer Phillips both remembered. "At the time," began Phillips, "she had the meningitis ... she was at John Gaston Hospital [in Memphis] and she had meningitis and yellow fever. The doctors give up on her. There wasn't no cure for her. And [her husband] went and got her a quart of corn whiskey and that saved her. The yellow fever and the meningitis, she made it, she stayed in the hospital, on charity, and you know how it was in the South. And she got treatment sometime. And she made the *Meningitis Blues* in the hospital! She recorded it in the hospital. And during that time, when she went into a coma, they pushed her away, back in the back room to die, and covered her up with a sheet. And the next morning that whiskey had sweated that fever out. The sheet was yellow and everything! And she survived. That whiskey cured her. How many times she told me!"[10] Whether or not it was meningitis or another serious infection, whether or not Minnie was treated in the hospital, whether or not it was Minnie. . . . We must leave these questions unanswered for now.

We may question, however, the unique symptom mentioned by Minnie in the first verse of her song.

I'm bending, I'm bending, my head is nearly down to my knees.

The avid listener will inspect the many vantage points of Minnie's piece, and will understand the sort of "seizure" that is poetically required: that of the fully imagined response. Further clarification may lie in the tension between *Memphis Minnie-Jitis Blues* as an artistic and poetic achievement and the reality of experience in which the blues singers ground their songs. For example, the puzzling line about "bending" may have referred to the black folk belief that if you had an infection and you bent over until your head was nearly touching your toes (or knees), you would die.[11] Or "I'm bending, I'm bending, my head is nearly down to my knees" may have been an image chosen for its imaginative power alone.

There were many vaudeville-derived duets (e.g. *Terrible Operation Blues*) where a male "doctor" (like Georgia Tom) treats a female patient (like Jane Lucas) who, it is discovered, needs a good dose of sex more than any orthodox medical treatment.[12] Typically in such performances, the woman complains that the doctor is taking too many liberties, only to be delighted later at how good the "treatment" felt, and could the doctor stop by, maybe tomorrow, too? It is worth noting, however, that no variant of *Terrible Operation Blues* appears in Minnie's and Joe's recorded repertoire, in spite of their success and capabilities in the performance of humorous duets. Perhaps such routines involved too many jokes and too little singing and playing, but it is also possible that Minnie had no desire to play the male doctor's passive victim. Certainly, no one in a Memphis Minnie song has to be tricked into having sex and is only later able to say she liked it!

Minnie was never again so clinical as she was in *Memphis Minnie-Jitis Blues,*[13] although she referred to doctors fairly often. The doctor mentioned in Plymouth Rock Blues might be a veterinarian, but it is more likely a conjure woman or root doctor. The doctor invoked in *Dirt Dauber Blues* is named only to be pronounced superflous in the wake of folk preparations. The doctor who appears in the first line of *Dirty Mother For You* appears so that his wife can draw status from her husband's profession, and for Minnie's original audience, a "doctor's wife" was a figure of some authority. The title of the song itself is one of several variations that attempt to take "dirty mother fucker" beyond the censors, successfully, we might add. Dirty Red recorded a version titled *Mother Fuyer* and Washboard Sam sang a version with the same title as Minnie's.[14] Here's Minnie's, the earliest version known:

DIRTY MOTHER FOR YOU

I ain't no doctor, but I'm the doctor's wife,
You better come to me
if you want to save your life
He's a dirty mother fuyer,
He don't mean no good.
He got drunk this morning,
Tore up the neighborhood.

I want you to come here, baby,
come here quick,
He done give me something
'bout to make me sick.
Awwww, dirty mother fuyer, etc.

Spoken: Play it, Dennis.

I went down to the station,
talked to the judge,
He said, "Don't bring me none
of that doggoned stuff you heard."
Awwww, dirty mother fuyer, etc.

I went down to the office(r),
fell out on the floor,
He done something to me,

now, he won't do no more.
Awwww, dirty mother fuyer, etc.

Spoken: Play it, Dennis, play it, boy.

Won't you look here, baby,
what you done done,
You done squeezed my lemon,
now you done broke and run.
Awwww, dirty mother fuyer, etc.

In *Down In New Orleans,* discussed more fully below, the lines,

My man is a doctor,
    and he lives off of rice and beans. (2x)
That's why he done gone and left me
back down in New Orleans.

conjure up the image of the root doctor more than the M.D., but
in *Doctor, Doctor Blues,* it is most assuredly a medical doctor whose
relationship to Minnie is sketched in the following terms:

DOCTOR, DOCTOR BLUES

Doctor stopped me from drinking,
    boys, I can't smoke no more. (2x)
And I can't see no peace,
seem like nowhere I go.

[The following verse is half-sung,
half-spoken:]

Oh, doctor, doctor,
    you know I got a lot of faith in you. (2x)
I'd trust you everywhere.
But it hurt me so bad,
when you say if I took another drink,
nothing you could do.

Oh, doctor, doctor,
 I ain't drinked in a great long time. (2x)
Spoken: Bring us a half a pint.
I'm gonna take a drink of this
if the good lord don't change my mind.

[First two lines are half-sung,
half-spoken:]

Now, lookahere, doctor,
 don't you know
 my mama's done gone blind? (2x)
Spoken: I know her trouble.
I was doing the best I could
but she wouldn't pay the doctor no mind.

Oh, doctor, doctor,
 tell me what's my trouble now. (2x)
"If you take another drink,
I bet they put you in the ground!"
Spoken: Doctor, you all right with me
anyhow.

The woman in the song sees the doctor as a prohibiting authority who has forbidden a few of those things that make life bearable,
liquor and cigarettes. She professes great faith in the doctor but
flubs the next line wherein the doctor hurt her by saying, presumably, "There's nothing I can do if you take another drink." Her
negative reaction to the doctor and his advice finally becomes so
strong that while she gives her assurance of not having "drinked
in a great long time," she also demands—off mike—"Bring us a
half-pint!" The song ends with a request for advice and a profession of faith, both of which are now unbelievable. The doctor's advice is no more *seriously* sought than it was in *Dirt Dauber
Blues.*
  The blues tradition expands the definitions of "doctor" in several other directions, reminding us of the inadequacy of dictionar-
ies when they are confronted by the cursed traditions of the night.
The reputation of the conjure doctor is indeed embedded in the

traditions of the night, and these doctors of "the other side" provide the basis for many songs.

No one has yet attempted to see the crossing of blues and voodoo as a nexus operating under a female sign, but the foundation for such a project has been established by Susan Cavin's "Missing Women: On the Voodoo Trail to Jazz."[15] Early accounts note the presence of women drummers in New Orleans' Congo Square ceremonies, where they also led chants and sang, and more than one commentator has called the Louisiana voodoo tradition matriarchal. Indeed, witch doctors were secondary to the queens and "the women always ruled,"[16] and it is no coincidence that the single best-known name in the annals of American voodoo is Marie Laveau. Voodoo queens were the overwhelming majority of those who presided over Congo Square ceremonies, just as they also appeared as drummers. Further, the queens drew white women into the ceremonies, a practice disapproved of by civil (male) authorities.[17] An analysis based on gender as well as class and race illuminates the historical factors that led to the ascendancy of these voodoo queens.

Cavin argues that African male sorcerers were more powerful and came from a higher class than female practioners, but their roles and the structures of their practices were crushed by slavery. Further, it was difficult for males to consolidate their power as magicians without becoming a psychosexual and social threat to the ruling white males. As African women were of lower caste and already outside the structure of established authority, it was possible for them to continue to practice midwifery, herbalism, and natural medicine as voodoo practitioners in the United States, without threatening the power of white rule. The witch and witchcraft traditions of Europe and the US provided soil in which the voodoo queens flourished.[18] Most of Cavin's findings are convincing, and they provide a useful background for our own analysis.

Minnie's references to voodoo, its practitioners and their paraphenalia, are not large in number, but our attention is justified by the critical importance attached to magic, conjure and hoodoo by many of Minnie's record-buying listeners. Further, for those of us who are interested in genuine poetic experience, we are drawn to the subject because it is through magic that oppressed peoples attempt to seize power over the repressive nature of everyday life. "Politically speaking, Voodoo is the triumph of the African way of life over the European, the triumph of freedom over slavery, the triumph of dignity over inhumanity."[19]

If poetry is created by the dissolution of the barriers between waking life and dream life, the blues songs about voodoo are compelling as they hint at a closer contact with unconscious powers of creativity and less alienated and less "rationalized" mental processes. The close relationship between magical thinking and primary process thinking succeeds in unearthing the source of powerful and fantastic imagery, and we see again how poetry can *only* be oppositional. Our appreciation of voodoo (not to mention blues) is based on the poetic affinity of the mental processes involved in each, and this will not be the first time we suggest that the blues can be viewed as a specific vehicle for the expression of voodoo.[20]

We are attempting here to illuminate the paths on which we see the convergence of women, the blues and witchcraft or voodoo, with negativity and contradiction as a means of propulsion. Many women artists have assumed the role of legitimate descendants of earlier alchemists and witches, and in so doing, have themselves become sources of power, leaders of rebellion in the revolt of the magicians. What unites the witch and the blueswoman is more than their opposition to social codes, for their very image is oppositional in a world where all representation is political. Through the centuries, this oppositional voice has taken many forms, but the message is the same. Women's spells become women's words, women's potions, women's gestures. What is repressed always returns: The herbalist is the cook, the flying figure is the dancer, the chanted spell is the song. New modes of repression fight new schemes of desire.[21] The asylum and the room with yellow wallpaper replaced the burning stake.

To accomodate the period of slavery and its aftermath, when black women and men were forced to act out the unconscious components of the witch hunt, only the stage directions were changed. In the 15th century, the repressed sexual conflicts were split and projected onto the Devil, the witch and the Virgin, while in the 19th and 20th centuries, the black male, the black female and the white woman became the objects of these projections. The Devil barely left the picture, of course, and we meet him frequently in blues lore, where he represents the repressed in the notion of the male blues singer learning music from the Devil at the crossroads.[22] This entire theme is repressed, however, when the adept is a woman, thus re-stigmatizing her by invoking her "secret" (from males) life, her preoccupation with "woman things," the things males are afraid to know, but allowing her to manifest these secrets within herself, these secrets that cannot otherwise be seen, by hysteria or witchcraft.[23] The symptom represents, symbolizes, the same inner tensions, at the same crash-marked junctions, the same dangerous intersections, whose activities are manifest (externalized) in witchcraft.

The analysis that follows will seek the presence of voodoo elements in the songs themselves. In doing so, we will try to maintain a sensitivity to the image and a willingness to follow it to its own limits. Further, we can come to understand the penetration of voodoo into other aspects of urban lore with which the blues is concerned. For example, a phrase like "laying the trick," seems to have an instantly recognizable meaning from the prostitute's point of view, (and we have seen how significant prostitution is in Minnie's world), but it is in fact a conjure expression for hoodooing someone. Indeed, the prostitute sense of "trick" probably derives from the conjure sense. If eroticism is the language of the blues, there is much evidence to suggest that it is spoken with a voodoo accent.[24] Both of these signs can be said to legitimately stake out the winding path of the poetic spirit that binds the listening community to the singer. And it is precisely this spirit, above all, that attracts the blues to voodoo and voodoo to the blues in search of a method of inspiration and a means to stimulate the latent faculties of the mind.

The blues singers are interpreters of the effects on the mind of the everyday life experiences of the black working class, but another name for root doctor or conjure woman is *interpreter*. It is from this point of departure that we continue our own exigesis. In our first example the voodoo references are slightly veiled:

DOWN IN NEW ORLEANS

I'm going back
   down in New Orleans. (2x)
Well, I'm going where
I can get my rice and beans.

We are the cookingest Creoles
   in the world you ever seen. (2x)
And if you don't believe me,
follow me back down to New Orleans.

Well, my man is a doctor
   and he lives off of rice and beans. (2x)
That's why he done gone and left me
back down in New Orleans.

I've got the cookingest sister
   in the world you ever seen. (2x)
But she can't cook nothing
but them rice and beans.

And you can't tell me nothing,
   baby, that I never seen. (2x)
And if you don't believe me,
follow me back to New Orleans.

Indeed, Minnie's *Down In New Orleans* is a good example of how an "ordinary" song may have many layers of meaning. At first glance, it seems to be a typical blues with its references to food and cooking, being abandoned, and going back (down)home, although the reference to Creoles is unusual. The usual "red beans and rice" used by Kokomo Arnold and countless others as an evocation of "back downhome" is here rendered as "rice and bean."[25] The city of New Orleans serves two purposes in the song. Throughout, it is used as an image of downhome, to which one returns,[26] where one has relatives, where one eats traditional meals. But in the last verse, it becomes the location of urban worldliness and experience, home of the cosmopolitan woman who has seen it all. This usage is echoed by Kokomo Arnold in *Set Down Gal:*

> I asked my mama not to be so mean
> She act like a gal
> from down in New Orleans.[27]

Peg Leg Howell and Jim Hill sketched the same idea this way in 1929:

> My woman do something, hon',
> I never seen.[28]
> She must be going
>   with a man from New Orleans. (3x)
> My woman do something
> I never have seen.

Clearly, New Orleans is where one learned to *do it*! But is *it* mistreatment (Arnold), unusual sex acts (Howell and Hill) or general sophistication? Or could the *it* that you learned how to do in New Orleans be the practice of conjure? Let us begin by hearing "root doctor" or conjure man where Minnie says "doctor," a reasonable interpretation as we can see from Elmore James' *Done Somebody Wrong:*

> Everything that happens,
>   you know, I am to blame. (2x)
> I'm gonna find me a doctor,
> maybe my luck will change.[29]

In James' example, there is no mistaking the "doctor" for an M.D!

Following this reading or hearing into Minnie's piece, her whole song can then be heard as a "conjuring up" of New Orleans as simultaneously one's home and the land of voodoo. Surrounded by root doctors, in the land of spells and potions, even the cooking begins to taste funny, and the "cookingest sisters" calls up the image of another voodoo practitioner, one known as Seven Sisters, and memorialized in the blues by J. T. "Funny Paper" Smith (The Howling Wolf).[30] Jazz Gillum underlines the vital connection between food and voodoo practices:

>I don't eat everybody's cooking,
>I am suspicious of my cornbread.[31]

Such suspicions, however, are not merely superstitions. The actual use of poisons by voodooists has since been "documented," of course, and if the discovery of the pharmaceutical basis of zombie-making (in Haiti) focuses a new light on the folk Negro's fear of "poison" and voodoo, an even sharper beam illuminates the scientists who until very recently collected such beliefs as only quaint superstitions.[32] Lines like Minnie's "done give me something about to make me sick" suddenly become clear. But there is a radical political dimension to the use of such chemicals and drugs, and the Haitian playwright Franck Etienne has remarked, "Today some Haitians still argue that voodoo ought to be wiped out. They call it superstition. They say that Christianity means progress. Who wants such progress?

"They talk about . . . how voodounists use poison against their enemies . . . And I say, I support it. . . . The Haitian peasant has against him the notary, the justice of the peace, the head of the rural section, the government employee, all in a complicated system of exploitation designed to strip him of what little he is able to cultivate. He has no access to justice. Poison is his only advocate, his only weapon. I believe in voodoo. It is the soul of the Haitian people. When you destroy voodoo, you destroy the people's souls. And all that will remain are zombies."[33]

In early 1936, at her third session with the newly revived Vocalion label, Minnie recorded two songs explicitly about hoodoo, *Hoodoo Lady* and *I'm A Gambling Woman*. In *Hoodoo Lady* Minnie cites instances of the hoodoo lady's power (by hearsay), makes several requests to benefit from these conjurations, warns us the doctor is tricky and assures us that she (Minnie) is scared of her. But throughout the song, the hoodoo lady never accomplishes a thing and her entire reputation is literally by repute alone, which may be one of the meanings of the song. Just as the listener contributes powerfully to a song's meaning, so do the objects, patients, clients, victims contribute largely to the root doctor's power.

HOODOO LADY

Hoodoo lady, how do you do?
They tell me you take a boot
and turn it to a brand new shoe.
But don't put that thing on me,
Don't put that thing on me,
Don't put that thing on me,
'Cause I'm going back to Tennessee.

Hoodoo lady, you can turn water to wine.
I been wondering
where have you been all this time.
I'm setting here, broke,
and I ain't got a dime.
You ought to put something
in these dukes of mine.
But don't put that thing on me, etc.

Spoken: Boy, you better watch it
'cause she's tricky.

Hoodoo lady,
I want you to unlock my door,
So I can get in and get all my clothes.
But don't put that thing on me, etc.

Now lookahere, hoodoo lady,
I want you to treat me right,
Bring my man back home
but don't let him stay all night.
And don't put that thing on me, etc.

Spoken: Boy, she's tricky as she can be.
Better watch her, too.

Why lookahere, hoodoo lady,
I'm your friend,
When you leave this time,
come back again.
But don't put that thing on me, etc.

Spoken: Boys, I'm scared of her!

The role of voodoo in the black community, as Minnie's song suggests, is multi-faceted and broad. The desire to control one's luck in gambling or to carry out divination so as to be able to predict the day's winning number in the policy game are also common uses to which voodoo is put. Further, these ideas are confined neither to the Louisiana/Chicago trail, nor to the 1920s and 1930s.

In some case, the voodoo aspects of a song may reverberate powerfully within the listening community, even though there are no specific or direct references to voodoo in the song. Minnie's *Black Cat Blues* is a nearly perfect example of this type of piece:

BLACK CAT BLUES

I got a big black cat
who sits in my back door.
He catches every rat run across my floor.
Now everybody wants to buy my kitty.
Everybody wants to buy my kitty.
Everybody wants to buy my kitty,
I wouldn't sell that cat
to save your soul.

If it wasn't for that cat
I wouldn't know what I would do.
Rats cutting up all
of my clothes and shoes.
Now everybody wants
to buy my kitty, etc.

I been had this old cat, now,
for three, four years.
Didn't nobody want him
till I brought him here.
Now everybody wants
to buy my kitty, etc.

Spoken: Catch a rat!

Before I got that cat,
rats had holes all in my walls.
Since I brought her home
you can't find no holes at all.
Now everybody wants
to buy my kitty, etc.

You have seen a-lots of cats
and you going to see a lots more.
I got one I carries everywhere I go.
Now everybody wants to buy my kitty, etc.

Spoken: Aw, play it now. Catch a rat.

Here, an animal that figures in dozens of beliefs so strongly
that its appearance cannot fail to elicit a reaction in those listeners who believe in the cat's powers, appears in a song totally
without references to its participation in the realm of magic,
luck and hoodoo, and yet it is the presence of the cat in the
song that is sufficient to invoke its power in the listener's mind.
Black Cat Blues is ostensibly about the virtues of a rat-catching
cat, although the third verse is ambiguous and the fifth verse is
directly sexual. Minnie may have omitted mention of voodoo,
bad luck or witchcraft, but ignoring these relevant attributes of
black cats is entirely insufficient to suppress them. For many
listeners, black cats meant bad luck as surely as did walking under a ladder or breaking a mirror. Some felt the cat was the
witch or even the Devil himself. Here we see the equation, the
Devil = the unconscious, or the forbidden, and Minnie, with
her black cat sitting at the *back* door (the back door leading
out to the alley, the back door as the front door to Hell), invoking the dark side of conjuration, the power of unconscious
desire, for what else is magic other than a clearing of desire's
own path?[34]
    At the level of conscious intention, Minnie may have kept her
cat free of voodoo references so that its relation to rats could pro-
ceed, without obstacle, directly to its realization as an image of
desire and sexuality. Regarding the objects (of desire?), the rats,
we may make a few preliminary observations. In the unconscious,

rats frequently represent the male genital,[35] and they can thus represent the male, as well. In fact, in Sippie Wallace's *Up The Country Blues,*[36] it is her *man* who, like Minnie's rats, had "torn up all my clothes," and the identical complaint is made by Kansas City Kitty to Georgia Tom in *The Doctor's Blues.*[37]

There is even a common folk belief that when rats or mice gnaw your clothes, it is a sure sign you are going to move or die. You must get someone outside the family to patch such clothes, rather than do it yourself which would bring more bad luck.[38] One material grounding of the belief may be the unspoken notion that if your man tears up all your clothes, it's time to move (or die). After all, the woman whose part is spoken by Kansas City Kitty in *The Doctor's Blues* is consulting the doctor because her man beat her up. The rat = man/penis equation, however, is directly confirmed by Minnie and Joe in *Hole In The Wall:*

HOLE IN THE WALL

KJ:
There is something wonderful,
We can't understand,
A rat come in here,
Cutting like a natural man.
KJ & MM:
He got a hole in the wall,
He got a hole in the wall,
And when he get to cutting,
You might have heard the poor girl squall.

MM:
Boys, that rat is a cutter,
You ought to understand,
He's cutting somebody
Everywhere he lands.
KJ & MM:
He got a hole in the wall, etc.

KJ:
I was over to old man Jones',

The other day.
He had cut his wife, and 'bout to do his baby
The same old way.
KJ & MM:
He got a hole in the wall, etc.

MM:
The cat jumped at him,
And he got away.
Boys, if you don't watch that rat,
he's gonna steal all your
Meat away.
KJ & MM:
He got a hole in the wall, etc.

KJ:
I saw old man Collins,
Might have heard him crying,
Boys, the way that woman cut him,
he's about to
Lose his mind.
KJ & MM:
He got a hole in the wall, etc.

One fact clearly emerges through all of our interpretations: Minnie's cat is a splendid symbolic weapon in the fight against male
supremacy, regardless of the level on which it operates.[39] After all,
in our dreams, the cat is frequently a symbol of the female genitals.[40] The common expression "pussy" for the female genitals reveals this to be so, of course, but as is so often the case, a person
who laughs at the word and its double meaning in a blues, nonetheless rejects the interpretation that their dream of cats may contain the same signification. But *Black Cat Blues* can be heard as a
restaged "battle of the sexes" with the male, for once, playing the
part of the vanquished. It is precisely this celebratory nature of
the blues, this life-affirming poetic current, that sets it apart from
the quasi-poetry so praised by leading literary critics.

13. DOORS

Mesmeric hunter of the unachieved
I run out my door
like the true aim of terror
like the desire of the general strike
—Nancy Joyce Peters

Each song is a door that must be kept open if poetry is to pass through. Thus a poet is forever opening the door: "I have seen myself opening a door, shutting it, opening it again," wrote André Breton, using the door for *conjuration*.[1] Indeed, we must become experts in the matter of doors, so important is it to understand "open" and "closed" as moments of the dialectic where poetry's ambition is to open the closed door of meaning.

Compared to the back door, references to the front door are relatively rare in the blues, although they do occur. What needs emphasizing is the unruly significance, the nocturnal function, of the back door in the world of the blues. In our discussion of crime, we linked the significance of the alley with the significance of the back door, suggesting that the back door and the front door function in different registers in the blues than in the diurnal white world of the bourgeoisie. Extending our analogy, we can say that just as the alley is a figure for the hidden and the repressed, so is the back door a representation of those things we would most like to hide.

The back door via the alley becomes a path for the revelation of the return of the repressed, a main byway of the blues journey, and it is no wonder that black music propagated in such fertile soil. The relationship between the vital currents of jazz developed in the nightclubs and the crime syndicates that supported such clubs is worth emphasizing. The nightlife in which the black musician participates mocks the "daylight" work ethic of white, bourgeois America.[2] What is important for blues and jazz alike is the growth of this spirit nourished in an atmosphere of opposition and rebellion, for jazz and blues are the music of "the other side," a location that can be reached only through the back door, a back door as "wide open" as the cities and clubs run by the crime syndicates.

The back door is as important for a poetic understanding of blues geography as are the famous Highways 49, 51 and 61 and cities like Memphis, Clarksdale and Chicago. And we may ask, who is the "back door man?" Does he use the "colored" entrance, the South's special back door? Ask Howlin' Wolf:

BACK DOOR MAN

I am a back door man. (2x)
Well, the men don't know
but the little girls understand.

When everybody trying to sleep,
I'm somewhere making my midnight creep.
Every morning the rooster crow,
Something tells me I've got to go
I am a back door man. (2x)
Well, the men don't know
but the little girls understand.

They take me to the doctor
shot full of holes
Nurse cried, "Please save his soul."
Accuse me for murder first degree
Judge's wife cried, "Let the man go free."
I am a back door man. (2x)
Well, the men don't know
but the little girls understand.[3]

Many of the stereotypes whites applied to blacks have been "accepted" and played back at a different speed, giving us not only the "back door man," but an entire platform for resistance and independent action, drawing unconsciously as well as consciously on all the associations that link blacks with evil, darkness, and night. The ramifications are endless: The badman, the hero, the sportsman, the lover and ultimately the trickster and the jokester, all have mocked the white man by carrying his ridiculous claims to their logical conclusions. From this technique, an important strand of black humor has developed which is still with us today,[4] for the back door can be humorous! The door itself can also evoke our feelings of hesitation, temptation and desire,[5] even as we dream of doors we never opened and doors that are yet to come.

MOANING THE BLUES

Oh, the blues got ways sometimes
    just like a natural man. (2x)
I don't care whichaway you turn,
they always is on your hands.

Won't you tell me, baby,
    how come you don't come back home? (2x)
I lay down last night
with my back door open all night long.

Here come the blues this morning,
    just 'fore day they shut my door. (2x)
But the lord forgive me,
I won't have them things no more.

This morning,
    setting on the side of my bed. (2)
(They done come) brought you a letter
(for) your plumb good man fell dead.

Spoken: Blues, what must I do?

Hmmmmm, Hmmmmm. (2x)
Hmmmmm, Hmmmmm.

My Strange Man presents the other side of the traditional
Stranger Blues theme. The latter's "I'm a stranger here, just rolled
in your town," becomes, for Minnie, "I met a strange man last
night, and I taken him home with me." The guitar technique pre-
dicts a style that would be brought to the Bluebird studio a few
years later by Tommy McClennan and Robert Petway.

MY STRANGE MAN

I met a strange man last night,
    and I taken him home with me. (2x)
Now he done gone and left me,
wonder where could my strange man be?

Strange man, strange man,
    won't you please come back to me? (2x)
You is my strange man,
you've got something that I really need.

Hmmm, wonder where is
    my strange man gone? (2x)
He left me this morning 'n
I've been lonesome all day long.

I woke up this morning,
Half past three,
I found my strange man,
Was standin' over me.
Strange man, strange man,
Tell me where you been.
Well, I sure feel happy
To see you back home again.

Strange man, strange man,
    please don't leave me no more. (2x)
Next time you leave me,
I'm gonna walk out and lock my door.

The blues personified, waiting at the back door in *Moaning The Blues* or merely hanging around as in *Tears On My Pillow*,[6] or "walking like a man" as Robert Johnson sang it,[7] all are attempts to wrest away misery by projection, a flinging away from the self, not only of misery but of responsibility. Externalization, whereby the singers actively and insistently place their troubles outside the back door, only to be "shocked" when they discover them there the next morning. But is the shock only a stage mechanism? Isn't there more to this than that?

It is important to see that the blues at the back door is the result of projection, but it is just as critical to be able to situate the contents of this projection within a social as well as a psychological context. By personifying the blues, and using the door as an agent of personification, the singers are able to portray the pain, oppression and misery of everyday life as socially situated ills with social causes; out of doors and personified, the blues comes to represent the repressive aspects of civilization.

Often the blues will have one meaning hidden beneath the layer(s) of another . . . like black vernacular speech. But to suggest that songs have a meaning other than the most obvious one suggested by the lyrics can hardly be shocking nowadays, especially to literary critics, although to many folklorists, this is still an unacceptable notion.[8] Related to the question of what meanings to attach to blues lyrics is the question, to what part of the lyrics is the meaning to be attached? We suggest that plot and narrative are the least important elements that give meaning to blues lyrics, whereas line and metaphor are crucial. The flashpoint of metaphor is the image, evoking emotional response from the listener, often in an instant, often through a succession of images. This is wholly consistent with the notion that blues songs are usually considered to be folk-lyrics, where a tune or a mood binds together a series or network of images.[9]

This also suggests that blues lyrics need not be grasped only by concentration and studied attention, but may be picked up on the fly, while dancing or drinking. Thus, there may be an analogy between how we listen to the blues and how surrealist poets listen to the unconscious. The surrealists unveiled a special mode of "listening," a non-directed, actively invoked passivity, at once the receptionist and receptor of the image as well as one's surprise. By simultaneously cultivating the network of obsession for paranoiac-critical reasons, one could establish the image's *context for projection*, and by such dislocation present oneself with new inspiration.

Indeed, there is an analogy between this position and the position of the listener to blues lyrics. In the blues, our comprehension of a phrase may be joined to the absorption of another phrase, later in the song. While these two phrases may be joined by conscious "sense," they are nonetheless arrayed in such a way before the listener that the images are, in fact, scattered. It is their gathering that is subjected to the whim of the listener's own actively occasioned passivity, i.e., to the whim of the listener's own obsessions.

We have everything to gain if we interrogate our own level of consciousness about what we hear and how we hear it, in an effort to plumb the depths of responsibility toward the determination of the nature of the revolutionary poetic voice. We hope to provide for the listener and the reader a new way to hear the blues. We shall refer the accusation that we have drawn from the songs more than the singer puts in, to the certainty that all creative forms engage the dreaming, active imagination of the audience with that of the performer in ways we will continue to describe. The precise content of our own interpretations are meant to suggest the links through which the listeners of today can preserve the vital function of comprehending the blues, and thereby assist in its survival.

14. DIRTY DOZENS

Poetry will be cannabilistic or will not be at all.
—Suzanne Césaire[1]

Dirty Dozens: "A black game of supposedly friendly rivalry and name-calling; in reality, a crucial exercise in learning how to absorb verbal abuse without faltering."—Audre Lorde[2]

Dirty Dozens: "a very elaborate game traditionally played by black boys, in which the participants insult each other's relatives, especially their mothers. The object of the game is to test emotional strength. The first person to give in to anger is the loser. See *signify.*"—Clarence Major[3]

These ideas suggest the dimensions of the dozens, and the literature devoted to this subject has grown to respectable size. Most of the literature is devoted to the verbal "game" rather than to the music, but we should not lose sight of the elective affinities between the dozens, signifying, and black vernacular speech, from which the musical form derives.[4] Indeed, one of our main themes is the flexible and angular deflection of meaning in such speech, as it appears in the blues.

Intrinsic to Minnie's songs is the fact that "dirty words" are, traditionally, for the use of men only. By treating such words as part of the male domain, women are divested of a significant amount of power, but men's power to abuse women with these words is mitigated and diffused by women's use of the same words. As H. Rap Brown notes, girls were among the best dozens players.[5]

Minnie, of course, created her own shock waves, many times, and her *New Dirty Dozen* contains a few examples of how she did so.

NEW DIRTY DOZEN

Come all you folks and start to walk,
I'm fixing to start my dozen talk.
What you're thinking about
ain't on my mind,
That stuff you got is the sorriest kind.
Now you're a sorry mistreater,
robber and a cheater,
Slip you in the dozens,
your papa and your cousin,
Your mama do the lordy lord.

Come all of you womens
oughta be in the can.
Out on the corner stopping every man,
Hollering "Soap is a nickel
and the towel is free,
I'm pigmeat, pappy, now who wants me?"
You's a old mistreater,
robber and a cheater,
Slip you in the dozen, etc.

Now the funniest thing I ever seen,
Tom cat jumping on a sewing machine.
Sewing machine run so fast,
Took 99 stitches in his yas, yas, yas.
Now he's a cruel mistreater,
robber and a cheater,
Slip you in the dozen, etc.

Now I'm gonna tell you
all about old man Bell.
He can't see but he sure can smell.
Fish-man passed here the other day.

Hollering "Hey, pretty mama,
I'm going your way."
I know all about
your pappy and your mammy,
Your big fat sister
and your little brother Sammy,
Your auntie and your uncle
and your ma's and pa's,
They all got drunk
and showed their Santa Claus
Now they're all drunken mistreaters,
robbers and a cheaters,
Slip you in the dozen, etc.

Both the melody and structure of Minnie's piece were based on Speckled Red's 1929-1930 Brunswick versions,[6] essentially the prototypes for most of the versions of the dozens that followed. Minnie's guitar adaptation of Speckled Red's characteristic piano figures was inventive and enticing. Her refrain was nearly Red's, as were some of her verse lines, but several of her verses were original and were used later by other purveyors of the song. This is not the only case where Minnie has created her own song, or a version of a song distinctively hers, out of someone else's popular and much covered hit, although numerically such cases are uncommon in Minnie's repertoire. Furthermore, it's instructive to see how uninventive are the lyrics of the versions by Kokomo Arnold and Leroy Carr, considering how inventive these singers could be on other occasions.

One of the most compelling images, that of the cat on the sewing machine, does not appear in Red's version, and is probably original with Minnie; Kokomo Arnold used it in combination with Red's verses four years later.[7] Earlier, Furry Lewis, another Memphis blues artist, sang this verse in his song about Casey Jones, and it evocatively foreshadows Minnie's verse.

Mrs. Casey said she dreamt a dream,
The night she bought her sewing machine.
The needle got broke, she could not sew.

> She loved Mr. Casey 'cause she told me so.
> Told me so.
> Loved Mr. Casey 'cause she told me so.[8]

Both Lewis's and Minnie's verses conjure up the words of Lautréamont:

> Beautiful as the chance meeting on a dissecting table
> of a sewing machine and an umbrella.[9]

"Soap is a nickel. . . ." would seem to be Minnie's verse, and it doesn't reappear on anyone else's record. Trying to trace the genesis of the "fishman" verse is difficult, although it is close to one verse in Minnie's later *You Can't Give It Away*. As should be clear, a goodly portion of Minnie's version used material that was original in concept or phrasing or both, and some of this material was taken up by later performers of the song. The complex interweaving of influence and creativity are pertinent subjects whenever someone as significant as Minnie comes before us, and it is not always easy to gauge the weight of these two factors in various pieces in her repertoire. We know already that Minnie was a highly original performer, a guitar innovator, and a composer of a great many songs, but in trying to follow an innovative path through a traditional form like the dozens, the matter can be especially complicated by the fact that Dozens songs don't always appear as such. For example, in Sam Chatman's *God Don't Like Ugly,* the singer insists "I don't play no dozens" while actually playing them in another name. Smokey Hogg's *You Gonna Look Like A Monkey* is also a dozens cousin.[10]

In "playing the dozens" or "signifying," one is often "called out of his (or her) name," and just as the dozens can, under certain conditions, lead to an actual (physical) fight and not just a verbal one,[11] being called out of one's name can be taken as an insult of high degree. Naming is itself a splendid facet of blue culture, where pseudonyms are frequently called upon to add intensity and vitality to the blues singer's powers of enchantment. Even a casual familiarity with the blues brings one into contact with names like Muddy Waters, Trilby Hargens, Howlin' Wolf, Kansas Joe, Blue Coat Tom

Nelson, "Sloppy" Henry, Guitar Slim, Jelly Belly, Ma Rainey, Banjo Joe, Doctor Clayton, Blues Birdhead, Big Mama Thornton, Jellyroll Anderson, Barbecue Bob, Mississippi Matilda, Shreveport Homewreckers, Snitcher Roberts, Sluefoot Joe, Chocolate Brown, Black Bottom McPhail, Red Hot Shakin' Davis, Papa Eggshell, Freezone, Moanin' Bernice, Mississippi Blacksnakes, Jack O'Diamonds, Blind Sammie, Washboard Sam, Za Zu Girl, Peetie Wheatstraw (The Devil's Son-in-Law, The High Sheriff of Hell), and two of our personal favorites, Peanut the Kidnapper, and Three Fifteen and His Squares.[12]

To name is to conjure, but also to envision, to redefine, and to reauthenicate.[13] But we also see the pseudonymous tendency in the blues as a movement (and moment) of refusal, a rejection of *standard procedure* wherein the blues singers assume a new stance beyond the range of white Christian authority. Everyday life where our names locate us firmly in the real is outmaneuvered by the refusal of the name.[14] Desire drifts into the space left vacant by the unused "proper" name, focused and refined into a sharper image by the pseudonym itself. The "totemic" significance of some of the pseudonyms is inescapable, but names draw their powers from many realms. The power of the name is often enough to cause a precipitation, and where once there was only an amorphous and congested solution, the sharp angles and planes of crystals are seen to form, after the evocation of the name. The pseudonym itself is the precipitate created by dissolving the name in the solvent of desire.

Pseudonyms were often subversive economic tools used to facilitate recording for many companies while contracts with other companies were still in force. As Fats Waller said,

Don't give your right name, no, no, no![15]

On a number of records featuring two or more singers, one musician will often say to another, at the instrumental break, "Aw, play it, Mr. Man," one way of maintaining a veiled identity on a record made under contract violation. It should also be heard as a note of direct opposition to the white habit of addressing adult black males as "Boy." A third inflection is the satire of treating

themselves as whites usually treated them, i.e. as nameless nobod-
ies. This is another use of *mimicry*.

Beyond the use of pseudonyms, another sort of naming frequently takes place in the blues. *Ma Rainey* is one of the most
interesting songs in Minnie's late repertoire, and it was made at
the June 27, 1940, session that also produced *Nothing in Rambling,
Finger Print Blues* and Lonesome Shack Blues. It was Minnie's only
session that year, but it produced several noteworthy songs.

MA RAINEY

> I was thinking about Ma Rainey,
>   wonder where could Ma Rainey be. (2x)
> I been looking for her,
> even been [in] old Tennessee.
>
> She was born in Georgia,
>   traveled all over this world. (2x)
> And she's the best blues singer,
> peoples, I ever heard.
>
> When she made Bo Weavil Blues,
>   I was living way down the line. (2x)
> Every time I hear that record,
> I just couldn't keep from crying.
>
> Hmmmm, hmmmmm. (2x)
> Hmmmm, hmmmmmmmm.
>
> People it sure look lonesome
>   since Ma Rainey been gone. (2x)
> But she left little Minnie
> to carry the good works on.

Minnie's tribute to Ma Rainey was recorded approximately six
months after Ma Rainey's death, and her song was a direct response to the news of the death of the "Mother of the Blues."
Minnie's first verse implies she's been looking all over for Ma
Rainey, but the final verse confirms that Minnie knows Ma is dead,
just as she knows that she's carrying on a tradition that Ma Rainey

helped to found. Minnie's song also gives factual details of Rainey's birth and career. *Bo-Weavil Blues,* recorded in December, 1923, was not only Ma Rainey's first record, it was also her first "hit". When she died, her death certificate gave her usual occupation as "housekeeping", but her legacy included *Louisiana Hoo Doo Blues,* which referred to Minnie's birthplace, "Down in Algiers where the hoodoos live in their dens."

Ma Rainey also compels our attention with Minnie's reference to herself in the last verse. There are many songs that have a last verse somewhat similar to the one in *Ma Rainey,* but end in the fashion of Julius Daniels' *My Mamma Was A Sailor:*

> If anybody asks you who
>   compose this song. (2x)
> Tell 'em Julius Daniels
> done been here and gone.[16]

Muddy Waters' *Sad Letter Blues* contains this verse:

> I got a letter this morning,
>   this is the way my letter read. (2x)
> Say "you better come on home, Muddy Waters,
> tell me your baby's dead."[17]

In all of these songs, and in others like them, where the singers mention their own names, we hear the desire to be known, to leave traces, to live in people's memories. This desire is also served by the label of the record which bears the singer's name, and many singers have bought copies of their records to give to friends as well as to show to disbelievers. Yet the current emphasis among certain blues scholars, on content as convention, as commonplace, which the above quoted *forms* are considered to be, contributes to the notion of the faceless singer at precisely the time and place where they are trying most to be remembered! Not "faceless" in the sense that anyone would argue that the singers don't want to be known, but "faceless" in the sense that the singer's *voicing a desire to be known* is covered over by the critical notion of "commonplace" form. Thus, we all grant the desire to be known when a singer buys fifty copies of her record and gives them away to her friends in the community, but we pretend *not to hear desire* when the singer inserts her name in the blanks, as in the above songs, because we presume we are hearing only a conventional form. How could this be desire, we say, when it's only a "convention?"

We pursue this issue because if "Julius Daniels" and "Muddy Waters" and "Little Minnie" are only conventional *routine* fillings-in of the blanks, we are ignoring the black woman or man as subjects with their own desires. How so? One example can be drawn from recent history. During the 1960s, critics, scholars and fans alike would express their pleasure at "finding" the object of their desire, a singer who hadn't recorded in 30 years. But the singer would remind the "discoverer," "I was never lost; I've been right here all the time." That is, I am only "found" if you see me as existing only to satisfy your desire (i.e., to find me), but as a subject with my own desires, the question of "lost" and "found" is irrelevant since I was never "lost." A sign of the depth of the crisis in consciousness is that the singer's remarks paraphrased above usually conjure up a smile at the "clever, folk witticism," while the profound insult to the subject carried out by the words of anyone so claiming to have "found" them is rarely if ever acknowledged.

Minnie . . . and Ma Rainey together: "Let the high wind cry the name of women long dead / or the sound of bitter old rain on a road."[18]

15. DUETS

Long ago the ancient flutes sang
under our smoking fingers
and we danced with lunar delight.
—Debra Taub

For black farm families of the 1920s, dancing to blues was a prime recreational focus. As wind-up record players needed no electricity, they were used outdoors as well as indoors to provide the music. As blues became more popular, the Saturday night dance became a significant institution, even while picnics and country suppers continued. Many female listeners were not allowed to go to the rough Saturday night dances at the juke joints, but families invited friends over for dancing or listening, sometimes on week nights. To hear the latest music for doing the newest dances, the blues was ideal.[1] Couples danced the Gator Wobble (a variation of the popular Shimmy), the Grind and the Eagle Rock, as well as the more traditional steps like the Charleston, the Two-Step, and the Lindberg Hop.[2] Many of these dances like the Buzzard Lope and the Eagle Rock were rarely danced by whites, and when they were, blacks abandoned those particular dances and went on to develop new ones, always keeping, literally, a few steps ahead.

Many duets, with their rhythmic emphasis, were especially well-suited to accompany dancers. Minnie and Joe recorded a duet at their first session for Columbia *(Goin' Back to Texas)* as well as at their first Vocalion session *(She Wouldn't Give Me None).* Most of these duets were about love and sex, and the songs must have been extremely popular, for they show up with some frequency on the collector's market. Minnie and Joe recorded over a dozen of them in the first five years of their career.[3] A number of Minnie's and Joe's duets are comic and no doubt derived from the vaudeville tradition, but with none of the naughty, cute and coy attributes associated with the vaudeville stage. Duets have other attractions, not the least of which is their drawing power at outdoor events where an added instrument and voice can double not only the appeal but also the power of a performance. But before discussing any more of the significant characteristics of duets, let's look at an early example, *What Fault You Find of Me?*, Part 1 and Part 2 of which took up both sides of Vocalion 1500.[4]

WHAT FAULT YOU FIND OF ME? PT 1

KJ:
Worked all summer and I worked all fall.
Had take my Christmas in my overalls.
Now I've got tired the way you treated me.
And I believe I'll go now,
back to my used to be.

MM:
Well, you know I love you baby,
I can't help myself.
I'd rather be with you than anyone else.
Lord, tell me baby,
what fault you find of me?
Ah, that you want to quit me, baby,
for your old time used to be.

KJ:
When I had you, wouldn't treat me right.
Stay out from me both day and night.
Now I've got tired, etc.

MM:
I been wondering, I been wondering,
I can't see to save my life.

How come we can't get along
like man and wife.
Now tell me baby, etc.

KJ:
Went to your house about half past ten.
Knocked on your door,
you wouldn't let me in.
I've got tired, etc.

WHAT FAULT YOU FIND OF ME? PT 2

MM:
I wouldn't mind being your hopping frog.
Drink muddy water, sleep in a hollow log.
Now tell me baby, etc.

KJ:
One thing certainly can't understand.
Corn-bread for me and biscuits for your man.
Now I've got tired, etc.

MM:
You know I been begging you so long, so long.
Quit your foolishness,
bring your clothes back home.
Now tell me baby, etc.

KJ:
Before I got you, I had my diamonds on.
Now I got you, they all in pawn.
Now I've got tired, etc.

MM:
If I could holler like a mountain jack.
Go up on the mountain,
call them diamonds back.
Now tell me baby, etc.

This 1930 piece is a typical example of a Minnie and Joe duet.
Joe makes a number of specific complaints about their erotic re-

lations, but Minnie's replies are never specific answers to Joe's complaints, except for the one verse where she insists she wishes she could retrieve the diamonds that he had to pawn because of her. In earlier verses she sings of the sincerity of her love, of her trying hard and of her puzzlement at their having such hard times. In each case, her verses have little to do with Joe's, and it's almost as if each had written their own verses or their own song, privately, with little or no knowledge of the other. Possibly, the duet's lyrics were relatively unrehearsed, and the casual relationship between each other's verses was entirely sufficient.

Or, the performance may have been rehearsed many times. But rather than discard the notion of each privately writing their own song, we can see it as an actual method of duet construction where one set of verses strung together loosely on a thematic string is intertwined with another, similar set of verses on a separate string, producing a finished, integrated performance. In this case, Joe sings a song of mistreated love while Minnie sings her song of devotion, sacrifice and dedication! This is not all there is to duet composition, of course. Joe's verses lead obviously and intentionally in one direction while Minnie intentionally opposes him, or not. But it is helpful to see the duets as two singer's separate songs if it allows us to draw conclusions about the creation of the song in its final form, so much enjoyed by their listeners. Whether or not this was the preferred form of duet composition is not the question here. But this seemingly "fragmented" aspect appears in other ways in other songs and is an important element in blues songs and their composition. When two singers alternate verses, the audience and the singers focus on the *verse* as the crucial element in the song.[5] Because the critical structural elements in blues tend to be metaphor, line, and image, this focus on the verse is successful.

Another typical, two-sided duet is *Can I Do It For You?*, a close relative of the folk song *Paper Of Pins,* also known as *The Keys Of Heaven,* and widely collected throughout the South.[6]

CAN I DO IT FOR YOU? PT 2

KJ:
I'll buy your wood and coal,

buy your wood and coal,
Buy your wood and coal,
if I can do something to you,
Hear me saying,
I want to do something to you.

MM:
I don't want no wood and coal,
I don't want no wood and coal.
I don't want nothing in the world you got
and you can't do nothing for me,
Hear me saying, you can't do nothing for me.

KJ:
Buy your shoes and clothes,
buy your shoes and clothes,
Buy your shoes and clothes,
if I can do something to you,
Hear me saying,
I want to do something to you.

MM:
I don't want no shoes and clothes,
I don't want no shoes and clothes,
I don't want nothing in the world you got,
and can't do nothing for me,
Hear me saying, you can't do nothing for me.

KJ:
I'll buy you a Chevrolet,
I'll buy you a Chevrolet,
Buy you a Chevrolet,
if I can do something to you,
Hear me saying,
I want to do something to you.

MM:
I don't want no Chevrolet,
I don't want no Chevrolet,
I don't want nothing in the world you got,
and you can't do nothing for me,

Hear me saying,
you can't do nothing for me.

KJ:

Buy you a baby calf, buy you a baby calf,
Buy you a baby calf
if I can do something to you,
Hear me saying,
if I can do something to you.

MM:

I don't want no baby calf,
I don't want no baby calf,
I don't want nothing in the world you got,
and you can't do nothing for me,
Hear me saying,
you can't do nothing for me.

KJ:

Can I do something to you,
can I do something to you?
Do anything in this world I can,
if I can do something to you,
Hear me saying,
if I can do something to you.

MM:

Naw, you can't do nothing to me,
naw, you can't do nothing to me.
I don't care what in the world you do, you
can't do nothing to me,
Hear me saying,
you can't do something to me.

KJ:

Buy you a sedan Ford,
buy you a sedan Ford,
Buy you a sedan Ford,
if I can do something to you,
Hear me saying,
if I can do something to you.

MM:
I will take a sedan Ford,
yes, I will take a sedan Ford,
I don't want nothing in the world you got,
but I will take a sedan Ford,
Hear me saying, I'll take a sedan Ford.

The song is worth hearing, if for no other reason than to hear Joe's perfectly dumbfounded voice as he asks, twice, while Minnie sings another refusal, "What kind of woman is this?" Can we answer Joe's question? Is this the disorderly woman, the wild woman of Ida Cox's song, *Wild Women Don't Have The Blues?* What functions does such an image have? The image of the wild and unruly woman represents new opportunities to escape the repressive norms of bourgeois family life, as we point out in our discussion of *Good Girl Blues.* Thus, the notion of disorder that it conjures up can be understood from a political perspective as well as from a personal one.

Minnie's choice of a Ford over a house or a Chevrolet is at first puzzling, as houses have great significance for her in other songs. But her preference for automobiles, which have even greater significance, demonstrates her desire for that object which is most symbolically useful, and in order to represent her triumph over the lack of status normally accorded the black woman, Minnie chooses conspicuous consumption as the typical weapon of our time. The Sedan Ford successfully conjures up the notion of luxury, as the Deluxe Fordor [4-door] Sedan or the Town Sedan sold for around $650, and were both considered top of the line, unlike the popular Model A Ford ($495 at the time). These bargaining songs should further remind us that even before white Americans began to use blacks as a medium of exchange, women themselves were gifts and objects for exchange between men of varying races.

Minnie's and Joe's duets occur in several forms. Fewest in number are those where Minnie sings harmony, only on the chorus, like *She Wouldn't Give Me None,* a song of great vocal beauty. Most frequently encountered are the traded verse songs like *Can I Do It For You?* or *What Fault You Find Of Me?* In these songs the structure of the song itself, the traded verses, specifies an equality that may not be supported by the lyrics, lyrics whose manifest content may carry the opposite meaning. For Minnie and Joe, the usual technique was for one partner to play the dominant role in an erotic relationship, difficult to please and preparing to leave the other behind. The other would plead, bribe and cajole, finally succeeding (as Joe does in *Can I Do It For You?*) or failing (as Joe does in the traded line song, *She Put Me Outdoors*). Both artists played both roles often enough that we quickly see the futility of applying an arithmetic solution to an essentially poetic problem. If the duets are dialogues in which the dramas of everyday life are re-enacted, it is the singer's specific comprehension of her role as a singing subject, no longer just an object, that represents an important step in the poetic assault on consciousness.

There are other duets where Joe is only a minimal participant, much like Minnie is on *She Wouldn't Give Me None*. On *What's The Matter With The Mill?*, with its superb guitar dynamics, and *You Stole My Cake,* Joe's vocal role is limited to supplying regularly spaced, coherent "answers" to Minnie's repeated questions or statements: "What's the matter with the mill?" or "You stole my cake."

WHAT'S THE MATTER WITH THE MILL?

Kansas Joe:
Spoken:
Say Minnie!
Where you going?

For what?
Aww, that old mill is
  done broke down.
I'm just from down there.
Aw, no, I went to get
my corn ground.
It done broke down.
Yeah, it done broke down.

Memphis Minnie:
Spoken:
What you want, Kansas Joe?
I'm going to the mill; what do
you think?
Have my corn ground.

How do you know?
Aw, and it broke you down.

What's the matter with the mill?
Done broke down?

Kansas Joe: Memphis Minnie:
                                            Sung:
                                     Can't get no grinding,
                                     tell me what's the matter with the mill.

                                            Sung:
                                     Well, I had a little corn,
                                     I put it in a sack,
                                     Brought it to the mill and
                                     Come right back.
                                     What's the matter with the mill?
It done broke down.   What's the matter with the mill?
It done broke down.   I can't get no grinding
                                     Tell me what's the matter with the mill.

                                         Spoken:
                                     Aww, grind it.

                                         Sung

                                     Now listen here folks,
                                     I don't want no stuff,
                                     You can't bring me my meal,
                                     Bring me the husks
                                     What's the matter with the mill?
It done broke down.   What's the matter with the mill?
It done broke down.   I can't get no grinding,
                                     Tell me what's the matter with the mill.

                                     Well, my papa sat and cried,
                                     My brother did, too.
                                     They both been to the mill,
                                     They can't get nothing to do.
                                     What's the matter with the mill?
It done broke down.   What's the matter with the mill?
It done broke down.   I can't get no grinding,
                                     Tell me what's the matter with the mill.

Kansas Joe:	Memphis Minnie:
	Now listen here folks,
	I want you to bear this in mind.
	If you're going to the mill,
	You're just losing time.
	What's the matter with the mill?
It done broke down.	What's the matter with the mill?
It done broke down.	I can't get no grinding,
	Tell me what's the matter with
	the mill.

Spoken
Aww, grind it again.

What's The Matter With The Mill? is easily one of Minnie and Joe's most exhilarating pieces, and certainly one of the most listenable. The double entendre of "grinding" is obvious, although the ancient roots of its derivation are less known:

> ... in antiquity women exclusively did this work. In symbolic language, however, the mill signifies the female organ and as the man is the miller, the satirist Petronius uses *molere mulierem* = (grind a woman) for coitus. ... [According to the Talmud:] By the grinding is always meant the sin of fornication (Beischlaf). Therefore all the mills in Rome stand still at the festival of the chaste Vesta. It is now demonstrated that every man is a miller and every woman a mill, from which alone it may be conceived that every marriage is a milling ... the child is the ground grain, the meal.[7]

Muddy Waters recorded a post-war version of *What's The Matter With The Mill?* for Chess, and he included it in his live performance repertoire as well. Another indication of the song's popularity was it's performance by Sam Walker at a Fort Valley State College folk music festival in 1953. The Heartfixers from Mississippi still do *What's The Matter With The Mill?*, as does Georgia's Jim Bunkley, and Memphis Jug Band veteran Charlie Burse recorded the song in 1939 as *What's The Matter With The Well?* Minnie's influence was by no means limited to blues figures, however, and *What's The Matter With The Mill?* was performed by hillbilly artist Moon Mullican and western swing star Bob Wills.[8]

There are other ways to hear Minnie's and Joe's duets, however, and we would like to explore a few of these. We would especially like to examine several of the *structural dimensions* of the blues, primarily, the role of *interruption* and the notion of *singing to each other,* and how they function in duets. While these ideas may sound unusual, they are by no means difficult to imagine. To begin, let us view the country blues terrain as a horizontal plane, a line full of bumps, gouges, valleys and hills, the peaks representing the eruption (interruption) of the forbidden. The repressed, the unconscious, the unspeakable is constantly returning in the blues, operating in unusual ways. The singers themselves, as well as their songs, come to represent and reproduce the return of the repressed for the white bourgeoisie. We are not speaking merely of abstractions, as an example from history makes clear.

In the section on hoboing and the outdoor blues we suggest the singers could be seen as wandering scholar/interpreters. In this fashion, the blues functions in the black working class as an educational medium, through which patterns of social communication (including "smart talk") are learned by example. Yet hundreds of years ago, street singers like Minnie fell under state supervision because of their educational potential, i.e., because they carried news the ruling class preferred to suppress. And this educational potential was condemned precisely as an *interruption.* Noise-making and subversive, they were denounced thusly in a police report of the times: "[These highly] disreputable people like beggars and women of ill repute, when they meddle in singing ... often *add things that are not in the song!*"[9]

Yet, within this mode of realization, there are numerous repressed voices clamoring to be heard, and these voices manifest themselves as interruptions that occur on many levels. Let's look at some of the other manifestations as they appear in Minnie's songs.

First, we can see Minnie's songs as the eruption of the female and female desire into the typically male country blues discourse, and we hope our entire book will function as an illumination of this mode of intervention, just as we see it as a structurally similar example of disruption itself.

Second, we can view the duets as structures in which such eruptions are given more graphic representation, as Minnie and Joe actually demonstrate various versions of male/female conflict and cooperation. Each can also be seen as trying to seize power from the other, through the structure of the song's shared vocals, as well as through the content of the lyrics. Minnie's success in this area can be seen against the fact that in normal conversation, women are "eminently interruptible" as well as unlikely to interrupt others; when they do, they are less likely to be successful at it.[10]

On a third level, silences, word play, moans, and nonsense sounds like scat singing can all represent the interruption of the conscious by unconscious material not yet speakable. A demonstration of this can be found in *Dirt Dauber Blues* and our discussion following it.

Fourth, the blues as a whole constantly and consistently interrupts white, bourgeois discourse. This happens whenever the blues is too primitive in exposing desire, or too "coarse," as in *You Can't Give It Away,* or too low-down with its songs of crime, voodoo and various other unsophisticated (non-alienated) subjects. It is this type of interruption that occurred in the case cited above where it was noted that "beggars and women of ill repute, when they meddle in singing ... often add things that are not in the song!"

Fifth, certain of Minnie's songs interrupt her work as a whole. Any plane that could be constructed to represent the smooth or irregular progress of her work, from song to song, would find itself pierced or stretched out of shape by the mark of the exceptional piece. *Call The Fire Wagon* with it's old style finger-picking has this effect on Minnie's other recordings of the later thirties. Here interruption acts as self-critique.

There are also those structural levels in the blues through which we can see operate the famous "call-and-response" that critics were so pleased to find in gospel music some years ago. Since then, we have often been shown how the guitar operates as a second voice, another form of call-and-response. But this form can also be found, rather obviously, in duets like Minnie and Joe's. *What's The Matter With The Mill?* is a typical example, with Joe's short replies to Minnie's full lines. Slightly less obvious are those pieces during which free-form calling and responding takes the shape of shouted exhortations from the sidemen or other personnel. Minnie's frequent whoops and shouts operate as a second voice, as does her occasional spoken words of encouragement to herself or to her guitar. But the whoops and cries can also remind us of the falsetto vocalizing in the style of Tommy Johnson's *Cool Drink Of Water Blues*. Are the falsetto parts the echo of a long lost responder, perhaps a caller from a track-lining crew, or are they the voice of a ghostly Maggie Campbell from generations before, still "walking too slow?"[11] Can we not also see the silent meaning of call-and-response as the poetic role of the community in the creative vision of the singer? This emphasis on participation and the community of response will sharpen our own vision of the singer's history as we pursue our investigation.

Let us invoke one more analogy in our effort to evoke all the possibilities of communication in duets. Together on an expedition through the Paris streets and into various shops, André Breton and Alberto Giacometti discovered a mask and a spoon, objects which seemed to reverberate with properties both magical and compelling. They confirmed Breton's poetic hypothesis that such an incident corresponded *not just to the desire of one of them but a desire of one with which the other was somehow connected,* i.e. it was a matter of shared preoccupations, to the extent that the *two of them together* "constitute[ed] a single influencing body, *primed*. . . . [In such cases] the sympathy existing between two or several beings seems to lead them toward solutions they would have never found on their own."[12] Yet the tension between the two objects, like the reverberation between the two friends and the threads taken up by two singers, draws upon the power of the still undisclosed revelation, acting on *the two parties.*

Musicians in a band where the heated passion of creativity seems to affect all of them or several of them at once, and where the instigator or the inspiration for the passion has not yet made itself known, and where the path of creativity seems to lead farther into the unknown rather than in a direction with which most are familiar, these musicians may say they have also pursued such an object and such a revelation. We will also assume that a musical couple working together like Minnie and her partner will have also found in their duets a destiny such as Breton describes.

The following note on the liberating potential of music, while not written specifically about duets, seems to describe them perfectly:

> An exchange between bodies—through work, not through objects. This constitutes the most fundamental subversion . . . to play for the other and by the others, to exchange the noises of bodies, to hear the noises of others in exchange for one's own, to create, in common, the code within which communication will take place. . . . Any noise, when two people decide to invest their imaginary and their desire in it, becomes a potential relationship, future order.[13]

16. FOOD AND COOKING

the common woman was common as the best of bread
and will rise
and will become strong—I swear it to you.
—Judy Grahn

I have never seen a wild poetic loaf of bread,
But if I did, I would eat it, crust and all.
—Bob Kaufman

So many of Minnie's songs deal with food or cooking that we would be justified in calling it one of the most significant and strategically important registers through which the meaning of her songs is transmitted. Among the relevant songs are the following, not a few of which are among her best: *I'm Gonna Bake My Biscuits, Plymouth Rock Blues, What's The Matter With The Mill, North Memphis Blues, Soo Cow Soo, Fishing Blues, You Stole My Cake, My Butcher Man, Selling My Pork Chops, Good Biscuits, Keep On Eating, Good Soppin', Fish Man Blues,* and others. The fact that in many of these songs the food appears as a figure or metaphor for sex doesn't change the fact that it was *food* that was chosen to stand in this particular relation.

In Minnie's songs, food, and especially cooking, also conjure up the notion of independence and privacy. For example, in *I'm Gonna Bake My Biscuits,* she's going to lock the doors and nail the windows down, and she repeatedly insists, "ain't gonna give nobody none." But because such references occur in the public language of the blues, they also accomplish unity through their content and elaboration and richness through their metaphor. Within these cooking songs we see the stirring of another vital sign. For the feminist critic who asked, "What if we turned recipes into poetry?" Minnie has supplied an answer that not only goes beyond the question of a "feminine aesthetics," but, hopefully, beyond aesthetics itself:[1]

I'M GONNA BAKE MY BISCUITS

I got a brand new skillet
and a brand new lid,
I ain't got no stove
but I bake my bread.
I'm gonna bake my biscuits,
I'm gonna bake my biscuits,
I'm gonna bake my biscuits,
Ain't gonna give nobody none.

I'm gonna lock my door,
nail my windows all down.
You know by that
I don't want no bums around.
I'm gonna bake my biscuits, etc.

I ain't got no flour
and ain't got no meal,
If you got no man you got to rob and steal.
I'm gonna bake my biscuits, etc.

I'm-a tell you something
I don't know if I'm wrong or right,
But if you want my bread,
you got to stay all night.
I'm gonna bake my biscuits, etc.

Ain't no need of you getting mad now, and
poking out your mouth.

You ain't gonna give me no bread
when my bread runs out.
I'm gonna bake my biscuits, etc.

Come here, come here,
I want you to come here now.
I ain't got tight for my bread ain't brown.
I'm gonna bake my biscuits, etc.

All baked goods in Minnie's song operate under the sign of Eros, as well as within the system of food preparation itself. It is noteworthy that in contrast to the many food and cooking references in Minnie's songs, references to drunkenness are relatively infrequent, even though Minnie was a heavy drinker. The absence of references to alcohol is balanced by an abundance of references to food and cooking. Is there a female rejection of the male preoccupation with drunkeness in favor of the malleable metaphors of cooking?

Other enticing ambiguities and contradictions appear in the lyrics of *I'm Gonna Bake My Biscuits*. Does "ain't gonna give nobody none" mean "I'm keeping them for myself" or "They're not free?" And what does "free" mean? "You got to stay all night" or some other form of exchange? Further, we are immediately struck by the tension between biscuit-baking as a solitary, creative activity for which no man is required ("ain't gonna give nobody none," "I'm gonna lock my door, nail my windows all down") and the erotic implications of a sexual partner ("if you want my bread, you got to stay all night," "I want you to come here now"). The latter position is opposed again and again in each chorus, almost as if the conflicts of present day eroticism are to be rehearsed again and again with each playing of the song. As in many blues, no resolution is offered, but only ambivalence and a portrayal of the conflicts themselves.

GOOD BISCUITS

Listen to my song, ladies,
    please take strictly understand. (2x)

Don't let no outside woman
make no biscuits for your man.

I'm going to give you all the lowdown,
    lowdown if I can. (2x)
Why I'm a single woman today
by letting other women feed my man.

So the next daddy I get, I'm going
    to take him to the restaurant. (2x)
Ain't gonna have him going around
eating biscuits, whoo, whoo,
made up with your nasty hands.

I just found out
    how come I can't keep a man. (2x)
I don't get no one buddy,
I have too many a-doggone friends.

You don't mean me no good,
    just a grin when I come in. (2x)
But if I catch you feeding my man, whoo, whoo,
Lord, I'm going to the pen.

In this song, it is presumed that the way to a man's heart is
indeed through his stomach, and that if you let another woman
feed your man, you're going to lose him. While the song's protagonist shows hostility toward other women who are seen as competitors in the third and fifth verse, the song itself is addressed, in
the first two verses, to all other women who may make the same
mistake as she did. This song demonstrates that competition over
a man is something devisive among women, a competition that can
be partly overcome by unifying around the issue of how to keep
one's lover. This song also shows how the subject or object in a
song may change from line to line and verse to verse, just as the
speaker or scene of action might change midway through a song.
Minnie capably uses many dramatic devices to increase the impact
of her pieces, and we will see other examples as we study her recorded repertoire. Of course, *Good Biscuits* cannot be seen as a
song wherein cooking loses its erotic message, for eroticism bubbles

along, barely beneath the surface, threatening to explode into full view at any moment. *Keep On Eating* actually begins "innocently" enough, but the eroticism breaks through in several places.

KEEP ON EATING

Everytime I cook,
look like you can't get enough,
Fix you a pot of soup
and make you drink it up.
So keep on a-eating,
Ooh, keep on a-eating,
Keep on eating, baby,
Till you get enough

You don't like nobody's cooking but mine.
Get up in the morning
and fix you a tenderloin.
So keep on a-eating, etc.

Don't tell nobody that I tried to be tough.
I just got a man so hard to fill up.
So keep on a-eating, etc.

Spoken: Oh, play it now, Mr. Charlie. Yes,
man! Just keep on eating.
You'll get through it someday.

I know you're crazy about your oysters and
your shrimp and crab,
Take you around the corner
and give you a chance to grab.
So keep on a-eating, etc.

I've cooked and cooked till I done got tired,
Can't fill you up off of my fried apple pie.
So keep on a-eating, etc.

I know you got a bad cold
and you can't smell.
I ain't gwine give you something that I can't sell.
So keep on a-eating, etc.

As to whether or not any of the songs under discussion ever free themselves entirely from erotic meanings, we would have to answer, "No," in agreement with the commentator who wrote that when the blues singers mention food, they usually mean sex.[2]

Minnie has several baking songs that refer specifically to cake, as opposed to biscuits or bread. *Wants Cake When I'm Hungry* is from 1937.

WANTS CAKE WHEN I'M HUNGRY

> I wants cake when I'm hungry,
>   "lightnin'" when I'm dry. (2x)
> And some good man to love me,
> and heaven when I die.
>
> Don't nobody want you
>   when you're stumbling all alone. (2x)
> You can find anything
> that'll wreck your happy home.
>
> I was up this morning,
>   going from door to door. (2x)
> Just sitting down wondering
> whichaway did my good man go.
>
> How a man expects for a woman to do right
>   when he won't do right himself? (2x)
> Well, it ain't no woman don't get tired of
> staying home all the time by herself.
>
> Call me, baby, call me around about 3. (2x)
> I'm having chills and fever
> and the doggone jinx got me.

Cake can inspire notions of luxury, dessert, cookies, birthdays and the passage of time, partially through the celebrations of anniversaries that we mark by serving cake. We are accustomed to thinking of cake as a luxury food, a food to satisfy desire more than need, but Minnie collapses this notion by demanding the satisfaction of desire (cake) as the satisfaction of a need (hunger).

The demand for cake and whiskey when only food and water are supposedly needed insists on the insufficiency of merely filling one's "needs," and by its nature underscores the insufficient nature of all such claims. It is not unusual to find "utopian" demands such as Minnie's in the blues, and the insistence that none of the typical compromises will suffice underscores one aspect of the surrealists' interest in blues: Both go far beyond the trivial "minimum demands" proposed by most seekers of social reform. In an essentially surrealist spirit, like so many other exemplars of "popular culture" at its best, Minnie not only insists that we can have our cake and eat it, too, but also forces us to ask ourselves: "Why settle for less?"[3]

Minnie not only wrote songs about food and cooking, but she also commemorated a local cafe, well known to the Memphis blues singers. George Sousoulas' North Memphis Cafe was located at 235 N. Main St. in Minnie's day,[4] and it operated from the same location for many years. Its former site is now occupied by the new convention center. As Baby Boy Warren recalled, "I knew [Minnie] when she come to Memphis and she started playing at the North Memphis Cafe up there on North Main,"[5] and Minnie's reference to the cafe is another indication of the degree to which she used autobiographical material as a basis and inspiration for her compositions.

NORTH MEMPHIS BLUES

I'll tell all you people,
you can rest and eat (at ease?).
You don't have to worry about cooking,
go to North Memphis Cafe and eat.
I'll tell all you people, you can rest and eat,
Because the North Memphis Cafe
got everything that you really need.

I don't buy no wood, even buy no coal,
I go to North Memphis Cafe and eat,
and don't be a dope.
I tell all you people, you can rest and eat.

You don't have to worry about cooking,
go to North Memphis Cafe and eat.

I will tell you all something,
I don't change like the wind.
If you go to the North Memphis Cafe and eat,
you'll go back again.
I tell all you people, you can rest and eat.
Because the North Memphis Cafe got every-
thing that you really need.

Now listen to me, good peole,
I don't aim to make you mad,
You go to the North Memphis Cafe
and get something you never had.
I tell all you people, you can rest and eat.
Because the North Memphis Cafe got every-
thing that you really need.

Not only did Minnie create a full range of songs about food
and cooking, but she herself was an excellent cook. On her visits
home to Walls, she would often do the cooking for the others who
were working in the fields, and throughout her life she never lost
her talent for baking biscuits.[6]

17. HORSES

Perhaps we are both wild horses,
we want to break fences but we don't know how.
—Rikki Ducornet

One of Minnie's most unusual songs is *Frankie Jean (That Trottin' Fool)*, a tale about a horse, spoken and whistled but never sung. Like the cow in *Soo Cow Soo*, the horse in this song is not overtly used to represent a sexual partner, a role Minnie seems to have reserved for small animals like spiders, snakes, roosters and bees. Nonetheless, this unusual song was widely heard and years later it was recorded by Bob Wills and His Texas Playboys.[1]

FRANKIE JEAN (THAT TROTTIN' FOOL)

Spoken:

One time my papa had a horse,
His name was Frankie Jean.
Man, that's the runningest horse
the world I ever seen,
And it just do me good
to ride old Frankie Jean.
And it do you good
to sit and listen at him sometimes
When he's coming down that plank road,
almost making his feet talk.

Man, that's the singlest-footing horse
the world I ever seen.
Something kind of like this:

(Instrumental break)

Go on, Frankie Jean, go on.

I had him out with me once
and he got loose.
I couldn't catch him to save my life.
I called Frankie Jean and I called him,
He didn't seem to pay me no mind.
I went and told my papa,
"How would you do
if you want to catch a horse?"
He said, "How did you do?"
I said, "I called mine; called Frankie Jean
and called him.
He didn't seem to pay me no attention."
Said, "That's a horse, you can't,
you didn't call him right.
You must whistle when you want
your horse to come to you.
Something like this:"

(Full verse whistled)

Then he come single-footing to me.

So I took him out again;
he got loose from me.
I called him and called him.
He didn't seem to pay me no attention.
I thought about what papa said.
You's a horse, I must whistle for you,
something like this:

(Full verse whistled)

Then he comes single-footing to me.

I had him out on a race once.

I had $5000 betting on Frankie Jean.
Folks, I wasn't scared at all,
Cause I know he wasn't going to let me lose.
'Fore he let me lose,
He'd run off all of his shoes.
Something like this:

(Instrumental break)

Go on, Frankie Jean.

Daisy Johnson told Mike Leadbitter (in 1963) that Frankie Jean may have been a mule as they never had a horse. Her son Lee confirms that it was "probably a mule."[2] As our study focuses on Minnie's songs as imaginative, creative products grounded in black, working-class experience, this uncertain lore emphasizes a segment of such experience that Minnie *transmuted* into the rich fabric of the fantasy, *Frankie Jean*. This process occurs in much the same way that, psychoanalytically speaking, the "day's residues," pieces of a previous day's moment of reality, are transformed into dreams. The actual experience is an essential ingredient, but the richness of Minnie's text derives from the poetic act itself. What Frankie Jean was in reality is less important than what he has become in song.

Frankie Jean also embodies an interesting structural dimension. The style of its performance qualifies it as a member of that uncommon genus, the "talking blues." Such pieces are scarce overall, although a number have been collected in Louisiana by Dr. Harry Oster.[3] Oster himself supplies a full definition of "talking blues":

Talking blues (contain) semi-rhythmic speaking or a mixture of speaking and singing, accompanied by rhythmic guitar. The speech has a fluid conversational flow though it is more rhythmic than ordinary conversation. At the same time it is less rhythmic than a Negro folk-sermon or than the talking blues of white performers in Southern mountain tradition, which usually have the poetic stresses coinciding exactly with the accented beats of the accompaniment. In the Negro talking blues

the lines are of approximately equal duration in time,
but may vary considerably in the number of words.
When the talking blues include singing, the performer
slips from speech to song and back so naturally that the
shift is scarcely perceptible. On records there is a significant number of examples of this tradition.[4]

As examples, Oster cites Bukka White's *Special Stream Line,*
Lightnin' Hopkins's *Come Go Home With Me* and six others,[5] but
one should not draw the conclusion that such pieces are in fact
common numerically.

For Minnie, Frankie Jean was a pet and companion. Her evocation of a race horse that her family owned and that won $5000
is meant as an entertaining fantasy for herself and her listeners,
for whom horses were almost entirely associated with physical labor
like ploughing. As Minnie's nephew said, the family had probably
owned a mule, and this was true for most of her listeners, if they
owned a work animal at all. It is *against* this association of mules
and work that Minnie constructs her song. By opposing play to
work in such a celebratory context, Minnie also accomplishes a utopian gesture of welcome to poetically insightful conceptions of the
relations of animals and human beings.

Indeed, all of our relationships are poetically restructured to
the extent that we allow our understanding of animals and our
relationship to animals to guide us in the poetic dimensions of
"normal" human relationships. This factor is responsible for
much of the appeal animal songs have for us, and while the dynamics of their vitality may remain unconscious in us, these
forces nonetheless account for much of the attraction animals
hold for humans. These notions are underscored by Minnie's father's instructing her that a "special" language with unconscious
meaning and power, whistling, is needed for communication with
her horse, and we are reminded here of the moans, shouts,
laughs and nonsense syllables that blues singers use to punctuate
their songs, moans and shouts which represent the unconscious,
the repressed and unknown, breaking through the web of conscious speech, just as whistling interrupts the futility of calling
Frankie Jean by name.

In Frankie Jean, whistling is emblematic of revolt from another point of view, for Minnie also breaks the taboo that insists that whistling is bad luck, especially when it's *women* that whistle. The notion that whistling is bad luck is common in the South, as is the rhyme,

> A whistling woman and a crowing hen
> Never come to any good end.[6]

In whistling for her horse, Minnie has told us so much more than we thought! Further, when she sang,

> One time my papa had a horse

she sang within a wider knowledge of meanings for "horse" than we may have realized: For her listeners, as well as for herself, "horse" was a word for conjuror, and it was used in New Orleans to refer to a voodoo priestess as well as a hoodoo doctor. Conjuration could even be carried out by a "Ponton," a cross between a man and a horse.[7] Conjure lore also refers to the riding of a possessed person as though he were a horse.[8] Against those who see the conveyance of a single concrete and specific meaning as the word's chief function, we remind them that words that are made for singing have no need of thought, for it is the imagination that engenders them. "The mind that imagines follows the opposite path of the mind that observes; the imagination does not want to end in a diagram that summarizes acquired learning."[9]

Our suggestions about listening to *Frankie Jean* are hardly the first time that women and horses have been linked within an imaginative fabric of liberation. In the iconography of the suffrage movment, the woman on a horse was an important symbol.[10] The horse has also been a figure of special autobiographical meaning in the work of surrealist painter and writer Leonora Carrington, and we may take it as a sign of another of those critical crossings that bid us to "stop and listen," to stop and understand, rather than to pass with only a casual glance. The listener who brings this special attention to Minnie's work will be amply rewarded.[11]

Five years later, Minnie took up the reins again. This time the impetus to do so came from a cow! Indeed, listening to Minnie's *Jockey Man Blues* (1935) and *Good Morning* (1936), it is impossible to miss the influence of Kokomo Arnold's extremely popular and influential *Milk Cow Blues* (1934), from which both of these songs derive in melody and in delivery.[12] Thematically, however, neither of Minnie's songs seem particularly close to Arnold's, but let's look more closely at *Jockey Man Blues*, where Minnie has heard Arnold's song about a milk cow/lover and has created an entirely different song about her own lover, her "jockey man." In spite of these textual differences, the songs have striking similarities in melody, rhythm, structure, and phrasing patterns.

JOCKEY MAN BLUES

Good morning, blues,
    please shake hands with me. (2x)
I've got the blues this morning,
just as low as I can be.

How can I sleep nights, baby,
    when you turn your back on me. (2x)
I'm gonna take my troubles,
go down by the sea.

You can eat 'n my kitchen, sleep in my bed,
Fall down in my arms, pretty papa,
Rest your worried head
Cause I need, need some loving now.
["need" done in falsetto]
I ain't got no one to love me, weeooo,
like you know how.

I woke up this morning
    with the rising sun. (2x)
My pretty papa's a jockey,
and he sure don't ride for fun.

If you see my jockey,
    I said please tell him hurry home. (2x)

I ain't had no loving, Lord,
Since my jockey been gone.

My jockey rode this morning,
   and my love come falling down. (2x)
Said, "I'll be your monkey woman,
but please don't lead me around."

Take a race horse to run,
A jockey to ride around,
Take a pretty sealskin papa,
Make my love come down.
Cause I don't feel welcome,
sleeping by myself.
Lord, since you went away and left me,
I don't want nobody else.

Kokomo Arnold's *Milk Cow Blues* and Memphis Minnie's *Jockey Man Blues* both begin with the same words, use similar phrasing, often share expressions, and even use falsetto delivery in similar parts of the songs. A like comparison could be made between *Milk Cow Blues* and Minnie's *Good Morning,* and while Minnie's text is farther removed in some ways, both songs are still very close in manner and melody.[13] Thus, an artist as creative as Minnie could rework another performer's song, in this case a hit, in such a way that it is at once recognizable as deriving from the other's song, while it is at the same time perceived as a new creation.[14]

Minnie's song is about her jockey who rides (her) in the morning, with great attention to her needs, i.e. "he sure don't ride for fun." This jockey, or lover, is a bit footloose, a "sealskin" (brown) papa whom she misses. Inspired by Arnold's barnyard metaphor, Minnie nonetheless delivers a more ambitious image by invoking a more glamorous animal, the racehorse, and by seizing the horse's rider for her own poetic needs, the jockey as opposed to the more standard "rider," suggesting superior, more experienced love-making skills. And yet an element of satire is maintained by the depiction of the male as a jockey, i.e. a tiny man.

The use of "jockey" by men as a blues convention meaning "rider" or lover does not contradict our idea as much as it reaffirms it. The satire, intentional or not, is more powerful because the usage is borrowed from the male to be used against him, as it were.[15] This is only another example of Minnie's *miniaturization of males by metaphor,* and it is interesting to note that of our two examples of songs about horses, *Jockey Blues* leads us back to the domain of bumble bees and insects, while *Frankie Jean* invokes an entirely different set of associations.

18. TRAINS AND TRAVEL

*We must have liberty. . . . Free air and free water! . . . Freedom
to move, to act, to speak; freedom to be still, to look, to be silent.*
— Ithell Colquhoun

The travel blues are as natural to a blues artist's repertoire as
the many blues on love and love's frustrations. Because the blues
originated in the minds of a disenfranchised people seeking liberation from geographically confining and repressive aspects of life,
because the blues artists and their listeners often fled the South
in search of freedom, travel became one of the primary *vital signs*
of the blues.

While it is impossible to understand the blues without some
comprehension of its relationship to migration patterns of blacks
leaving, and returning to, the South, such an understanding is often
a self-imposed dead-end for the literal-minded and demographi-
cally-minded listeners who too easily come to see travel as only a
physical, geographic activity. For example, not all migrants abandoned the South irrevocably, and many returned to the South to
visit friends and relatives, to help with chores, or to convince
friends to come North with them. Some even returned to the South
to live.[1] Memphis and other Southern cities were regular performance stops for touring Northern musicians, especially in the vaudeville years when TOBA theaters were scattered across the South.
But the journey, in any direction, is only one dimension of traveling.

Because both the blues and travel can be mental activities, as well, we are justified in turning to the travel blues in an attempt to understand the appeal of both the blues and traveling. Within the desire to escape the South can be found the affection for family and friends who remain behind, and ambivalence marks the travel songs just as it marks our desire to travel. Minnie's songs are no exception, of course, and in many of her pieces, the ambivalence that may run beneath the surface of a song like *'Frisco Town* appears as sexual conflict in most of the song's verses.

Other singers have specified their reasons for travel, and while many have sung that they were going away "just to wear you off my mind,"[2] commentary has been more diverse. Charlie Patton sang of traveling to flee the flood waters of the Mississippi River,[3] and others sang of traveling North to find new employment[4] or of traveling back to the South where the weather was warm.[5] Kokomo Arnold sang a variation on that theme, when he bemoaned his run of hard luck:

> Lord, if the black cat blues
> don't leave me, mama, Lord,
> I got to get further on down the road.[6]

Son Bonds' contention reminds us that the usual catalog of "reasons" for the travel blues is rarely exhaustive and only plumbs the surface:

> Now the reason I'm traveling,
> just to make you lonesome here.[7]

Travel also operates as a status symbol for the blues singer who invokes glamorous locales, of and about which many listeners may have only heard.[8] Memphis, Detroit, Chicago, Texas, Tennessee, Walls, Algiers, Louisiana, these place names work their magic upon the mind with little difficulty, so willing are we to integrate journeys and destinations into the complex nature of our lives and plans. The magic of place names and the power of personal names unite at a critical junction where pseudonyms like "Texas Slim," "Chicago Sunny Boy," and "Memphis Minnie" create a totemic geography of their own.

We may also approach the travel blues from the perspective of the various means of transportation employed. In Minnie's repertoire, the car as symbolic object gains ascendancy over the highway number and the train. First, however, let us look at Minnie's songs that are about trains. *Mr. Tango Blues* is about a lover leaving town by train, whereas *Chickasaw Train Blues* depicts the train as a powerful separator of lovers.

CHICKASAW TRAIN BLUES
(LOW DOWN DIRTY THING)

I'm gonna tell everybody what that
   Chickasaw have done done for me. (2x)
She done stole my man away
and blowed that doggone smoke on me,
She's a low down dirty dog.

[I] ain't no woman
   like to ride that Chickasaw. (2x)
Because everywhere she stops,
she's stealing some woman's good man off,
She's a low down dirty dog.

I told the depot agent this morning,
   I don't think he treats me right. (2x)
He done sold my man a ticket and
know that Chickasaw leaving town tonight,
He's a low down dirty dog.

I walked down the railroad track,
   that Chickasaw wouldn't even let me ride
   the blinds. (2X)
And she stops, picking up men,
all up and down the line,
She's a low down dirty dog.

> Hmmm, Chickasaw don't pay
> > no woman no mind. (2x)
> And she stops, picking up men
> all up and down the line.

In this song, the train is a woman who takes other women's men, and not the typical masculine symbol of power. Where Minnie does say *"he's* a low down dirty dog," she is referring to the depot agent and not the train. It has long been thought that *Chickasaw Train Blues* referred to a local freight train in the Memphis/Ripley area, but the Chickasaw was actually a fast *passenger* train run by the Illinois Central. It was christened January 13, 1924, ten years before Minnie's record was issued.[9] The Chickasaw ran from Memphis north to St. Louis, and its route carried it through Ripley, Tennessee, birthplace of Sleepy John Estes, into the western tip of Kentucky and into Cairo, at the southern tip of Illinois, before arriving at Carbondale, Illinois, a principal stop. The train then wound through many Illinois hamlets into Belleville and East St. Louis before finally crossing the state line into Missouri and St. Louis. The trip took about eight hours, and as late as 1962, you could still ride the Chickasaw from Memphis to St. Louis.

In *I'm Going Don't You Know*, an upbeat song about a pleasant trip, Minnie misses the train entirely.

I'M GOING DON'T YOU KNOW

> Train's at the station, don't you know,
> Who all goin'? Let me hear you blow.
> Hey, hey,
> Hey, hey,
> Everybody going,
> Yes, I'm going, don't you know.
>
> Everybody's got their ticket, where is mine?
> Look like to me I'm gonna be left behind.
> Hey, hey, etc.
>
> *Spoken:* Now, play it for me this time.
>
> Now, go home and pack up everything you got.

Please don't bring that old run down clock.
Hey, hey, etc.

Now don't keep me waiting
on the corner so long,
Train's at the station and she soon be gone.
Hey, hey, etc.

Spoken: Now, swing you cats.

You done fooled around here
and made me miss that train.
Now I got to catch me a air-o-plane.
Hey, hey, etc.

Well, everybody going, baby,
and I wants to go, too.
Don't you hear me talking
that sweet talk to you.
Hey, hey, etc.

Many blues singers are mighty travelers and the vicissitudes of rail travel can strongly affect their lives.[10] While Minnie and Joe began their recording career traveling 1100 miles to New York to record for Columbia, by that time, Minnie was in her early thirties and had traveled and performed in many states of the South, Texas probably among them, and she may have been to Chicago several times as well. *Goin' Back to Texas* was the first song Minnie sang on record; it was the third song of the session, the first two having been solo vocals by Joe McCoy, *I Want That* and *That Will Be Alright*. Like *Goin' Back to Texas*, *'Frisco Town* also evoked far away places.

FRISCO TOWN

That old 'Frisco train
   makes a mile a minute. (2x)
Well, in that old coach,
I'm gonna sit right in it.
I'm on my way, to 'Frisco town.

You can toot your whistle,
   you can ring your bell. (2x)
But I know you been wanting it
by the way you smell.
I'm on my way to 'Frisco town.

There's a boa constrictor
   and a lemon stick. (2x)
I don't mind being with you
but my mama's sick.
I'm on my way to 'Frisco town.

I would tell you what's they matter,
   but I done got scared. (2x)
You got to wait now, until we go to bed.
I'm on my way to 'Frisco town.

If you was sick, I wouldn't worry you. (2x)
I wouldn't want you to do
something that you couldn't do.
I'm on my way to 'Frisco town.

Well, if you want it, you can get it,
   and I ain't mad.(2x)
If you tell me this is something
that you ain't never had.
I'm on my way to 'Frisco town.

Lookahere, you get mad
   everytime I call your name. (2x)
I ain't never told you
that you couldn't get that thing.
I'm on my way to 'Frisco town.

I woke up this morning
   about half past five. (2x)
My baby turned over,
cried just like a child.
I'm on my way to 'Frisco town.

I got something to tell you,
   I don't want to make you mad. (2x)

I got something for you,
make you feel glad.
I'm on my way to 'Frisco town.

Lookahere, lookahere,
   what you want me to do. (2x)
Give you my jelly, then die for you.
I'm on my way to 'Frisco town.

I got something to tell you,
   gonna break your heart. (2x)
We been together so far,
we gotta get apart.
I'm on my way to 'Frisco town.

Like many of Minnie's songs, *'Frisco Town* was taken up by other performers. Only a few months after Minnie's first record was released, pianist James "Boodle It" Wiggins recorded it for Paramount as *Frisco Bound*.[11] More recently, the modern folk blues guitarist Larry Johnson, also performed *'Frisco Town*.[12]

The title, as well as the lyrics, suggested to many that the 'Frisco Train was simply the train bound for San Francisco. Actually, the Frisco Railway was formed by the merger of the St. Louis and San Francisco lines, and it was a major transportation company in Minnie's Memphis. It not only ran trains from Memphis to Kansas City, Chicago, St. Louis, and other cities, but it also ran a commuter train from the outskirts of Memphis to the center of town.

The travel blues can signify liberation in diverse ways. When Minnie is on her way to 'Frisco Town, or on the way back to Texas, she is outdoors and *beyond confinement*, beyond the standard conception of the role a black girl from a deep South farm family was expected to fill. The highly rhythmic guitar artistry we hear on songs like *She Wouldn't Give Me None, New Dirty Dozen* or *'Frisco Town* easily evokes the notion of Minnie moving, while the lyrics of the travel blues represent a linguistic outmaneuvering of confinement itself. The implicit hope of freedom was often lodged in the location of the recording studio, either in the promised land of Chicago or New York. But the train that carried one there could represent despair as well as hope. What signaled rambling freedom for the male who was on his way north to record, might represent only desertion for the female left behind.[13] In our case, however, it was the female herself who was on the way north to record. Minnie's repertoire contains references to more orthodox travel. *'Frisco Town* began with Minnie sitting in the coach section of the 'Frisco train, and in *Poor and Wandering Woman*, she isn't thinking about "riding the blinds" as she was in *Chickasaw Train Blues*; rather, she sings "I've got my ticket in my hand." Yet at other times, she took to the highways on foot.

We know that Minnie began traveling at an early age, as young as thirteen years old, according to some reports. In *In My Girlish Days*, she notes she was "Trying to run away from that home of mine" in "1917," i.e. at the age of twenty. This information is not necessarily autobiographical, however, or it may refer to one of many such incidents, but we do know the truth of her traveling and that life on the road for a wandering girl or woman must have been exceedingly difficult. Unlike the male blues singer/wanderer, Minnie had no coterie of female hobos with whom to make common cause. In spite of the many references in the blues to hoboing, few are made by or about women. Indeed, female hobos and wanderers were uncommon during the earlier years that Minnie made her own way from town to town. By the time she gave up this mode of travel, female hobos were becoming much more common and the Depression was deepening. The Depression put many women on the road, just as it multiplied the number of men already wandering, but women never accounted for more than a tiny percent of the hoboing population.[14]

It is easy to imagine the degree of opposition against which Minnie had to struggle as a maker and performer of black women's hobo songs.[15] Facing powerful odds, she achieved visibility and audibility by the process of transforming the content and shape of her wanderings into the subject of her songs, and ultimately, into her own subjectivity. The songs themselves became the currency of her fame.

Isolated references to hoboing are scattered throughout her work, like this line from *Drunken Barrel House Blues*: "Folks, I ain't got no money, but I can hobo on out of town."

But the hobo experience is fully articulated in two late songs, *Nothing in Rambling* (1940) and *In My Girlish Days* (1941).

NOTHING IN RAMBLING

I was born in Louisiana,
I was raised in Algiers,
And everywhere I been, the peoples all say,
Ain't nothing in rambling,
Either running around.
Well, I believe I'll marry,
Oooo, wooo, Lord, and settle down.

I first left home, I stopped in Tennessee,
The peoples all begging,
"Come and stay with me."
'Cause ain't nothing in rambling, etc.

I was walking through the alley
with my hand in my coat.
The police start to shoot me,
thought it was something I stole.
You know it ain't nothing in rambling, etc.

The peoples on the highway
is walking and crying,
Some is starving, some is dying.
You know it ain't nothing in rambling, etc.

You may go to Hollywood
and try to get on the screen.
But I'm gonna stay right here
and eat these old charity beans.
'Cause it ain't nothing in rambling, etc.

IN MY GIRLISH DAYS

Late hours at night, trying to play my hand,
Through my window, out stepped a man.
I didn't know no better,

Oh boys,
In my girlish days.

My mama cried, Papa did, too,
Ooh, daughter, look what a shame on you.
I didn't know no better, etc.

I flagged a train, didn't have a dime,
Trying to run away from that home of mine.
I didn't know no better, etc.

I hit the highway, caught me a truck,
Nineteen and seventeen,
when the winter was tough.
I didn't know no better, etc.

Spoken: Lord, play it for me now.

All of my playmates is not surprised,
I had to travel 'fore I got wise.
I found out better,
And I still got my girlish ways.

In the latter song we see a "shameful" incident as the motive
for flagging a train or hitting the highway, the difficulty of life on
the road, and the suggestion that she got wise during her travels,
as her friends thought she would. But, Minnie continues, she hasn't
changed that much; in fact, she's "still got [her] girlish ways."

Nothing in Rambling may have been built around an incident
from Minnie's life and experience. Daisy recalled, "I heard her say
something about she was walking down the street and they arrested
her, but they turned her loose. She had her hand in her pocket
and I guess they thought she had something. She didn't have nothing."[16] The ending of the song is a bit more "mature," i.e. pessi-
mistic and conservative. There is in fact *nothing* in rambling, and
as a consequence, she has given it up. A youthful sense of adventure is replaced with an adult fondness for security. Or is it? Is
life on the road so hard that even a diet of welfare beans is pref-
erable, or is there irony in the punch line as Minnie reminds us
that the temptation in adulthood is the regressive desire to place
the imagination on a bland diet?

As a blues singer, Minnie is both a self-appointed and freely elected representative of the black working class, subject to recall and kept in office mainly by popular vote. This constituency also provides the contexts which are transformed through the poetic act. The blues serves an educational as well as an inspirational function as poetically transformed ideas are returned to the lives of the listeners. As their songs can be the vehicles for the substance and making of black history, the singers become wandering scholar/interpreters, stopping here and there to give short lectures to an admiring populace, in each instance acquiring new material to be presented at the next occasion.[17]

It would be unreasonable, of course, to expect the forces of repression to not notice this, too, and their typical response was a demand for censorship. In 1835, for example, the editor of a French music magazine insisted that street singers, whose critical function was similar to that of the blues singer, be brought under government control. Instead of celebrating the good life, i.e. alcohol and sex, "the people would hear praise for the love of labor, sobriety, economy, charity and above all the love of humanity."[18]

To the same end, the street singer was and is often classed as a bum or vagrant, relieving those in power from the formality of having to justify police surveillance. With or without guitar, however, their fate is often the same, and a hundred years after the source quoted above, the Mississippi Sheiks reminded their listeners:

> Times seem so hard
>   look like my road have turned to stone. (2x)
> When every friend you have done
> shook hands and gone.
>
> There's a man named Pete,
>   he walks the street each and every day. (2x)
> And if the time don't get better,
> he will run the loafing man away.[19]

Nearly every society has their minstrels, or street singers, or they have someone who performs this function.[20] Close to the blues singers in many ways are the *griots*, traveling African musicians whose role in the community is analogous to the blues singer's role in the black communities of the US, although many differences still prevail: Some griots become rich (as only a few blues singers have), while others are hired to sing the praises of the rich (which few blues singers are likely to do). Others are poor and lowly. They are often able to sing lengthy epic histories of various tribes and families,[21] and one critic called them walking libraries of generations of living books.[22]

Another group of Minnie's songs that are linked by the themes of wandering and hoboing includes *Outdoor Blues, Out in the Cold* and World of Trouble. In all of them, the cold plays a prominent role. Here is the earliest of the three, *Outdoor Blues* (1932):

OUTDOOR BLUES

One cold night,
   I was out in the frost and snow. (2x)
I didn't have a penny,
I couldn't find no place to go.

Way down the lane,
   I thought I see'd a fire. (2x)
'Fore I could make it there to warm my hands,
the hobos had put it out.
I was so cold
   my feets was near about froze. (2x)
And I didn't have a penny,
I couldn't find no place to go.

I come to a house,
   I knocked up on the door. (2x)
They wouldn't accept my company
because I didn't have on no clothes.

Hmmm, my feets was near about froze. (2x)
I didn't have a penny,
I couldn't find no place to go.

I looked and saw

old lady standing in the door. (2x)
She said, "Come in, daughter,
how in the world that you trying to go?"

Several significant and recurring themes appear in this song:
Homelessness, the freezing cold, lack of money and, implicitly, running away. The scene is vividly drawn where the song's protagonist
arrives at the hobo jungle only to find the fire extinguished. Many
of the themes in *Outdoors Blues* recur in *Out in the Cold*, although
in the latter song, the woman's homelessness has been explicitly
forced upon her. Again the freezing cold is used to give substance
and materiality to loneliness, as it is also in *World of Trouble*, and
she is thus able to intensify our perception of the cruelty being
thrust upon her when her shocked voice sings:

That was *me* last night, hoo, hoo, you drove from your door!

The full lyrics of both songs follow. *Out in the Cold* was supported by a stubbornly insistent rhythm and the lilting clarity of
Black Bob's piano. *World of Trouble* was a two-fisted, Chicago,
postwar blues.

OUT IN THE COLD

I dreamt a dream last night
    I never dreamt before. (2x)
And when I woke up this morning,
(My trunk was setting outdoors).

I didn't have no money,
    I couldn't find me no place to go. (2x)
So that left me and my trunk,
(setting) out in the cold.

That was me last night, hoo, hoo,
you drove from your door. (2x)
Why you wouldn't let me in,
the reason I sure don't know.

So that left me out here wandering
   up and down this old lonesome road. (2x)
I'm just wandering, wondering,
whichaway must I go.

Hmmmmm,
   my feets are near about froze. (2x)
I've been to a many house this morning,
and won't nobody open the door.

WORLD OF TROUBLE

It's a cold, cold morning,
   I was out in the rain and snow. (2x)
Yes, in a world of trouble,
I couldn't find no place to go.

The wind was blowing
   and the rain began to freeze. (2x)
So much of trouble,
Lord, have mercy on me.

Standing on the corner,
   my friends all was passing by. (2x)
Well, I cried so much,
Lord, I didn't have no tears to dry.

My brother, he's in trouble,
my Dad he just broke jail,
My man, he's in trouble,
and the law is on his trail.
It's a cold, cold morning,
and I'm out in the rain and snow.
Yes, in a world of trouble,
I had no place to go.

The cold is a time-honored theme in the blues, and many singers refer to it, especially in the context of the cold and unfriendly North that has been disappointing and has evoked the desire to return to the warm and familiar South. As the Mississippi Sheiks sang,

> I'm staying in the house,
>> I'd just as soon be outdoors. (2x)
> I'll have to go back South
> where the weather suits my clothes.[23]

Jazz Gillum's *Down South Blues* expresses similar sentiments, but in Bobo Jenkins's *10 Below Zero*, as in Minnie's *Out in the Cold*, it is the lover's decision that has caused the songs' protagonists to be out in the cold in the first place.[24]

Out in the Cold also has an ambiguous quality precipitated by its initial verse, and it is unclear whether or not the entire song is a dream, a dream that *begins* with the second line, i.e. "I dreamed that I woke to find my trunk outdoors." Or does only the first line refer to the dream, with the rest of the song describing what happened when she woke from the dream? There is no final or correct answer to this question, but there are many occasions in blues and in other varieties of folklore where dreams are interpreted either as predictors of the immediate future or in the light of the stimulus that is said to "cause" them. If Minnie's dream in *Out in the Cold* is one of the former class, let us quote two of the latter class as well. In *Broken Bed Blues*, the Kansas City Blues Strummers sang,

> I dreamt last night
>> my bed was falling down (2x)
> It must have been my sweetie
> certainly leaving town.

Furry Lewis sang a variation of the same idea:

> I dreamt last night
>> the world was caving in. (2x)
> Wasn't nothing a'tall
> but my girl coming home again.[25]

Dreams can be significant in blues from other perspectives, as well. Charlie Patton's niece said that Patton used to "dream a song, and he'd get up and write them"—sometimes his wife would write them down and Patton would then go off in a room by himself and work up the tune.[26] Eugene Powell noted that he learned at least one excellent guitar piece from a dream, adding that the "jet black man [with the] long fingers" who played guitar in his dream was "nothing but the devil."[27] J. B. Lenoir said that he dreamed his best lyrics,[28] and James "Son" Thomas, blues singer and sculptor, also specifies the inspirational function of dreams:

> The futures come in dreams. The dreams just come to me. I lay down and dream about the sculpture, about how to fix one of the heads, things like that. I'm liable to dream anything. That give you in your head what to do.[29]

Memphis Minnie, having dreamed herself outdoors, has, in her song, suggested a new way to hear her songs: The outdoor blues, with their imagery of deprivation, pain, and cold can be heard not only as a metaphoric reenactment of black working-class life under white capitalism, and beneath that, the life of the black woman under male domination, but also as a metaphor for the dangers inherent in trying to step *outside* white domination and the domination of male lovers and parents.[30]

These are not the only perspectives through which Minnie's travel blues can be viewed, however. Unlike many male singers, Minnie does not often sing about the much traveled highways and their numbers: *49 Highway*, by Big Joe Williams; *New Highway 51*, by Tommy McClennan; *80 Highway Blues*, by Son Bonds; *101 Highway* by Jimmy McCracklin.[31] No doubt Minnie heard most or all of these, but she felt no desire or need to make room for such pieces in her recorded repertoire. For Minnie, the highways may have been more cold and hostile than tempting and enticing, and this is reflected in her songs. Indeed, in Minnie's case, one is struck more by the mechanics of travel than by the path or destination. Propelled by eroticism, it is the automobile that travels through an entire range of meaning in Minnie's songs.

Her interest in automobiles first surfaces in *Can I Do It For You?*, recorded in 1930 at her third recording session.[32] In this latter song, Joe makes nine offers, the first eight of which are refused, before Minnie decides to accept a "Sedan Ford" in exchange for letting Joe "do something" to, or for, her. The listener is surprised, especially as she had already refused a Chevrolet! Then we realize that in seeing Minnie as hard to please, we are taken in the same way Joe was... she intended to accept all along! And of course, this is the axis around which the song's humor revolves. If to the male singer, the car is pervasively sexual, Minnie is not only capable of seizing this usually male perogative, but of extending the car's emblematic significance as a sign of status, wealth and success; to this she will add the notion of freedom as one of the automobile's metaphoric possibilities.

Six months after her third session, Minnie recorded the richly textured *Garage Fire Blues*, which along with *Grandpa and Grandma Blues* was released as by "Memphis Minnie and Her Jug Band," actually her Memphis colleagues, Jed Davenport and His Beale Street Jug Band. In *Garage Fire Blues*, the threat of fire is actually transformed by the flames until there emerges from the smoke and ashes, Minnie's two magisterial road agents, the car and the chauffeur. We say "ashes" because the lyrics suggest the chauffeur saved the car(s) rather than the garage.

GARAGE FIRE BLUES

My house on fire,
    where's the fire wagon now? (2x)
Ain't but the one thing,
I don't want my garage to burn down.

I got a Hudson Super Six,
    I gotta big old model Cadillac 8. (2x)
I woke up this morning,
my Cadillac standing at my back gate.

Oh, boys, boys,
    I got the best chauffeur in town. (2x)
He saved my Hudson Super Six,
my Cadillac didn't get burned down.

Oh, lord, lord,
    wonder where is my chauffeur now? (2x)

'Cause my Cadillac 8
done Cadillac'd out of town.

I tell the whole wide world,
   I ain't gonna walk no more. (2x)
I got a Cadillac 8,
take me anywhere I want to go.

In Minnie's lexicon, "chauffeur" is not just another word for
lover. If a chauffeur is, in fact, a "hired driver, usually on long
term lease," Minnie may be telling us that man's lack of dependability is so chronic that the only way a woman can have a comfortable relationship with a man is to hire one! And by the fourth
verse, this "best chauffeur in town" has already disappeared, along
with the Cadillac 8. Minnie seems perfectly content by the fifth
verse, however, because the *car* is back in her possession, the
chauffeur wandering aimlessly, to be beckoned back to recording
ten years later, just in time to star in Minnie's biggest hit song:

ME AND MY CHAUFFEUR BLUES

Wants to see my chauffeur,
Wants to see my chauffeur,
I wants him to drive me,
I wants him to drive me downtown.
Says he drives so easy,
I can't turn him down.

But I don't want him,
But I don't want him,
To be riding these girls,
To be riding these girls around.
So I'm gonna steal me a pistol,
shoot my chauffeur down.

Well, I must buy him,
Well, I must buy him,
A brand new V-8,
A brand new V-8 Ford.
Then he won't need no passengers,

I will be his load.

Spoken: Yeah, take it away.

Going to let my chauffeur,
Going to let my chauffeur,
Drive me around the,
Drive me around the world.
Then he can be my little boy,
Yes, I'll be his girl.[33]

Me and My Chauffeur became so widely identified with Minnie that Lightnin' Hopkins felt compelled to "answer" her with a song of his own, *Automobile*:

I saw you riding around,
   you riding in a brand new automobile. (2x)
Yes, you were sitting there happy
with your handsome driver at the wheel,
in your brand new automobile.[34]

In Minnie's *Me and My Chauffeur*, the driver and the ride itself most obviously referred to a lover and sexual activity, but without the metaphoric maneuverability of *Garage Fire*. And if, earlier, there had been a puzzling excitability to "cadillac'd out of town," *Me and My Chauffeur* didn't clarify the situation. Neither did Big Bill who "explained" it this way in 1935, again demonstrating how many songs seem to be about other songs, and how often the singers seem to sing to each other.

Some low-down man learned my baby
   how to Cadillac 8. (2x)
Now, Lord,
ever since she's learned that position,
I can't keep my business straight.[35]

Walter Roland commands the same principles into a different configuration:

These here women
  what call theyselves a Cadillac
  ought to be a T-Model Ford. (2x)
You know, they got the shape alright, but
they can't carry no heavy load.[36]

We have included the 1939 *Call the Fire Wagon* here because
it is connected to the above song(s) not only through the medium
of *fire,* but because it, too, is about a car, or in this case, a wagon.

CALL THE FIRE WAGON

I was talking to the people that lives in town,
Y' ever had the shack
and your clothes burn down?
So call the fire wagon,
Call the fire wagon,
Call the fire wagon,
Ain't no fire wagon in town.

Saved my baby and my wardrobe trunk,
I lost everything else I had in front.
So call the fire wagon, etc.

Standing on the streets
in my sleeping gown,
Watching that shack
and my clothes burn down.
Call the fire wagon, etc.

Fast asleep laying in my bed.
Lord, this smoke is 'bout to kill me dead.
So call the fire wagon, etc.

Spoken: Play it till the fire wagon comes.
Yeah.

This big city's all right
but I'm so far from town,

> A shack catches fire,
> you know it's got to burn down.
> So call the fire wagon, etc.
>
> Well, the jinx overtaken us, now,
> and carrying us down,
> Me and my baby got to leave this town.
> So call the fire wagon, etc.

Minnie tells us that this song about a personal tragedy is not a tragedy itself when she offers the spoken comment, "Play it till the fire wagon comes." We are reminded that we are at a song, not at a houseburning where such a comment would be inappropriate.[37] Thus, Minnie herself guards against a too-literal interpretation, while the song itself redefines her role, temporarily, as a traditional one, for it has always been the women, "professional mourners, who rendered grief public, be it in regard to death, to suffering, or to the victims of massacres. . . ." But because this was one of the few public roles for women, it was already easy to ignore them when they began decrying their own lot.[38]

Fire changes everything, and Minnie's song depicts changes on two levels. The song itself depicts a sudden and dramatic change in the life of the person whose house and belongings were destroyed by the fire. Even more dramatically *Call the Fire Wagon* is distinguished by a change in style: The song has an intense rural flavor, with the intricate guitar picking evoking a 1930 Vocalion rather than a 1939 one. That Minnie could do this is interesting; that she did so is unusual. Perhaps she missed the old style, perhaps a fan persuaded her to do an older-sounding piece, perhaps she wanted to test the market for her old sound versus the market for the style she had been playing in since around 1935. What she thought about it and why she did it are likely to remain secrets.

With the style of nine years earlier, Minnie also recalls a subject from that period, flames and fire. But in the earlier song, *Garage Fire Blues*, fire as a burning passion was quickly seized and the flames of destruction evaporated within the progression of the metaphor, not to mention the humorous attitude a jug band often helped to evoke. Indeed *Garage Fire Blues* was really a heated incubation tank for *Me and My Chauffeur Blues*. Further, *Garage Fire Blues* is only a starting point for a vehicular discourse on lovemaking, and we may see it as a sort of erotic kindling. But in *Call the Fire Wagon*, fire is a destroyer whose unconscious sexual aspects creep beneath the burning house to hint at the destruction of love as well.

The creative/destructive role of fire is only hinted at in *Garage Fire Blues*. Yet its importance in our lives is demonstrated by the importance of fire and the dream of change at the heart of alchemy,[39] which has proved to be so powerful an influence on surrealism and the most inspired of modern poets. For the dream of change is at the heart of so many blues, particularly those songs that seem to be carefully balanced on a razor's edge of high emotion, daring the least event to detonate into chaos.

In Minnie's songs, much of this transformative power is shared by the automobile, which ultimately comes to represent *a vehicle for desire*. Yet this notion hardly exhausts the liberating potential of this image of transport. For example, Simone de Beauvoir has reminded us of how a woman's freedom may be only illusory, how the Virginia Woolf of *A Room of One's Own* may have had the freedom to go for a ride on an omnibus, but not in such a way as to protect her from what Beauvoir called "disagreeable incidents." Indeed, Beauvoir noted that a woman's preoccupation with the possibility of such incidents "rivets her to the ground. 'Your wings droop.' "[40] Such incidents still occur, of course, but they were strongly opposed by Memphis Minnie's "I drink anywhere I please," and routed terribly, if not ultimately, when the omnibus carrying Woolf, Beauvoir and the fantasies of all women smarting under the pain of "disagreeable incidents" stopped on that December afternoon in Montgomery, Alabama, in 1955 and picked up Rosa Parks on her way home from work.

19. MAD LOVE

Long poem as a long river
Go to whoever will love.
—Valentine Penrose

Songs about madness are not unusual in the blues, but there are not a great number of them. Passing references, however, are numerous and somewhat consistent: The low-down ways of the spouse or lover are causing the song's protagonist to "lose my mind." Minnie's scattered references to going crazy or being driven insane stretch from one end of her work to the other, from *Crazy Crying Blues* in 1931 to *Mean Mistreater Blues* in 1944 and *Tears On My Pillow* in 1949.

MEAN MISTREATER BLUES

I have the blues at all times,
   they worry me night and day. (2x)
They fall so hard at times,
till they send my mind away.

Once I had a mistreater,
   kept accusing me of someone else. (2x)
When it come to a showdown,
he was stepping out himself.

I give him all of my money, my love,
   my everything. (2x)

He stays sweet all the winter,
jumps salty in the spring.

Spoken: Low down dog. That's a nasty man.

I give up all of my pleasure,
    forsaken all of my friends. (2x)
But now the way he been doing,
I declare it's a crying sin.

Such ideas receive their sharpest and most intense focus in *Crazy Crying Blues:*

CRAZY CRYING BLUES

I been going crazy,
    I just can't help myself.
    Ahhhhuuuuhahhhh. (2x)
Because the man I'm loving,
he's loving someone else.

Spoken: You know I'm bound to cry.

Ahhhhaaahhhhuuuuhhuh. (2x)
Ahhhhaaahhhhuuuuhhuh.

I was locked outdoors,
    sat on my steps all night long and cried.
    Ahhhhaaahhhuuuhhhaaah. (2x)
I'm going crazy, crazy as I can be.

I got up this morning,
    I made a fire in my stove.
    Ahhhhaaahhhuuuhhhaaah. (2x)
I made up my bread and sat my pan outdoors.

I'm crazy, I'm crazy, just can't help myself.
    Ahhhhaaahhhuuuhhhaaah. (2x)
I'm just as crazy, crazy as a poor girl can be.

Ahhhhaaahhhhuuuuhhuh. (2x)
Ahhhhaaahhhhuuuuhhuh.

By establishing her position outside the limits of normal experience, in a bleak and dark terrain where the sane principles of daily living seem banned, Minnie insists we focus our attention on certain dangers: The choice between challenging the norms of her time and possibly risking madness, or accepting the normal roles of gender assignment and living a life of diurnal quietude and barren hopes. Minnie chose to challenge the limitations and to go beyond them, echoing the risk in a song that, on the surface, implies that a disruption in erotic relations can indeed drive one mad, so much so that even the automatic gestures of living become disorganized. Most compelling is the image of the locked out woman, sitting on her porch steps crying all night long, her back turned in vain on the house that has turned its back on her.

And yet this song has a haunting quality that takes us beyond its obvious meaning. Minnie achieved distinction by choosing the life of a blues-singing guitarist. Not satisfied with being able to "play like a man" or "as good as any man," she became better than most of them. She was an extraordinary artist who placed herself in a position that must have caused (and been caused by) extraordinary pleasure, extraordinary pressure and extraordinary pain. Thus, the crying and the tears that are so often mentioned in her songs, like the song above about madness itself,[1] these images help us to understand how truly *heroic* her life really was. The very victory of her achievement always outshines and outlasts the depictions of conflict in the lyrics themselves. Thus, Minnie's "motto," as it were, might be a paraphrase of Shelley's *Ozymandias* (1817). Where Shelley wrote, "Look on my works, ye Mighty, and despair." Minnie declares:

> LOOK ON MY WORKS,
> YE DESPAIRING, AND BE MIGHTY!

Another way in which the blues is radical and revolutionary is how it functions as a visionary means: Even when sung in repressive language of the present, it still reaches for a liberated future. In much the same way, but through a more complex skein of the dialectic, the mad and the insane act as the harbingers of progess. For it is only through the disreputable and the disrupting, the profane and the sinister, i.e., through evil itself, that progress first manifests itself, usually in the form of transitional beings who venture into the unexplored and dangerous land to return to civilization with strange acquisitions, the methods and tools of progress, inevitably denounced by the society for whom the gifts are gathered. The price is the explorer's sanity, even while the "civilization" continues to go forward because of her. The insane and the mad are thus essential to society's progress, and they stand at all crossroads, "resting upon the historical faults" that produced them, embodying and declaiming the very text of the junction for all travelers everywhere.[2] The best known example of such a being is, of course, the Ancient Mariner, but history is full of such ferryman who appear as if by magic, not only at the crossroads, but at the very gates of hell itself.

To struggle against the oppressive forces of the times, one may risk madness and defeat, but the fruits of even a partial victory are the rents in the fabric of white male bourgeois rule. Madness, like crime, provides its own critique of society, but at a high cost to the subject, who can easily be declared "mad" as a means of social control. The successful evasion of the punitive hand of "justice" can be accomplished by the "monster woman" who is selfish because she refuses to be selfless. These women have given themselves the mission of having a story to tell because they have determined that their life will have a story of its own (and not just a footnote in someone else's biography.)

Minnie was one of these women, and heeding Fourier's cry of "Absolute Divergence," she determined she would go where others had not. In a culture where a constant danger was the precipitation into invisibility, Minnie became the "visible woman," perhaps a new metaphor for a blues novel of tomorrow. Her celebration of her own sexuality, her straight forward presentation of her own needs and desires according to her own rules, but in terms and methods, words and phrases, usually reserved for male speech, should remind us again and again how many steps forward the blueswoman has taken for us all. Minnie sang these words in her *Walking And Crying Blues:*

Mens walk on womens nowadays
    just like tramping on the grass. (2x)
Anytime you walk on me, wheeoo,
that's your yas, yas, yas.

If these notes on madness and alienated states flow naturally to and from the blues, it is no accident that we find love nearby, for we are used to the notion of extreme passion as at once the most delirious and the most liberating of mental states. Of course, the blues would be at home on such a ground! As the blues reflects our desires, it projects the imaginative possibilities of an eros-affirming existence, and provides us with an equally accurate picture of the frustration of this desire. But love is the power that can extend eros into our daily living, and, as Franklin Rosemont has argued, the struggle for a non-alienated eros should be a principal task of all radical as well as poetic activists.[3] Long ago Romanian surrealists Gherasim Luca and Trost declared that "love is the revolutionary method proper to surrealism," and in 1968 other surrealists specified, "The role of surrealism is to tear language away from the repressive system and to make it the instrument of desire."[4] As we invoke one more assessment of the role of eros in our daily lives, we can't help but notice that in all three observations, the subject of commentary could as easily have been the blues as surrealism: "To love, above all. There always will be time later to interrogate ourselves about what we love enough to want to be ignorant of nothing. Before and after such an inquiry, intimate resonance counts most; without it at the outset one is almost irremediably deprived, and nothing to be learned can replace it if it be lost on the way. The evidence of this is daily reinforced by many '*textual analyses*' seeking to reduce the obscurities of a poem while what matters first and foremost is that, on the affective level, the *contact* spontaneously establish itself and the *current* pass, carrying its receiver to the point where no obstacle may be made of these very obscurities. . . . We must insist: *Only the gates of emotion provide access to the royal road; the roads of knowledge, otherwise, lead nowhere.*"[5]

But the basic, poetic relationships taken for granted in the blues often come as a shock to more sophisticated critics. How can this be? Are poets remiss? Is the *erotic message* for which poets are responsible a secret?

> Poetry is made in a bed like love
> Its rumpled sheets
> are the dawn of things. . . .[6]

> Love
> like anybody else,
> comes to those who wait actively
> and leave their windows open.[7]

If we exalt love as possessing within itself a perfect self-sufficiency, we insist that it establishes a structural precedent for solutions of every kind: the disavowal of the logical method and the abandonment of the self to strictly internal principles. Only in this way can the fever of desire properly confront the diagnosis of one's agitation.

In this line from *I'm Gonna Bake My Biscuits,* is Minnie delineating a different path?

> I'm gonna lock my doors,
> nail my windows all down

Or is she only agreeing with the notion that "there is no solution outside of love?"[8] If there are things the blues can teach us, one of them will be the knowledge of the endless variety of love's approaches, an array of erotic references that can be used to obliterate the objection that the blues is too often about the same old thing! Fortunately, the very act of being an avid listener can inform intelligent critical opinion of the diversity of the blues lexicon.

Two of Minnie's songs that were recorded in the early thirties focus on eroticism from two different perspectives. *My Butcher Man* and *Stinging Snake Blues* were recorded in 1933 and 1934, years of severe economic depression. In 1930 and 1931 Minnie and Joe made constant trips to the Vocalion studio in Chicago in addition to their earlier sessions in Memphis and their first session in 1929 in New York. But in 1932 there were only two sessions for Vocalion, this time in New York. One could even call this a single, two-day session. Joe sang on five songs, Minnie sang on six, and Joe provided the spoken commentary on Minnie's *You Stole My Cake*, making it one of their best duets. But in 1933, Minnie recorded only four sides, without Joe, and were it not for this isolated session for Okeh, for whom she had never before recorded, Minnie would have faced two years of (un)recorded silence. In March, 1934, Minnie returned to the Vocalion studio by herself. *Stinging Snake Blues*, coupled with *Drunken Barrel House Blues*, was recorded at this session, while *My Butcher Man* was one of the songs recorded at the 1933 Okeh session. Here the complexity of the interwoven guitar figures established in her duets with Kansas Joe is diminished in favor of a stronger rhythmic thumbstroke, foreshadowing her future session-mates: various combinations of rhythm guitar, piano, bass and drums.

MY BUTCHER MAN

Spoken: Wonder where is my butcher man now?
I've been looking for him all day long!

Butcher man, butcher man,
   where have you been so long? (2x)
I can't catch you at the butcher shop
and you're so hard to find at home.

I'm going to tell everybody
   I've got the best butcher man in town. (2x)
He can slice your ham,
he can cut it from the fat on down.

He slice my pork chops
   and he grinds my sausage, too. (2x)
Ain't nothing in the line of butcherin'
that my butcherman can't do.

Butcher man, in the morning,
  won't you please stop by my house. (2x)
I've got enough butcherin' for you to do
if you promise me
(you just only hush your mouth?)

Butcher man, butcher man,
  I got a ham I cannot slice. (2x)
If you can't stop in the morning,
please stop by tomorrow night.

If anybody asks you, "Butcher man,
  where have you been?" (2x)
Show 'em that long-bladed knife,
tell 'em you been butchering
out in the slaughter pens.

Spoken:
Let's go, butcher man, for me.

    The butcher man is a lover whose, slicing, cutting, grinding and slaughtering (!) skills are so in demand that the protagonist of the song, can rarely find him at home or get him to visit often enough. This is the manifest content of the song, and in the last verse, he is reproached for his running around with other women. The harshness of the imagery in this song is unusual, even for someone as forthright as Minnie. This is signaled by the dislocation the listener feels when hearing the last sung line, for even in the blues, love-making is not usually compared to the butchering of cattle, sheep and hogs in slaughtering pens.[9]

    The harsh imagery of *My Butcher Man* radically depicts the woman as a desiring subject, for whom passion is primary. The question of human freedom is raised whenever desire is placed above necessity, whenever love and hate are placed beyond contradiction. As complex as these issues may be, the blues singers raise them at each occurrence of an extreme image, for even the simplest moment of an extremity is still defined by its position on the boundary of confinement, ever struggling to enlarge these boundaries and, one day, to break through.

STINGING SNAKE BLUES

This house is full of stinging snakes,
   crawling all in my bed. (2x)
I can't rest at night
from them crawling all under my head.

I got up this morning,
   one stung me on my leg. (2x)
I can't sleep at night
because they keeps me awake.

Hmmmmmmm,
   wonder where my stinging snake gone? (2x)
I can't see no peace
since my stinging snake left me home.

I got a stinging snake,
   I love sometimes better   than I do myself. (2x)
If the Lord has to take him,
I won't be stung by nobody else.

Hmmmmmmm,
   where's my stinging snake now? (2x)
I believe to my soul,
that my stinging snake's trying
to put me down.

Stinging Snake Blues, is a fairly orthodox blues on a common subject using typical blues imagery. While snakes have often been used by the singers as representations of the penis, or male sexuality, for blues listeners the snake has other associations, as well. Many believed the snake to be the representative of the Devil, and this belief is of particular interest for in the blues when the Devil is evoked, we know that desire is struggling to break free of repression. "The Devil, in the completed shape in which he stands before us today, represents, one might say, the personification of the unconscious and repressed instincts, of the repressed sexual components of man. . . ."[10] Learning the blues from the Devil at a crossroads is a significant theme in the lives of several blues singers.[11] Julio Finn emphasizes the crossroads as a critical (male) metaphor for the bluesman, as the sign of multiple and powerful presences: Robert Johnson (the hero of Finn's book) made a pact with the Devil at the crossroads, and the same crossroads is the sign of Johnson's hoodoo initiation by the root doctor.[12]

If Finn had stayed a little longer at the crossroads, he would have seen another presence there. For the crossroads also comes to represent the symptom as that point at which the return of the repressed crosses its denial, and as such, it becomes the point at which the unconscious acquires conscious representation and visibility. Yet what is most *symptomatic* in Finn's description of Johnson's world, i.e. the blues*man*'s world, as well as in Finn's entire text, is the absence of the blues*woman*. The repressed blues woman, however, is no more successfully excluded than any other repressed psychical component that returns within the very symptom designed to ward it off. Thus, it is at the same crossroads, already marked for her by a primary, primal sign of darkness and the unconscious, the Devil, that the blueswoman (re-)appears to haunt the male country blues text that Finn has created.[13] The crossroads is, after all, the main entrance to "les Invisibles" and is a powerful and vital sign in voodoo.[14]

The snake-handler, hawking the blues at the crossing, and singing the songs that only the Devil knows, such figures who specialize in the summoning of repressed desires help us to more easily understand how the snake becomes the embodiment of eroticism as it sinuously wends its way through the terrain staked out by the singers. As representatives of sexuality in the blues, these reptiles draw not only on unconscious meanings and fears but on consciously held beliefs as well. Through identification the singers and their listeners can share in the snake's magical power or participate in a struggle with this image of potent sexuality.

20. WORK

Withdraw your attachment to the slave system! Revolt against work!
Assert your right to dream, to make love, to be lazy!
Throw the floodgates through an open window!
—Penelope Rosemont

LIVING THE BEST I CAN

Everybody talking 'bout how I'm living,
But I'm living the best I can.
Everybody talking 'bout how I'm living,
But I'm living the best I can.
When you see me up around about four,
Down on my knees
scrubbing somebody's floor.
Everybody talking 'bout how I'm living,
But I'm gitting it the best I can.

Minnie's *Living The Best I Can* refers to an occupation often reserved for working-class black women, floor scrubbing, though it is one of the few of Minnie's blues to actually mention such jobs. Many aspects of daily toil are referred to in the blues, but this is not the case with Minnie's songs. This line of thought will inevitably bring us face to face with the dubious aesthetic of "social realism" and its sorry function in modern times, and it is noteworthy how well Minnie acquits herself in the matter of work and its portrayal. Her blues confront the social basis of art with a demand for the satisfaction of desire, rather than with a realistic depiction of work itself. Couched within this demand is an illumination of the nature of the connection between work and desire itself.

SOCKET BLUES

Down in my old home town,
put the irons on the stove,
But I'm got to have a socket
everywhere I go.
I need a socket, oohhh, I need a socket.
Babe, I've got to have a socket,
if you want me to iron your clothes.

I got the clothes on the bed,
all sprinkled down,
I can't find no socket around,
I need a socket, etc.

Well, the last socket I had,
you threw it out of doors,
How in the world you expect
for me to iron your clothes,
I need a socket, etc.

Well, the reason I love my baby
and love him so,
He carry me a socket everywhere he go.
I need a socket, etc.

I got an electric iron, I got plenty of steam,
But a socket, now,
is all in the world I need.
I need a socket, etc.

The woman in *Socket Blues* is willing to exchange her labor for her own sexual pleasure, but the terms of this high energy transaction are of her own making, as we are reminded by the socket's teasing oscillation between male and female representation. As in other blues, the instruments of daily toil appear here freed from their repressive context, their future significance sketched mostly by desire.

But as we have seen, the material base of the blues is always in evidence, and for working-class black women, domestic drudgery has always been a stark reality. Indeed, focusing on black/white domestic labor relations reveals the dimensions of white exploitation of black women,[1] and one cannot overemphasize the actual disablement and the degradation of the work itself. A number of blueswomen who were popular in the Classic era of the 1920s had to take jobs as domestics when their fortunes turned for the worst,[2] and we are not surprised to find that other references to domestic work appear in the blueswomen's songs. In *Itching Heel Blues,* Irene Scruggs refers to domestic work as

busting suds in the white folks yard . . .[3]

While the phrase is a commonplace, it is none the worse for that. Such words still carry meaning and not even those attached to the most mundane aspects of life lose their poetic possibilities. Thus, Scruggs's line must still be considered to *mean what it says,* among other things, regardless of whether or not Scruggs ever worked as a washwoman, or whether or not the line is a conventional one. It is within the experience of the members of the working-class black community and not necessarily within the experience of the singer that one finds the "truth" of blues lyrics. That such a commonplace phrase as the one found in Scruggs's song reverberates powerfully within the social consciousness of the working-class black woman is demonstrated retroactively by the very experiences that gave birth to such songs, like the militant strike by the Washerwomen's Association of Atlanta in 1881, where $1 for 12 pounds of laundry was their demand.[4]

Blues singing is itself work, of course, and we would like to assess the dimensions of one of the most important aspects of such work, the wages received for recording. We have only a little "hard" data on the wages of Minnie, Joe McCoy or Ernest Lawlars, but from the facts at our disposable, and the wages of other singers, we can extrapolate some meaningful figures. Bluesman Sylvester Weaver's scrapbook contained royalty statements from Clarence

Williams Music Publishing Company, for the period 1924 to 1928, as well as various documents from Okeh. Weaver received less than $50 composer's royalties from Williams for his hits *Guitar Rag/Guitar Blues,* but he also received $25 per side from Okeh for his recording work.[5] At that, he was making more than many famous artists of the 1930s and considerably more than some of his compatriots like Barbecue Bob. In 1930, Bukka White was paid $240 for recording 14 sides, only four of which were issued. Son House supplied the figure of $15 per side from Paramount in 1930-1931, although the figure $40 for nine sides was also mentioned.[6] John Hurt was given $20 per accepted side, plus travel expenses, by Okeh in 1928.[7] Bessie Smith was paid $125 per side, then $200 per side,[8] but such a figure is probably beyond useful analogy. More to the point is the fact that top *country blues* stars for Columbia, like Barbecue Bob and Peg Leg Howell, made only $15 per side.[9]

It seems clear that first-generation country blues recording artists were getting from $15-$25 per side for the recording work, with the possibility of composing royalties on some of their songs. But more money was to be had through live engagements. Even in poor, rural areas, an extremely popular singer like Charlie Patton might make $50-$100 a week. (A sharecropper in the same area would be lucky to clear several hundred dollars in a year.) One singer asserted that he always made at least $10 a night, sometimes as much as $75, playing for picnics, parties or in juke joints in the 1920s and 1930s in Mississippi.[10] The money to be made at live performances thus exceeded the artists' fees as recording "stars," and we may assume that Minnie earned the same sort of wages, playing in the Mississippi Delta country and in the small towns around Memphis. We know she frequently returned to Memphis where she commonly played for friends, and she probably earned a few dollars at these jobs, too; no doubt such jobs were interspersed with better paying ones.

By the late 1930s, Minnie was only getting $12.50 per side, and still besting the salaries of some of her colleagues. Curtis Jones, for example, who also recorded for Vocalion, was only making $7.50 per side,[11] and in 1939 in Memphis, Vocalion paid Little Buddy Doyle $5 per side, issued or not.[12] Buddy Moss was an American Record Corporation regular, but he was never a star of the stature of Minnie. In 1934-1935, he was paid only $5 per issued side. By the summer of 1935, this figure was raised to $10.[13] Small wonder that some of the "rediscovered" blues artists didn't feel much like recording again.[14]

For Minnie, things would soon be looking up, however. The recording ban kept her out of the studio for 1942 and 1943, and while she signed a new contract in 1945, she didn't begin to record under its terms until 1946. By then, her wages had tripled since her 1939 rate of $12.50 per side, so that now she was receiving $35.00 per side.[15] For her 1948/1949 contract, she was making $45 per side, more than the union scale of $41.25 per side, which had been set at the end of the 1948 recording ban. It's ironic that the sides for which Minnie was paid the most—*Tears On My Pillow, Jump Little Rabbit*—sold quite poorly, and she probably made considerably less on her big, but earlier, hits like *Me And My Chauffeur Blues.*

Looking at Minnie's recording contracts tells only part of the story. For example, whatever her early "wages" were, a measure of her success is provided by Johnnie Temple's testimony that she and Joe appeared in Jackson one year in a brand new Winton automobile,[16] and that she and Joe owned the first steel-bodied National guitar that the residents of Jackson had ever seen. Minnie's sister Daisy also remembers Minnie coming home in a shiny new car, but the details concerning Minnie's guitars were never imparted to her.

Yet to be remembered for a new shiny car, as well as for shiny guitars, is an established sign in the blues culture, as Memphis Slim emphasized:

> I mean, well, she came and made it and then she came back down there in her big car. She had a big car called a Mormon [Marmon], I had never heard of it but it was a fine car. *Bumble Bee Blues.* And then she bought a steel guitar. She and her husband Joe, they had two steel guitars, they was big stuff.[17]

The first National arrived on the market in the Fall of 1928. They were so successful that National went from their three-man

shop in 1927 to a twenty-two-man shop in 1928! The price of the
National steel was closer to that of a better Martin than a lesser
guitar when Sears introduced them in their Fall/Winter catalog for
1929-1930. The National Triolian Metal Guitar with polychrome
finish was $46, while lesser guitars ran from $3.89 to $27.95 (Su-
pertone) in the catalog of a year before. Clearly, these self-ampli-
fying guitars with the metal resonators could be heard above the
noises of a loud and boisterous crowd, and their shiny, chrome
appearance had the look of success. "You should have seen them
when they was new," remembered Johnny Shines. "They looked
like a piece of silver." For many entertainers, they must have
seemed ideal.[18]

Minnie may have had automobiles and guitars befitting a star,
but her stardom was of a limited sort. Blues singers rarely become big stars, and this has helped them maintain their unusual
level of rapport with their audiences. Another significant factor,
especially among downhome and more rural artists, is the
ground-level relationship between singer and audience at picnics
as well as at juke joints. Bluesman Johnny Shines was discussing
playing in juke joints when he said, "When you were playing in
a place like that, you just sat there on the floor on a cane-bot-
tomed chair, just rear back and cut loose. There were no mi-
crophones or PA set-ups there; you just sing out as loud as you
can."[19]

That the blues was one of the first examples of a working-class
music available on phonograph records served to narrow the distance between singer and listener that had existed at tent shows
or on the TOBA stage. Simultaneously this distance was attacked
from within, as it were, as the vaudeville oriented stage performers
like Bessie Smith and Ma Rainey began to share the record lists
with country blues performers who left the stage behind to play in
the midst of their audience at country suppers, chock houses and
juke joints. This notion of "ground level" already embodies the
objections made by the black bourgeoisie and rising class of petit
bourgeoisie to the *lower*-class nature of the (country) blues. These
classes will prefer their music to return to the stage, and the "ideal"
middle-class critic will ask of blues to give up its downhome vocals,
also.

But it was the phonograph record—listened to at home, with a guitar only a few steps away—that played such a powerful role in reducing the distance between performer and audience, and it's noteworthy that the blues' continued penetration into black working-class markets paralleled the rise of the country blues. Minnie and her generation of performers were among the first black singers to be idolized by aspiring young performers as paid recording artists.[20] Most of these aspirants would have already become familiar with the singers in their own homes, via the phonograph. From our modern viewpoint, let us look more carefully at the phonograph record and its impact on Minnie's original audience, by focussing on one particular piece.

Among Minnie's early releases, the versions of *I'm Talking About You* show up with some frequency on the collector's market, their worn and scratched appearance and sound a testament to their popularity with their former owners. As on many of their records, the fast-paced, highly rhythmic but delicately articulated two-guitar sound that Minnie and Joe developed was partly responsible for the record's success. One writer situates Minnie's most lasting contribution to the blues in the "intricate two guitar style of Memphis,"[21] and certainly Minnie and Joe's guitar artistry was a strong factor in their success. Much of their guitar interplay could have been inspired by the Memphis team of Frank Stokes and Dan Sane (the Beale Street Sheiks), although even a casual listener will hear similar reverberations in, for example, the two guitars accompanying Sammy Hill's *Cryin' for You Blues,*[22] recorded in Dallas. Still, the site, the sound and the idea of "Memphis" legitimately evoke an identifiable band of the blues spectrum, along which can be located performers as diverse as Gus Cannon and his Jug Stompers, Hattie Hart, Robert Wilkins, Furry Lewis and, of course, Memphis Minnie and Kansas Joe.

I'm Talking 'bout You No. 2 has nearly twice the verses as the first, and it's delivered at nearly twice the pace. Its striking energy level and compelling guitar virtuousity has made it a highly infectious favorite among Minnie's fans. All eleven verses deal with a woman's unhappiness at her man's behavior, and, thematically, it's a descendant of *Going Back to Texas/I'm Going Back Home.* Hearing verse after verse of complaint and misery, the modern critic must be careful not to dismiss the song as repetitious or boring, without first understanding how a song's content relates to its popularity. For example, one critic dismissed Minnie as a "middling-type country [blues] singer," thus demonstrating in an instant the distance separating the modern critic from Minnie's original listener.[23]

Many of these modern critics and fans have 78s and LPs of Minnie's work in staggering quantities. These listeners can, in a relatively short period of time, survey most of Minnie's repertoire. But accumulating Minnie's entire repertoire, or even a sizeable portion of it, would take the original listener over twenty-five years, more if one counted LP reissues, and by the time the purchaser acquired late pieces like *Kissing in the Dark,* many of the early records would probably be broken, lost or worn gray. Record prices varied from the standard .75 to .35 for releases on cheaper labels, but even these were expensive for the typical working-class black blues fan, many of whom were sharecroppers or tenant farmers. The fact that a number of these farm families had phonographs and more had records is a striking confirmation of the importance of the blues in the lives of these listeners.[24]

Most important, the average purchaser of *I'm Talking 'bout You No. 2* may not have heard or purchased a Memphis Minnie record for months. They may not have even purchased a blues record for a year. Their last purchase may have been *I'm Talking About You* (No. 1), *Mr. Tango Blues,* or a Barbecue Bob or Bessie Smith record. But the field of easily heard records hadn't even a vague resemblance to the record libraries one finds in the possession of the modern critic or listener. Thus, a reviewer calls one prolific recording artist a member of "the Bill Gaither/Bumble Bee Slim school of '30s singers who churned out tedious record after tedious record."[25] Neither Leroy's Buddy (Bill Gaither) nor Bumble Bee Slim attract collectors the way Robert Johnson and Charlie Patton do, but Gaither's and Slim's records were far more popular than Johnson's or Patton's, even when the former were issued in rapid succession. Thus, the predilections of the modern collector or fan can easily obscure the actual pattern of the blues' popularity in earlier decades.

Plainly, hearing a new Memphis Minnie record—one that might be called "boring" by a modern critic—could be extremely exciting to the 1930 purchaser who played her copy of *I'm Gonna Bake My Biscuits* until it was gray with wear. Our purpose isn't so much to defend a particular song as it is to understand the source of some of the values embedded in modern criticism as well as in earlier black blues culture. If we want our "modern" criticism to resonate in the space between Minnie and her original audience as well as in the space between her and her audience of today, this understanding is a necessity.[26]

We know very little about the world of the blues listener, but we do know that women were the primary listeners to blues records. Farm women and their children listened to records on the phonograph during the day, while their husbands joined them after work in the fields. Some women listened while sewing.[27] Blues harp man Phil Wiggins remembered that his mother was the record collector/purchaser in his family, and she bought records by Sleepy John Estes, Brownie McGhee and Sonny Terry, Meade Lux Lewis and others.[28] "My father had a lot of blues," said Joe Louis Walker. "He had more blues records than anybody I know except my mother."[29] This pattern has persisted into modern times and Billy Boy Arnold commented that a club that featured jazz more frequently than blues, McKie's Show Lounge, had its ladies night on its blues night.[30] Chess Records's Phil Chess estimated that women accounted for 80% of Chess's blues record sales, and the same study notes that women were also the most loyal listeners to blues disc jockeys.[31] Marshall Chess spoke this way of Muddy Waters' success: "It was sex. If you had ever seen Muddy then, the effect he had on women. Because blues, you know, has always been a women's market. On Saturday night, they'd be lined up ten deep."[32]

It has been estimated that blacks were buying 10,000,000 race records a year by 1927, and that 10-20% of black farm families had phonographs; more had records,[33] many of which they purchased from pullman porters who purchased them in the larger cities farther north, and who sold them farther south, along with copies of the Chicago *Defender* (which also carried mail order advertisements for the same records).[34] Very little has been written

on patterns of actual record sales and distribution, although even
a survey of the dealer's stickers and tags that are often found on
the labels of vintage blues records would be interesting. For example, our copy of George Hannah's *Gutter Man Blues* has a label
showing it was sold in a tailor shop. Whether as a new record or
second hand, we'll never know. Blues singer Floyd Jones told an
interviewer, "Them times [the late 1920s] you mostly bought your
records from a drug store. And you'd go in and say, 'What you
got new'?. . . . That's the only way you knowed there was a new
number coming out. . . ." He added that often someone would sit
outside playing the new records.[35] Furniture stores were also
among the principal record outlets in the South, and even some
plantation commissaries carried records.[36] Many residents ordered
their records by mail, and it was through mail order that companies
like Paramount did a large proportion of their business. *I'm Talking
About You,* recorded at Minnie's and Joe's second Vocalion session, February 21, 1930, was released as the reverse of *Bumble Bee,*
and both songs were hits. *I'm Talking 'bout You No. 2* was recorded
on July 8, 1930. While Vocalion released it backed with *Bumble
Bee No. 2,* it was coupled with *I'm Talking About You* (No. 1) for
its release on the cheaper Banner, Oriole, Perfect and Romeo labels. Oriole was sold only in McCrory stores, Romeo was sold only
in Kress stores, and each of these dime store labels were sold
through a specific retail outlet on an exclusive basis.[37] Here are
the lyrics for *No. 2:*

I'M TALKING
'BOUT YOU NO. 2

> You can quit me,
> do anything you want to do,
> Someday you'll want me
> and I won't want you.
> I'm talking about you,
> I'm talking about you,
> I'm talking about you,
> I don't care what you do.

You's a man running from hand to hand,
You can get you a woman,
I got another man.
I'm talking about you, etc.

You will mistreat me,
and you won't do right,
You can take it on back
where you had it last night.
I'm talking about you, etc.

Well, you can't be mine,
somebody else's, too,
I ain't gonna stand that way you do.
I'm talking about you, etc.

Sho' as you's a married man
and you got a wife,
You keep running around here,
you'll lose your life.
I'm talking about you, etc.

That (what?) you had
for me the other night.
You can turn it around,
bring it home tonight.
I'm talking about you, etc.

When I was at home, I was with my man,
Now you got me here,
from hand to hand.
I'm talking about you, etc.

Ain't no need of you walking
around with your mouth poked out.
That is something just as well cut it out.
I'm talking about you, etc.

You know when I met you
from house to house,
I know some of your womens

had put you out.
I'm talking about you, etc.

It wouldn't have been so bad,
but you didn't have a dime.
That I wouldn't mind helping you,
no man of mine.
I'm talking about you, etc.

Well, looka here, what you expect for me to do?
Want me to be your mammy
and your doctor, too.
I'm talking about you, etc.

I'm Talking About You (and *I'm Talking 'bout You No. 2*) was one of Minnie's most widely copied songs. Delta stalwart Big Joe Williams, accompanied by Erwin Helfer on piano, recorded a stomping version in Chicago in 1957, while Houston Stackhouse took the refrain and tune from *I'm Talking About You* and added entirely different stanzas. A similar "version" was performed by Eddie Lee Jones which consisted of the melody, chorus, and verses of the song with verses added from other songs of Minnie's. East Coaster Frank Hovington also recorded the piece. Finally, the song was cut by the hillbilly group, Norman Phelps' Virginia Rounders[38] as well as other blues artists and Western Swing performers like Milton Brown. It is interesting to note that the versions cited range from shortly after the piece was released in 1930 up to nearly the present day.

The degree to which a song is copied is an excellent measure of the popularity of the piece itself, and it shows us the degree to which Minnie was able to reach and emotionally move her listeners. Listeners, like readers, if their passion is genuine, struggle against the desire to become performers (or writers).[39] The active listener is constantly hovering on the edge of becoming a blues singer. For some, it may only be a question of defeating a hesitation sufficiently to cause a failure of repression. A new pattern of projections and introjections is then freed and we find a singer where once a listener stood.

Thus we can become *new* listeners as we realize that much of the blues' power lies in the effect it has on the listener and its power to transform both participants in a given "blues conversation." The listeners then become singers, while the singers become the new audience for the former listeners, now singers themselves. But if listeners are transformed by hearing blues, it is clear that the nature of the transformation is accomplished by the nature of the hearing. Thus, we partially control the effect the blues has on us by the way in which we understand it . . . and, of course, here is where the radical prospect of the blues finds fruition: A new reading, a new hearing, a new understanding transforms the consciousness of the listener/poet, and it is the politicized consciousness that is most capable of accomplishing the revolutionary project of changing the world.

During an informal blues session when the downhome musicians are playing close to the listeners and dancers, the listeners influence the length and structure of the songs by forcing the singer, actively, to integrate their responses back into the performance.[40] Blues is truly a participatory art, and not simply another occasion of performer/audience contexts,[41] for it is *within* that relationship that participation takes place. The listeners, by hearing the singers and making the songs their own are able to form and participate in a "blues community" from which they can draw feelings of solidarity and strength. The blues thus finds its true object in the history of the new subject, the listener, especially the listener-becoming-singer. Thus, when Lonnie Johnson recorded *You Don't See Into the Blues Like Me* on a Friday the 13th, it was in order to enable the original purchaser to speak or sing the words of the title,[42] as well as the words of the song. This dynamic is a another reminder of Lautréamont's dictum that poetry is to be made by all.[43]

This participatory aspect of the blues can be evoked in numerous ways. Often a song speaks of the work being done or even the work site itself, as in *North Memphis Blues,* about the North Memphis Cafe, or Minnie's *Hot Stuff*:

HOT STUFF

I was sitting in a beer tavern
playing the blues one night,
A man walked up
and wanted to take my life,
Hollering hot stuff, hot stuff,
Well it's hot stuff here,
And it's everywhere I go.

The humorous *Sylvester and His Mule Blues* deals not only with
work on the farm, but with FDR and the New Deal:

SYLVESTER AND HIS MULE

Sylvester went out on his lot,
he looked at his mule,
And he decided he send
the President some news.
Sylvester went out on his lot,
and he looked at his mule.
And he decided he send
the President some news.

Sylvester walked out across his field,
begin to pray and moan,
He cried, "Oh, lord,
believe I'm gonna lose my home."
(Repeat verse.)

Spoken: Play it, Dennis.

He thought about the President,
he got on the wire.
"If I lose my home,
I believe I'll die." (Repeat verse.)

First time he called,
he get him somebody else.
"I don't want to talk to that man,

I want to speak to Mr. President Roosevelt."
(Repeat verse.)

He said, "Now, Sylvester,
you can rest at ease,
Catch that big, black jackass
and go [ ] the field." (Repeat verse.)

Clearly, *Sylvester and His Mule Blues* is a sarcastic jab at the gap between New Deal promises and hard realities for blacks in the South. While the song depicts a black farmer appealing to the President for assistance, with Roosevelt assuring Sylvester that he can rest at ease, the President never promises (or delivers) anything concrete. As the ultimate demonstration of his lack of sincerity, Minnie has Roosevelt telling Sylvester, "Catch that big black jackass," in characteristically unpresidential diction! No factual source for this song has yet surfaced, although it has the ring of an actual event. Certainly a rural black's desperate call to the White House and Roosevelt's personal "concern" and reply would be typical news of the day.

We have examined the idea of work as it appears in a few of Minnie's songs and as it relates to certain aspects of the lives of Minnie's listeners. That Minnie rarely refers to work, *per se,* in her songs is not surprising. But we can also see this "absence" not simply as an area of women's activity needing validation in Minnie's songs, but as a reminder that life can only be truly liveable above and beyond *work,* that the notion of *play* can never be fulfilled as long as it is continually dismantled by the *work* that historically defines it.

And, of course, blues artists, by the very nature of their musicianship, participate in play while they are working; instruments are said to be played because we comprehend that in spite of the fact that musicians work as hard as other workers, they also "play" at their work, i.e. there is a potential for gratification that is not present in other, more alienated types of work. Blues artists do improvise more than many other types of musicians, and this, too, determines the contribution of play to the activity of blues singing. The singers also maintain this distinction. Arthur "Big Boy" Crudup exclusively used the term *work* to refer to *non-musical* employment. In the South, he farmed or worked in a sawmill or did anything he could to feed his family, but he only occasionally played music in the South, in spite of his success as a recording artist. He seemed nearly awestruck by the notion that a southern bluesman could avoid working non-musical jobs. "If Sonny Boy [Rice Miller] say he never work in his life, he's a damn liar. I lived in Mississippi all my life and there's no colored people there that don't work. . . . See, me, him and Elmo [Elmore James] all worked on farms then 'round Belzoni [Mississippi]. Elmore drove a tractor, me, I drove a tractor and Sonny Boy, he drove a tractor. He didn't play no music but on the weekend."[44]

Eloquent testimony to the special and playful nature of blues performance! If blues singing partakes of play as well as work, it does so in content as well as in form. Ben Sidran has elaborated on this fact:

> Work, in the traditional sense, became equated with be-
> ing within the realm of white economics, with working
> for the white man. . . . Even today, black musicians call
> their day job 'a slave.' Work within the world of black
> culture, however, was quite a different proposition: a
> musician's work *is* his play. . . . The black culture was
> defining work as pleasure rather than as service, duty
> or obligation.

Continuing this point, Sidran links improvisation with the idea of play:

> As jazz playing broke out of the restrictions imposed
> by the swing formulas, albeit at first informally, the no-
> tion of music being work rather than play seemed to
> fall by the wayside. This provided a basis for the black
> musician to establish himself, once more, as one indi-
> vidual who was saying and doing what he pleased—out-
> side the pale of white economics. . . .[45]

There is nothing wrong with seeing the blues singer as someone who plays while she works, as long as we understand that she also works while she plays. But beyond that, the blues singer—and Minnie is especially exemplary here—prefigures and prepares the dialectical resolution of the two. The abolition of work is the first big step toward the realization of poetry and freedom.

Minnie's attitude toward "the abolition of work" provides a fitting and emblematic closing for our study:

Interviewer: When she would visit you in Walls, was she ever interested in working, like on the farm, or . . .

Daisy: I never knowed her to go to a field, did you Ethel? [laughter]

Ethel: Naw. [laughter] Now, she would go out in the field and pick tomatoes and come home and cook 'em. Now, I don't know what she did before I knowed her.

Daisy: She didn't work then either! [laughter]

Ethel: She would really go out in the fields and pick tomatoes, and she loved to cook tomato dumplings.

Daisy: She was a good cook.

Ethel: Sweet tomato dumplings. And she would go out, and say, "Don't you all cut those tomatoes up." And she would cook, make the best tasting dumplings and every thing. But she not going to chop no cotton and pick no cotton. She stayed at the house. 'Kid' loved to cook, but she sure didn't do nothing else . . . much. [laughter] She'd stay here and practice on her songs.[46]

A DISCOGRAPHY OF
MEMPHIS MINNIE

This discography is based on the pioneer work of Dixon and Godrich's *Blues and Gospel Records 1902-1943*, as well as on Daniel Groslier's excellent modification[1], but many corrections have been made. We have amended the personnel or instrumentation of various sessions, and access to file material has also enabled us to correct a few dates. Further, the availablility of reissued 78s on LP, CD or cassette has made it possible for us to list them here, so that the ardent listener can hear most of Minnie's repertoire. However, we have restricted our enumeration of these reissues to LPs, CDs or cassettes *by* Memphis Minnie, and we have made no attempt to list every single song that appears on LP, CD or cassette collections that contain work by other artists as well, although we have listed a representative few of these.

Minnie sang on 184 issued sides, 212 if you count those pieces on which she played but did not sing. If you count unissued songs (but not alternate takes), she sang on 212 sides, most of which have been issued, finally. If you count unissued songs (but not alternate takes) on which she played but did not sing, she performed on a total of 246 pieces. This latter figure becomes 252 if you presume she plays on the six Jed Davenport and His Beale Street Jug Band sides (See Appendix, below).

The first parenthetical expression after the title shows the composer of the song according to Library of Congress registration information. () means not searched; (-) means that the search shows no registration; (Minnie McCoy) means that according to Library of Congress copyright registration records, "Minnie McCoy" is the composer of the song.

The second parenthetical expression shows information as provided on the label of the record itself. () means no record has been examined; (-) means no composer credit is given on the record; (Minnie McCoy) means that "Minnie McCoy" appears on the record label itself as a composer credit.[2]

Label names are given in all capitals only if the issue is an LP, CD or cassette reissue and not an original 78rpm issue. Thus, Columbia 30176 refers to a 78 issue cut at Minnie's April 25, 1949 session, whereas COLUMBIA CK-46775 refers to a 1991 Columbia compact disc reissue.

The artist credit on the label is coded by a system of asterisks (*) and pluses (+), unless all sides from the session are issued under the same artist credit. For example, all the sides from Minnie and Joe's first session were issued as by **KANSAS JOE AND MEMPHIS MINNIE**. This credit appears at the beginning of the session, below, and no "*" or "+" is necessary. For the session of February 17, 1930, however, three different artist credits were (eventually) used: **MEMPHIS MINNIE**, signaled by a "*", **KANSAS JOE**, signaled by a "+", and **KANSAS JOE AND MEMPHIS MINNIE**, signaled by a "+*". Each side from this session has a code to signify the artist credit that appeared on the label for that particular song. It may be noted that we have coded even unissued songs. Without this practice, however, it would be difficult to assess the level of each artist's participation in the sessions. Thus, one might not realize that two of the three unissued sides on the February 17, 1930, session were by **KANSAS JOE** or **KANSAS JOE AND MEMPHIS MINNIE**, and not simply by **MEMPHIS MINNIE**.

Session personnel are coded using standard techniques. Thus in the first session below, both Minnie's and Joe's guitars appear on all sides. Joe's vocals, however, *only* appear on sides coded -2 and Minnie's vocals *only* appear on sides coded -1. They both sing on songs coded -1,2. Both of their guitars appear on all sides, so no guitar coding is necessary for this session.

KANSAS JOE AND MEMPHIS MINNIE　　　　NEW YORK, JUNE 18, 1929

Memphis Minnie, vo (-1), gtr; Joe McCoy., vo (-2), gtr.

148707-2	I WANT THAT (THING)-2 ()(-)	Columbia 14542-D, EARL BD-603, DOCUMENT DOCD-5028
148708-3	THAT WILL BE ALRIGHT-2 () (-)	Columbia 14439-D, CBS LP 66.232, YAZOO LP 1021, EARL BD-603, K.O.B. LP, DOCUMENT DOCD-5028
148709-2	GOIN' BACK TO TEXAS-1,2 (-) (-)	Columbia 14455-D, PALTRAM LP 101, EARL BD-617, DOCUMENT DOCD-5028
148710-1,2	'FRISCO TOWN-1 (-) (-)	Columbia 14455-D, YAZOO LP 1008, EARL BD-608, DOCUMENT DOCD-5028
148711-1	WHEN THE LEVEE BREAKS-2 () (-)	Columbia 14439-D, YAZOO LP 1063, BLUES CLASSICS LP 1, DOCUMENT DOCD-5028
148712-2	BUMBLE BEE-1 (Minnie McCoy)(-)	Columbia 14542-D, HISTORICAL LP 2, EARL BD-608, DOCUMENT DOCD-5028

KANSAS JOE AND MEMPHIS MINNIE　　　　NEW YORK, JUNE 19, 1929

Joe McCoy, vo, gtr; Memphis Minnie, gtr.

148717-2	NO MO' CHERRY BALL	Columbia unissued
148718-2	YOU CAN'T DO IT TO ME	Columbia unissued

MEMPHIS MINNIE* KANSAS JOE AND MEMPHIS MINNIE+*

KANSAS JOE+　　　　MEMPHIS, FEBRUARY 17, 1930

See also the Appendix for other songs from this session.

Memphis Minnie, vo (-1), gtr (-2); Joe McCoy, vo (-3), gtr (-4).

MEM-730	I'M GONNA BAKE MY BISCUITS-1,2,4* (-) (McCoy)	Vocalion 1512, TRAVELIN' MAN TM-803, DOCUMENT DOCD-5028
MEM-731	MISTER TANGO BLUES-1,-2,4* (-) (McCoy)	Vocalion 1512, MAGNOLIA LP 501, TRAVELIN' MAN TM-803, DOCUMENT DOCD-5028
MEM-732	SHE WOULDN'T GIVE ME NONE-1,2,3,4+* ()(McCoy)	Vocalion 1576, MAGNOLIA LP 501, TRAVELIN' MAN TM-803, DOCUMENT DOCD-5028
MEM-733	MY MARY BLUES-3,4+	Vocalion unissued

MEM-738	I CALLED YOU THIS MORNING-1,2,3,4+*	Vocalion unissued
MEM-739-B	PLYMOUTH ROCK BLUES-1,2*	Vocalion unissued
MEM-765	WHAT FAULT YOU FIND OF ME? PART 1-1,2,3,4+* (Minnie McCoy) (M.McCoy-J.McCoy)	Vocalion 1500, TRAVELIN' MAN TM-803, DOCU-MENT DOCD-5028
MEM-766	WHAT FAULT YOU FIND OF ME? PART 2-1,2,3,4+* (Minnie McCoy) (M. McCoy-J. McCoy)	Vocalion 1500, TRAVELIN' MAN TM-803, DOCU-MENT DOCD-5028
MEM-772-A	I'M TALKING ABOUT YOU-1,2,4* (Minnie McCoy) (McCoy)	Vocalion 1476, Banner 32556, Oriole 8165, Perfect 0214, Romeo 5165, PALTRAM LP 101, TRAVELIN' MAN TM-803, DOCUMENT DOCD-5028
MEM-773-A	BUMBLE BEE-1,2,4* (Minnie McCoy) (McCoy)	Vocalion 1476, Banner 32525, Oriole 8157, Perfect 0211, Romeo 5157, PALTRAM LP 101, TRAVELIN' MAN TM-803, DOCUMENT DOCD-5028
MEM-790	CAN I DO IT FOR YOU? PART 1-1,2,3,4+* (-) (M. McCoy-J. McCoy)	Vocalion 1523, OLD TRAMP OT-1207, DOCUMENT DOCD-5028
MEM-791	CAN I DO IT FOR YOU? PART 2-1,2,3,4+* (-) (M. McCoy-J. McCoy)	Vocalion 1523, ORIGIN LP 6, EARL BD-603, DOCUMENT DOCD-5028

Where Minnie's name appears as a solo artist credit, ("Memphis Minnie" instead of "Kansas Joe and Memphis Minnie"), as on MISTER TANGO BLUES, or I'M GONNA BAKE MY BISCUITS, the legend "Minnie McCoy" appears beneath her name. This practice was followed fairly consistently through 1932. This notation is not to be confused with the "McCoy" *composer credit* that appears beneath the song title.

MCCOY AND JOHNSON (MINNIE MCCOY AND JOE JOHNSON?)

MEMPHIS, MAY 26, 1930

Memphis Minnie vo, gtr; Joe McCoy, vo, gtr.

59992	I'M GOING BACK HOME () (Joe Johnson)	Victor 23352, PALTRAM LP 101, HISTORICAL LP 32, RCA LP 47377, EARL BD-617, DOCU-MENT DOCD-5028

MEMPHIS JUG BAND

MEMPHIS, MAY 26, 1930

Memphis Minnie, vo, gtr; Charlie Burse, gtr; Will Shade, hca; Hambone Lewis, jug.

59993-2	BUMBLE BEE BLUES (Minnie McCoy)(Minnie McCoy)	Victor V-38599, JOKER LP 3104, RCA LP 47377, DOCUMENT DOCD-5028

| 59994 | MENINGITIS BLUES () () | Victor 23421, DOCUMENT DOCD-5028 |

WASHINGTON WHITE   MEMPHIS, MAY 26, 1930
Washington "Bukka" White, vo, gtr; probably Memphis Minnie ("Miss Minnie"), vo.

| 62506-2 | I AM IN THE HEAVENLY WAY | Victor V-38615, ORIGIN LP 12 |
| 62508-1 | PROMISE TRUE AND GRAND | Victor V-38615, ORIGIN LP 13 |

MINNIE AND BESSIE MCCOY   MEMPHIS, MAY 29, 1930
Probably Memphis Minnie, vo, gtr; Bessie McCoy, vo.

| 62537-2 | MIDNIGHT SPECIAL | Victor unissued |

MCCOY AND JOHNSON   MEMPHIS, MAY 29, 1930
Memphis Minnie, vo (-1), gtr; Joe McCoy, vo (-2), gtr.

62538	I NEVER TOLD A LIE-1 (Minnie McCoy)(Minnie McCoy)	Victor 23313, Bluebird B-5385, Sunrise S-3466, RCA LP 47377, OLD TRAMP OT-1207, DOCUMENT DOCD-5028
62539	DON'T WANT NO WOMAN-1,2 (-) (Joe Johnson)	Victor 23313, Bluebird B-5385, Sunrise S-3466, PALTRAM LP 101, EARL BD-617, DOCUMENT DOCD-5028
62540	GEORGIA SKIN-1 (Minnie McCoy) (Minnie McCoy)	Victor 23352, PALTRAM LP 101, HISTORICAL LP 32, RCA LP 47377, EARL BD-617, DOCU-MENT DOCD-5028

MEMPHIS MINNIE* KANSAS JOE AND MEMPHIS MINNIE+*
KANSAS JOE+   CHICAGO, JUNE 5, 1930
Memphis Minnie, vo (-1), gtr (-2); Joe McCoy, vo (-3), gtr (-4).

C-5817	I DON'T WANT NO WOMAN I HAVE TO GIVE MY MONEY TO-1,2,3,4+* () (McCoy)	Vocalion 1535, PALTRAM LP 101, EARL BD-617, DOCUMENT DOCD-5028
C-5818	BUMBLE BEE NO. 2-1,2*	ARC unissued
C-5819	BOTHERIN' THAT THING-2,3,4+	ARC unissued
C-5820-A	I'M WILD ABOUT MY STUFF-2,3,4+ () (McCoy)	Vocalion 1570, PALTRAM LP 101, HISTORICAL LP 32, EARL BD-617, DOCUMENT DOCD-5028
C-5821	CHERRY BALL BLUES-2,3,4+	ARC unissued
C-5822-A	MEMPHIS MINNIE-JITIS BLUES-1,2,4* (-) (McCoy)	Vocalion 1588, BLUES CLASSICS LP 13, DOWN WITH THE GAME LP 200, DOCUMENT DOCD-5029

C-5823	GOOD GIRL BLUES-1,2,4* (Minnie McCoy)()	Vocalion 1603, DOCU- MENT DOCD-5029
C-5824	GEORGIA SKIN BLUES-1,2*	ARC unissued
C-5829	I CALLED YOU THIS MORNING-1,2,3,4+*	ARC unissued
C-5830	MY MARY BLUES-2,3,4+ () ()	Vocalion 1576, PALTRAM LP 101, EARL BD-617, DOCUMENT DOCD-5029
C-5831	PLYMOUTH ROCK BLUES-1,2,4* (-) (McCoy)	Vocalion 1631, BLUES CLASSICS LP 13, DOCU- MENT DOCD-5029

MEMPHIS MINNIE* KANSAS JOE+   CHICAGO, JUNE 24, 1930
Memphis Minnie, vo (-1), gtr (-2); Joe McCoy, vo (-3), gtr (-4)

C-5864-A	CHERRY BALL BLUES-2,3,4+ (Minnie McCoy) (McCoy)	Vocalion 1535, PALTRAM LP 101, EARL BD-617, DOCUMENT DOCD-5029
C-5865-A	BOTHERIN' THAT THING-2,3,4+() (McCoy)	Vocalion 1570, PALTRAM LP 101, HISTORICAL LP 32, EARL BD-617, DOCUMENT DOCD-5029
C-5866-A	BUMBLE BEE NO. 2-1,2,4* (Minnie McCoy) (McCoy)	Vocalion 1556, Banner 32525, Oriole 8157, Perfect 0211, Romeo 5157, RST (BLUES DOCUMENTS) BD-2048, DOCUMENT DOCD-5029
C-5867	GEORGIA SKIN BLUES-1,2,4* (Minnie McCoy)()	Vocalion 1603, DOCUMENT DOCD-5029

Although the liner notes and label of RST (BLUES DOCUMENTS) BD-2048 note
that C-5867 appears there, it does not.

MEMPHIS MINNIE   CHICAGO, JULY 1, 1930
Memphis Minnie, vo, gtr; Joe McCoy, gtr.

| C-5894 | NEW DIRTY DOZEN (-)(Perryman) | Vocalion 1618, BLUES
 CLASSICS LP 13, DOCU-
 MENT DOCD-5029 |
| C-5895 | NEW BUMBLE BEE (-)(McCoy) | Vocalion 1618, BLUES
 CLASSICS LP 13, DOCU-
 MENT DOCD-5029 |

MEMPHIS MINNIE* KANSAS JOE AND MEMPHIS MINNIE+*
KANSAS JOE +   CHICAGO, JULY 8, 1930
Memphis Minnie, vo (-1), gtr (-2); Joe McCoy, vo (-3), gtr (-4).

| C-6009-A | FRANKIE JEAN (THAT TROTTIN'
 FOOL)-1,2,4*(-)(McCoy) | Vocalion 1588, BLUES
 CLASSICS LP 13, DOWN
 WITH THE GAME LP 200,
 DOCUMENT DOCD-5029 |

C-6010-A	I'M TALKING 'BOUT YOU NO. 2-1,2,4*(Minnie McCoy?) (McCoy)	Vocalion 1556, Banner 32556, Oriole 8165, Perfect 0214, Romeo 5165, HISTORICAL LP 2, TRAVELIN' MAN TM-803, DOCUMENT DOCD-5029
C-6011	SHE PUT ME OUTDOORS-1,2,3,4+* (-)()	Vocalion 1612, BLUES CLASSICS LP 13, ALBA-TROSS LP 8189, K.O.B. LP, DOCUMENT DOCD-5029
C-6012	PILE DRIVIN' BLUES-2,3,4+ (-)()	Vocalion 1612, EARL BD-603, DOCUMENT DOCD-5029
C-6013	I CALLED YOU THIS MORNING-1,2,3,4+* (-) (McCoy)	Vocalion 1631, BLUES CLASSICS LP 13, DOCU-MENT DOCD-5029

MEMPHIS MINNIE AND HER JUG BAND

CHICAGO, SEPTEMBER 9, 1930

Memphis Minnie, vo, gtr; Joe McCoy, gtr; Jed Davenport, hca; probably Hambone Lewis, jug.

C-6082	GRANDPA AND GRANDMA BLUES (-) (McCoy)	Vocalion 1601, ORIGIN LP 4, EARL BD-608, DOCUMENT DOCD-5029
C-6083	GARAGE FIRE BLUES (-) (McCoy)	Vocalion 1601, ROOTS LP 307, EARL BD-608, DOCUMENT DOCD-5029

MEMPHIS MINNIE   CHICAGO, OCTOBER 9, 1930

Memphis Minnie, vo, gtr; Joe McCoy, gtr.

C-6433-A	DIRT DAUBER BLUES (-) (McCoy)	Vocalion 1638
C-6434-A	YOU DIRTY MISTREATER (-) (McCoy)	Vocalion 1638

MEMPHIS MINNIE* KANSAS JOE AND MEMPHIS MINNIE+*
KANSAS JOE+   CHICAGO, OCTOBER 11, 1930

Memphis Minnie, vo (-1), gtr (-2); Joe McCoy, vo (-3), gtr (-4).

C-6440	THAT'S YOUR YAS YAS YAS-2,3,4+ () ()	Vocalion 1677 (see also the session for February 9, 1931)
C-6441	I'M FIXED FOR YOU-2,3,4+ () ()	Vocalion 1677
C-6442	WHAT'S THE MATTER WITH THE MILL?-1,2,3,4+* (Minnie McCoy) (McCoy)	Vocalion 1550, BLUES CLASSICS LP 13, MCA LP 1370 (MCA LP 1370 shows the matrix number 64428-A), DOCUMENT DOCD-5029

| C-6443 | NORTH MEMPHIS BLUES-1,2,4* (Minnie McCoy) (McCoy) | Vocalion 1550, BLUES CLASSICS LP 13, DOCU-MENT DOCD-5029 |

MEMPHIS MINNIE   CHICAGO, JANUARY 19, 1931
Memphis Minnie, vo, gtr; Joe McCoy, gtr.

C-7240-B	DON'T BOTHER IT	Vocalion unissued
C-7241-B	TODAY TODAY BLUES	Vocalion unissued
C-7244-B	LAY MONEY DOWN (IF YOU RUN AROUND)	Vocalion unissued
C-7245-B	HARD DOWN LIE	Vocalion unissued

KANSAS JOE AND MEMPHIS MINNIE+* KANSAS JOE+
                                          CHICAGO, JANUARY 21, 1931
Memphis Minnie, vo (-1), gtr (-2); Joe McCoy, vo (-3), gtr (-4).

C-7246	BEAT IT RIGHT-2,3,4+ () ()	Vocalion 1643, PALTRAM LP 101, EARL BD-617, DOCUMENT DOCD-5029
C-7247	PREACHER'S BLUES-2,3,4+ () ()	Vocalion 1643, BLUES CLASSICS LP 13 DOCUMENT DOCD-5029
C-7248-B	LET'S GO TO TOWN-2,4+*	Vocalion unissued
C-7249-B	PICKIN' THE BLUES-2,4+*	Vocalion unissued

MEMPHIS MINNIE* KANSAS JOE+   CHICAGO, JANUARY 30, 1931
Memphis Minnie, vo (-1), gtr (-2); Joe McCoy, vo (-3), gtr (-4).

VO-109-A	SHAKE MATTIE-2,3,4+ (-) (McCoy)	Vocalion 1668, MAMLISH LP 3803, EARL BD-603, DOCUMENT DOCD-5029
VO-110-A	MY WASH WOMAN'S GONE-2,3,4+ (-) (McCoy)	Vocalion 1668, MAMLISH LP 3803, YAZOO LP 1026, MCA LP 3529, EARL BD-603, DOCUMENT DOCD-5029
VO-111-A	I DON'T WANT THAT JUNK OUTA YOU-1,2,4*(-) ()	Vocalion 1678, YAZOO LP 1008, EARL BD-608, DOCUMENT DOCD-5030
VO-112-A	CRAZY CRYIN' BLUES-1,2,4* (-) ()	Vocalion 1678, BLUES CLASSICS LP 13, MCA LP 3529, DOCUMENT DOCD-5030
VO-113-A	TRICKS AIN'T WALKING NO MORE-1,2,4* (-) (Bogan)	Vocalion 1653, DOCU-MENT DOCD-5030

MEMPHIS MINNIE* KANSAS JOE AND MEMPHIS MINNIE+*
KANSAS JOE+   CHICAGO, FEBRUARY 9, 1931
Memphis Minnie, vo (-1), gtr (-2); Joe McCoy, vo (-3), gtr (-4).

VO-116-B	SOMEBODY'S GOT TO HELP YOU-1,2,3,4+*	Vocalion unissued
VO-117-B	THAT'S YOUR YAS YAS YAS-2,3,4+ () ()	Vocalion 1677 (It is not known whether this matrix or C-6440 [see October 11, 1930] is used on Vocalion 1677.)
VO-118	DON'T BOTHER IT-1,2,4* (-) (McCoy)	Vocalion 1673, DOCU-MENT DLP 559, DOCU-MENT DOCD-5030
VO-119	TODAY TODAY BLUES-1,2,4* (-) (McCoy)	Vocalion 1673, DOCUMENT DLP 559, DOCUMENT DOCD-5030

MEMPHIS MINNIE* KANSAS JOE AND MEMPHIS MINNIE+*
                                     CHICAGO, FEBRUARY 11, 1931
Memphis Minnie, vo (-1), gtr (-2); Joe McCoy, vo (-3), gtr (-4).

VO-122-B	HARD DOWN LIE-1,2*	Vocalion unissued
VO-123-B	LAY MONEY DOWN (IF YOU RUN AROUND)-1,2*	Vocalion unissued
VO-124-B	PICKIN' THE BLUES-2,4+*	Vocalion unissued
VO-125-B	LET'S GO TO TOWN-2,4+*	Vocalion unissued

KANSAS JOE AND MEMPHIS MINNIE
                                     CHICAGO, FEBRUARY 24, 1931
Memphis Minnie, vo, gtr; Joe McCoy, vo, gtr.

VO-116	SOMEBODY'S GOT TO HELP YOU	Vocalion unissued

MEMPHIS MINNIE   CHICAGO, MARCH 13, 1931
Memphis Minnie, vo, gtr; Kansas Joe, gtr.

VO-135-A	LAY MY MONEY DOWN (IF YOU RUN AROUND) (-) ()	Vocalion 1665, RST (BLUES DOCUMENTS) BD-2048, DOCUMENT DOCD-5030
VO-136-A	HARD DOWN LIE (-) ()	Vocalion 1665, RST (BLUES DOCUMENTS) BD-2048, DOCUMENT DOCD-5030

KANSAS JOE AND MEMPHIS MINNIE+* THE HILLBILLY PLOWBOY++
                                     CHICAGO, MARCH 16, 1931
Memphis Minnie, vo (-1), gtr (-2); Joe McCoy, vo (-3), gtr (-4).

VO-137-A	SOMEBODY'S GOT TO HELP YOU-1,2,3,4+* (-) (McCoy)	Vocalion 1653, YAZOO LP 1021, RST (BLUES DOCUMENTS) BD-2048, DOCUMENT DOCD-5030

VO-138-A	PICKIN' THE BLUES-2,4+* (-) (McCoy)	Vocalion 1660, BLUES CLASSICS LP 13, DOCUMENT DOCD-5030
VO-139-A	LET'S GO TO TOWN-2,4+* (-) (McCoy)	Vocalion 1660, BLUES CLASSICS LP 13, DOCUMENT DOCD-5030
VO-140-A	ROWDY OLD SOUL-3,4++	Vocalion unissued

When Vocalion thought that a record might be marketable in Latin America—for example, the instrumentals PICKIN' THE BLUES and LET'S GO TO TOWN—the song titles were also given in Spanish on the label. In this case, COGIENDO LOS BLUES and VAMOS A LA CIUDAD.

MEMPHIS MINNIE CHICAGO, MARCH 23, 1931
Memphis Minnie, vo (-1), gtr (-2); Joe McCoy, vo (-3), gtr (-4);
probably Memphis Minnie, mandolin (-5).

VO-151-A	SOO COW SOO-1,2,4 (-) (McCoy)	Vocalion 1658, YAZOO LP 1021, EARL BD-608, DOCUMENT DOCD-5030
VO-152-A	AFTER WHILE BLUES-1,4,5 (-) (McCoy)	Vocalion 1658, BLUES CLASSICS LP 13, DOCUMENT DOCD-5030

We suggest that Minnie plays mandolin on AFTER WHILE BLUES because the guitar sounds like Joe McCoy, and Minnie is said to have been able to play mandolin, as she may on the December 15, 1937 session.

MEMPHIS MINNIE* KANSAS JOE AND MEMPHIS MINNIE+*
KANSAS JOE+ NEW YORK, FEBRUARY 3, 1932
Memphis Minnie, vo (-1), gtr (-2); Joe McCoy, vo (-3), gtr (-4).

11213-A	FISHIN' BLUES-1,2,4*(-) (McCoy)	Vocalion 1711, Banner 32796, Melotone 12729, Oriole 8242, Perfect 0245, Romeo 5242, TRAVELIN' MAN TM-803, DOCUMENT DOCD-5030
11214-A	JAILHOUSE TROUBLE BLUES-1,2,4* (-) (M.McCoy)	Vocalion 1718, TRAVELIN' MAN TM-803, DOCUMENT DOCD-5030
11215-A,B	OUTDOOR BLUES-1,2,4* (-) (McCoy)	Vocalion 1698, Banner 32796, Melotone 12729, Oriole 8242, Perfect 0245, Romeo 5242, RST (BLUES DOCUMENTS) BD-2048, DOCUMENT DOCD-5030
11216-A	WHERE IS MY GOOD MAN?-1,2,4* (-) (McCoy)	Vocalion 1698, Banner 32797, Melotone 12730, Oriole 8243, Perfect 0246, Romeo 5243, ORIGIN LP 6, EARL BD-608, DOCUMENT DOCD-5030

11217-A	YOU STOLE MY CAKE-1,2,3,4+* (-) (M.McCoy)	Vocalion 1688, RST (BLUES DOCUMENTS) LP 2032, DOCUMENT DOCD-5030
11218-A	KIND TREATMENT BLUES-1,2,4*	Vocalion unissued, TRAVELIN' MAN TM-803, DOCUMENT DOCD-5030
11218-B	KIND TREATMENT BLUES-1,2,4* (-) (M.McCoy)	Vocalion 1711, Banner 32797, Melotone 12730, Oriole 8243, Perfect 0246, Romeo 5243
11219-A	YOU KNOW YOU DONE ME WRONG-2,3,4+ () ()	Vocalion 1718, EARL BD-603, DOCUMENT DOCD-5030
11220-A	JOLIET BOUND-2,3,4+ (-)(-)	Vocalion 1686, YAZOO LP 1021, EARL BD-603, DOCUMENT DOCD-5030
11221	I'M GOING CRAZY-2,3,4+ () ()	Vocalion 1705
11222-A	STRANGER'S BLUES-2,3,4+ () ()	Vocalion 1686, DOCUMENT DOCD-5030

MEMPHIS MINNIE* MEMPHIS MINNIE, GEORGIA TOM, TAMPA RED AND KANSAS JOE++ KANSAS JOE+

NEW YORK, FEBRUARY 4, 1932

Memphis Minnie, vo (-1), gtr (-2); Joe McCoy, vo (-3), gtr (-4); Charlie McCoy, mnd (-5); Tampa Red, vo, gtr (-6); Georgia Tom, vo, pno (-7).

11230	DRESSER DRAWER BLUES-3,4,5+ () ()	Vocalion 1705
11231-A	SOCKET BLUES-1,2,4* (-) (M. McCoy)	Vocalion 1688, DOCUMENT DLP 559, DOCUMENT DOCD-5030
11232-A	MINNIE MINNIE BUMBLE BEE-1,2,3,4,6,7++ (-) ()	Vocalion 1682

MEMPHIS MINNIE CHICAGO, NOVEMBER 27, 1933

Memphis Minnie, vo, gtr.

152534-2	MY BUTCHER MAN (-) (-)	Okeh 8948, EARL BD-608, COLUMBIA CK-46775, DOCUMENT DOCD-5031
152535-2	TOO LATE (-) (-)	Okeh 8948, EARL BD-608, DOCUMENT DOCD-5031
152536-2	LAKE MICHIGAN BLUES (-)()	Okeh unissued
152537-2	AIN'T NO USE TRYING TO TELL ON ME (I KNOW SOMETHING ON YOU) () ()	Okeh unissued, YAZOO LP 1021, EARL BD-608, COLUMBIA CK-46775, DOCUMENT DOCD-5031

MEMPHIS MINNIE   CHICAGO, MARCH 24, 1934
Memphis Minnie, vo, gtr.

CP-1069-1	STINGING SNAKE BLUES (-) (-)	Vocalion 02711, PALTRAM LP 101, EARL BD-617, DOCUMENT DOCD-5031
CP-1070-1	DRUNKEN BARRELHOUSE BLUES (-) (-)	Vocalion 02711, YAZOO LP 1021, EARL BD-608, DOCUMENT DOCD-5031

MEMPHIS MINNIE* MEMPHIS MINNIE AND KANSAS JOE*+

CHICAGO, AUGUST 24, 1934

Memphis Minnie, vo (-1), gtr (-2); Joe McCoy, vo (-3), gtr (-4).

C-9380	YOU GOT TO MOVE (YOU AIN'T GOT TO MOVE) PART 1-1,2,3,4*+ (-)(McCoy)	Decca 7038, MCA LP 1370, BLUES CLASSICS LP 1, DOCUMENT DOCD-5031
C-9381	KEEP IT TO YOURSELF-1,2* (-) (McCoy)	Decca 7037, MCA LP 3529, TRAVELIN' MAN TM-803, DOCUMENT DOCD-5031
C-9381	KEEP IT TO YOURSELF-1,2* (Alternate take)	Decca unissued, MAMLISH LP 3801, OLD TRAMP OT-1207, DOCUMENT DOCD-5031
C-9382	CHICKASAW TRAIN BLUES (LOW DOWN DIRTY THING)-1,2* (Memphis Minnie McCoy)(McCoy)	Decca 7019, MCA LP 1370, MCA LP 1352, ACE OF HEARTS LP 72, PAL-TRAM LP 101, DECCA DL 4434, DOCUMENT DOCD-5031
C-9383	BANANA MAN BLUES (I DON'T WANT THAT THING)-1,2* (-) (McCoy)	Decca 7019, YAZOO LP 1043, OLD TRAMP OT-1207, DOCUMENT DOCD-5031

MEMPHIS MINNIE AND KANSAS JOE   CHICAGO, AUGUST 31, 1934
Memphis Minnie, vo, gtr; Joe McCoy, vo, gtr.

C-9389	YOU GOT TO MOVE (YOU AIN'T GOT TO MOVE) PART 2 (-) (McCoy)	Decca 7038, RST (BLUES DOCUMENTS) LP 2032, DOCUMENT DOCD-5031

MEMPHIS MINNIE AND KANSAS JOE   CHICAGO, SEPTEMBER 6, 1934
Memphis Minnie, vo, gtr; Joe McCoy, vo, gtr.

C-9402	HOLE IN THE WALL (-) (McCoy)	Decca 7023, MCA LP 3529, EARL BD-603, DOCU-MENT DOCD-5031
C-9407	GIVE IT TO ME IN MY HAND (CAN I GO HOME WITH YOU) (-) (McCoy)	Decca 7023, MCA LP 1370, FLYRIGHT LP 108, MAG-NOLIA LP 501, DOCU-MENT DOCD-5031

MEMPHIS MINNIE   CHICAGO, SEPTEMBER 10, 1934
Memphis Minnie, vo, gtr; Joe McCoy, gtr.

C-9426-A	SQUAT IT (-) (McCoy)	Decca 7146, MCA LP 1370, ROOTS LP 329, DOCU-MENT DOCD-5031
C-9427	MOANING THE BLUES (-) (McCoy)	Decca 7037, MCA LP 1370, WHOOPEE LP 104, MCA LP 3529, RST (BLUES DOCUMENTS) BD-2048, DOCUMENT DOCD-5031

1.) C-9427 appears on RST (BLUES DOCUMENTS) BD-2048, although GEOR-GIA SKIN (C-5867) is called for in the liner notes and on the label. 2.) The reverse of Decca 7146 is by Sam Theard. 3.) Joe McCoy's presence is impossible to aurally confirm on the above session, and he may not be present.

MEMPHIS MINNIE   CHICAGO, JANUARY 10, 1935
Memphis Minnie, vo, gtr. poss. Jimmy Gordon, pno.

C-9641-A	DIRTY MOTHER FOR YOU (Roosevelt Sykes) (McCoy)	Decca 7048, PALTRAM LP 101, TRAVELIN' MAN TM-803
C-9642-A	SYLVESTER AND HIS MULE BLUES (-) (McCoy)	Decca 7084, MCA LP 3529, TRAVELIN' MAN TM-803
C-9643-A	WHEN YOU'RE ASLEEP (-) (McCoy)	Decca 7084, DOCUMENT DLP 559
C-9644-A	YOU CAN'T GIVE IT AWAY (-) (McCoy)	Decca 7048, PALTRAM LP 101, TRAVELIN' MAN TM-803

DIRTY MOTHER FOR YOU was registered at the Library of Congress by State Street Music on November 6, 1936, naming Roosevelt Sykes as composer. This was done nearly two years after Minnie's version (and nine months after Sykes' own version), and these facts, combined with Big Bill's attributing the song to Minnie, suggests that Minnie was composer of this famous song, as the label indicates.

GOSPEL MINNIE   CHICAGO, JANUARY 15, 1935
Memphis Minnie, vo, gtr; accompanied by unknown pno, female vo and male vo.

C-9657-A	LET ME RIDE (-) (Dennis-McCoy)	Decca 7063, MCA LP 1370
C-9658-A	WHEN THE SAINTS GO MARCHING HOME (-) (Dennis-McCoy)	Decca 7063, MCA LP 1370

MEMPHIS MINNIE   CHICAGO, MAY 27, 1935
Memphis Minnie, vo, gtr.

90016-A	JOCKEY MAN BLUES (-) ()	Decca 7125, DOCUMENT DLP 559
90017-A	WEARY WOMAN'S BLUES (-) ()	Decca 7125, MCA LP 1370
90018-A	REACHIN' PETE (-) (McCoy)	Decca 7102, MCA LP 1370, MAMLISH LP 3803
90019-A	DOWN IN NEW ORLEANS (-) (McCoy)	Decca 7102, MCA LP 3529, EARL BD-608

TEXAS TESSIE   CHICAGO, JULY 27, 1935
Memphis Minnie, vo, gtr; unknown 2nd gtr, (possibly Big Bill Broonzy on at
least 91421-1)

91419-1	GOOD MORNIN'	Bluebird unissued
91420	YOU WRECKED MY	Bluebird B-6429, EARL
	HAPPY HOME(-) (-)	BD-608, TRAVELIN' MAN
		TM-803
91421-1	I'M WAITING ON YOU (-) (Minnie	Bluebird B-6141, DOCU-
	McCoy)	MENT DLP 559
91422-1	KEEP ON GOIN' (-) (Minnie McCoy)	Bluebird B-6141, DOCU-
		MENT DLP 559

The reverse of Bluebird 6429 is by Trixie Butler.

MEMPHIS MINNIE* MEMPHIS MINNIE, BLACK BOB, BILL SETTLES+
                                            CHICAGO, AUGUST 22, 1935
Memphis Minnie, vo (-1), gtr; Black Bob, pno; Bill Settles, b.

C-1098-B	BALL AND CHAIN BLUES-1* (-)	Vocalion 03541, OLD
	(Minnie McCoy)	TRAMP OT-1207
C-1099-B	HE'S IN THE RING (DOING THAT	Vocalion 03046, CBS LP
	SAME OLD THING)-1* (Minnie	63.288, PALTRAM LP 101,
	McCoy) (-)	K.O.B. LP, EARL
		BD-617
C-1099-A	HE'S IN THE RING (DOING THAT	Vocalion unissued, DOCU-
	SAME OLD THING) -1	MENT DLP 559
C-1100-A	JOE LOUIS STRUT-1+(-) (-)	Vocalion 03046, CBS LP
		63.288, BLUES CLASSICS
		LP 1, MAGPIE LP 4413

MEMPHIS MINNIE   CHICAGO, OCTOBER 31, 1935
Memphis Minnie, vo, gtr; Casey Bill Weldon, steel gtr (-1); Black Bob, pno;
Bill Settles, b.

96226-1	WHEN THE SUN GOES DOWN,	Bluebird B-6187, OLD
	PART 2-1 (-) (L. Carr)	TRAMP OT-1207
96227-1	HUSTLIN' WOMAN BLUES-1 (-)	Bluebird B-6202, FLY-
	(Minnie McCoy)	RIGHT LP 108, STASH
		LP 117
96228-1	SELLING MY PORK CHOPS (-)	Bluebird B-6199, EARL
	(Minnie McCoy)	BD-608
96229-1	DOCTOR, DOCTOR BLUES	Bluebird B-6199, EARL
	(Minnie McCoy) (Minnie McCoy)	BD-608

The reverse of Bluebird 6187 is by Chasey Collins; the reverse of Bluebird 6202 is
by Pine Top (Aaron Sparks).

MEMPHIS MINNIE   CHICAGO, DECEMBER 16, 1935
Memphis Minnie, vo, gtr; Black Bob, pno; unknown b.

C-1183-2	BITING BUG BLUES (-) ()	Vocalion 03144, RST
		(BLUES DOCUMENTS)
		BD-2048

C-1184-1	MINNIE'S LONESOME SONG (-) (Minnie McCoy)	Vocalion 03187, RST (BLUES DOCUMENTS) BD-2048
C-1184-3	MINNIE'S LONESOME SONG (-) (Minnie McCoy)	Vocalion 03187
C-1185-1	YOU AIN'T DONE NOTHING TO ME (-)()	Vocalion 03144, RST (BLUES DOCUMENTS) BD-2048
C-1186-1	AIN'T NOBODY HOME BUT ME	Vocalion unissued, OLD TRAMP OT-1207
C-1186-2	AIN'T NOBODY HOME BUT ME (-) (Minnie McCoy)	Vocalion 03187, RST (BLUES DOCUMENTS) BD-2048

BUMBLE BEE SLIM   CHICAGO, FEBRUARY 5, 1936
Bumble Bee Slim, vo; Myrtle Jenkins, pno; Memphis Minnie (?), gtr. Other songs
from this session feature Casey Bill Weldon on steel guitar, rather than Minnie.
On the unissued take -2, Slim clearly says, "Play the guitar, Minnie, 'cause you
done lost, too." Minnie may not appear on the issued take -1, however.

| C-1223-2 | WHEN SOMEBODY LOSES (THEN
SOMEBODY WINS) () (Amos Easton) | Vocalion unissued |

BUMBLE BEE SLIM AND MEMPHIS MINNIE
                              CHICAGO, FEBRUARY 6, 1936
Bumble Bee Slim, vo; Memphis Minnie, vo, probably gtr; Casey Bill Weldon, steel
gtr; unknown b; unknown tapping. Minnie does not appear on other songs from
this session.

| C-1227-2 | NEW ORLEANS STOP TIME (-)
(Amos Easton) | Vocalion 03197, MAGPIE
LP 4414 |

MEMPHIS MINNIE   CHICAGO, FEBRUARY 18, 1936
Memphis Minnie, vo, gtr; unknown b.

C-1263-1	ICE MAN (COME ON UP) (-) (Minnie McCoy)	Vocalion 03222, FLY- RIGHT LP 108, COLUMBIA CK-46775
C-1264-1	HOODOO LADY (-) (Minnie McCoy)	Vocalion 03222, FLY- RIGHT LP 108, COLUM- BIA CK-46775
C-1265-1	MY STRANGE MAN (-) (Minnie McCoy)	Vocalion 03285, FLY- RIGHT LP 108, COLUM- BIA CK-46775
C-1266-1	I'M A GAMBLIN' WOMAN (-) (Minnie McCoy)	Vocalion 03258, Conqueror 9025, DOCUMENT DLP 559

MEMPHIS MINNIE   CHICAGO, MAY 27, 1936
Memphis Minnie, vo, gtr; Black Bob, pno (-1); unknown b;
unknown woodblocks.

C-1384-1	I'M A BAD LUCK WOMAN (-) (Minnie McCoy)	Vocalion 03541, DOCU-MENT DLP 559, COLUM-BIA CK-46775
C-1385-2	CAUGHT ME WRONG AGAIN (Minnie McCoy) (Minnie McCoy)	Vocalion 03258, Conqueror 9025, DOCUMENT DLP 559, COLUMBIA CK-46775
C-1386-1	BLACK CAT BLUES (-) (Minnie McCoy)	Vocalion 03581, PALTRAM LP 101, EARL BD-617, COLUMBIA CK-46775
C-1386-2	BLACK CAT BLUES	ARC unissued, EARL BD-617
C-1387-1	GOOD MORNING (-) (Minnie McCoy)	Vocalion 03436, MAGPIE LP 1806, COLUMBIA CK-46775
C-1388-2	MAN YOU WON'T GIVE ME NO MONEY (-) (Minnie McCoy)	Vocalion 03474, BLUES CLASSICS LP 1, COLUM-BIA CK-46775
C-1389-1	IF YOU SEE MY ROOSTER (PLEASE RUN HIM HOME)-1 (-) (Minnie McCoy)	Vocalion 03285, FLYRIGHT LP 108, COLUMBIA CK-46775

The title of CAUGHT ME WRONG AGAIN in the copyright records of the Library of Congress, is given as I CAN'T SAY NOTHING YOU CAUGHT ME WRONG AGAIN.

MEMPHIS MINNIE   CHICAGO, NOVEMBER 12, 1936
Memphis Minnie, vo, gtr; possibly Alfred Bell, tpt; probably Black Bob, pno;
unknown b.

C-1667-2	I DON'T WANT YOU NO MORE (-) (Minnie McCoy)	Vocalion 03436, FLY-RIGHT LP 108
C-1668-1	OUT IN THE COLD (-) (Minnie McCoy)	Vocalion 03398, OLD TRAMP OT-1207
C-1669-2	DRAGGING MY HEART AROUND (-) (Minnie McCoy)	Vocalion 03398, OLD TRAMP OT-1207
C-1670-1	MOONSHINE (-) (Minnie McCoy)	Vocalion 03894, BLUES CLASSICS LP 1
C-1671-1	IT'S HARD TO BE MISTREATED (-) (Minnie McCoy)	Vocalion 03474, BLUES CLASSICS LP 1
C-1672-2	HAUNTED BLUES (-) (Minnie McCoy)	Vocalion 03581
C-1672-1	HAUNTED BLUES	Vocalion unissued, RST (BLUES DOCUMENTS) BD-2048

C-1672-1 is mistitled HAUNTED HOUSE on RST (BLUES DOCUMENTS) BD-2048.

MEMPHIS MINNIE CHICAGO, JUNE 9, 1937
Memphis Minnie, vo, gtr; probably Alfred Bell, tpt; probably Black Bob, pno;
Fred Williams, d.

C-1925-2	HOT STUFF (Minnie McCoy) (Minnie McCoy)	Vocalion 03651, MAGPIE LP 1806
C-1925-1	HOT STUFF	Vocalion unissued, DOCU-MENT DLP 559
C-1926-1	LIVING THE BEST I CAN (-) (Minnie McCoy)	Vocalion 03768, DOCU-MENT DLP 559
C-1927-1	YOU CAN'T RULE ME (-) (Minnie McCoy)	Vocalion 03697, EARL BD-617
C-1928-1	NO NEED YOU DOGGIN' ME (-) (Minnie McCoy)	Vocalion 03697, DOCU-MENT DLP 559
C-1929-2	LOOK WHAT YOU GOT (Memphis Minnie McCoy) (Minnie McCoy)	Vocalion 03612, RST (BLUES DOCUMENTS) BD-2048
C-1929-1	LOOK WHAT YOU GOT	Vocalion unissued, OLD TRAMP OT-1207

MEMPHIS MINNIE* YAS YAS GIRL+ CHICAGO, JUNE 17, 1937
Memphis Minnie, vo, gtr; probably Black Bob, pno; Fred Williams, d.

C-1936-1	MY BABY DON'T WANT ME NO MORE* (-) (Minnie McCoy)	Vocalion 03894, BLUES CLASSICS LP 1
C-1936-2	MY BABY DON'T WANT ME NO MORE*	Vocalion unissued, COLUMBIA CK-46775
C-1937-2	WANTS CAKE WHEN I'M HUNGRY* (-) (Minnie McCoy)	Vocalion 03768, OLD TRAMP OT-1207
C-1938-2	DOWN IN THE ALLEY* (-) (Minnie McCoy)	Vocalion 03612, DOCU-MENT DLP 559, COLUMBIA CK-46775
C-1939-3	BLUES EVERYWHERE+ (-) (Casey Bill)	Vocalion 03638, ARC 7-09-66, Conqueror 8922, MAGPIE LP 1806

All issues of C-1939-3 were mis-credited to YAS YAS GIRL, a *nom de disque* of
Merline Johnson, but as Dixon and Godrich note, this is by Memphis Minnie. The
reverse of Vocalion 03638, ARC 7-09-66 and Conqueror 8922 is by Merline Johnson.

MEMPHIS MINNIE CHICAGO, JUNE 22, 1937
Memphis Minnie, vo, gtr; probably Black Bob, pno; Fred Williams, d.

C-1942-1	KEEP ON SAILING (-) (Minnie McCoy)	Vocalion 03651

MEMPHIS MINNIE CHICAGO, DECEMBER 15, 1937
Memphis Minnie, vo, gtr; Arnett Nelson, clt (-1); unknown [or Minnie], mand
(-2); Blind John Davis, pno; unknown, b.

C-2052-1	PLEASE DON'T STOP HIM-1 (-)(Minnie McCoy)	Vocalion unissued, OLD TRAMP OT-1207, COLUMBIA CK-46775

C-2052-2	PLEASE DON'T STOP HIM-1,2	Vocalion unissued
C-2053-1	WALKING AND CRYING BLUES-1 (-) (Minnie McCoy)	Vocalion 03966, Conqueror 9026, OLD TRAMP OT-1207
C-2054-2	I'M GOING DON'T YOU KNOW-1	Vocalion unissued
C-2054-1	I'M GOING DON'T YOU KNOW-1 (-)(Minnie McCoy)	Vocalion unissued, DOCU-MENT DLP 559, COLUM-BIA CK-46775
C-2055-1	RUNNING AND DODGING BLUES-1,2 (-)()	Vocalion unissued, OLD TRAMP OT-1207
C-2055-2	RUNNING AND DODGING BLUES-1,2	Vocalion unissued
C-2056-1	NEW CAUGHT ME WRONG AGAIN (-) (Minnie McCoy)	Vocalion 03966, Conqueror 9026, EARL BD-608
C-2057-2	STOP LYING ON ME-1	Vocalion unissued
C-2057-1	STOP LYING ON ME-1 (-)()	Vocalion unissued, DOCU-MENT DLP 559

Composer credit information for C-2052 and C-2054 appears on the compact disc reissue, CK-46775.

MEMPHIS MINNIE   CHICAGO, JUNE 23, 1938
Memphis Minnie, vo, gtr; probably Black Bob, pno; Charlie McCoy, mand; unknown b.

C-2280-1	I HATE TO SEE THE SUN GO DOWN (-) (McCoy)	Vocalion 04356, RST (BLUES DOCUMENTS) BD-2048, COLUMBIA CK-46775
C-2281-1	LONG AS I CAN SEE YOU SMILE (-) (McCoy)	Vocalion 04506, Conqueror 9162, EARL BD-608
C-2282-1	HAS ANYONE SEEN MY MAN? (-) (McCoy)	Vocalion 04250, RST (BLUES DOCUMENTS) BD-2048, COLUMBIA CK-46775
C-2283-1	GOOD BISCUITS (-) (McCoy)	Vocalion 04295, OLD TRAMP OT-1207, COLUMBIA CK-46775
C-2284-1	I'VE BEEN TREATED WRONG (-) (McCoy)	Vocalion 04250, BLUES CLASSICS LP 26, EARL BD-617, COLUMBIA CK-46775
C-2285-1	KEEP ON WALKING (-) (McCoy)	Vocalion 04356, RST (BLUES DOCUMENTS) BD-2048
C-2286-1	KEEP ON EATING (-) (McCoy)	Vocalion 04295, OLD TRAMP OT-1207, COLUMBIA CK-46775
C-2287-1	I'D RATHER SEE HIM DEAD (-) (McCoy)	Vocalion 04506, Conqueror 9162, EARL BD-608

MEMPHIS MINNIE* LITTLE SON JOE +

CHICAGO, FEBRUARY 3, 1939

Memphis Minnie, vo (-1), gtr; Little Son Joe, vo (-2), gtr; prob. Fred Williams, d.

C-2446-1	DIGGIN' MY POTATOES-2+ () (-)	Vocalion 04707
C-2447-1	A.B.C. BLUES-2+ () ()	Vocalion 04776
C-2448-1	BONE YARD BLUES-2+ () ()	Vocalion 04776
C-2449-1	MY BLACK BUFFALO-2+ () (-)	Vocalion 04978, MAGPIE LP 1806
C-2450-1	TUFF LUCK BLUES-2+ () (-)	Vocalion 04707
C-2451-1	KEY TO THE WORLD-2+ () (-)	Vocalion 05004
C-2452-1	BLACK WIDOW STINGER-1* (-) (-)	Vocalion 04694, Conqueror 9198, MAGPIE LP 1806
C-2453-1,4	GOOD SOPPIN'-1* (-) (-)	Vocalion 04694, Conqueror 9198, MAGPIE LP 1806

The reverse of Vo 04978 is by Monkey Joe (Jesse Coleman)

MEMPHIS MINNIE

CHICAGO, FEBRUARY 6, 1939

Memphis Minnie, vo, gtr; Little Son Joe, gtr; Fred Williams, d.

C-2454-1	WORRIED BABY BLUES (-) ()	Vocalion 04898, RST (BLUES DOCUMENTS) BD-2048
C-2455-1	CALL THE FIRE WAGON (-)(-)	Vocalion 04858, Conqueror 9282, K.O.B. LP, EARL BD-617
C-2456-1	POOR AND WANDERING WOMAN BLUES (-) (-)	Vocalion 05004, RST (BLUES DOCUMENTS) BD-2048
C-2457-1	BAD OUTSIDE FRIENDS (-) (-)	Vocalion 04797, Conqueror 9275, FLYRIGHT LP 108, K.O.B. LP
C-2458-1	LOW DOWN MAN BLUES (-)(-)	Vocalion 04797, Conqueror 9275, FLYRIGHT LP 108, K.O.B. LP
C-2459-1	DON'T LEAD MY BABY WRONG (-) ()	Vocalion 04898, OLD TRAMP OT-1207
C-2460-1	KEEP YOUR BIG MOUTH CLOSED (-)(-)	Vocalion 04858, Conqueror 9282, K.O.B. LP, OLD TRAMP OT-1207

MEMPHIS MINNIE

CHICAGO, JUNE 27, 1940

Memphis Minnie, vo, gtr; Little Son Joe, gtr.

WC-3166-A	LONESOME SHACK BLUES (-) (McCoy)	Okeh 05728, Conqueror 9764, Columbia 30067, 37690, BLUES CLASSICS LP 1
WC-3167-A	NOTHING IN RAMBLING (-) (McCoy)	Okeh 05670, Conqueror 9764, Columbia 30066, 37689, BLUES CLASSICS LP 1

WC-3168-A BOY FRIEND BLUES (-) (McCoy)   Okeh 05670, Conqueror
                                                  9372, Columbia 30066,
                                                  37689, BLUES CLASSICS
                                                  LP 1
WC-3169-A FINGER PRINT BLUES (-) (-)   Okeh 05811, Conqueror
                                                  9763, FLYRIGHT LP 108,
                                                  K.O.B. LP
WC-3170-A IT'S HARD TO PLEASE MY MAN   Okeh 05728, Conqueror
           (-) (McCoy)   9372, Columbia 30067,
                                                  37690, BLUES CLASSICS
                                                  LP 1
WC-3171-A MA RAINEY (-) (-)   Okeh 05811, Conqueror
                                                  9763, FLYRIGHT LP 108,
                                                  K.O.B. LP

No composer credits are given on Conqueror 9763, but Okeh 05811 may show them.

MEMPHIS MINNIE   CHICAGO, MAY 21, 1941
Memphis Minnie, vo, gtr; Little Son Joe, gtr; unknown, b.

C-3764-1   IN MY GIRLISH DAYS   Okeh 06410, Conqueror
           (Ernest Lawler) (Lawlar)   9933, BLUES CLASSICS
                                                  LP 1
C-3765-1   ME AND MY CHAUFFEUR BLUES   Okeh 06288, Conqueror
           (Ernest Lawler) (Lawlar)   9933, Columbia 30124,
                                                  CBS LP 66426, LP 30008,
                                                  LP 22135, BLUES
                                                  CLASSICS LP 1, CBS LP
                                                  66218, CBS PORTRAIT
                                                  MASTERS RK 44072
C-3766-1   DOWN BY THE RIVERSIDE (-)   Conqueror 9936, CBS
           (Lawlar)   PORTRAIT MASTERS
                                                  RK 44072, RST (BLUES
                                                  DOCUMENTS) BD-2048
C-3767-1   I GOT TO MAKE A CHANGE   Conqueror 9935, CBS POR-
           BLUES (-) (See note)   TRAIT MASTERS RK 44072,
                                                  OLD TRAMP OT-1207
C-3768-1   PIG MEAT ON THE LINE (-)   Okeh 06505, Conqueror
           (Lawlar)   9935, FLYRIGHT LP 108,
                                                  K.O.B. LP
C-3769-1   MY GAGE IS GOING UP (-)   Okeh 06410, Conqueror
           (Lawlar)   9934, FLYRIGHT LP 109
C-3770-1   THIS IS YOUR LAST CHANCE   Okeh 06505, Conqueror
           (-) (Lawlar)   9936, FLYRIGHT LP 108
C-3771-1   CAN'T AFFORD TO LOSE   Okeh 06288, Conqueror
           MY MAN (Ernest Lawler) (Lawlar)   9934, Columbia 30124,
                                                  FLYRIGHT LP 109,
                                                  CBS PORTRAIT
                                                  MASTERS RK 44072

C-3765-1, C-3766-1, C-3767-1 and C-3771-1 have been reissued on a CBS compact
disc (RK 44072), where the composer credit for all songs is given as "E. Lawler".

MEMPHIS MINNIE* LITTLE SON JOE+
MR. MEMPHIS MINNIE, or (on some copies) LITTLE SON JOE++

CHICAGO, DECEMBER 12, 1941

Memphis Minnie, vo (-1), gtr; Little Son Joe, vo (-2), gtr; prob. Alfred Elkins, b.

C-4090-1	I'M NOT A BAD GAL-1* (-) (Lawlar)	Okeh 06624, Columbia 30029, 37462, MAGPIE LP 1806, SAYDISC/ MATCHBOX SDR 182, CBS PORTRAIT MASTERS RK 44072
C-4091-1	YOU GOT TO GET OUT OF HERE-1* (-) (Lawlar)	Columbia 30134, FLY-RIGHT LP 108, CBS PORTRAIT MASTERS RK 44072
C-4092-1	DON'T TURN THE CARD-1* (-) (See Note)	Columbia unissued, CBS PORTRAIT MASTERS RK 44072, DOCUMENT DLP 559
C-4093-1	LOOKING THE WORLD OVER-1* (-) (Lawlar)	Okeh 06707, Columbia 30025, 37458, FLYRIGHT LP 109, CBS PORTRAIT MASTERS RK 44072
C-4094-1	IT WAS YOU BABY-1* (-) (Lawlar)	Okeh 06624, Columbia 30029, 37462, SAYDISC/ MATCHBOX SDR 182,CBS PORTRAIT MASTERS RK 44072, EARL BD-617
C-4095-1	YOU NEED A FRIEND-1* (-) (See Note)	Columbia unissued, CBS PORTRAIT MASTERS RK 44072, DOCUMENT DLP 559
C-4096-1	I AM SAILIN'-1* (-) (See Note)	Columbia unissued, EPIC LP 37318, LP 22123, CBS PORTRAIT MASTERS RK 44072, EARL BD-617
C-4097-1	REMEMBER ME BLUES-1* (-) (See Note)	Columbia unissued, CBS PORTRAIT MASTERS RK 44072, DOCUMENT DLP 559
C-4098-1	BLACK RAT SWING-2++ (Willie Mae Thornton and Minnie Lawler) (Lawlar)	Okeh 06707, Columbia 30025, 37458, FLYRIGHT LP 109, BLUES CLASSICS LP 1
C-4099-1	JUST HAD TO HOLLER-2+ ()()	Columbia unissued, EPIC LP 37318, LP 22123

The entire session for December 12, 1941, with the exception of the last two titles (C-4098-1 and C-4099-1) has been reissued on a CBS compact disc (RK 44072), where the composer credit for all songs is given as "E. Lawler".

MEMPHIS MINNIE   CHICAGO, DECEMBER 19, 1944
Memphis Minnie, vo, gtr; Little Son Joe, gtr; unknown, d.

C-4302	FASHION PLATE DADDY (Ernest Lawler) ()	Columbia unissued, ORIGIN LP 24
C-4303	WHEN YOU LOVE ME (Ernest Lawler) (Lawlar)	Okeh 06733, Columbia 37455, 30022, FLYRIGHT LP 109
C-4304	PLEASE SET A DATE (Ernest Lawler) (Lawlar)	Columbia 36895, 30003, FLYRIGHT LP 109
C-4305	MEAN MISTREATER BLUES (Ernest Lawler) (Lawlar)	Columbia 37295, 30015, MAGPIE LP 1806, K.O.B. LP
C-4306	LOVE COME AND GO (Ernest Lawler) (Lawlar)	Okeh 06733, Columbia 37455, 30022, FLYRIGHT LP 109
C-4307	TRUE LOVE (-) (Lawlar)	Columbia 36895, 30003, FLYRIGHT LP 109
C-4308	WHEN MY MAN COMES HOME (-) ()	Columbia unissued, ORIGIN LP 24

MEMPHIS MINNIE   CHICAGO, FEBRUARY 26, 1946
Memphis Minnie, vo, gtr; Little Son Joe, gtr; unknown, b.

CC-04504	I'M SO GLAD (-) (Lawlar)	Columbia 37295, 30015, BLUES CLASSICS LP 1, MAGPIE LP 1806, COLUMBIA LP 3356, K.O.B. LP
CC-04505	HOLD ME BLUES	Columbia unissued, ORIGIN LP 24
CC-04506	KILLER DILLER FROM THE SOUTH	Columbia unissued, ORIGIN LP 24
CC-04507	MOANING BLUES (NO. 1)	Columbia unissued, ORIGIN LP 24
CC-04508	GOT TO LEAVE YOU (NO. 1)	Columbia unissued, ORIGIN LP 24
CC-04509	THE MAN I LOVE (-) ()	Columbia unissued, ORIGIN LP 24

MEMPHIS MINNIE   CHICAGO, SEPTEMBER 20, 1946
Memphis Minnie, vo, gtr; Little Son Joe, gtr; unknown, b; unknown, d.

CC-04625	GOT TO LEAVE YOU (NO. 2) (-) ()	Columbia unissued, ORIGIN LP 24
CC-04626	KILLER DILLER BLUES (-) (Lawlar)	Columbia 37977, 30102, RBF LP 16, FLYRIGHT LP 109
CC-04627	MOANING BLUES (NO. 2) (Little Son Lawlar, i.e. Ernest Lawlers)()	Columbia unissued, ORIGIN LP 24
CC-04628	HOLD ME BLUES (Little Son Lawlar) (Lawlar)	Columbia 37977, 30102, RBF LP 16, FLYRIGHT LP 109, ORIGIN LP 24

CC-04629	FISH MAN BLUES (Words by Little Son Lawlar [Ernest Lawlers]; music by Lester F. Melrose) (Lawlar)	Columbia 37579, 30054, MAGPIE LP 1806, K.O.B. LP
CC-04630	WESTERN UNION (Words by Little Son Lawlers, music by Lester Melrose) (Lawlar)	Columbia 30134, MAGPIE LP 1806
CC-04631	MY MAN IS GONE (AGAIN) (-) ()	Columbia unissued, ORIGIN LP 24
CC-04632	LEAN MEAT WON'T FRY (Ernest Lawlar) (Lawlar)	Columbia 37579, 30054, MAGPIE LP 1806, K.O.B. LP

MEMPHIS MINNIE   CHICAGO, DECEMBER 27, 1947

Memphis Minnie, vo, gtr; Little Son Joe, gtr; Blind John Davis, pno; unknown, b; unknown, d; vo chorus by sidemen, -2

CC-04968	THREE TIMES SEVEN BLUES (-) (Lawlars)	Columbia 38099, 30111, MAGPIE LP 1806, K.O.B. LP
CC-04969	DAYBREAK BLUES (-) (Lawlars)	Columbia 30120, FLY-RIGHT LP 109
CC-04969	BLUE MONDAY BLUES (Alt. take of DAYBREAK BLUES)	Columbia unissued, ORIGIN LP 24
CC-04970	MILLION DOLLAR BLUES (Ernest Lawlar) (Lawlars)	Columbia 30120, FLY-RIGHT LP 109
CC-04970	MILLION DOLLAR BLUES (Alt. take)	Columbia unissued, ORIGIN LP 24
CC-04971	SHOUT THE BOOGIE-2 (-) (Lawlars)	Columbia 38099, 30111, MAGPIE LP 1806, K.O.B. LP
CC-04971	SHOUT THE BOOGIE-2 (Alt. take)	Columbia unissued, ORIGIN LP 24

MEMPHIS MINNIE AND LITTLE SON JOE   CHICAGO, APRIL 23, 1949

Memphis Minnie, vo, gtr; Little Son Joe, gtr; Blind John Davis (?), piano; unknown, b; vo chorus by sidemen, -2

CC-05043	TEARS ON MY PILLOW (-) (Lawlars)	Columbia 30176, FLY-RIGHT LP 4713, K.O.B. LP
CC-05044	SWEET MAN (-) (Lawlars)	Columbia 30176, MAGPIE LP 1806, K.O.B. LP
CC-05044	SWEET MAN (Alt. take)	Columbia unissued, ORIGIN LP 24
CC-05045	I HOPE LOVE WILL CHANGE SOME DAY (LUCK WILL CHANGE SOME DAY) (-) ()	Columbia unissued, ORIGIN LP 24
CC-05046	OH BELIEVE ME (BELIEVE ME) (-) ()	Columbia unissued, ORIGIN LP 24
CC-05047	TONIGHT I SMILE WITH YOU (-) (Lawlars)	Columbia 30146, FLY-RIGHT LP 109

CC-05048   JUMP LITTLE RABBIT-2 (-) (Lawlars) Columbia 30146, FLY-
                                                              RIGHT LP 109

Little Son Joe's presence is impossible to aurally confirm on the above session, and
he may not be present.

MEMPHIS MINNIE   CHICAGO, 1949

Memphis Minnie, vo, gtr; Sunnyland Slim, pno; poss. Ernest "Big" Crawford, b;
unknown, d.

1214-1	DOWN HOME GIRL (-) ()	Regal unissued, BIO-GRAPH LP 12035
1215-1	NIGHT WATCHMAN BLUES (-) ()	Regal unissued, BIO-GRAPH LP 12035
1215-2	NIGHT WATCHMAN BLUES	Regal unissued, BIO-GRAPH LP 12035
1216-1	WHY DID I MAKE YOU CRY (-) (Lawlars)	Regal 3529, BIOGRAPH LP 12035
1217-1	KIDMAN BLUES (-) (Lawlars)	Regal 3529, SAVOY LP 16000, MUSIDISC LP 955, LP 2705, MUSE LP 5212
1217-2	KIDMAN BLUES (KID MAN BLUES)	Regal unissued, BIO-GRAPH LP 12035

MEMPHIS MINNIE WITH LITTLE JOE AND HIS BAND

                                                    CHICAGO, JULY 11, 1952

Memphis Minnie, vo, gtr; Little Son Joe, gtr; Little Walter, hca (-1); possibly
Black Bob, pno (-2); possibly Elga Edmonds, d.

C-1024	BROKEN HEART-2 (-) (M. Minnie)	Checker 771, CHESS LP 6641.047
C-1025	CONJUR MAN-1 (-)()	Checker unissued
C-1026	LAKE MICHIGAN-1 (-)()	Checker unissued
C-1027	ME AND MY CHAUFFEUR-1 (Ernest Lawlar)(M. Minnie)	Checker 771, CHESS LP 6641.047

**MEMPHIS MINNIE AND HER COMBO* LITTLE SON JOE+ LITTLE
BROTHER MONTGOMERY++**   CHICAGO, OCTOBER 5, 1953

Memphis Minnie, vo (-1), gtr; Little Son Joe, vo (-2), gtr; Little Brother
Montgomery, vo (-3), pno; unknown, d.

2606-3	KISSING IN THE DARK-1*	JOB unissued
2606-4	KISSING IN THE DARK-1* (Earnest Lawlars) (E. Lawlars)	JOB 1101, FLYRIGHT LP 585, P. VINE LP 9022, BOOGIE DISEASE LP 101/102
2607-1	WORLD OF TROUBLE-1* (Earnest Lawlars) (E. Lawlars)	JOB 1101, FLYRIGHT LP 585, JUKE JOINT LP 1501, BOOGIE DISEASE LP 101/102
2608	IN LOVE AGAIN-1* () ()	JOB unissued, FLYRIGHT LP 585
2609-1	WHAT A NIGHT-1* () ()	JOB unissued, FLYRIGHT LP 585

2610	KEEP DRINKIN'-3++	JOB unissued, FLYRIGHT LP 577, P. VINE LP 9022
2611	BOOGIE-3++	JOB unissued, FLYRIGHT LP 577
2612	ETHEL BEA-2+ ()()	JOB unissued, FLYRIGHT LP 585, JUKE JOINT LP 1501
2613	A LITTLE TOO LATE-2+ ()()	JOB unissued, FLYRIGHT LP 585
	I'D WRITE A LETTER-2+ ()()	JOB unissued, P. VINE LP 9022

MEMPHIS MINNIE   MEMPHIS, 1959
Memphis Minnie, vo, gtr; Little Son Joe, d. (Presence of other personnel unconfirmed.)

	A FEW DROPS OF LOVE	Audiodisc
	IN YOUR HEART	
	UNLUCKY TOWN	Audiodisc

The above issue is a private test pressing, and no copy can be located, although Georges Adins was able to hear it when he visited Minnie shortly after it was made.

Appendix
The Jed Davenport Session

JED DAVENPORT AND HIS BEALE STREET JUG BAND
                                   MEMPHIS, FEBRUARY 17, 1930
Jed Davenport, hca, vo (-1), comments (-2); Joe McCoy, gtr, vo (-3), comments (-2); Memphis Minnie, gtr (-4), mandolin (-5), vo (-6), comments (-7); Hambone Lewis, jug; Milton Robey, violin, imitation cornet (-8).

MEM-734	BEALE STREET BREAKDOWN-2,5 (Jed Davenport) ()	Vocalion 1478, MATCHBOX LP 213, ORIGIN LP 19, HISTORICAL LP 36
MEM-735	YOU OUGHT TO MOVE OUT OF TOWN-3,4,6 (-) (Davenport)	Vocalion 1513, MATCHBOX LP 213, HISTORICAL LP 36
MEM-763	THE DIRTY DOZEN-4 (Rufus Perryman) ()	Vocalion 1478, MATCHBOX LP 213, HISTORICAL LP 36
MEM-764	JUG BLUES-4 (Jed Davenport) ()	Vocalion 1504, MATCHBOX LP 213, WHOOPEE 102
MEM-774	SAVE ME SOME-1,3,4,7 (Charlie McCoy) (Davenport)	Vocalion 1513, MATCHBOX LP 213, ORIGIN LP 19, HISTORICAL LP 36
MEM-775	PICCOLO BLUES-4,8 (Jed Davenport) ()	Vocalion 1504, MATCHBOX LP 213, WHOOPEE LP 102

Note: The above session is as given by Richard Metson in "Jed Davenport, The Recordings, Part 1," JUKE BLUES 9, Summer 1987, p. 20. Our main reason for listing it here is that it would make indecipherable the already-complicated session notes for the February 17, 1930, session (q.v.). Too, Minnie's instrumental contribution to the Jed Davenport sides is difficult to establish.

NOTES

Chapter 1: THE HEROINE

1. Ron Weinstock. Record review, in *Living Blues* 66. 1985. p. 29.
2. Steve LaVere. "Memphis Minnie". *Living Blues* 14. Autumn 1973. p. 5.
3. Sheldon Harris. *Blues Who's Who*. New Rochelle: Arlington House, 1979. Reprint. NY: Da Capo, 1981. p. 162. Harris is quoting Chris Strachwitz, folklorist and owner of Arhoolie Records.
4. The Winter 1980-1981 *Living Blues* (#49) published the results of the first annual W. C. Handy Awards. Twenty performers were elected to the Hall of Fame, and Minnie was one of these. Bessie Smith was the only other woman elected. Ma Rainey was elected to the Hall of Fame some years later.
5. "BU Poll." *Blues Unlimited* 100. April 1973. p. 6.
6. Helen Oakley Dance. *Stormy Monday. The T-Bone Walker Story.* Baton Rouge: Louisiana State University Press, 1987. Reprint. NY: Da Capo, 1990. p. 1
7. Darlene Gavron Stevens. "Koko Taylor." *Chicago Sunday Tribune.* February 24, 1991. Section 6, p. 3.
8. Wesley Race. "Hound Dog Taylor." *Blues Unlimited* 93. July 1972. p. 16. At this time, Minnie would have been playing with Son Joe, and not her first husband.
9. Mike Rowe and Mike Leadbitter. "I Was the Baby Boy: Baby Boy Warren Talks to Mike Rowe and Mike Leadbitter". *Blues Unlimited* 96. November 1972. p. 5.
10. Bukka White, quoted in Margaret McKee and Fred Chisenhall. *Beale Black and Blue. Life and Music on Black America's Main Street.* Baton Rouge: Louisiana State University Press, 1981. p. 126.
11. While Langston Hughes, who wrote about Minnie in the 1940s, wrote a poem entitled "Minnie Sings Her Blues" that appears in *Fine Clothes to the Jew* (NY: Knopf, 1927, p. 64) in a chapter titled "Beale Street Love," the poem is too early and too jazz-oriented to be about Memphis Minnie.
12. As we note in the discography, Minnie recorded 184 (or 252) sides, depending on how you count them.
13. Pete Welding wrote that the Johnny Shines LP, *Standing at the Crossroads,* Testament LP 2221, "handily demonstrates that Shines' basic musical orientation is midway between those of Son House and Robert Johnson, with an additional overlay of Memphis blues, the most prominent source of which derives from Mem-

phis Minnie." "The Testament Story—Conclusion." *Blues World* 44. Autumn 1972. p. 5.

Bob Groom. "The Library of Congress Blues and Gospel Recordings, 4: Sampson Pittman, Calvin Frazier, The Frazier Family." *Blues World* 44. Autumn 1972. p. 17.

Jim and Amy O'Neal. "Living Blues Interview: Eddie Boyd, Part One". *Living Blues* 35. November/December 1977.p. 12.

Dave Weld "Living Blues Interview: J. B. Hutto". *Living Blues* 30. November/December, 1976. p. 19.

Bruce Iglauer, Jim O'Neal, and Bea Van Geffen. "Living Blues Interview: Lowell Fulson, Part One". *Living Blues* 2:5, Summer 1971. p. 20.

John J. Broven. "J. B. Lenoir: Yet Another Forgotten Artist." *Blues Unlimited* 15. September 1964. p. 5

14. Howard DeWitt, with research assistance and discography by Morton Reff. *Chuck Berry: Rock N Roll Music.* Second Edition. Ann Arbor: Pierian Press, 1985. p. 166.

15. Daisy Douglas Johnson, interviewed by Paul Garon and Beth Garon, Memphis, June 23, 1989.

16. Adins was able to question Minnie about a number of matters, and Leadbitter did as well, although the latter suggests much of his information also came from Daisy and her husband. Adins, too, corresponded with Daisy. Georges Adins, personal communication to the authors, August 17, 1987. See also Georges Adins, "Memphis Minnie", *Rhythm and Blues Panorama* 24, March 24, 1963. Reprinted in *Soul Bag* 97. January/February 1984. For Leadbitter's report, see Mike Leadbitter, "My Girlish Days." *Blues Unlimited* 78. December 1970. pp. 8-9.

17. For June 24, 1894, see Mike Leadbitter, "My Girlish Days", p. 8.

For June 3, 1896, see Jeff Titon. *Early Downhome Blues.* Urbana: University of Illinois Press, 1977. p. 94, or Samuel Charters. *Sweet as the Showers of Rain.* NY: Oak Publication, 1977. p. 85. (*Sweet as the Showers of Rain* has been reprinted, along with *The Bluesmen,* as *The Bluesmakers.* NY: Da Capo, 1991.)

For June 24, 1900, see William Broonzy, as told to Yannick Bruynoghe. *Big Bill Blues.* London: Cassell and Company, 1955. p. 106.

Chapter 2: THE RISE OF MEMPHIS MINNIE

1. Sung by Mamie Smith for Okeh, in a session arranged by Okeh's Fred Hager and black songwriter/bandleader Perry Bradford. Mamie Smith recorded *That Thing Called Love* and *You Can't Keep a Good Man Down,* on February 14, 1920, and the songs were released on Okeh 4113. On August 10, 1920, she cut her first blues, *Crazy Blues,* and *It's Right Here For You (If You Don't Get It - 'tain't No Fault O' Mine).* The record was released as Okeh 4169.

2. In the liner notes to Yazoo LP 1071, *Ma Rainey's Black Bottom,* Stephen Calt notes that "Classic" blues is "a nonsensical term devised by jazz enthusiasts. In reality [such songs] are black vaudeville blues; there is nothing 'classic' about them." Considering that "classic" can mean: "of recognized value," "traditional, enduring," "a typical example," "authentic, authoritative," or "noted because of special literary or historical associations," it is difficult to understand why Calt could not find a link between the meaning of the word and its "Classic" application. Derrick Stewart-

Baxter has denounced the term as well, even though the title of his *Ma Rainey and the Classic Blues Singers* (NY: Stein and Day, 1970) inevitably helped promote its use.

3. The most complete discussion of classic blues is in Daphne Duval Harrison. *Black Pearls. Blues Queens of the 1920s*. New Brunswick: Rutgers University Press, 1988. See also Sandra Lieb's *Mother of the Blues. A Study of Ma Rainey*. Amherst: University of Massachusetts Press, 1981.

4. Detailed discussions of the structure, form and function of country blues can be found in David Evans. *Big Road Blues*. Berkeley: University of California Press, 1982. Reprint. NY: Da Capo, 1987, and in Titon, *Early Downhome Blues*, pp. xiv-v. Titon emphasizes that downhome is a feeling as well as a style: downhome "locates the feeling as a place in the mental landscape of black America."

5. Evans, *Big Road Blues*, p. 48. Thanks also to Don Kent for helping us refine these ideas.

6. Recent studies are attempting to correct such distortions. In addition to Harrison's and Lieb's work, cited above, there is Hazel V. Carby's "It Just Be's Dat Way Sometime: The Sexual Politics of Women's Blues". *Radical America* 20:4. June/July 1986. pp. 9-22.

7. Chris Albertson, who provided the above figures in *Bessie* (NY: Stein and Day, 1973. pp. 98, 181, 165.), noted about Howell, "Male blues singers were not likely to get rich from their records." That is to say, he treats the difference between Smith and Howell's pay scales as an essentially gendered issue. The degree to which this is correct, or not, is at the heart of our investigation.

8. Relatively few country blues artists from before the Depression continued to record after the Depression *in a rural style:* Sleepy John Estes, Kokomo Arnold, Bukka White and a few others did so, but Peg Leg Howell, Tommy Johnson, Ishman Bracey, Walter Hawkins, and dozens of others did not. Robert Johnson never recorded before the Depression.

9. Pete Welding. "Teddy Darby". *Blues World* 31. June 1970. p. 3.

10. John G. Allinson. "The McKinley James Story." *Blues Unlimited* 135/136. July/September 1979. p. 12. Robert Springer. " 'Being Yourself Is More Than Trying to Be Somebody Else'. An Interview with Robert Shaw." *Blues Unlimited* 129. March/April 1978. pp. 13-14. Bill Greensmith. "Just Whaling" (Louis Myers Interview). *Blues Unlimited* 122. November/December 1976 p. 5. Mike Rowe. *Chicago Breakdown*. London: Eddison Press, 1973. Reprinted as *Chicago Blues*. NY: Da Capo, 1981. p. 99. Pete Lowry. Obituary for Tommie Lee Russell. *Living Blues* 32. May/June 1977. p. 6.

11. James Watt, interviewed by Jim O'Neal, Chicago, June 15, 1984.

12. Minnie poses other, unresolved tensions. For example, in spite of her well-known ferocity and indpendence, she chose to enter the male-dominated country blues field as the partner/wife of a male performer.

13. The number of blues singers who said they took up the blues and/or came North to escape a life of cotton-picking is legion.

Chapter 3: SOUTHERN NIGHTS

1. This is the birthdate that appears on Minnie's death certificate.

2. Daisy was born September 3, 1915, in Walls, Mississippi. Ethel Douglas, Minnie's sister-in-law, and one of her few surviving family members, has also been very helpful in reconstructing details of Minnie's early life.

3. Brewer Phillips, interviewed by Steve Cushing, Chicago, July 8 and 9, 1989.

4. For an account of the "first instrument" motif in blues singers' autobiographies, see Barry Lee Pearson. *"Sounds So Good To Me"*. Philadelphia: University of Pennsylvania Press, 1984. For notes on the childhood of musicians, see Martin Nass, PhD. "The Development of Creative Imagination in Composers." *Psychoanalytic Explorations In Music*. Ed. by Stuart Feder, Richard L. Karmel and George H. Pollock. Madison, CT: International Universities Press, 1990. p. 279.

5. Leadbitter, "My Girlish Days", p. 8. Adins, "Memphis Minnie", 1984. pp. 5-8. Grard Herzhaft. "Memphis Minnie Revisited", *Soul Bag 97,* January/February, 1984. pp. 8-9.

6. Cushing, Brewer Phillips interview.

7. O'Neal, James Watt interview.

8. Johnny Shines, quoted in Rowe, *Chicago Breakdown,* p. 43. Johnny Shines, interviewed by Paul Garon and Beth Garon, Tuscaloosa, June 20, 1989. Guitarist/vocalist Johnny Shines was born in Tennessee in 1915, traveled with Robert Johnson, and captured the most pleasing characteristics of Johnson's style. Comfortable in both a rural acoustic mode and a postwar, electric band setting, his ringing eloquence has made him a champion Delta practitioner.

9. Garon, Daisy Douglas Johnson interview.

10. Garon, Daisy Douglas Johnson interview.

11. Herbert R. Northrup. *Organized Labor and the Negro.* NY: Harper, 1944. Second Edition, pp. 44-45.

12. Margaret McKee and Fred Chisenhall, *Beale Black & Blue,* p. 73.

13. David M. Tucker. *Lieutenant Lee of Beale Street.* Nashville: Vanderbilt University Press, 1971. pp. 145-146.

14. Margaret McKee and Fred Chisenhall, *Beale Black & Blue,* p. 23. McKee and Chisenhall are quoting a 1932 issue of the *Memphis World.*

15. [Will Shade, "Days of Nineteen-Hundred," from *Conversation with the Blues. A Documentary of Field Recordings* by Paul Oliver. Recorded July 20, 1960. Decca LK 4664.] See also, Paul Oliver. *Conversation with the Blues.* London: Cassell, 1965. pp. 85-86.

16. George W. Lee. *Beale Street. Where the Blues Began.* NY: Robert O. Ballou, 1934. p. 90.

17. See his remarks in the chapter, "Me and My Chauffeur."

18. Herzhaft, "Memphis Minnie Revisited".

19. Richard K. Spottswood. "Rev. Robert Wilkins." *Blues Unlimited* 13. July 1964. p. 5.

20. In the liner notes to Yazoo 1050, *Furry Lewis, in His Prime,* Stephen Calt suggests that Minnie, along with Frank Stokes and Jim Jackson, was Memphis' "reigning blues favorite."

21. Don Kent, personal communication to the authors, April, 1988.

22. Memphis Slim, interviewed by Jim O'Neal, Chicago, December 30, 1975. Piano man Memphis Slim, born Peter Chatman in 1915 in Memphis, was the best known of the expatriate bluesmen living in Europe. He recorded prolifically.

23. Babysitting for Eddie Taylor is confirmed by Homesick James. Interviewed by Jim O'Neal, Atlanta, October, 1988. Taylor's own claim is a bit more extravagant: "Eddie [Taylor] often said that he'd been nursed by Memphis Minnie—a wonderful claim whether taken figuratively or literally as he meant it. . . ." Justin O'Brien. "Eddie Taylor 1923-1985." *Living Blues* 72. 1986. p. 32.

24. Pee Wee Whittaker to David Evans, and David Evans, personal communication to the authors, February 16, 1987; O'Neal, Homesick James interview.

25. Harris, *Blues Who's Who.* p. 547.

26. Victor 21134. Recorded October 20, 1927.

27. Steve Calt. Liner notes to *Bottleneck Trendsetters,* Yazoo 1049. Herzhaft, "Memphis Minnie Revisited."

28. Especially if the 1920s Weldon, who lived in Memphis and played with the Memphis Jug Band, was an entirely different person.

29. Jimmy Rogers, interviewed by Jim O'Neal, Atlanta, October, 1988.

30. Stephen Calt and Gayle Wardlow. *King of the Delta Blues. The Life and Music of Charlie Patton.* Newton, NJ: Rock Chapel Press, 1988. p. 154.

31. Gayle Dean Wardlow. "Can't Tell My Future: The Mystery of Willie Brown." *Blues Unlimited* 147. Spring 1986. p. 8.

32. Calt and Wardlow, *King of the Delta Blues,* p. 157. Some listeners will remember that this is almost exactly the way J. D. Short described Charlie Patton's guitar skills, although Short specified "Lord have mercy" instead of "Fare thee well." J. D. Short. "Charlie Patton." On *Son House and J. D. Short. Blues from the Mississippi Delta.* Folkways FA 2467.

33. *How Come You Do Me Like You Do* (by Austin and Bergere) was a hit in 1924.

34. Calt and Wardlow, *King of the Delta Blues,* pp. 158-159. Calt and Wardlow's report suggests that Minnie was the dominant personality in her relationship with Brown. While this is no surprise—later we will hear Johnny Shines insist that Minnie won *all* her arguments—the weakness of *King of the Delta Blues* is the authors' fanatical need to disparage nearly every singer who came in contact with Charlie Patton, especially Brown. One of the few exceptions was Memphis Minnie.

35. Steve Calt. Liner notes to *Roots of Rock.* Yazoo 1063.

36. A far cry from the downhome blues of Memphis in the 1920s, the Hamfats was a bluesy, driving jazz band, at once earthy and relatively sophisticated, that usually consisted of Morand on trumpet; Odell Rand, clarinet; Horace Malcolm, piano; Joe McCoy, guitar and vocals; Charlie McCoy, guitar and/or mandolin; Ransom Knowling, or another, bass; and Pearlis Williams on drums.

37. Leadbitter, "My Girlish Days," p.9. Other sources confirm this general idea.

38. Adins, "Memphis Minnie."

39. We use the term "common law" less in its legal sense than as a term indicating "by mutual consent."

40. Sunnyland Slim, interviewed by Beverly Zeldin, Chicago, 1987. Memphis Slim to David Evans, and David Evans, personal communication to the authors. Alas, Memphis Slim never amplified his remarks about his father's connection with Minnie.

41. Garon, Johnny Shines interview.

42. Ethel Douglas and Daisy Douglas Johnson, interviewed by Paul Garon and Beth Garon, Memphis, June 23, 1989. An A and R man, for "artist and repertoire," was usually the person in charge of the recording artist and their recording session.

43. Zeldin, Sunnyland Slim interview. Born Albert Luandrew in 1907 in Tennessee, pianist Sunnyland became a mainstay of the Chicago blues tradition, and helped dozens of singers newly arrived from the South to secure jobs and find their way around the Chicago blues scene. He has been an active bluesman for seven decades! "Sunnyland was really the one that got her in with Chess. He's the one that got her recording with Chess. No, they wasn't lovers, never was. Sunnyland Slim, that old scoundrel, I like him," said Brewer Phillips.

44. Cab Calloway. *Of Minnie the Moocher and Me.* NY: Crowell, 1976.

45. The suggestions that Minnie's name was derived from the cartoon character, Minnie Mouse is attributed to Mike Leadbitter by Herzhaft, in "Memphis Minnie Revisited," but, Leadbitter does not mention Minnie Mouse, at least not in "My Girlish Days." The "Minnie Mouse" theory is pure speculation, although the Disney character did debut around the time of Minnie's first session.

46. Garon, Ethel Douglas and Daisy Johnson interview. Unlike Daisy Douglas Johnson, Ethel Douglas was familiar with Minnie's repertoire in the old days, and it was completely without prompting, or without having played any of Minnie's pieces for her ourselves, that she made her remarks about *When the Levee Breaks,* a side cut at Minnie and Joe's first session in 1929, but since then issued on LP.

47. Other unissued songs have now been issued by specialist record companies like Yazoo, Blues Documents, or Mamlish. For example, Minnie's *Ain't No Use Trying To Tell on Me (I Know Something on You),* recorded for Okeh in 1933, appears only on Yazoo LP 1021, and was never issued by Okeh. The alternate take of *Keep It To Yourself,* recorded for Decca in 1934, appears only on Mamlish LP 3801.

In their discography, Dixon and Godrich note that "The Hillbilly Plowboy" is probably Joe McCoy. R. M. W. Dixon and John Godrich, *Blues and Gospel Records, 1902-1943.* Chigwell: Storyville Publications, 1982. Third Edition, Fully Revised. p. 466.

48. Jim Jackson. *Jim Jackson's Kansas City Blues.* Vocalion 1144. Recorded October 10, 1927. Tampa Red and Georgia Tom. *It's Tight Like That.* Vocalion 1216. Recorded October 24, 1928. Leroy Carr. *How Long — How Long Blues.* Vocalion 1191. Recorded June 19, 1928.

49. Quoted in Barry Lee Pearson, *"Sounds So Good To Me,"* p. 126.

50. Bill wrote that Minnie and her husband often returned to Memphis after their Chicago recording dates. Broonzy, *Big Bill Blues.* p. 105.

51. Arthur "Big Boy" Crudup, quoted in Mike Leadbitter. "Big Boy Crudup." *Blues Unlimited* 75. September 1970. pp. 16-17.

52. This may be Lenlow, Tennessee.

53. Garon, Daisy Douglas Johnson interview.

54. Garon, Ethel Douglas and Daisy Johnson interview.

55. Richard Metson. "Jed Davenport, The Recordings, Part 1." *Juke Blues* 9. Summer 1987. pp. 18-20. See also Richard Metson. "Jed Davenport, The Recordings, Part 2." *Juke Blues* 10. Autumn 1987. pp. 15-16. As many of the discographical details concerning Minnie's role in this session are speculative, the Davenport discography is appended to the main discography of Minnie's work. See our note there.

56. Harris, *Blues Who's Who,* p. 161.

57. Willie Moore, quoted in Calt and Wardlow, *King of the Delta Blues*, p. 158.

58. As if any more proof were needed that this was Minnie and Joe McCoy, "Memphis Minnie and Kansas Joe" were credited on the Victor session sheet for the "Minnie McCoy and Joe Johnson" outing. The session actually took place on two days, May 26 and 29, 1930. Dixon and Godrich, *Blues and Gospel Records*, p. 510.

59. Many details about Victor can be found in Brian Rust. *The Victor Master Book, Volume 2* (1925-1936). Indexes by Malcolm Shaw and Nevil Skrimshire. Stanhope: Walter C. Allen, 1970. See also the lengthy Victor section in Brian Rust, *The American Record Label Book*. New Rochelle: Arlington House, 1978. Reprint. NY: Da Capo, 1984, and Dick Spottswood. "When the Wolf Knocked on Victor's Door." *78 Quarterly*. 1:5. 1990. pp. 68-69. Spottswood gives the figure of 990 and 165 copies for Minnie and Joe's Victor releases, but notes that the figures may mean anything from quantity pressed to quantity sold.

60. See, for example, Richard Lieberson. "Guitar Duos." *The Guitar Player Book,* Revised and Updated Edition. Cupertino: Guitar Player Books and NY: Grove Press, 1979. p. 262.

61. Quoted in Gayle Dean Wardlowe, "Garfield Akers and Mississippi Joe Calicott: From the Hernando Cottonfields." *Living Blues 50*. Spring 1981. p. 26.

62. Wardlowe, "Garfield Akers," p. 27. From a taped interview with Johnny Temple.

63. Garon, Johnny Shines interview.

64. Richard Metson credits Bob Groom for this observation. Metson, "Jed Davenport, Part 1," p. 20. Minnie may have also called her song <u>New</u> Dirty Dozen because it followed Speckled Red's piano versions. Either is consistent with naming conventions of the time.

65. Mississippi Sheiks. *Sitting on Top of the World*. Okeh 8784. Recorded February 17, 1930. This was a race record hit and should not be confused with the popular song, *I'm Sitting on Top of the World*, by Henderson, Lewis and King (1925).

Chapter 4: CHICAGO DAYS

1. St. Clair Drake and Horace Cayton. *Black Metropolis*. NY: Harper Torchbooks, 1962. Revised and Enlarged Edition. Volume 1, pp. 8.

2. Paul Oliver. *The Story of the Blues*. Philadelphia: Chilton, 1969. p. 74.

3. St. Clair Drake and Horace Cayton, *Black Metropolis*. Volume 1, pp. 8, xlii. See also Mike Rowe, *Chicago Breakdown*, pp. 27, 35.

4. St. Clair Drake and Horace Cayton, *Black Metropolis*. Volume 1, pp. 63, 65-76.

5. St. Clair Drake and Horace Cayton, *Black Metropolis*. Volume 1, pp. 218-219.

6. Jacqueline Jones, *Labor of Love, Labor of Sorrow*. NY: Vintage, 1986. (Orig. 1985.) p. 168.

7. Rowe, *Chicago Breakdown*, p. 27.

8. Jacqueline Jones, *Labor of Love, Labor of Sorrow*. p. 159.

9. St. Clair Drake and Horace Cayton, *Black Metropolis*. Volume 1, pp. 218-219.

10. Nor did Joe have any session of his own in that economically desolate year.

11. For more details, see Rust, *The American Record Label Book*, pp. 94-95.

12. Victor may have been the most prestigious label, but it's doubtful whether Minnie or her listeners knew or cared. By the time Minnie recorded for them back in 1930, their second race series, the 23250 series was well under way. But the Depression was also well under way and Minnie's Victor items are very scarce.

13. Cushing, Brewer Phillips interview.

14. Leadbitter, "My Girlish Days," p. 9. Alan Balfour, in the liner notes to *In My Girlish Days Memphis Minnie 1930-1935* (Traveling Man TM 803), gives the date as "late 1934." Daisy knows nothing about when or why Minnie and Joe broke up, and she never heard Minnie refer to it. Daisy saw Joe McCoy once or twice, but knows nothing of him.

15. Broonzy, *Big Bill Blues*, p. 94.

16. Harlem Hamfats. *Hallelujah Joe Ain't Preachin' No More*. Decca 7299. Recorded January 14, 1937. Of course it's also possible that McCoy turned to preaching toward the end of his life, after he retired from the music world.

17. Comparatively speaking, few of Minnie and Joe's early records were registered at the copyright office, so we have relatively sparse evidence about Joe's songwriting skills. The Library of Congress records do show that Joe's *Cherry Ball Blues* was registered, with "words and melody by Minnie McCoy." Thus Joe may have written few of his own compositions in the days with Minnie. The composer credit to "McCoy" on the many Harlem Hamfats records doesn't point to Minnie, of course, so it may point to Joe, but it might also point to Charlie McCoy, who is known to have been a capable songwriter, if not a prolific one.

18. We hope even this short summary makes it clear that Joe McCoy had a successful career after his separation from Minnie. Mike Leadbitter's piece implies that after the separation, Joe did little else but die in 1949.

19. Broonzy, *Big Bill Blues*, p. 94.

20. O'Neal, Memphis Slim interview. The role of Lester Melrose is dicussed at length below. Joe's song was first recorded by him with the Harlem Hamfats, as *Weed Smoker's Dream* (recorded October 2, 1936), but it was re-issued as *Why Don't You Do Now?* Lil Green recorded it in 1941, as *Why Don't You Do Right?* Like many songs taken up by more sophisticated singers, *Weed Smoker's Dream*, was thoroughly detoxified before crossing race, class and gender lines. The man's original exhortation to the woman to "put her stuff on the market" isn't retained in Lil Green's version, much less Peggy Lee's. In *Black Metropolis* (Volume 2, p. 584), Drake and Cayton call *Why Don't You Do Right?* "one of the most popular juke-box songs."

21. O'Neal, Jimmy Rogers interview.

22. O'Neal, Homesick James interview. Homesick James, born James Williamson in 1910 in Tennessee, is a highly esteemed guitarist playing in the style of Elmore James. Like Shines, his few vintage recordings are outstanding and widely sought. He has traveled and toured extensively.

23. Cushing, Brewer Phillips interview.

24. Michel and Pierre Chaigne have nominated Carl Martin as guitarist here. While Martin was in the studio the same day, so was Big Bill, and it is Big Bill's matrix numbers that are immediately adjacent to Minnie's. Finally, the solo on *I'm Waiting On You* sounds to us more like Broonzy than Martin. Michel Chaigne, personal communication to the authors.

25. Ernest Virgo finally unearthed the real name of Black Bob, Ed Hudson. A surprisingly difficult piece of information to come by, the inability of any source to

produce Bob's real name had vexed researchers for decades. Ernest Virgo, personal communication to the authors.

26. *When the Sun Goes Down, Part 1,* cannot be traced to Minnie. However, Minnie's title may refer to Leroy Carr's original *When the Sun Goes Down,* which was recorded on February 25, 1935, and released on Bluebird 5877.

27. O'Neal, Homesick James interview.

28. Zeldin, Sunnyland Slim interview.

29. Bruce Iglauer, Jim O'Neal, and Nigel Watson. "Living Blues Interview: Bobo Jenkins." *Living Blues* 3. Autumn 1970. p. 11.

30. Fiddlin' Joe Martin to David Evans, correspondence with the authors, February 16, 1987. See also, David Evans. "The Fiddlin' Joe Martin Story." *Blues World* 20. July 1968. p. 4. Harris, *Blues Who's Who,* p. 349.

31. Blind John Davis, interviewed by Jim O'Neal in Chicago, March 21, 1977.

32. "Singers trained in one blues style can rarely break away and play for new tastes, and for this reason most blues singers appeal primarily to listeners of their own generation," wrote William Ferris. *Blues From the Delta.* Garden City: AnchorPress/Doubleday, 1978. Reprint. NY: Da Capo, 1988. p. 48. One tends to forget that Minnie was really a first generation blues artist.

33. Reviewing the LP *In My Girlish Days,* Tony Russell remarked that Minnie "stepped easily into [the] role ... of a female Big Bill" after her first recording years. *Blues Unlimited* 147. Spring 1986. p. 34.

34. This would include Minnie's Vocalions made after 1934. Lester Melrose. "My Life in Recording." *American Folk Music Occasional.* Compiled and Edited by Chris Strachwitz and Pete Welding. NY: Oak Publications, 1970. p. 60. Our description of Melrose's career is taken largely from this article.

35. Willie Dixon. "I Am the Blues." *Living Blues* 36. January/February 1978. p. 8.

36. Samuel Charters coined the phrase the "Bluebird Beat" in *The Country Blues.* NY: Rinehart, 1959. Reprint. NY: Da Capo, 1975. pp. 182-194. Rowe has given us the other two in *Chicago Breakdown,* p. 17.

37. Big Bill Broonzy to Yannick Bruynoghe. "Who Got the Money"? *Living Blues* 55. Winter 1982/1983. p. 21.

38. Cushing, Brewer Phillips interview.

39. Bob Koester. "Lester Melrose: An Appreciation." *American Folk Music Occasional.* p. 58.

40. It was released on Vocalion 1191, as well as on Banner, Oriole, Perfect, and Romeo.

41. Nick Perls, personal communication to the authors.

42. We make no attempt here to analyze the allied and often parallel roles of Louis Jordan, mainstream black bands, and rhythm and blues, all of which developed from, through, or around the Melrose sound.

43. As blues critic Peter Guralnick wrote, Minnie was "a pioneer both in the prewar and postwar band styles of Chicago." Peter Guralnick. *A Listener's Guide to the Blues.* n.p. Facts on File, 1982. p. 53.

44. Jas Obrecht. "Johnny Shines, Whupped around and Screwed around, but Still Hanging on." *Living Blues* 90. March/April, 1990. p. 29.

45. "Memphis Minnie: Opens at Tramor Hotel and Cafe, 740 E. 47th St., Chicago, records for Vocalion; blues singer, will be accompanied by 'Black Bob', piano; Arnett Nelson on clarinet," is how it appeared in *The Chicago Defender,* September

26, 1936; quoted in Walter C. Allen's "Chicago 'Defender' Clippings." *Blues Unlimited* 69. January 1970. p. 2.

46. Broonzy, *Big Bill Blues,* p. 106.

47. Ernest Virgo, personal communication to the authors, May 8, 1987

48. Moody Jones, quoted in Mike Rowe. "The Old Swingmasters." *Blues Unlimited* 137/138. Spring 1980. p. 7.

49. Milton Rector's father was with the Rabbit Foot and Silas Green shows.

50. Sunnyland Slim, interviewed by Jim O'Neal, Chicago, September 2, 1981.

51. O'Neal, Homesick James interview.

52. Garon, Johnny Shines interview.

53. Ernest Virgo suggests Black Bob as the pianist on Minnie's June 23, 1938, session, as noted in *Blues Unlimited* 148/149, p. 5, as well as in Virgo's correspondence to us. Black Bob may also appear on several earlier sessions.

54. Tom Tsotsi. "Listening in the Amen Corner." *Joslin's Jazz Journal,* November, 1985. pp. 14 and 16; "Listening in the Amen Corner." *Joslin's Jazz Journal.* August, 1987. p. 4. Tsotsi also suggests that Blind John Davis is not the pianist on the June, 1937, sessions for which he is cited by Dixon and Godrich. See the discography for our own amendations to the personnel on these various sessions.

55. Rowe, *Chicago Breakdown,* p. 25.

56. We are grateful to Michel and Pierre Chaigne for discovering the mandolin on the unissued test of C-2055-2, *Running and Dodging Blues,* as well as for the suggestion that Minnie plays it.

57. As noted earlier, Minnie's union with Son may have been common-law and not by license. No license has yet been found, in any case.

58. Cushing, Brewer Phillips interview.

Chapter 5: ME AND MY CHAUFFEUR

1. Moody Jones, quoted in Rowe, "The Old Swingmasters", p. 10.

2. G. P. Jackson, quoted in Mike Leadbitter. "One of the Best." *Blues Unlimited* 104. October/November 1973. p. 14.

3. Adins, "Memphis Minnie".

4. Walter and Byrd. *Wasn't It Sad About Lemon.* Paramount 12945. Recorded March, 1930. Bumble Bee Slim. *The Death of Leroy Carr.* Decca 7098. Recorded July 7, 1935. Brownie McGhee. *Death of Blind Boy Fuller.* Okeh 06265. Recorded May 22, 1941.

5. Sonny Boy Williamson. *Good Morning, School Girl.* Bluebird 7059. Recorded May 5, 1937. *School Girl* was the first song Williamson sang at his first session, but it was issued after the later-recorded *Got the Bottle Up and Gone* and *Skinny Woman. Garage Fire Blues* is discussed in the section on travel.

6. Rockin' Dopsie and The Cajun Twisters. *Me and My Chauffeur.* GNP Crescendo 2154, *Big Bad Zydeco.* Clifton Chenier. *Be My Chauffeur,* on Avco-Embassy LP 33006, recorded in late 1966. Eddie "One String" Jones. *I'll Be Your Chauffeur.* On *Eddie "One String" Jones and Edward Hazelton.* Portent 2. Lightnin' Hopkins. *Automobile.* Gold Star 666. Recorded 1948?

7. Homesick James also does *Kissing in the Dark,* on *Home Sweet Homesick James.* Big Bear 10. His *Can't Afford To Do It* and *Set a Date* were recorded in 1962 and released on Colt 632.

8. Big Mama Thornton. *Black Rat.* On *Big Mama Thornton with Muddy Waters' Blues Band.* Arhoolie LP F 1032. Recorded April 25, 1966.

Lightnin' Hopkins. *Black Cat.* RPM 388. Recorded 1951?

Big Joe Williams does *Black Rat* on the LP *Malvina My Sweet Woman.* Oldie Blues OL 2804. Recorded March 24, 1973, in Holland.

Big Joe Duskin said he always liked Minnie because "she played this song called *You're One Black Rat and One Day I'm Gonna Find Your Trail.* Well, I named it and redone it." (Big Joe Duskin, interviewed by Norman Darwen, London, 1988.)

On the LP *James 'Son' Thomas Plays and Sings Delta Classics.* (Dutch) Swingmaster 2102, Thomas does *Black Rat,* recorded in the Netherlands, 1981.

Pernell Charity, from Weaver, Virginia, recorded *Black Rat Swing* for Trix in the mid to late 70s, on Trix 3309, *The Virginian.*

Mike Rowe unearthed an unissued Aristocrat version of *Black Rat Swing* by Muddy Waters and Johnnie Jones. Mike Rowe. "Mike Rowe's Numerology Guide." *Blues Unlimited* 104. October/November 1973. p. 23.

Whispering Smith does *Looking the World Over* on *Swamp Blues.* Excello LP 8015/8016.

9. Dixon and Godrich *(Blues and Gospel Records,* 3rd Edition) note that only "some" copies bear this label, and presumably the others are labeled as by "Little Son Joe." The many copies we've examined have all borne the "Mr. Memphis Minnie" legend.

10. It is also possible that Minnie held some post wherein her presence at meetings was required, but it has not been possible to confirm this.

11. Clark Halker. "Banding Together." *Chicago History* 18:2. Summer 1989. pp. 40-59. Halker's piece is an informal history of Chicago's black local 208.

12. Robert Leiter. *The Musicians and Petrillo.* NY: Bookman Associates, 1953. Bruce Bastin. *Red River Blues.* Urbana: University of Illinois Press, 1986. p. 261. See also Bruce Bastin. "Letters," in *Blues Unlimited* 145. Winter 1983. pp. 16-17.

13. Robert Palmer. *Deep Blues.* NY: Viking, 1981. p. 146.

14. Melvyn Hirst reviewed a Minnie LP in *Blues World* 29. April 1970. p. 11, and noted, *"Tears on my Pillow* and *Sweet Man* were recorded in 1949, and after a recording career of twenty years, the decline in ability is considerable." Hirst's remarks are typical, and it is difficult to disagree. Another example: Of Minnie's 1949 sides cut for Regal, blues scholar Kip Lornell noted unenthusiastically, and with some kindness, that they "drag somewhat." Kip Lornell. Review of *Love Changin' Blues* (Biograph 12035). *Living Blues* 7. Winter 1971-2. p. 36.

15. Georges Adins was among the first to credit Minnie with having written her own material. Adins, "Memphis Minnie."

16. While we've not been able to examine a copy of every single Minnie record, we've examined all but a few. We have been able to *hear* every one.

17. From the transitional session of June 27, 1940, some labels bear the legend "McCoy," others bear no composer credits at all (not uncommon for Minnie's records of the thirties and forties), and some may bear the legend "Lawlars."

18. Cushing, Brewer Phillips interview. Phillips specifically mentioned Willie Love's *V-8 Ford,* recorded in Jackson, Mississippi, in 1952 for the Trumpet label, but this song was Buddy Moss's and dates from an earlier decade.

19. O'Neal, Sunnyland Slim interview.

20. Dean and Nancy Tudor wrote that Minnie's guitar skills were "probably equal to the best of the country bluesmen guitar pickers...." Dean and Nancy Tudor.

Black Music. Littleton: Libraries Unlimited, 1979. p. 106. Their high estimation of Minnie's work is representative of the view of other critics.

21. O'Neal, Homesick James interview. Moody Jones, quoted in Rowe, "The Old Swingmasters," p. 10.

22. Amy O'Neal. "Snooky Pryor." *Living Blues* 6. Autumn, 1971. p. 5. Pryor and Moody are quoted in Rowe, "The Old Swingmasters," pp. 10, 20.

23. O'Neal, Memphis Slim interview.

24. Pete Welding. "Rambling Johnny Shines." *Living Blues* 22. July/August 1975. p. 31 Lonnie Johnson played at Gatewood's too, but noted that it was often hard to get paid there. See Paul Oliver's *Conversation With Blues.* London: Cassell, 1965. pp. 148-9.

25. Jim O'Neal. "Blues Questions and Answers." *Living Blues* 12. Spring 1973. p. 37.

26. "Muddy Waters." Interview by Jim and Amy O'Neal. *Living Blues* 64. March/April 1985. p. 31.

27. O'Neal, Sunnyland Slim interview.

28. Bill Greensmith. "Payton's Place." *Blues Unlimited* 109. August/September 1974. p. 15

29. O'Neal, Jimmy Rogers interview.

30. Armand "Jump" Jackson, interviewed by Jim and Amy O'Neal. Chicago, March 21, 1976.

31. Jim O'Neal and Bill Greensmith. "Living Blues Interview: Jimmy Rogers." *Living Blues* 14. Autumn 1973. p. 20.

32. Minnie cut an alternate take of *Daybreak Blues,* which has been issued on Origin LP 24 as *Blue Monday Blues.*

33. Sellers is quoted in Oliver, *Conversation with the Blues,* p. 149. Brother John Sellers was born in Clarksdale in 1924. He learned the guitar and performed gospel, blues and folk music. He was a relatively sophisticated performer who numbered Big Bill among his influences.

34. J. B. Lenoir, quoted in Oliver, *Conversation with the Blues,* p. 152. J. B. Lenoir, a unique and inventive singer, was born in Mississippi in 1929 and killed in an automobile accident in 1967. By then, he had already secured his reputation as a noted postwar Chicago performer.

35. Paul Oliver, *Story of the Blues,* p. 110

36. Mike Rowe. "'I Was Really Dedicated', An Interview with Billy Boy Arnold, Part 2: Very Exciting Times." *Blues Unlimited* 127. November/December 1977. p. 12. Postwar Chicago harp player Billy Boy Arnold was born in Chicago in 1935, and his second record, the latin-beat *I Wish You Would* (1955), was an instant hit.

37. Garon, Daisy Douglas Johnson interview.

38. Garon, Ethel Douglas and Daisy Johnson interview.

39. Broonzy, *Big Bill Blues,* pp. 104-106.

40. O'Neal, Jimmy Rogers interview.

41. The Blues Rockers was a Chicago band that recorded for Aristocrat and Chess in 1949-1950.

42. O'Neal, James Watt interview.

43. Champion Jack Dupree, interviewed by Norman Darwen, London (The 100 Club), March 23, 1989.

44. Jim O'Neal. "Chicago Blues Yesterday and Today: Blue Smitty." *Living Blues* 44. Autumn 1979. p. 11.

45. O'Neal, Memphis Slim interview.

46. In Lightnin' Hopkins' *Get Off My Toe* (Recorded May 12, 1959, Tradition LP 1040), Hopkins recreates a sidewalk scene where the singer is continually being crowded by a drunk whom he rebukes repeatedly.

47. Darwen, Joe Duskin interview.

48. Bill Dicey, interviewed by Norman Darwen, July 16, 1987. Dicey could no longer remember whether he saw Minnie at Carl's Beach or Sparrow's Beach.

49. In a 1959 interview with Ted Watts, Scrapper Blackwell referred in passing to Minnie's presence in Indianapolis, but he never amplified his remarks; he said nothing of her owning a club, however. Ted Watts, personal communication to the authors, January 12, 1989.

50. Ted Joans, personal communication to the authors, October 2, 1989.

51. Mike Rowe, personal communication to the authors, July 20, 1989. From information provided by Jim Gallert (Detroit, June, 1989).

52. Minnie does occasionally refer to her man's looks, as in *What a Night* or *Jockey Man Blues.*

53. Mimi Clar Melnick. "I Can Peep through Water and Spy Dry Land: Boasts in the Blues." *Mother Wit From the Laughing Barrel.* Ed. by Alan Dundes. Englewood Cliffs: Prentice-Hall, 1973. p. 271.

54. Brother John Sellers, interviewed by Jim O'Neal, New Orleans. April 27, 1986.

55. Steve Cushing, personal communication to the authors, Chicago, July 14, 1989.

56. Leadbitter, "My Girlish Days," p. 9.

57. (Daisy herself is quite short, and this may be the basis for her opinion that Minnie was tall). See also, Broonzy, *Big Bill Blues.* p. 106. Charles Sweningsen, correspondence with the authors, March 22, 1987. O'Neal, Homesick James interview.

58. Cushing, Brewer Phillips interview.

59. Garon, Ethel Douglas and Daisy Johnson interview.

60. O'Neal, Jimmy Rogers interview.

61. Garon, Johnny Shines interview.

62. Richard Spottswood, correspondence with the authors, June 5, 1987. Minnie was also clearly embarrassed by her condition, and Spottswood did not prolong the interview.

63. Willie Moore, quoted in Calt and Wardlow, *King of the Delta Blues,* p. 159.

Chapter 6: "I DRINK ANYWHERE I PLEASE"

1. Brewer Phillips, phone interview with Paul Garon, January 4, 1991. Big Lucky Carter, phone interview with Paul Garon, January 6, 1991.

2. Rowe, *Chicago Breakdown,* p. 126.

3. O'Neal, Jimmy Rogers interview.

4. Wardlowe, "Garfield Akers," p. 26.

5. Johnny Shines, quoted in Rowe, *Chicago Breakdown,* p. 43. Shines was referring to 1941 or later.

6. Darwen, Joe Duskin interview. O'Neal, James Watt interview. Jim O'Neal. "Chicago Blues, Yesterday and Today: Blue Smitty, Part Two." *Living Blues* 45/46. Spring 1980. p. 56.

7. Bev Zeldin, personal communication to the authors, n.d.

8. O'Neal and O'Neal, "Muddy Waters," p. 40

9. O'Neal, Jimmy Rogers interview.

10. Johnny Shines, quoted in Rowe, *Chicago Breakdown,* p. 43.

11. Garon, Johnny Shines interview.

12. O'Neal, Homesick James interview.

13. Cushing, Brewer Phillips interview.

14. Brother John Sellers, quoted in Oliver, *Conversation with the Blues,* p. 149.

15. Cushing, Brewer Phillips interview.

16. Mike Rowe, "'I Was Really Dedicated,' Part 2: Very Exciting Times," p. 12.

17. Brother John Sellers, quoted in Oliver, *Conversation with the Blues,* p. 149.

18. O'Neal, James Watt interview..

19. O'Neal and Greensmith, "Jimmy Rogers," p. 14

20. Garon, Johnny Shines interview. O'Neal, Sunnyland Slim interview.

21. Cushing, Brewer Phillips interview. When we interviewed Johnny Shines, he was enrolled in an upholstery course at C. A. Fred Technical College in Tuscaloosa.

22. Cushing, Brewer Phillips interview.

23. Charles Sweningsen, personal correspondence with the authors, March 27, 1987.

24. Gene Santoro. "The Main Man" (Buddy Guy interview). *Guitar World* 8:3. April 1987. p. 30.

25. O'Neal, Homesick James interview.

26. Cushing, Brewer Phillips interview.

27. Steve Cushing, personal communication to the authors, Chicago, July 14, 1989. Blues guitarist James Wheeler also confirms that most blues singer/guitarists were sitting down as they played, until the late 1950s. James Wheeler, personal communication to the authors, April 11, 1987.

28. Studs Terkel, personal communication to the authors, October 14, 1986. Broonzy had been a frequent guest on Terkel's radio shows.

29. Garon, Ethel Douglas and Daisy Johnson interview. See also, Leadbitter, "My Girlish Days," p. 9.

30. Garon, Ethel Douglas and Daisy Johnson interview.

31. Garon, Ethel Douglas and Daisy Johnson interview.

32. Garon, Ethel Douglas and Daisy Johnson interview.

33. Sleepy John Estes. *Down South Blues.* Champion 50001. Recorded July 9, 1935. Estes sang, "Now I get up every morning and I walk up to Third and Beale (2x) / And I'm just studying and I'm wondering, Lord, just how to make a meal."

34. William "Boogie Man" Hubbard to David Evans, correspondence with the authors, February 16, 1987.

35. Big Lucky Carter, phone interview with the authors, August 4, 1987. O'Neal, Homesick James interview.

36. Cushing, Brewer Phillips interview.

37. Zeldin, Brewer Phillips interview.

38. Paul Garon. *The Devil's-Son-in-Law. The Story of Peetie Wheatstraw and His Songs.* London: Studio Vista, 1971. p. 25.

39. Cushing, Brewer Phillips interview.

40. Cushing, Brewer Phillips interview. Zeldin, Brewer Phillips interview. While Minnie seems definitely to have been featured on WDIA, the exact dimensions of her connection with the station are unknown. Further, it is possible that Phillips has conflated Minnie's appearances on WDIA and KFFA.

41. Adins, "Memphis Minnie."

42. Big Lucky Carter, phone interview with the authors, August 4, 1987.

43. Steve Gronda "Eddie Kirkland: 'Detroit was Flooded with Blues'" (Interview) (Transcribed and edited by Bez Turner.) *Juke Blues* 4. Spring 1986. p. 6 Baby Boy Warren also saw Minnie in Detroit, but he recalled her difficult financial straits. "She wasn't doing too good when she come to Detroit.... She stayed in Detroit about three years with some friends of mine." Rowe and Leadbitter, "I Was the Baby Boy," p. 5. While it has been difficult to unearth any concrete proof that Minnie and Son actually lived in Detroit, we think they did.

44. O'Neal, Homesick James interview.

45. Cushing, Brewer Phillips interview.

46. Cushing, Brewer Phillips interview.

47. Cushing, Brewer Phillips interview.

48. Cushing, Brewer Phillips interview.

49. Zeldin, Brewer Phillips interview.

50. Cushing, Brewer Phillips interview.

Chapter 7: "THE BEST THING GOIN' "

1. Garon, Ethel Douglas and Daisy Johnson interview.

2. Adins, "Memphis Minnie."

3. Garon, Daisy Douglas Johnson interview.

4. Garon, Ethel Douglas and Daisy Johnson interview.

5. Wade Walton, interviewed by Paul Garon, Clarksdale, June 21, 1989.

6. Bukka White, quoted in Bruce Cook. *Listen to the Blues*. NY: Scribners, 1973. pp. 128-129.

7. Jo Ann Kelly, correspondence with the authors, Nov 1, 1987. Jo Ann Kelly also has a thank-you note from Minnie from early 1969, probably written by Daisy. There is also extant a tape of the benefit. The exact amount raised was $117.50, the equivalent of $450 in 1990. See, also, James Cortese. "Blues Bring Joy to an Old Heart." *Commercial-Appeal*. May 25, 1968.

8. The letter from Minnie and Daisy appears in "Letters." *Blues Unlimited* 82. June 1971, p. 20.

9. This alledgedly "common occurrence" has never been given close scrutiny to determine how many blues singers do *not* repent at the end of their lives. Probably more than is generally believed.

10. Garon, Daisy Douglas Johnson interview.

11. *Commercial-Appeal,* August 7, 1973. *Billboard,* August 25, 1973. *The Black Perspective in Music,* Fall, 1974. p. 226. LaVere, "Memphis Minnie." Paul Garon. "Memphis Minnie." *Living Blues* 14. Autumn 1973. p. 5.

12. Thomas Millroth, "Från 'Kid' Douglas till Memphis Minnie." *Jefferson* 55 (1982), pp. 10-14.

13. Studs Terkel. *Chicago*. NY: Pantheon, 1986. p. 186.

14. Titon, *Early Downhome Blues*, p. 94. 15. Paul Oliver. "Memphis Minnie (Mc-Coy)." In *Jazz on Record*. Albert McCarthy, Max Harrison, Alun Morgan and Paul Oliver. London: Hanover Books, 1968. p. 196.

16. Tudor, *Black Music*, p. 106.

17. CJ's is described as "a fashionable club and restaurant . . . [where] the only black people . . . are the busboys and the weekend's featured vocalist, Joyce Cobb." Bill Barlow. "Delta Blues Festival '87." *Living Blues* 78. January/February 1988. p. 60.

18. Eunice Davis. *Eunice Davis Sings the Classic Blues of Victoria Spively, Memphis Minnie and Eunice Davis*. L&R 42.016. Victoria Spivey felt especially close to Minnie. See John Godrich, "Victoria Spivey." *Blues Unlimited* 19. February 1965. p. 5

19. Bob Groom. *The Blues Revival*. London: Studio Vista, 1971. p. 105. Johnny Shines commented on the similarity between Minnie's style and that of Jessie Mae Hemphill. Garon, Johnny Shines interview.

20. Big Mama Thornton's *Bumble Bee, Looking the World Over,* and *Black Rat* are on Arhoolie LP F 1032, *Big Mama with Muddy Waters' Blues Band*. Recorded April 25, 1966.

21. See Introduction.

22. For example, in the 1982 W. C. Handy National Blues Awards, Minnie's album, *Gonna Take the Dirt Road Home* (Origin Jazz Library) tied for sixth place in the category, "Vintage or Reissue Album of the Year (U.S.)" See *Living Blues* 54. Autumn/Winter 1982.

In the 1983, Fourth Annual W. C. Handy Awards, Minnie's MCA LP, *Moaning the Blues* was voted #8 in the competition for "Vintage or Reissue Album of the Year. U.S." See *Living Blues* 58. Winter 1983. p. 16.

23. Peter Moody. *Memphis Minnie: The Life and Recording History of the Great Female Country Blues Singer*. n.p. the author, November 1967. 36pp.

24. Eileen Southern. *Biographical Dictionary of Afro-American and African Musicians*. Westport: Greenwood Press, 1982. p. 113.

25. Roger D. Kinkle. *The Complete Encyclopedia of Popular Music and Jazz*. 1900-1950. New Rochelle: Arlington House, 1974. Volume 3, p. 1421.

Chapter 8: TO MAKE HEARD THE INTERIOR VOICE

1. Jacques Attali. *Noise. The Political Economy of Music*. Minneapolis: University of Minnesota Press, 1985. p. 11.

2. Gaston Bachelard. *Water and Dreams*. Dallas: The Bachelard Foundation, 1983.

3. André Breton. "Hector Hyppolite." *Surrealism and Painting*. NY: Icon/Harper, 1972. p. 309.

4. This material is touched on by André Breton in *Communicating Vessels*. Lincoln: University of Nebraska Press, 1990. p. 19.

5. André Breton. "Rising Sign." *What Is Surrealism? Selected Writings*. Edited by Franklin Rosemont. NY: Monad, 1978. II. pp. 280-282. Emphasis added.

6. Joseph Jablonski. "Adventure or Experiment? (Surrealism or Scientific Method?)." *Surrealist Enlightenment* 1. January 1988. (non-paginated)

7. Sandra Harding. *The Science Question in Feminism.* Ithaca: Cornell University Press, 1986. pp. 193, 245.

8. Adrien Dax. "Interview de Malcolm de Chazal." *Medium: Communication Surrealiste* 3. New Series. May 1954. p. 12. This interview is quoted by Franklin Rosemont in "Malcolm de Chazal." *Arsenal: Surrealist Subversion* 4. 1989. p. 125.

9. André Breton. "Interview with Jean Duche." *What Is Surrealism.* II. p. 264.

10. Joseph Jablonski. "Letter to Michael Richardson." *Surrealist Enlightenment* 1. January 1988. (non-paginated). Franklin Rosemont's anthology, *Surrealism and Its Popular Accomplices* (San Francisco: City Lights, 1980), includes many texts that explore this theme. See also his "Black Music, By Any Means Necessary," in *Living Blues* 25. January/February 1976. p. 23.

11. Cheikh Tidiane Sylla. "Surrealism and Black African Art." *Arsenal: Surrealism Subversion* 4. 1989. p. 129.

12. Robert Goffin. "Hot Jazz." *Negro: An Anthology.* Edited by Nancy Cunard. NY: Frederick Ungar, 1970. Edited, abridged, and with an Introduction by Hugh Ford. p. 239. Earlier surrealist references to blues and black music are noted in Paul Garon. *Blues and the Poetic Spirit.* London: Eddison Press, 1975. Reprint. NY: Da Capo, 1979. See also Franklin Rosemont. "Black Music and the Surrealist Revolution." *Arsenal: Surrealist Subversion* 3. Chicago: Black Swan Press, 1976. p. 17.

13. André Breton. "Prolegomena to a Third Manifesto of Surrealism, or Else." *What Is Surrealism.* II. pp. 213-214.

14. Tommy Johnson. *Maggie Campbell Blues.* Victor 21409. Recorded February 24, 1928.

15. Michele Russell. "Slave Codes and Liner Notes." In Gloria T. Hull, Patricia Bell Scott and Barbara Smith, eds. *But Some of Us Are Brave.* Old Westbury: Feminist Press, 1982. p. 130.

16. Russell, "Slave Codes and Liner Notes," pp. 130-131.

17. Ora Williams. Preliminary note to Ora Williams, et. al. "American Black Women Composers: A Selected Annotated Bibliography." In Hull, et. al. *But Some of Us Are Brave.* p. 298.

18. Michele Wallace. *Invisibility Blues.* London: Verso, 1990. p. 70.

19. See the section on travel for the lyrics of *Me and My Chauffeur.*

20. Betsy Wing. "Glossary," in Hélène Cixous and Catherine Clément. *The Newly Born Woman.* Translated by Betsy Wing. Minneapolis: University of Minnesota Press, 1986. p. 168. Emphasis added.

21. Dick Waterman. Obituary for Son House. *Living Blues* 84. January/February 1989. p. 49.

22. Benjamin Péret. "The Dishonor of Poets." *Radical America* IV:6. August 1970. p. 20. This text has been reprinted in Benjamin Pret. *Death to the Pigs.* Lincoln: University of Nebraska Press, 1988.

23. Terry Eagleton. *Marxism and Literary Criticism.* Berkeley: University of California Press, 1976. pp. 47, 57. As Eagleton remarks, "what needs to be added is Marx and Engels' 'principle of contradiction': that the political views of an author may run counter to what his work objectively reveals." In addition to the writings we've already cited, there have been at least two lengthy articles on the blues from a Marxist perspective, and these pieces deserve wider exposure. One is by Carl Boggs. "The Blues Tradition: From Poetic Revolt to Cultural Impasse." *Socialist Review* 8:2 (#38). March/April 1978. pp. 115-134. The other is Larry Portis' "The

Cultural Dialectic of the Blues." *Canadian Journal of Political and Social Theory/Revue Canadienne de Theorie Politique et Sociale.* IX:3. (Fall 1985). pp. 23-36.

24. Penelope Rosemont. "The Golden Goose." *Arsenal: Surrealist Subversion 4.* Chicago: Black Swan Press, 1989. p. 27

25. Michel Leiris. "Glossary." *The Autobiography of Surrealism.* Ed. by Marcel Jean. NY: Viking, 1980. p. 108.

Chapter 9: BUMBLE BEE

1. Rust, *The American Record Label Book,* p. 321.

2. Big Bill. *Long Tall Mama.* Banner 33085. Recorded March 30, 1932.

3. Recording data for the songs mentioned is as follows: Muddy Waters. *Honey Bee.* Chess 1468. Recorded January 23, 1951. Slim Harpo. *I'm a King Bee.* Excello 2113. Recorded 1957. Bo Carter. *I'm an Old Bumble Bee.* Okeh 8852. Recorded December 15, 1930. Mae Glover. *Skeeter Blues.* Champion 16238. Recorded February 24, 1931. At his first session for Paramount in 1931, Bumble Bee Slim recorded *Honey Bee Blues* (Paramount 13132), but no copy of this record has yet been found.

4. Titon. *Early Downhome Blues,* p. 64. Buddy Guy has testified that he was so nervous the first time he was hired to play with a band that he was fired. He was able to keep the job after another try six months later by getting drunk enough to cure his stage-fright. See Rowe, *Chicago Breakdown,* p. 179.

5. The lyrics of *'Frisco Town* appear in the section on travel.

6. But this should not lead one to misapprehend the very real character of male domination.

7. Peg Leg Howell. *Fo' Day Blues.* Co 14177. Recorded November 8, 1926.

8. The French psychoanalyst Luce Irigaray calls 'mimicry,'

> An interim strategy for dealing with a realm of discourse (where the speaking subject is posited as masculine) in which the woman deliberately assumes the feminine style and posture assigned to her within this discourse in order to uncover the mechanisms by which it exploits her.

Luce Irigaray. *This Sex Which Is not One.* Ithaca: Cornell University Press, 1985. p. 220 ("Notes on Selected Terms")

9. Newbell Niles Puckett. *Folk Beliefs of the Southern Negro.* Chapel Hill: University of North Carolina Press, 1926. pp. 82, 492, 503. Others believed that fire or another type of disaster would occur if a bee settled in a house. J. Mason Brewer. *American Negro Folklore.* NY: Quadrangle/New York Times Book Co. 1968. p. 293. Ideas associated with bees have also found their way into dreams and dream interpretation, and again we meet images of death (swarming bees in a dream) and betrayal (the dream of bees stinging you).

10. Sigmund Freud. *The Interpretation of Dreams. The Standard Edition of the Complete Psychological Works of Sigmund Freud.* Vol 5. London: Hogarth Press and the Institute of Psycho-Analysis, 1968. p. 357. Hereafter, references to the Standard Edition of Freud's works will be shortened to SE, thus: [SE 5. p. 357.]

11. See also, for example, Johnny Shines. *Black Spider Blues.* Vanguard LP VRS 9218. Recorded 1965.

12. The most casual inspection of the boll weevil songs reveals a path of instant identification for the black singers who saw the boll weevil's tenacity as an emblem of the sort of endurance that their own people had gone through. No amount of harassment, punishment or torture could vanquish the boll weevil or the black Americans who identified with the tiny insect, in spite of the damage it wrought to their cotton crop.

13. Gaston Bachelard. *The Poetics of Space.* Boston: Beacon Press, pp. 226-227; 150, 151, 155.

14. J. T. 'Funny Paper' Smith (The Howling Wolf). *Hopping Toad Frog.* Vocalion 1655. Recorded July 10, 1931.

15. Bruce Jackson. *Wake Up Dead Man: Afro-American Worksongs From Texas Prisons.* Cambridge: Harvard University Press, 1972. pp. 151, 154. We will return to the topic of miniaturization in our discussion of Minnie's *Jockey Blues* in the section on horses.

16. Carolyn Heilbrun has written, "A word or name must bear, I agree with Coleridge, all the meanings that connotations attach to it." *Writing a Woman's Life.* NY: Norton, 1988. p. 116.

17. Charlotte Perkins Gilman. *The Man-Made World: Or Our Androcentric Culture.* NY: Johnson Reprint, 1971. (Orig. 1911) pp. 101-102.

Chapter 10: CRIME

1. André Breton. *Mad Love.* Lincoln: University of Nebraska Press, 1987. p. 95.

2. An anonymous writer for *Cornhill Magazine* wrote, "It is notorious that a bad man . . . is not so vile as a bad woman . . . Women of this stamp may be [more] justly compared to wild beasts than to women." Quoted by Elizabeth Windschuttle. "Women, Crime and Punishment." In *Women and Crime.* Ed. by S. K. Mukherjee and Jocelynne A. Scutt. Sydney: Australian Institute of Criminology/George Allen and Unwin, 1981. p. 41 (pp. 31-50). Unfortunately, this is not an obsolete attitude of the 19th century. Modern writers also have noted "the punitive police attitudes to certain types of criminal women—particularly those who are perceived to repudiate their femininity." Ngaire Naffine. *Female Crime.* Sydney: Allen and Unwin, 1987. p. 2. See also, M. Chesney-Lynd. "Chivalry Re-Examined: Women and the Criminal Justice System." In *Women, Crime and the Criminal Justice System.* Ed. by L. H. Bowker. Lexington: Lexington Books, 1979. p. 197.

3. Boggs, "The Blues Tradition: From Poetic Revolt to Cultural Impasse," p. 124.

4. Bob Coleman. *Cincinnati Underworld Woman.* Paramount 12731. Recorded January, 1929.

5. Attali, *Noise.* pp. 12, 13.

6. Hélène Cixous and Catherine Clément. *The Newly Born Woman.* p. 25.

7. Francis J. Braceland, M.D. *The Institute of Living. The Hartford Retreat. 1822-1972.* Hartford: Institute of Living, 1972. p. 152, quoting the annals of New Haven colony for 1727. Emphasis added.

8. Charters, *The Country Blues,* pp. 161-162.

9. Quoted in Paul Avrich. *The Russian Anarchists.* Westport: Greenwood Press, 1980. (Orig. 1967) pp.106-107. Thanks to Brian Myers for this quotation.

10. Paul Garon. *Blues and the Poetic Spirit.* London: Eddison Press, 1975. Reprint. NY: Da Capo, 1979. p. 136.

11. Walter Davis. *Howling Wind Blues.* Victor 23308, recorded September 29, 1931.

12. Walter Beasley. *Georgia Skin.* Okeh 8540. Recorded November 30, 1927. Zora Neale Hurston discusses the game of Georgia Skin in *Mules and Men.* Bloomington: Indiana University Press, 1978. (Orig. 1935). pp. 255-256.

13. Lawrence Levine, *Black Culture and Black Consciousness.* NY: Oxford University Press, 1977, pp. 326-328.

14. Wole Soyinka. "The Critic and Society: Barthes, Leftocracy and Other Mythologies." Edited by Henry Louis Gates, Jr. *Black Literature and Literary Theory.* NY: Methuen, 1984. p. 40. In *Black Pearls,* p. 64, Daphne Duval Harrison emphasizes how the early blueswomen "sought escape from the oppressive controls of the black church. . . ."

15. Rayna R. Reiter, quoted in Chris Kramarae and Paula A. Treichler. *A Feminist Dictionary.* Boston: Pandora Press, 1985. p. 127.

16. André Breton, quoted in *The Autobiography of Surrealism.* Edited by Marcel Jean. NY: Viking, 1980. p. 441. The quotation is taken from Breton's *Les Pas Perdus.*

17. Richard M. Jones. *Trouble in Mind.* Bluebird 6569. Recorded August 5, 1936.

18. Lucille Bogan ("Bessie Jackson") sings this line as "change my tricking name." Minnie seems not to sing "tricking," but another word which sounds somewhat like "second." Bessie Jackson's *Tricks Ain't Walking No More* was released on Romeo 5121. Recorded mid-December, 1930.

19. One of the key messages of Albert Murray's *Stomping the Blues* (NY: McGraw, 1976. Reprint. NY: Da Capo, 1989) is that by designating "blues" as a *jazz mode,* we can have a *respectable* blues, rescued from its lower class purveyors, the blues singers. Indeed, the very twistings and turnings that make Murray's "Folk Art and Fine Art" chapter such a hostile dissertation in an otherwise congenial work are themselves proof of the great power of class antagonisms.

20. O'Neal, Homesick James interview.

21. Nixon had been hired to drive the artists to the session. He made this report to David Evans. David Evans, correspondence with the authors, July 21, 1988.

22. At one level, the late appearance of an early-sounding song like *Call the Fire Wagon* supports this notion of the country, although it does not tally at all with the way most people remember Minnie.

23. "The Women Prostitutes of Lyon Speak to the People." *New French Feminisms. An Anthology.* Edited by Elaine Marks and Isabelle de Courtivron. NY: Schocken, 1981. p. 196.

24. See the chapter on the the Dirty Dozens.

25. Paul Oliver. "Got Cut All to Pieces: Bessie Tucker and Ida May Mack." *Blues Off the Record.* NY: Hippocrene, 1985. Reprint. NY: Da Capo, 1988. p. 280.

26. Isadore Ducasse, Comte de Lautramont. "Poesies" in *Maldoror (Les Chants De Maldoror).* NY: New Directions, 1965, p. 333.

Chapter 11: DIRT DAUBER BLUES

1. August Spies is quoted in Dave Roediger and Franklin Rosemont. *Haymarket Scrapbook.* Chicago: Charles H. Kerr, 1986. p. 7.

2. Puckett, *Folk Beliefs of the Southern Negro,* pp. 375, 508, 333. "In Florida, Izzelly Haines [a midwife] prescribed concoctions of . . . 'dauber nests' to hasten the expulsion of the afterbirth." Jacqueline Jones. *Labor of Love, Labor of Sorrow.* NY: Vintage, 1986. (orig. 1985). p. 214. Harry M. Hyatt also cites several similar beliefs, calling the wasps both mud-daubers and dirt-daubers. *Folklore From Adams County Illinois.* NY: Memoirs of the Alma Egan Hyatt Foundation, 1935. pp. 152, 241.

3. Here is a fine example of such a meaning remaining veiled: On one of Joe McCoy's first sessions without Minnie (for Decca, on August 13, 1934), he recorded *Someday I'll Be in the Clay* and *I Got To Have a Little More.* The artist credit on both sides of Decca 7008 was "The Mississippi Mudder (Mud-Dauber Joe)".

4. Bluesman Yank Rachell calls such moaning "mumbling" in *Rachel Blues,* Bluebird 7525, recorded March 13, 1938.

5. Sigmund Freud. "The Unconscious." SE XIV. Freud's actual statement was "conscious presentation comprises the presentation of the thing plus the presentation of the word belonging to it, while the unconscious presentation is the presentation of the thing alone." p. 201.

6. Sigmund Freud. "Negation." SE XIX. On page 235, Freud remarks about the mother dream, "In our interpretation, we take the liberty of disregarding the negation and of picking out the subject matter alone of the association. It is a though the patient had said: 'It's true that my mother came into my mind as I thought of this person [in the dream], but I don't feel inclined to let the association count.'"

7. Chris South. "Collective Comments." *Feminary* II:1/2. p. 5. As Jill Johnston wrote, "*Passivity* is *the* dragon that every woman has to murder in her quest for independence." Quoted in Kramarae and Treichler, *A Feminist Dictionary,* p. 322.

8. This is especially clear in the inability of so many critics to comprehend the blues as protest music; the "protest" is missing. Note also that D. K. Wilgus defines a "folk-lyric" as "A folk-song lacking a coherent, developed narrative, often consisting of images held together by a tune or mood." D. K. Wilgus. *Anglo-American Folksong Scholarship Since 1898.* New Brunswick: Rutgers University Press, 1959. p. 432. Even here, folk-lyrics are defined by what is missing: plot and narrative. Of course, "something missing," from the point of view of Freud (and Lacan) implies "woman."

9. Giving the singers the opportunity to not say things can also be understood as operating symbolically when we hear the way Sonny Boy Williamson (Rice Miller) does *not* say "won't be back no more" at the end of *One Way Out* (Checker 1003, recorded September, 1961), or how Smokey Hogg does *not* say "hell" in *Low Down Woman Blues* (Speciality 356, recorded October 3, 1949). This swallowing of the last word of the last line, often turning the job of articulation over to the guitar or harmonica, has always been a compelling feature in the blues.

10. On one level, the reference to work has a specific feminine cast. Jacqueline Jones notes the importance of the money obtained by selling eggs. "Some women peddled berries, chickens, eggs and vegetables along the roads and in towns. . . . The saying 'chickens for shoes' referred to women's practice of using the money they earned selling eggs and chickens to buy shoes for their children so that they could attend school in the winter." *Labor of Love,* pp. 56, 96; see also, pp. 81, 89.

11. André Breton. "Interview with *View* Magazine" *What is Surrealism? Selected Writings.* II. p. 204.

12. "The Secret of Internal Laughter," collective text of the Surrealist Group of Prague, 1966. Quoted in Petr Kral. *Le Surrealisme en Tchecoslovaquie*. Paris: Gallimard, 1983. p. 333

13. Evans, *Big Road Blues*, p. 165. Emphasis added.

14. Ira Selkowitz and Susan Day. "Wilburt 'Big Chief' Ellis." *Living Blues* 63. January/February 1985. p. 33. Etta Baker is quoted by Walter Liniger. "Blues Workshop in Elkins, West Virginia." *Living Blues* 64. March/April 1985. p. 49.

15. Calt and Wardlow trace the notion that "blues" are sad to Tin Pan Alley and the rise of the black vaudeville-oriented blues singers, and especially to W. C. Handy and other composers of their songs. Calt and Wardlow, *King of the Delta Blues*, pp. 18, 105. Albert Murray, in *Stomping the Blues*, discusses at great length the false notion that blues is a "sad" music.

16. Thus, we find confirmed what we already surmised when we come upon Lawrence Levine's suggestion that many parallel "contours and functions of black laughter resembled those of black music, especially the blues, for which a sense of commentary was also fundamental." Levine, *Black Culture and Black Consciousness*, p. 359.

17. This phenomenon is analyzed in Nancy Walker. *"A Very Serious Thing": Women's Humor and American Culture*. Minneapolis: University of Minnesota Press, 1988.

18. Mary Douglas has defined "dirt" as "matter out of place." An intriguing discussion of the issues involved in the concept of "purity" can be found in her *Purity and Danger: An Analysis of the Concepts of Pollution and Taboo*. London: RKP, 1979. (orig. 1966). p. 40.

19. One could easily draw a line of descent from Minnie's *Plymouth Rock* and *If You See My Rooster* to Polly Boyden's *The Pink Egg* (Truro, MA: Pamet Press, 1942), a proletarian novel where all the characters are birds. Birds are often used as images of freedom because they are able to fly, from the *The Cutty Wren* to the "snitching" bird in *Henry Lee (Young Hunting*, Child #68), to the eagle who builds its nest in the Rocky Mountains, "way out in the West," in so many blues.

Chapter 12: DOCTORS AND DISEASE

1. Kramarae and Treichler, *A Feminist Dictionary*, pp. 126-127. The first quotation is from Mary Ritter Beard; the second from "Our Grandmothers." *The New Century For Women*. July 29, 1876. p. 92.

2. Clyde Vernon Kiser. *Sea Island To City. A Study of St. Helena Islanders in Harlem and Other Urban Centers*. NY: Atheneum, 1969. (orig. 1932). p. 37. Gilbert Osofsky. *Harlem: The Making of a Ghetto*. NY: Harper, 1968. (orig. 1966). pp. 143-144. Jones, *Labor of Love, Labor of Sorrow*, p. 192. Jones notes that "Midwives and older women knowledgeable in folk medicine continued to occupy an honored place in Afro-American culture [in the 1930s]." p. 214. The interested reader should also consult Ellen J. Stekert's "Focus for Conflict: Southern Mountain Medical Beliefs in Detroit" and Marion Pearsall's "Prepared Comments" on Stekert's paper. *The Urban Experience and Folk Tradition*. Ed. by Americo Paredes and Ellen J. Stekert. Austin: University of Texas Press for the American Folklore Society, 1971. pp. 95-136.

3. The term "doctor" was also used to refer to the type of patent medicine entrepreneur that Minnie might have played for in her medicine show or traveling show days.

4. Jones, *Labor of Love, Labor of Sorrow*, p. 288.

5. G. Frank Lydston. *The Diseases of Society (The Vice and Crime Problem)*. Philadelphia: Lippincott, 1904. pp. 319, 320-321.

6. For a less extreme example, see John E. Lind's "The Dream As A Simple Wish-fulfillment in the Negro." *Psychoanalytic Review I*. 1914. pp. 295-300. Early issues of the *Review* contain other, similar articles.

7. Lydston, *The Diseases of Society*, pp. 393, 394, 396-397.

8. Osofsky, *Harlem: The Making of a Ghetto*, p. 141.

9. Osofsky, *Harlem: The Making of a Ghetto*, p. 153. As recently as 1990, newspapers could still accurately note, "Death Rate for Blacks on the Rise," Jean Latz Griffin. *Chicago Sunday Tribune*. December 2, 1990. Section 2, p. 3.

10. Cushing, Brewer Phillips interview. Zeldin, Brewer Phillips interview.

11. Reported by a black physician from Texas. Quotation supplied by Samuel Lehman.

12. Jane Lucas and Georgia Tom. *Terrible Operation Blues*. Champion 16171. Recorded November 19, 1930.

13. Even this "personal" song was recorded by Minnie and Joe's neice, Ethel McCoy. *Meningitis Blues* appears on Adelphi AD 1004, recorded in East St. Louis, 1969. George and Ethel McCoy's repertoires contained a number of Minnie's songs.

14. Dirty Red (Nelson Wilborn, aka Red Nelson). *Mother Fuyer*. Aladdin 194. Recorded June 2, 1947. Washboard Sam's piece was issued as by Shufflin' Sam and His Rhythm. *Dirty Mother for You*. Vocalion 03329. Recorded September 16, 1936. The song was also recorded by Shorty Bob Parker as *Ridin' Dirty Motorsickle* in 1938, and released on Decca 7488, and by Mack Rhinehart and Brownie Stubblefield as *Dirty No Gooder*. ARC 7-01-66, recorded October 26, 1936.

15. Susan Cavin. "Missing Women: On the Voodoo Trail to Jazz." *Journal of Jazz Studies* 3:1. Fall 1975. pp. 4-27. There has been much recent and excellent work on the history of women in jazz. See, for example, Sally Placksin. *American Women in Jazz*. NY: Seaview Books, 1982, and Linda Dahl. *Stormy Weather*. NY: Pantheon, 1984. Julio Finn's *The Bluesman* (NY: Morrow, 1986) contains an excellent political history of voodoo.

16. Early accounts like those quoted in Stearns (Marshall Stearns. *The Story of Jazz*. NY: Oxford University Press, 1956), Jones (LeRoi Jones. *Blues People*. NY: Morrow, 1963) and Cavin note that women drummers were active in the Congo Square ceremonies, where they also led chants and sang. Robert Tallant prints a first-person song about a voodoo queen and notes that voodoo was a matriarchy "almost from its first days in Louisiana." (Robert Tallant. *Voodoo in New Orleans*. NY: Macmillan, 1946. pp. 20-21, 43).

17. Cavin, "Missing Women . . . ," pp. 21-23. Also, images of women predominate on the covers and in the titles of those later printed offshoots of voodoo, the dream- and number-books.

18. Cavin, "Missing Women . . . ," pp. 22-24.

19. Finn. *The Bluesman*, p. 36

20. Garon. *Blues and the Poetic Spirit*, pp. 143-144. In this earlier work, we also emphasized the link between primitive magic and revolutionary currents of modern poetry and thought.

21. See Joseph Jablonski. "Notes on the Revolution of Witchcraft." *Arsenal: Surrealist Subversion* 2. Summer, 1973. pp. 6-8.

22. We discuss this subject in the section on madness.

23. Clément, "The Guilty One" p. 23.

24. One advocate of such a view is J. L. Dillard; see his *Lexicon of Black English.* NY: Seabury Press, 1977.

25. Kokomo Arnold. *Red Beans and Rice.* Decca 7347. Recorded March 30, 1937. Louis Armstrong signed at least one picture, "Red Beans and Ricely Yours...," according to Charles Keil. *Urban Blues.* Chicago: University of Chicago Press, 1966, p. 169. But Minnie later uses "beans" (in *Nothing in Rambling*) as "charity beans," another meaning that may circulate around her use of "rice and beans," although even in *Nothing in Rambling,* the connotation of staying *home* is clearly present.

26. The motto of the Mississippi Delta Blues Festival is "The Blues Is Like Coming Home."

27. Kokomo Arnold. *Set Down Gal.* Decca 7361. Recorded March 30, 1987.

28. Peg Leg Howell and Jim Hill. *Chittlin' Supper.* Co 14426. Recorded April 13, 1929.

29. Elmore James. *Done Somebody Wrong.* Fire 1031. Recorded 1961.

30. J. T. "Funny Paper" Smith (The Howling Wolf). *Seven Sisters Blues.* Vocalion 1641. Recorded July 10, 1931. J. T. Smith is a different singer than the post-war Chicago bluesman, Howlin' Wolf (Chester Burnett).

31. Jazz Gillum. *The Blues What Am.* Victor 20-2580. Recorded April 24, 1947.

32. See Wade Davis. *The Serpent and the Rainbow* (NY: Simon and Schuster, 1985) pp. 162-167, for a recent and popular treatment of drug-induced zombieism. Davis' bibliography contains technical/scientific, historical and popular references. A more technical version with some of the anecdotal material (and spark) removed is *Passage of Darkness: The Ethnobiology of the Haitian Zombie.* Chapel Hill: University of North Carolina Press, 1988.

33. Quoted in Amy Wilentz. "Voodoo in Haiti Today." *Grand Street* 6:2. Winter 1987. p. 123. Wade Davis also underscores the political dimension of zombification, calling it the "ultimate social sanction" and emphasizing its cultural role as punishment for those who have "transgressed the established and acknowledged codes of his or her society," *Passage of Darkness,* p. 284, but as another critic makes clear, Davis tends to minimize the abuses of the Duvaliers and their coterie. See Erika Bourguignon. Book Review of *Passage of Darkness. The Ethnobiology of the Haitian Zombie* (Chapel Hill: University of North Carolina Press, 1988), in *Journal of American Folklore* 102. October/December 1989, p. 497.

34. Interesting, too, is the extent to which Minnie's song fits in so well with the Industrial Workers of the World image of the black cat as the symbol of proletarian sabotage, and thus as the workers' friend. Halloween-like black cats abound in IWW songs and cartoons during the 1910s and 1920s, and were certainly known in the black communities of the Deep South, since Louisiana and East Texas were black IWW strongholds. Joyce L. Kornbluh. *Rebel Voices. An IWW Anthology.* Chicago: Charles H. Kerr, 1988. New Edition. p. 251.

35. Sigmund Freud. "Notes Upon A Case of Obsessional Neurosis" (1909). SE X. p. 214. See also Sandor Ferenczi. "Gulliver Fantasies." *Final Contributions to the Problems and Methods of Psycho-Analysis.* Volume III of *The Selected Papers of Sandor Ferenczi.* NY: Basic Books, 1955. p. 53.

36. Sippie Wallace. *Up the Country Blues*. Okeh 8106. Recorded c. October 26, 1923.

37. Kansas City Kitty (Possibly Thelma Holmes or Skippy Brown). *The Doctor's Blues*. Vocalion 1508. Recorded c. May 13, 1930.

38. Brewer, *American Negro Folklore*, p. 303. See the identical belief reported by the Editors, "Folklore and Ethnology," in *Southern Workman* 24:8. (Sept, 1895). pp. 154-156. Reprinted in Bruce Jackson. *The Negro and His Folklore in Nineteenth-Century Periodicals*. Austin: University of Texas Press for the American Folklore Society, 1967. pp. 274-283.

39. While we habitually resist the inclination to psychoanalyze the blues singer, it is worth remembering that Freud ("Notes Upon A Case of Obsessional Neurosis" (1909). SE X. p. 214.) suggested that vermin, e.g. rats, could often represent unwanted brothers and sisters. This should be kept in mind when hearing a song about a rat-destroying cat sung by a singer who grew up with 12 siblings.

40. Freud, *The Interpretation of Dreams*. 1900. SE V. p. 357.

Chapter 13: DOORS

1. Breton, *Mad Love*, p. 15.

2. See Ben Sidran. *Black Talk*. NY: Holt, 1970. Reprint. NY: Da Capo, 1983. p. 89. See also Ronald L. Morris. *Wait Until Dark. Jazz and the Underworld 1880-1940*. Bowling Green: Popular Press, 1980.

3. Howlin' Wolf. *Back Door Man*. Chess 1777. Recorded June, 1960.

4. Levine, *Black Culture and Black Consciousness*, p. 309.

5. Bachelard, *The Poetics of Space*, pp. 222, 224.

6. See the section on madness for the lyrics to *Tears on My Pillow*.

7. Robert Johnson. *Preachin' Blues*. Vocalion 04630. Recorded November 27, 1936.

8. Bruce Jackson, an editor of the *Journal of American Folklore*, has insisted that if we limit our interest in a song's content to its most superficial aspects, we will have turned our back on much of what the social sciences have taught us in this century, but his lesson still goes unheeded in many folklore circles. Jackson, *Wake Up Dead Man*, p. 37.

9. Levine, *Black Culture and Black Consciousness*, p. 240, quotes Bruce Jackson on the accumulation of images.

Chapter 14: DIRTY DOZENS

1. Césaire's comment springs humorously from the famous ending of *Nadja:* "Beauty will be convulsive or it will not be."

2. Audre Lorde. "Eye to Eye: Black Women, Hatred, and Anger." *Sister Outsider*. Trumansburg: Crossing Press, 1984. p. 171.

3. Clarence Major. *Dictionary of Afro-American Slang*. NY: International Publishers, 1970. p. 46.

4. See Paul Garon. "The Dirty Dozens," (*Living Blues* 97. May/June 1991. pp. 33-35) and Henry Louis Gates, Jr. *The Signifying Monkey*. (NY: Oxford University

Press, 1988.) for recent treatments of the Dozens. Also germane for our own study, is Paul Oliver's lengthy study of the dozens, as song, in "The Blue Blues," a section of his *Screening the Blues*. London: Cassell, 1968. Reprint. NY: Da Capo, 1989.

5. Noted by Gates, *The Signifying Monkey*, p. 72.

6. Speckled Red. *The Dirty Dozen*. Brunswick 7116. Recorded September 22, 1929. Speckled Red. *The Dirty Dozen—No. 2*. Brunswick 7151. Recorded April 8, 1930.

7. Kokomo Arnold. *The Twelves (Dirty Dozens)*. Decca 7083. Recorded January 18, 1935.

8. Furry Lewis. *Kassie Jones* Pt. 1. Victor 21664. Recorded August 28, 1928.

9. Comte de Lautréamont. *Maldoror and Poems*. Harmondsworth: Penguin, p. 217. In the special supplement to *Living Blues* 25, "Surrealism and Blues," several pages are devoted to the intersection of the phonograph record and the sewing machine in the works of the surrealists. *Living Blues* 25. January/February 1976. pp. 19-34, especially pp. 24-25.

10. Sam Chatman. *God Don't Like Ugly*. On *Blues n' Trouble*. Arhoolie LP F1006. Recorded July 25, 1960. Smokey Hogg. *You Gonna Look Like a Monkey (When You Get Old)*. Modern 20-758. Recorded 1949.

11. Roger Abrahams. *Deep Down in the Jungle*. Hatboro: Folklore Associates, 1964. p. 51-52.

12. The first edition of Dixon and Godrich's *Blues and Gospel Records* (1964) contained nearly 900 pseudonyms that appeared on records between 1921 and 1945, from which co-author John Godrich compiled a list of "Blues and Gospel Record Label Pseudonyms".

13. Finn, *The Bluesman*, p. 196.

14. Gaston Bachelard. *The Psychoanalysis of Fire*. Boston: Beacon Press, 1968. pp. 39-40.

15. Waller's remark is quoted by John Langston Gwaltney in the context of his decision to use pseudonyms to disguise his informants's names in *Drylongso*. NY: Vintage, 1981. (orig. 1980).

16. Julius Daniels. *My Mamma Was a Sailor*. Victor 20658. Recorded February 19, 1927.

17. Muddy Waters. *Sad Letter Blues*. Chess 1434. Recorded 1950.

18. O. W. de L. Milosz, quoted in Bachelard, *The Poetics of Space*, p. 179.

Chapter 15: DUETS

1. Titon, *Early Downhome Blues*, pp. 28, 31-32. Titon's Appendix A, "Patterns of Record Purchase and Listening" has been invaluable in providing information on early blues listeners.

2. Coot Grant, quoted in Marshall and Jean Stearns. *Jazz Dance. The Story of American Vernacular Dance*. NY: Macmillan, 1968. pp. 24, 27. See also Calt and Wardlow, *King of the Delta Blues*, pp. 91 and 18.

3. In 1936, shortly after Minnie and Joe separated, Minnie recorded her final duet, this time with the popular Bumble Bee Slim. Minnie and Slim cut the humorous *New Orleans Stop Time*, on which the sound effects and dialogue combine to suggest that Slim and Minnie are demonstrating dance steps to each other. Bum-

ble Bee Slim and Memphis Minnie. *New Orleans Stop Time.* Vocalion 03197. Recorded February 6, 1936. Minnie accompanied Slim on at least one other side from this session. While her presence is impossible to detect on Slim's issued version of *When Somebody Loses (Then Somebody Wins),* a test pressing of an unissued take (-1) reveals her presence, as Slim clearly remarks, "Play the guitar, Minnie, 'cause you done lost, too." This information was supplied by Michel and Pierre Chaigne, who own the test pressing of C-1223-1.

4. King Solomon Hill used some of its lines in his *Tell Me Baby,* issued on Paramount 13129. Recorded January, 1932.

5. Ferris, *Blues from the Delta,* p. 69. Ferris is describing a verse-trading competition between singers, but we think his point has the further application we suggest.

6. Arthur Palmer Hudson collected a dozen texts of *Paper of Pins* in Mississippi, while Cecil Sharp collected a number of variants of *The Keys of Heaven* in North Carolina, Virginia, and Kentucky. See Arthur Palmer Hudson. *Folksongs of Mississippi and Their Background.* Chapel Hill: University of North Carolina Press, 1936. p. 276. Cecil Sharp. *English Folk-Songs from the Southern Appalachians.* Edited by Maud Karpeles. London: Oxford University Press, 1973. II. pp. 45-49.

7. Herbert Silberer. *Problems of Mysticism and Its Symbolism.* NY: Moffat, Yard and Co., 1917. pp. 97-98. (Here Silberer is quoting F. Nork's *Mythologie de Volkssagen and Volksmarchen* (Stuttgart: 1848), although it is not always clear where Nork ends and Silberer begins.)

8. Muddy Waters. *Can't Get No Grindin'.* Chess 2143. Recorded March 1972. See also, Rita Scala. "Muddy Waters in Italy." *Living Blues* 31. March/April 1977. p. 29. The song provides a striking example of the survival of the most vintage songs in the most modern of repertoires. Bruce Bastin. "Fort Valley Blues, Part 2." *Blues Unlimited* 112. March/April 1975. pp. 16, 13. Guitarist Edward Slappy performed *Me and My Chauffer Blues* [sic] at the same festival ten years earlier. The Heartfixers do *What's the Matter with the Mill?* on *The Heartfixers,* Southland LP SLP-12. Jim Bunkley recorded Minnie's *What's the Matter with the Mill?* in 1968. *Jim Bunkley and George Henry Bussey.* Rounder 2001. Charlie Burse and His Memphis Mudcats. *What's the Matter with the Well?* Vocalion 05299. Recorded July 8, 1939. Moon Mullican. *What's the Matter with the Mill?* King 1447. Bob Wills and His Texas Playboys. *What's the Matter with the Mill.* Vocalion 03424. Recorded September 29, 1936. Wills also recorded Minnie's *Frankie Jean (That Trottin' Fool).*

9. Quoted by Attali, *Noise,* p. 73. Emphasis added. As we note elsewhere, Minnie may have been a "star," but she did her share of street singing as well.

10. Nancy M. Henley. *Body Politics.* Englewood Cliffs: Prentice-Hall, 1977. p. 74.

11. Tommy Johnson. *Cool Drink of Water Blues.* Victor 21279. Recorded February 3, 1928. Tommy Johnson. *Maggie Campbell Blues.* Victor 21409. Recorded February 4, 1928. Barrelhouse piano players sang their songs in falsetto so as to be heard above the noise of the crowd; for the same reason, work-gang song leaders tend to be tenors.

12. Breton, *Mad Love,* pp. 32-33, 34. Emphasis added.

13. Attali, *Noise,* p. 143.

Chapter 16: FOOD AND COOKING

1. Sylva Bovenschen. "Is There a Feminine Aesthetic"? *New German Critique* 10. Winter 1977. p. 133. See also Gisela Ecker, ed. *Feminist Aesthetics.* Boston: Beacon Press, 1985. pp. 23-50, where this article is reprinted. It is important to consider the fact that *all* surrealist women who have been asked have pronounced themselves vigorously against "feminine aesthetics."

2. Lieb, *Mother of the Blues,* p. 104. Most blues authorities who have concentrated on the meaning of the blues support this position. See, for example, Paul Oliver's *Blues Fell This Morning* (NY: Horizon, 1960) or *Screening the Blues,* Samuel Charters' *The Poetry of the Blues* (NY: Oak, 1963), or our own *Blues and the Poetic Spirit.*

3. Franklin Rosemont. *Surrealism and Its Popular Accomplices,* p. 3

4. The North Memphis Cafe was listed in the Memphis city directories as early as 1926.

5. Rowe and Leadbitter, "I Was the Baby Boy," p. 5. Eric Townley. *Tell Your Story.* Chigwell, Essex: Storyville, 1976. p. 247. Harris, *Blues Who's Who,* p. 161.

Bluesman James "Yank" Rachell also refers to the North Memphis Cafe in his *Expressman Blues.* Sleepy John Estes. *Expressman Blues.* Victor 23318. Recorded May 17, 1930. Although Rachell sings on this side, it was credited to Estes on the label. "Hon, I'll sing this song, James ain't going to sing no more. (2x) / I'm gonna put this mandolin under my arm, to the North Memphis Cafe I'll go."

6. Garon, Ethel Douglas and Daisy Johnson interview.

Chapter 17: HORSES

1. *Frankie Jean.* By Bob Wills and His Texas Playboys. Kaleidoscope LP F.20 (1984), *The Tiffany Transcriptions, Vol 3.* Originally recorded April 8, 1946. Vocal by Tommy Duncan and Bob Wills.

2. Leadbitter, "My Girlish Days," p. 9. Garon, Daisy Douglas Johnson interview.

3. Minnie, of course, was originally from Louisiana, and she may have heard talking blues in her childhood or the tradition could have been carried North to Walls by others in her family or social circle. Oster's work has revealed not only a number of "talking blues" but a related "stream of consciousness blues" that drew neither from the pool of traditional blues verses nor from commercial phonograph records. (See Evans, *Big Road Blues,* p. 102) Robert Pete Williams was the leading exponent of this latter form.

4. Harry Oster. *Living Country Blues.* Detroit: Folklore Associates, 1969. p. 23.

5. Bukka White. *Special Stream Line.* Vocalion 05526. Recorded March 8, 1940. Lightnin' Hopkins. *Come Go Home with Me.* On Folkways LP 3822. Recorded January 16, 1959.

6. Puckett, *Folk Beliefs of the Southern Negro,* pp. 394, 412, 487. Puckett also found the Mississippi belief that whistling in the woods is dangerous as it can attract snakes. p. 436. Wayland Hand, ed. *The Frank C. Brown Collection of North Carolina Folklore* (Series Editor, Newman Ivey White). Volume 7. *Popular Beliefs and Superstitions From North Carolina.* Durham: Duke University Press, 1964. p. 568-569, items #8488-8495.

7. Puckett, *Folk Beliefs of the Southern Negro*, pp. 201, 159, 204, 291. Horses were thought to be able to "detect" voodoo. A. M. Bacon. "Folklore and Ethnology: Conjuring and Conjure Doctors." *Southern Workman* 24:11. November, 1895, and 24:12. December 1895. Reprinted in Jackson, *The Negro and His Folklore in Nineteenth Century Periodicals*, p. 287.

"Horse" is also the spirit that *possesses* in Haitian voodoo, and among the voodooists, "the word 'horse' is universally understood." Dr. Louis Mars, *The Crisis of Possession in Voodoo*. n.p. Reed, Cannon and Johnson, 1977. p. 29. Further, Michel Leiris, cited in Mars, pp. 55-56, has delineated the Ethiopian roots of this usage.

8. Dillard, *Lexicon of Black English*, p. 113

9. Bachelard, *The Poetics of Space*, pp. 151-152.

10. Edith P. Mayo. "Redemption and Reform: Iconography of the U.S. Suffrage Movement." Eighth Biennial Convention of the American Studies Association. October, 1981.

11. The interested reader will want to consult Nancy Joyce Peters' "Women and Surrealism." *Arsenal: Surrealist Subversion 4*. Chicago: Black Swan Press, 1989. pp. 5-12.

12. Kokomo Arnold. *Milk Cow Blues*. Decca 7026. Recorded September 10, 1934. *Milk Cow Blues* was pressed, repressed and reissued by Decca in their later race series of the 1940s. It was widely copied and covered, a fairly late version being Elvis Presley's *Milk Cow Blues Boogie*, on Sun 215, recorded January 8, 1955.

13. We can only speculate on the text and style of the rejected *Good Morning* that Minnie recorded for Bluebird a year earlier than the issued Vocalion version.

14. For a detailed analysis of how blues artists have worked and reworked certain songs associated with Tommy Johnson and specific regions of Mississippi, see Evans's *Big Road Blues*.

15. Jazz Gillum refers to his *woman* as a jockey in *Jockey Blues*, by Bill Gillum. Bluebird 6409. Recorded April 4, 1936. Another male singer acknowledges that being a "jockey" isn't always sufficient. Texas Alexander, in *Johnny Behrens Blues*, tells how he once was a jockey who taught his woman how to ride, but the song ends with the woman leaving him. Texas Alexander, *Johnny Behrens Blues*. Okeh 8745. Recorded June 15, 1929

Chapter 18: *TRAINS AND TRAVEL*

1. As a recent newspaper headline reveals, "Report Shows Blacks Returning to South: Census Bureau confirms exodus from North. . . ." *The Milwaukee Journal*. January 10, 1990. pp. 1A, 6A

2. See, for example, the Kansas City Blues Strummers. *Broken Bed Blues*. Vocalion 1048. Recorded July 27, 1926.

3. Charlie Patton. *High Water Everywhere*. Paramount 12909. Recorded October, 1929.

4. Bob Campbell. *Starvation Farm Blues*. Vocalion 02798. Recorded August 1, 1934.

5. Jazz Gillum. *Down South Blues*. Bluebird 9004. Recorded December 4, 1941.

6. Kokomo Arnold. *Old Black Cat Blues (Jinx Blues)*. Decca 7050. Recorded January 15, 1935.

7. Son Bonds. *She Walks Like My Woman*. Decca 7022. Recorded September 6, 1934.

8. Melnick, " 'I Can Peep through Water and Spy Dry Land,'" p. 274

9. Untitled clipping, *Memphis Chamber of Commerce Journal*, February, 1924.

10. Indeed, for the barrelhouses that depended on out-of-town patrons for their weekend livelihood, the cancellation of passenger service by one rail line in the Delta in the early 1930s was fatal. Calt and Wardlow, *King of the Delta Blues*, p. 230.

11. James Wiggins. *Frisco Bound*. Paramount 12860. Recorded October 12, 1929. Lee Green used a few of its lines and part of its melody for *Memphis Fives*, but *The Fives* was a classic virtuso piano piece with a life of its own. Lee Green. *Memphis Fives*. Vocalion 1501. Recorded c. January 16, 1930.

12. A note by Bob Groom in *Blues World* 37, Dec 1970, pp. 10-11, refers to a Larry Johnson performance at the Manchester Sports Guild (UK) on December 5, 1970, where Johnson performed *Frisco Town* in a manner derived from Minnie's version, followed by *Ain't no Use Tellin' on Me*, probably also derived from Minnie.

13. Carby, "It Jus Be's Dat Way Sometime: The Sexual Politics of Women's Blues," pp. 14-16.

14. A tramp who had just covered 8000 miles in six months, remarked "I even saw two women on the road and last summer I saw a woman beating her way in a box car." Nels Anderson. *The Hobo*. Chicago: University of Chicago Press, 1923. Quoted in Kenneth Allsop. *Hard Travellin'*. NY: New American Library, 1967, p. 220. According to a study of 200,000 unattached migrants served by the Federal Transient Program, only 2-3% were women. John N. Webb. *The Transient Unemployed*. WPA Research Monograph III. Washington: USGPO, 1935. p. 32.

15. Anderson's *The Hobo* contains a number of hobo songs, but none of them are blues or black songs. George Milburn *(The Hobo's Hornbook*, Ives Washburn, 1930), on the other hand, includes a few such pieces. Most startling, however, is John Greenway's *American Folk Songs of Protest*. Philadelphia: University of Pennsylvania Press, 1953. pp. 173-208. In his chapter on "The Migratory Worker," he sees hobo songs as a rich lode of folk materials, but completely ignores the blues, hobo songs *par excellence!* The exceptional commentator is Kenneth Allsop who devotes several chapters of *Hard Travellin'* to the blues as hobo song.

16. It is difficult to assess such reports wherein the informant's words seem to almost perfectly echo the words of a song. While Daisy rarely listened to Minnie's records, a past or present interviewer's leading questions may have enabled her to read the incident back into the song. In the earliest days of blues research, probing for the "reality" behind the song was a predominant mode of interviewing. Thus, the song may have preceded any such incident, although it now seems as if the incident was first.

17. This idea has some affinity with the ones expressed by the poets Nikki Giovanni and Alice Walker. Giovanni suggested the people could use Harlem's churches and bars for lectures in black history, medical science and more. See "One Day I Fell Off the Roof (A View of the Black University)." *The Black Woman*. Ed. by Toni Cade. NY: Mentor, 1970. p. 135. Alice Walker explained the role of the "black revolutionary artist" in this way: "He must be a walking filing cabinet of poems and songs and stories, of people, of places, of deeds and misdeeds." From

"The Unglamorous but Worthwhile Duties of the Black Revolutionary Artist, or Of the Black Writer Who Simply Works and Writes." *In Search of Our Mothers' Gardens.* NY: Harcourt, 1983. p. 136. Giovanni's notion of the reinscription of various institutions is supported by Houston Baker, who writes that in black culture, even the university is inscribed by music as a condition of existence. See his notes on the "chapel of melody" in his meditation on Fisk University and W. E. B. DuBois' *The Souls of Black Folks,* in *Modernism and the Harlem Renaissance.* Chicago: University of Chicago Press, 1987. pp. 65-66.

18. Quoted in Attali, *Noise,* p. 74.

19. Mississippi Sheiks. *Times Done Got Hard.* Okeh 8854. Recorded December 15, 1930.

20. In his study of the Big Rock Candy Mountain, surrealist writer/artist Hal Rammel refers to a 13th-century ode by the "rebellious vagabond scholars and poets," the Goliards, to the patrons of dice and intoxication! But as Rammel mentions, the Goliards wrote for the educated, Latin-speaking people. Hal Rammel, *Nowhere in America.* Urbana: University of Illinois Press, 1990, p. 13.

21. Paul Oliver. *Savannah Syncopators.* London: Studio Vista, 1970. p. 45. See pp. 43-52 on *griots.*

22. Maurice Delafosse. *The Negroes of Africa.* Washington: Associated Publishers, 1931. p. 271.

23. Mississippi Sheiks. *Winter Time Blues.* Okeh 8773. Recorded February 17, 1930.

24. Jazz Gillum. *Down South Blues.* Bluebird 9004. Recorded December 4, 1941. Bobo Jenkins. *Ten Below Zero.* Fortune 838. Recorded 1956.

25. Kansas City Blues Strummers. Vocalion 1048. Recorded July 27, 1926. Furry Lewis. *Why Don't You Come Home Blues.* Vocalion 1134. Recorded October 9, 1927.

26. David Evans. "Charlie Patton, Conscience of the Delta." *Voice of the Delta....* Edited by Robert Sacré. Liège: Presses Universitaires Liège, 1987. pp. 175, 176.

27. Simon J. Bronner. "Living Blues Interview: Eugene Powell—Sonny Boy Nelson." p. 23. *Living Blues* 43. Summer 1979.

28. Keil. *Urban Blues,* p. 145. Many composers report similar experiences. For example Max Bruch remarked, "My most beautiful melodies have come to me in dreams." Quoted in Martin Nass, PhD, "On Hearing and Inspiration in the Composition of Music." *Psychoanalytic Explorations in Music.* Ed. by Stuart Feder, Richard L. Karmel and George Pollock. Madison, CT: International Universities Press, 1990. p. 185.

29. William Ferris. "James 'Son Ford' Thomas, Sculptor." *Local Color: A Sense of Place in Folk Art.* By William Ferris. NY: McGraw-Hill, 1982. p. 150.

30. It is hardly necessary here to justify the expansive power of the idea of the *outsider,* but it is worth noting that some aspects of language and place within the social structure have changed little since Minnie's heyday. On August 24, 1986, the front page of the *Chicago Sun-Times* carried the headline, "Mayor's staff—*outsiders* are in. Many women, blacks ..." (emphasis added).

31. Big Joe Williams. *49 Highway Blues.* Bluebird 5996. Recorded February 25, 1935. Tommy McClennan. *New Highway No. 51.* Bluebird 8499. Recorded May 10, 1940. Son Bonds. *80 Highway Blues.* Bluebird 8927. Recorded September 24, 1941. Jimmy McCracklin. *Highway 101.* Globe 104. Recorded 1945.

32. See the section on duets for the lyrics of *Can I Do It for You?*

33. Minnie remade her hit eleven years later for Checker; since the middle of 1930 she had been recording almost exclusively in Chicago, but this session for the Chicago-based Chess label group, like many of her earliest songs, was recorded in Memphis.

34. Lightnin' Hopkins. *Automobile*. Gold Star 666. Recorded in 1949.

35. State Street Boys. *She Caught the Train*. Okeh 8962. Recorded January 10, 1935.

36. Walter Roland. *T Model Blues*. Perfect 0265. Recorded July 17, 1933.

37. Minnie may have found that such comments as "Play it till the fire wagon comes" made it easier for her to perform songs like *Call the Fire Wagon*, that would otherwise be uncomfortable. We do not mean to suggest that the comments spoken by blues singers during their songs can be so easily accounted for, or analyzed in such a linear and superficial manner, but we are suggesting the possibility of another dimension, to be considered with the already accepted notions of the motivations behind such comments: e.g. convention; reassurance; evocation of a second person, or of an instrument-as-person; to (re)produce audience involvement, and more.

38. Silvia Bovenschen, "Is There A Feminine Aesthetic"? p. 111. This is echoed in Puckett, *Folk Beliefs of the Southern Negro*, p. 90. "It is the women and not the men who are the mourners."

39. Bachelard, *Psychoanalysis of Fire*, pp. 7, 18, 51.

40. Simone de Beauvoir. *The Second Sex*. NY: Knopf, 1953, p. 712.

Chapter 19: MAD LOVE

1. Can we avoid remembering, precisely here, Bukka White's dismal report about Minnie's last years, "all she do is sit in her wheelchair and cry and cry."

2. Catherine Clément. *The Weary Sons of Freud*. London: Verso Books, 1987. p. 64. "They control, through their very aberrations, the mechanisms of how others eat, dress, marry."

3. "The project of revolution must be eroticized ... revolutionists must be made increasingly aware of the erotic implications of the ... transformation of society.... The dissemination of a revolutionary erotic consciousness ... remains a programmatic constant of surrealism." Franklin Rosemont. "The 100th Anniversary of Hysteria". *Surrealism in 1978*. (Exhibition catalog for an international surrealist exhibition in Cedarburg, Wisconsin, 1978). p. 7. See also Audre Lorde. "Uses of the Erotic: The Erotic as Power." *Sister Outsider*. Trumansburg: Crossing Press, 1984. pp. 53-59.

4. Luca and Trost's *Dialectic of Dialectic* (1945) is quoted in André Breton. *What Is Surrealism*. I, p. 65. Excerpts from "The Platform of Prague," a joint declaration of the Surrealist Groups of Paris and Prague, appeared in *Radical America*, January 1970. Special Issue, "Surrealism in the Service of the Revolution." p. 89.

5. André Breton. "First Hand," in *What Is Surrealism? Selected Writings*. II, p. 308-9. Final emphasis added. This text was the Preface to Karel Kupka's study of Australian aboriginal art.

6. André Breton. From "On the Road to San Romano." *Selected Poems*. London: Jonathan Cape, 1969. p. 105.

7. Judy Grahn. "Confrontations with the Devil in the Form of Love." *The Work of a Common Woman.* NY: St. Martins, 1978. p. 148.

8. André Breton. "Exhibition X ... Y...." *What Is Surrealism? Selected Writings.* II, p. 43

9. Minnie uses the image of a "fattening pen" in her 1935 recording of *Ball and Chain Blues* as the sign of her lover's death ("He got to die") and as a place to keep *him* for *her* use. The image is especially significant in the latter song where Minnie jousts with the idea of suicide as a reaction to her not being able to marry her true love!

10. Sigmund Freud. *Minutes of the Vienna Psychoanalytic Society.* Edited by Herman Nunberg and Ernst Federn. Volume II. 1908-1910. NY: International Universities Press, 1967. Session 66, p. 122.

11. David Evans. *Tommy Johnson.* London: Studio Vista, 1971. p. 108 n. 6. See Arna Bontemps. *Lonesome Boy.* Boston: Houghton Mifflin, 1955, for a moving literary application of this theme. The story has been reprinted in Langston Hughes and Arna Bontemps. *The Book of Negro Folklore.* NY: Dodd, Mead, 1959. In Illinois, Hyatt found a similar story of learning to play the fiddle from a big black man who first appears as (or who is first heralded by) a "big black snake." *Folk-lore From Adams County Illinois,* Item 9073, p. 457. See elsewhere in this book where Eugene Powell refers to learning a song from the devil, in a dream.

12. The crossroads has received imaginative treatment in another work, as well. Houston Baker's *Blues, Ideology and Afro-American Literature.* Chicago: University of Chicago Press, 1984. Baker analyzes several examples of black literature using the junction, or crossroads, as a *blues figure* through which he orchestrates a new interpretation of various works of black literature.

13. Finn's only mention of Minnie is as a name among the many he cites as examples of pseudonyms taken by blues singers. She isn't mentioned in his two-page section on women that closes the book (in case you wondered where they were) and this special, little section contains Finn's tribute to the blueswomen: High praise, but mentioned as an afterthought and consigned to the margin.

14. The crossroads is "more than a metaphysical principle.... It is at this point of intersection that the abstract and ancestral principles which are the loa—whose location is in an absolute time and in an absolute space—become a living organism of this immediate moment and this particular place." Maya Deren. *Divine Horsemen: Voodoo Gods of Haiti.* NY: Delta 1972. p. 35, 75.

Chapter 20: WORK

1. Jacqueline Jones. *Labor of Love, Labor of Sorrow.* p. 206.

2. Daphne Duvall Harrison. *Black Pearls. Blues Queens of the 1920s.* p. 263 n.12.

3. Irene Scruggs. *Itching Heel Blues.* Paramount 12944. Recorded c. May 26, 1930.

4. Jones, *Labor of Love, Labor of Sorrow,* p. 148.

5. Sylvester Weaver. *Guitar Blues/Guitar Rag.* Okeh 8109. Recorded October 19, 1923 and November 2, 1923. *Guitar Rag* was recorded in 1936 by Bob Wills, although at no gain for Weaver. As was Wills' habitual practice, the black artists from whose works he profited were not mentioned or credited for their work.

For other details, see "The Sylvester Weaver Scrapbook" in *Living Blues 52.* Spring 1982. pp. 15-25. The section includes articles by Jim O'Neal and Paul Garon, a Weaver discography and facsimile reproductions of many of the documents from the scrapbook, including letters from J. C. Johnson, Clarence Williams, and Helen Humes.

6. Titon, *Early Down Home Blues*, p. 220. Son House told Julius Lester that he received $40 for the session. "Interview with Son House." *Sing Out* XV:3. 1965. pp. 38-45.

7. John Fahey. *Charley Patton.* London: Studio Vista, 1970. p. 8.

8. Albertson, *Bessie*, pp. 44-46.

9. Albertson, *Bessie.* p. 165. Albertson's information is taken from the Columbia files, whereas Howell remembered a much higher figure. "I got paid $50 for my first record. And I got royalties, too—they came in twice a year." Pete Welding. "I'm Peg Leg Howell." Interviewed by George Mitchell. *Blues Unlimited 10.* March 1964. p. 7.

10. Evans, "Charlie Patton, The Conscience of the Delta," p. 149.

11. Dixon and Godrich, *Recording the Blues,* p. 92.

12. Dixon and Godrich, *Recording the Blues,* p. 92. On the next page, they add, "It appears that singers were being paid rather less than they had been ten years before...."

13. "News," citing Larry Cohn. *Blues Unlimited 91.* May 1972. p. 17. Bastin, *Red River Blues,* p. 126.

14. Of course, many of them did want to record again, partly because they were still interested in a chance at fame, and partly because they needed the money. Even now, Yank Rachell says he does not enjoy traveling and playing blues, but does it for the money. Interview with Yank Rachell, by Jim O'Neal and Patricia Johnson, Atlanta, October, 1988.

15. The contract specified that her wages be paid to Lester Melrose, and one can only guess whether or not she received the full amount. Robert Koester suggests that Melrose probably did pay Minnie the full amount as he made most of his money through publishing his artists' songs, and Bukka White agreed with this positive assessment of Melrose. (See Bruce Cook, *Listening to the Blues,* p. 128.) Other informants close to CBS feel that Melrose probably kept a goodly portion. $45 was the equivalent of about $240 today (1990).

16. Gayle Dean Wardlow, personal communication to the authors. The Winton was manufactured from 1896 until 1924, and it was quite an expensive car, selling for around $4000 when a Model T Ford was selling for $300!

17. On the Marmon, Jim O'Neal, Memphis Slim interview. The car may have been a Marmon, if not a Winton, or there may have been several cars.

18. Garon, Johnny Shines interview. Information on National guitars can be found in the appropriate year's Sears catalogs and in "The Story of the Dobro," by Ed Dopera as told to Michael Brooks. *The Guitar Player Book.* Revised and Updated Edition, by the Editors of *Guitar Player Magazine.* Cupertino: Guitar Player Books and NY: Grove Press, 1979. pp. 361-364. See also "The Guitar in Early Country Music," by Douglas Green. *The Guitar Player Book,* pp. 281-283. The list of blues singers who we know played National steel guitars includes Tampa Red, Tommy McClennan, Robert Petway, Walter Vinson, Peetie Wheatstraw, Bo Carter and many others.

19. Welding, "Rambling Johnny Shines," p. 27.

20. We don't always realize that singers like Charlie Patton (b. 1891), Peg Leg Howell (1888) and Memphis Minnie (1896) were contemporaries of Ma Rainey (1886) and Bessie Smith (1894) and that all of them are considered "first generation" blues singers.

21. Guralnick, *The Listener's Guide to the Blues*, p. 53.

22. Sammy Hill. *Cryin' For You Blues*. Victor 38588. Recorded in Dallas, August 9, 1929.

23. Al Wilson. "Rare Blues of the Twenties." *Little Sandy Review* 2:2. November 1966. p. 7.

24. Titon, *Early Downhome Blues*, p. 23.

25. David Harrison, review of *The Yas Yas Girl* 1938-1941 (Earl Archives BD601). *Blues Unlimited* 148/149. Winter 1987. p. 31.

26. We will only add that the early and continued rejection of 1930s urban blues by collectors is another one of the signs of the white blues phenomemon. While the rise of white blues musicians has been the occasion for comment, white blues fandom has been less so, although the latter's roots and effects are worth tracing. Our *Blues and the Poetic Spirit* criticizes white blues at length.

27. Titon, *Early Downhome Blues*, pp. 272-273.

28. Barry Lee Pearson. "Bowling Green John Cephas and Harmonica Phil Wiggins." *Living Blues* 63. January/February 1985. p. 20.

29. Joe Louis Walker, quoted in Mary Katherine Aldin. "Interview: Joe Louis Walker. 'My Whole Thing Was Playing Music.'" *Living Blues* 87. August 1989. p. 15.

30. Mike Rowe. "'I Was Really Dedicated:' An Interview with Billy Boy Arnold. Part 3: 'Whatever I did it was me and I'm proud of it'." *Blues Unlimited* 128. January/February 178. p. 24

31. Keil, *Urban Blues*, p. 156.

32. Peter Guralnick. *Feel Like Going Home*. NY: Outerbridge and Dienstfrey, 1971. p. 49.

33. Titon, *Early Downhome Blues*, pp. 205, 23.

34. Nelson George. *The Death of Rhythm & Blues*. NY: Pantheon, 1988. p. 11. Johnny Otis substantiates George's comments, although he may also be George's source: "The porters who worked on the trains used to bring in records from Chicago and places, and would play them on Saturdays or Sundays in the neighborhood—we liked them because they were 'risky,' you know." Johnny Otis, quoted in John Broven. "A Rap with Johnny Otis." *Blues Unlimited* 100, April 1973. p.

35. Justin O'Brien, "The Dark Road of Floyd Jones-Part 1," *Living Blues 58*. Winter 1983. p. 7.

36. Calt and Wardlow, *King of the Delta Blues*, p. 180.

37. See Dixon and Godrich *Recording the Blues*, and Rust, *The American Record Label Book*.

38. Poor Joe Williams. *I'm Talking About You*. Collector *Jen 3*. Recorded September 1-3, 1957. (This is a 45 rpm extended-play release.) Eddie Lee Jones does *I'm Talking 'bout You* on *Yonder Go That Old Black Dog: Blues, Spirituals and Folksongs From Rural Georgia* by Eddie Lee Jones and Family. Testament T-2224. Recorded August, 1965. Frank Hovington. *I'm Talking About You*. On *Lonesome Road Blues*, Rounder LP 2017. Norman Phelps Virginia Rounders. *Talkin' 'bout You*. Decca 5237. Recorded February 24, 1936.

39. Bachelard, *The Poetics of Space*, pp. xxii.

40. Ferris, *Blues from the Delta*, p. 103.

41. Levine, *Black Culture and Black Consciousness*, p. 203.

42. Lonnie Johnson. *You Don't See Into the Blues Like Me.* Okeh 8451, recorded August 13, 1926.

43. Lautréamont, "Poesies," p. 333.

44. Arthur "Big Boy" Crudup, quoted in Leadbitter, "Big Boy Crudup," pp. 17-18.

45. Sidran, *Black Talk*, pp. 38, 88.

46. Garon, Ethel Douglas and Daisy Johnson interview.

DISCOGRAPHY

1. Daniel Groslier. "Memphis Minnie/Discographie," in *Soul Bag* 97. January/February, 1984. pp. 9-15.

2. While we've tried to track the registration of all of Minnie's song, funding was not available to do the same for every song recorded by Joe McCoy or Son Joe. We've examined as many of Minnie's records as possible, and collectors around the world have offered valuable assistance. Nonetheless, 20 sides eluded our inspection. Some exist only as test pressings, of course, on which there are no composer credits to be found.

INDEX

Action Committee of Women Prostitutes, 128
Adins, Georges, 5, 83
After While Blues, 29
Agar, Eileen, 65
Alchemy, 228
Algren, Nelson, 115, 131
Alley, meaning and function of, 123, 124
Analogy, 91, 98; as revolutionary principle, 94-95
Aragon, Louis, 97
Arnold, Billy Boy, 56, 71; on Minnie's temper, 71; on women as blues fans, 247
Arnold, Kokomo, 155, 171, 204, 208; influence of Memphis Minnie on, 171
As Long As I Can See You Smile, 65
ASP (Association of Seattle Prostitutes), 128
Attali, Jacques, 91
Automobile (Lightnin' Hopkins), 225

Baby Face Leroy, 52, 67
Bachelard, Gaston, 112, 113
Back Door Man (Howlin' Wolf), 164
Baker, Etta, 140
Barbecue Bob, 139, 246; wages of, 10, 242
Barnes, George, 44
Beale Street, 17-18, 59, 76
Beale Street Blues (W. C. Handy), 18
Beale Street Sheiks, 245
Beard, Mary Ritter, 143
Beasley, Walter, 120
Beauvoir, Simone de, 228
Beehive, as utopian model, 113
Bell, Alfred, 45
Bergh, Kajsa, 47
Berlin, Irving, 37

Berry, Chuck, influence of Memphis Minnie on, 4
Bidbei, 116
Big Maceo, 41, 86
Biographical Dictionary of Afro-American and African Musicians (Eileen Southern), 87
Biting Bug Blues, 63; (lyrics), 111
Black Bob, 4; accompanies Memphis Minnie, 39, 44, 45
Black Cat Blues, 160, 162; (lyrics), 159
Black humor, 94, 139, 165
Black Pearls (Daphne Duval Harrison), 99
Black Rat (Johnny Shines), 24
Black Rat Swing, 48
Black vernacular speech, 167, 169
Black women as leaders, 143
Blue Smitty, on street singing, 60
Blues, and realism, 239, 241; animal imagery in, 113, 141, 202; as antagonistic to middle-class values, 127, 188, 244; as autobiography, 214, 241; as diverse commentary, 99; as educational medium, 187, 217; as folk-lyrics, 167; as historical documents, 98, 217; as product of imagination, 201, 202, 203; as subversive, 92; conventions and commonplace in, 110, 175, 241; function of projection in, 167, 168; importance of class, race and gendered aspects, 92; interpretation of, 100; liberating aspects of, 97, 189, 197, 213, 231, 251; nature of, 6; nonsense sounds in, 135, 188, 202; political imagery and, 100; sexual references in, 193, 194, 233, 234, 236, 237, 240; structure and content, 136, 188, 189; subversive character, 92, 137

Blues as dance music, 177
Blues contests, 57, 59
Blues criticism, 75, 247
Blues, meaning in, 94, 99, 100, 102, 112, 155, 167, 180, 241; class and race aspects of, 102; unconscious, 101
Blues on record, history of, 7
Blues singer, and anonymity, 173; and listener, 244, 245, 251; and "singing to each other", 187, 225; and stardom, 244; as traveler, 211; as visionary, 94; compared with *griots*, 218; function of, 217; politics of, 101; wages of, 241-242
Blues singing, as play, 253, 254; as work, 241, 253
Bo Diddley, 67
Bo-Weavil Blues (Ma Rainey), 175
Bogan, Lucille, 32, 99, 124, 131
Bonds, Son, 208, 222
Botherin' That Thing, 30, 31
Boyd, Eddie, 67; influence of Memphis Minnie on, 4
Bradford, Perry, 9
Breton, André, 91, 97, 163, 189
Brim, Grace, 67
Brim, John, 67
Broken Bed Blues (Kansas City Blues Strummers), 221
Broken Heart, 67
Broonzy, Big Bill, 4, 27, 37, 38, 41, 50, 53, 55, 66, 71, 86, 225; accompanies Memphis Minnie, 72; as Melrose artist, 42; influence of Memphis Minnie on, 103; memorial show for, 76; on blues contest, 57; on Minnie's travels, 44
Brown, H. Rap, 169
Brown, Joe, 67
Brown, Milton, influence of Memphis Minnie on, 250
Brown, Willie, 16, 20, 24, 40
Bumble Bee, 20, 24, 25, 29, 31, 68, 103, 109, 248; (lyrics of Columbia version), 104; (lyrics of Vocalion version), 105; Columbia and Vocalion versions compared, 107
Bumble Bee Blues (Victor), 29

Bumble Bee No. 2, 30, 103, 106, 248; (lyrics), 107
Bumble Bee Slim, 41, 104, 246
Bumble bees, beliefs concerning, 110
Bunkley, Jim, influence of Memphis Minnie on, 186
Burr Clover Blues (Muddy Waters), 16
Burse, Charlie, influence of Memphis Minnie on, 186

Cakes and baking, meaning of, 196
Caldonia (Louis Jordan), 66
Calicott, Joe, 30, 68
Call the Fire Wagon, 28, 46, 188, 227, 228; (lyrics), 226
Calloway, Cab, 25
Can I Do It for You?, 28, 183, 222; (lyrics), 180
Can't Afford to Lose My Man, 48
Can't Get No Grinding (Muddy Waters), 68, 186
Cannon, Gus, 16, 245
Carr, Leroy, 171; influence of on 1930s sound, 42
Carrington, Leonora, 3, 203
Cars, meaning of, 223
Carter, Big Lucky, 65, 77
Carter, Bo. *See* Chatman, Bo
Cats, 160, 162
Caught Me Wrong Again, 140
Cavin, Susan, 152
Césaire, Suzanne, 169
Chatman, Bo ("Bo Carter"), 23; influence of Memphis Minnie on, 103
Chatman, Lonnie, 23
Chatman, Peter, Sr. (father of Memphis Slim), 24
Chatman, Sam, 23, 172
Chauffeur, meaning of, 224
Chauffeur Blues (Jefferson Airplane), 86
Checker Records, 4, 48
Chenier, Clifton, influence of Memphis Minnie on, 4, 48
Cherry Ball Blues, 30
Chess Records, 4, 247
Chicago, racial demographics of, 33-34
Chicago Defender, 34, 54, 247

Chickasaw Train Blues (Low Down Dirty Thing), 35, 210, 214; (lyrics), 209

Chirico, Giorgio de, 97

Church, as image of repression and object of humor, 121-122

Church's Park, 19

Clark, James "Beale Street", 54

Classic blues, 7; as subject of critical attention, 99; compared to country blues, 8, 127

Clubs and taverns, *230 Club*, 54; *640 Club*, 73; *708 Club*, 4, 44, 53, 55, 65, 69; *2200 Club*, 73; Blue Flame, 55; Blue Note, 76; Club DeLisa, 53; Du Drop Lounge, 55, 59; The Flame, 54; Gatewood's Tavern, 53, 55; H & T, 73; Indiana Theatre, 54, 73; Joe's L. A. Bar, 73; Joe's Rendezvous, 73; Koppin Theatre, 61; Little Eddie's, 73; Martin's Corner, 53; McKie's Show Lounge, 247; Mona Lisa, 61; Music Box, 53; Painted Doll, 73; Square Deal, 54; Sylvio's, 54, 55, 73; Tiny Davis' Lounge, 73; Tramor Hotel and Cafe, 44; White Elephant (Don's Den), 53; as criminal locale, 164. *See also under Southern Clubs.*

Cobb, Joyce, influence of Memphis Minnie on, 86

Cole, Nat King, 66

Coleman, "Beale Street", accompanies Memphis Minnie, 77

Coleman, Bob, 116

Coleman, Sam, accompanies Memphis Minnie, 77

Collins, Lee, 54

Colquhoun, Ithell, 207

Come Go Home with Me (Lightnin' Hopkins), 202

Complete Encyclopedia of Popular Music and Jazz, 1900-1950 (Roger D. Kinkle), 87

Composer credits and song authorship, 51, 52

Congo Square, 152

Cool Drink of Water Blues (Tommy Johnson), 189

Cortez, Jayne, 13

Country blues, description and social meaning of, 8-9

Cox, Ida, 7, 183

Crackentine, Kid, 29

Crazy Crying Blues, 32, 229; (lyrics), 230

Crime, as critique of bourgeois society, 164, 115, 117

Critics, 93, 94, 246; condescension in, 176, 245, 246;

Crossroads, 94, 154, 232, 237, 238

Crudup, Arthur "Big Boy", 27, 41, 253; as Melrose artist, 42

Cryin' for You Blues (Sammy Hill), 245

Cunard, Nancy, 97

Cushing, Steve, 61

Dance, Helen Oakley, 3

Darby, Teddy, 11

Davenport, Jed, 24, 28, 31; accompanies Memphis Minnie, 20, 223

Davis, Blind John, 4, 24, 40, 41, 71; accompanies Memphis Minnie, 45

Davis, Eunice, influence of Memphis Minnie on, 87

Davis, Walter, 41, 117; at Memphis rehearsal hall, 78

Daybreak Blues, 53; (lyrics), 55

Death of Blind Boy Fuller (Brownie McGhee), 48

Death of Leroy Carr (Bumble Bee Slim), 48

Debs, Eugene V., 18, 131

Delany, Mattie, 11

Depression, effects of on blues recording, 10, 34, 103, 235

Devil, 154, 237, 238

Dicey, Bill, 61

Dirt Dauber Blues, 32, 149, 151, 188; (lyrics), 134

Dirt-daubers, beliefs concerning, 133

Dirty dozens, defined, 169. *See also New Dirty Dozen.*

Dirty Mother for You, 35, 149; (lyrics), 149

Dirty words, women's use of, 169

Dixon, Willie, on Lester Melrose, 41

Dobbins, Joe, plays at benefit for Minnie, 84
Doctor, meaning of, 156
Doctor Clayton, 41
Doctor, Doctor Blues, 39; (lyrics), 150
Doctor's Blues, The (Kansas City Kitty and Georgia Tom), 161
Don't Want No Woman, 30
Don't Worry About that Mule (Louis Jordan), 66
Done Somebody Wrong (Elmore James), 156
Douglas family, 28; and fires, 28; farm, 15; members of, 14; moves to Brunswick, Tennessee, 28; moves to Memphis from Walls, 76
Douglas, Abe (father), 14, 28
Douglas, Dovie (sister), 62
Douglas, Edward (brother), 84
Douglas, Ethel (sister-in-law), 255; and 1927 flood, 26; on Casey Bill, 21; on Joe McCoy, 37; on Minnie playing for family and friends, 76
Douglas, Gertrude (mother), 14, 28
Douglas, Lizzie. *See* Memphis Minnie.
Douglas, Leo (brother), 37
Down in New Orleans, 38, 150; as voodoo song, 155, 156; (lyrics), 155
Down in the Alley (lyrics), 122
Down South Blues (Jazz Gillum), 221
Doyle, Little Buddy, 4; wages of, 242
Dreams, 201, 221; inspirational function of, 221, 222
Drunken Barrel House Blues, 214, 235
Dry Well Blues (Charlie Patton), 16
Ducornet, Rikki, 199
Duets, 148; composition of, 180; structural aspects of, 183, 184, 187, 188
Dupree, Champion Jack, 139; on street singing and Memphis Minnie, 59
Duskin, Joe, 60; on Minnie's temper, 68

80 Highway
Ekstine, Billy, 66
Elective affinities, 91
Ellis, Wilbert "Big Chief", 140

Ernst, Max, 97
Estes, Sleepy John, 57, 77, 210, 247
Etienne, Franck, 157
Evil, as progress, 232

Female country blues artists, 11, 136
Female drummers, 152
Female healers, 143, 154
Female territory, as depicted in *Plymouth Rock Blues*, 141
Finger Print Blues, 117, 174
Finn, Julio, 238
Fire, meaning of, 227, 228
Fish Man Blues, 191
Fishing Blues, 191
Fitzgerald, Ella, 66
Five Long Years (Eddie Boyd), 67
Flamingos, The, 67
Folk beliefs, 134, 148
Folk healers, 135, 143, 144, 152
Food and cooking, as metaphor for sex, 191, 196; privacy and independence associated with, 191; songs, ambiguous references in, 193
49 Highway (Big Joe Williams), 222
Fort Valley State College, 186
Fourier, Charles, 9, 232
Frankie Jean (That Trottin' Fool), 15, 51, 199, 203; (lyrics), 199
Franklin, Aretha, 79
Frazier, Calvin, influence of Memphis Minnie on, 4
Freud, Sigmund, 136
Frisco Bound (James Wiggins), 213
Frisco Railway, 213
'Frisco Town, 25, 109, 208, 213, 214; (lyrics), 211
Fuller, Blind Boy, 86
Fulson, Lowell, influence of Memphis Minnie on, 4

Gaither, Bill. *See* Leroy's Buddy.
Gambling songs, 119
Garage Fire Blues, 48, 223, 227, 228; (lyrics), 223
Georgia Skin, 30; (lyrics), 119
Georgia Skin (Walter Beasley), 120
Georgia Tom, 148, 161
Giacometti, Alberto, 189

Gillum, Jazz, 156, 221

Gilman, Charlotte Perkins, 114

Glover, Mae, 104

God Don't Like Ugly (Sam Chatman), 172

Godwin, Harry, 84

Goffin, Robert, on surrealism and jazz, 97

Goin' Back to Texas, 25, 29, 177, 211, 245

Good Biscuits, 63, 140, 191, 194; (lyrics), 193

Good Girl Blues, 183; (lyrics), 121

Good Mornin' (Bluebird), 38

Good Morning (Vocalion), 204, 205

Good Morning, School Girl (Sonny Boy Williamson), 40, 48

Good Soppin', 15, 191

Goodman, Benny, 66

Gordon, Jimmy, 4, 35

Grahn, Judy, 191

Grandpa and Grandma Blues, 223

Green, Lil, 41, 52

Guilt, exteriorization of, 98

Guitar Blues (Sylvester Weaver), 242

Guitar Rag (Sylvester Weaver), 242

Guitar Slim, 74

Gutter Man Blues (George Hannah), 248

Guy, Buddy, on playing standing up, 74

Hager, Fred, 9

Hallelujah Joe Ain't Preachin' No More (Harlem Hamfats), 36

Hampton, Lionel, 66

Handy, W. C., 18

Hannah, George, 248

Harlem Hamfats, 24, 36, 86

Harpo, Slim, 103

Harris, Homer, accompanies Memphis Minnie, 54

Harrison, Daphne Duval, 99

Hart, Hattie, 245

He's in the Ring (Doing that Same Old Thing), 39

Heartfixers, influence of Memphis Minnie on, 186

Helfer, Erwin, 250

Hemphill, Jessie Mae, 11

Hesitating Blues (W. C. Handy), 18

Hill, Big Bill, 55

Hill, Jim, 156

Hill, Rose Lee, 11

Hill, Sammy, 245

Hitch Me to Your Buggy, and Drive Me Like a Mule (Will Weldon), 20

Hite, Les, 66

Hobos, 215; paucity of female, 214, songs of female, 214

Hogg, Smokey, 172

Hole in the Wall, 35; (lyrics), 161

Holiday, Billie, 99

Hollywood Rag (Gus Cannon), 16

Homesick James, 24, 39, 127; accompanies Memphis Minnie, 77; influence of Memphis Minnie on, 48; on Minnie as mentor, 78; on Minnie's gambling, 45; on Minnie's guitar skills, 53; on Minnie's temper, 70; on Minnie's tobacco chewing, 38; on Minnie's travels, 39; on playing standing up, 74; on Sonny Boy Williamson and Memphis Minnie, 70

Hoodoo Lady, 157; (lyrics), 158

Hooker, John Lee, influence of Memphis Minnie on, 103

Hopkins, Lightnin', influence of Memphis Minnie on, 48, 225; sings "talking blues", 202

Horse, and woman, 203; "horse" as voodoo term, 203. See also *Frankie Jean (That Trottin' Fool)*

Hot Stuff, (lyrics), 252

House, Son, 16, 20, 100; wages of, 242

Hovington, Frank, influence of Memphis Minnie on, 250

How Come You Do Me Like You Do? (popular song), 22, 65

How High the Moon (Lionel Hampton), 66

How Long — How Long Blues (Leroy Carr and Scrapper Blackwell), 27, 42

Howard, Rosetta, 86

Howell, Peg Leg, 109, 156; wages of, 10, 242

Howlin' Wolf, 66, 164; as urban
    stylist, 8
Howling Wind Blues (Walter Davis),
    117
Hubbard, William "Boogie Man",
    accompanies Memphis Minnie,
    77
Hughes, Langston, on Memphis
    Minnie, 54
Hunter, Alberta, 99
Hurt, Mississippi John, wages of, 242
Hustlin' Woman Blues, 39; (lyrics),
    125
Hutto, J. B., as urban stylist, 74; influ-
    ence of Memphis Minnie on, 4

I Am in the Heavenly Way (Bukka
    White), 29
*I Don't Want No Woman I Have To
    Give My Money To*, 30
I Love You for Sentimental Reasons
    (Nat King Cole), 66
I Never Told a Lie, 30
I Want That, 25, 211
I'm a Gambling Woman, 45, 157
I'm Fixed For You, 32
I'm Going Back Home, 29, 30, 245;
I'm Going Don't You Know (lyrics),
    210
I'm Gonna Bake My Biscuits, 51, 191,
    193, 234, 247; (lyrics), 192
I'm So Glad, 50
I'm Talking 'bout You No. 2, 245, 246,
    248; (lyrics), 248
I'm Talking About You, 31, 245, 246,
    248, 250
I'm Waiting On You, 65
*If I Had My Way I'd Tear This Build-
    ing Down* (Blind Willie Johnson),
    116
*If You See My Rooster (Please Run
    Him Home)*, (lyrics), 137
Illinois Central Railroad, 16, 210
Imagination, as instrument of interpre-
    tation, 93, 112, 148
In My Girlish Days, 51, 86, 214, 215;
    (lyrics), 215
Ink Spots, 66
Insects, 111, 112, 133

Interpretation, gendered aspects of, 98
"Interpreters," singers and root doc-
    tors as, 93, 154
Interruption, 187, 188
Into Each Life (Ink Spots, Ella
    Fitzgerald), 66
It's Tight Like That (Tampa Red and
    Georgia Tom), 27
Itching Heel Blues (Irene Scruggs),
    241

Jackson, Bruce, 113
Jackson, G. P., 47
Jackson, Jim, 19
Jackson, Jump, on Langston Hughes,
    54
Jailhouse Trouble Blues, 117
James, Elmore, 156, 254
James, McKinley, 11
Jelly Jelly (Billy Ekstine), 66
Jenkins, Bobo, 39, 221
Jersey Bounce (Les Hite, Benny Good-
    man, Red Norvo), 66
Jim Jackson's Kansas City Blues (Jim
    Jackson), 27
Joans, Ted, sees Minnie perform, 61
Jockey, as lover, 205
Jockey Man Blues, 38, 204, 205; (lyr-
    ics), 204
Joe Louis Strut, 39
Johnson, Blind Willie, 116
Johnson, Daisy, 14, 62, 255; as inform-
    ant, 5; on *Frankie Jean (That Trot-
    tin' Fool)*, 201; on Minnie's last
    years, 84; on *Nothing in Rambling*,
    216; on the "Gospel Minnie" sides,
    36; visits Minnie in Chicago, 56
Johnson, Larry, influence of Memphis
    Minnie on, 213
Johnson, Lonnie, 41, 251
Johnson, Merline, 41
Johnson, Robert, 16, 167; Julio Finn
    on, 238; record sales, 246
Johnson, Tommy, 23, 98, 189
Jones, Curtis, 41; wages of, 242
Jones, Eddie "One String", influence
    of Memphis Minnie on, 48
Jones, Eddie Lee, influence of Mem-
    phis Minnie on, 250

Jones, Floyd, 67, 75; on buying blues records, 248

Jones, Moody, 53; on Black Bob, 44; on Minnie's guitar skills, 53; on Son Joe as guitarist, 47

Jones, Richard M., 57

Jordan, Charlie, 77

Jordan, Louis, 66

Jump Little Rabbit, 50, 243

Just A Dream (Big Bill), 57

Kansas City Blues Strummers, 221

Kansas City Kitty, 161

Kaufman, Bob, 191

Keep It To Yourself, 35

Keep On Eating, 191; (lyrics), 195

Keep On Sailing (lyrics), 23

Kelly, Jack, 20

Kelly, Jo Ann, influence of Memphis Minnie on, 87; stages benefit for Minnie, 84

Key To The World, 46

Keys of Heaven, The (traditional song), 180

KFFA, 78

Kidman Blues, 66

Killer Diller, 50

Kimbrough, Lottie, 8

King, B. B., 44

Kinkle, Roger D., 87

Kirkland, Eddie, influence of Memphis Minnie on, 78

Kissing in the Dark, 246

Koester, Bob, on Lester Melrose, 42

Lacey, Willie, 44

Lacy, Rube, 140

Lake Michigan, 67

Lautréamont, Comte de, 131, 172, 251

Laveau, Marie, 152

Lawlars, Ernest, 5; as song writer, 51, 52; as traveler, 47; birth and death dates, 46; death of, 83; first accompanies Memphis Minnie, 45; first recording session, 46; heart condition, 79, 83; reputation as guitarist, 47

Leadbelly (Huddie Leadbetter), 22

Leadbitter, Mike, 5, 62, 201

Lee, (Patton), Bertha , influence of Memphis Minnie on, 103

Lee, Peggy, 37

Left Me with a Broken Heart (Jimmy Rogers), 67

Lenoir, J. B., 11, 67; influence of Memphis Minnie on, 4; on dreams and blues, 222; on Memphis Minnie's Blue Monday parties, 56

Leroy's Buddy (Bill Gaither), 246

Lewis, Dee, 74

Lewis, Furry, 19, 171, 221, 245

Lewis, Meade Lux, 247

Library of Congress copyright registration, and authorship of songs, 51, 52

Lieb, Sandra, 99

Lincoln, Charley, 139

Lipscomb, Mance, influence of Memphis Minnie on, 4

Listener, characteristics and role of, 93, 94, 113, 189, 247, 251

Listening, special modes of, 167, 168

Litherland, Gina, 133

Little Esther. *See* Esther Phillips.

Little Walter, 66, 67; accompanies Memphis Minnie, 67; as urban stylist, 43

Little, Robert, sees Minnie perform, 62, 74

Littlejohn, Johnny, 39

Living the Best I Can, (lyrics), 239

Lockwood, Robert Jr., 53, 70, 78

Lonesome Shack Blues, 174

Looking the World Over, 48, 58

Lorde, Audre, 169

Louis, Joe, 39

Louis, Joe Hill, 70, 79

Louisiana Hoo Doo Blues (Ma Rainey), 175

Love, as revolutionary principle, 233

Love. *See* also under Blues, Sexual references.

Love, Willie, 47, 52, 78

Low, Mary, 103

Loy, Mina, 133

Luca, Gherasim, 233

Lucas, Jane, 148
Lydston, G. Frank, racist and sexist views of, 145

Ma Rainey, 47, 174, 175; (lyrics), 174
Maggie Campbell Blues (Tommy Johnson), 98
Major, Clarence, 169
Make Me One Pallet on the Floor (W. C. Handy), 18
Make My Getaway (Big Bill), 58
Mama Don't Allow No Easy Riders Here (W. C. Handy), 19
Mansour, Joyce, 115
Martin, Fiddlin' Joe, 16, 24; accompanies Memphis Minnie, 40
Mayes, Dave, 74
McClennan, Tommy, 41, 222; influence of Memphis Minnie on, 166
McCoy, Bessie, 26, 30
McCoy, Charlie, 4, 23, 37, 45
McCoy, Ethel, 11
McCoy, Joe, 5, 23, 24; becomes preacher, 36; death of, 37; leads small washboard bands, 37; pseudonyms, 26, 29, 36; records for Decca, 36; records with Harlem Hamfats, 36; slide guitar by, 32
McCoy, Robert Lee, 37, 52
McCoy, Virginia, 37
McCracklin, Jimmy, 222
McDowell, Fred, 63
McGhee, Brownie, 73, 247
Me and My Chauffeur (Checker), 67
Me and My Chauffeur Blues (Okeh), 4, 40, 48, 51, 58, 67, 100, 225, 227, 243; (lyrics), 224
Mean Mistreater Blues (lyrics), 229
Melrose, Lester, role of in recorded blues, 41, 42, 52
Memorial songs, 48, 174
Memphis, early history of blacks in, 17
Memphis Jug Band, 29
Memphis Minnie, addresses in Chicago, 46, 56, 76; addresses in Memphis, 77, 83; appearance in standard reference works, 87; as mentor to younger artists, 56, 68, 78; asthma and, 83; automobiles

and, 183, 222, 223, 226, 228, 243; birth of, 14; Blue Monday parties, 55, 56; Burial place of, 16, 85; Casey Bill Weldon and, 21; Chicago Federation of Musicians, dues records, 49, 73; childhood of, 14; competitive attitude toward other performers, 63; cooking and, 80, 198, 255; death of, 85; drinking and, 68, 71; farm work and, 63, 255; fires and, 223, 226; gambling and, 45; guitar and performance style of, 10, 35, 40, 43, 44, 227, 235; guitars and, 30, 31, 80; illness, 83, 84; influence of others on, 171, 204, 205, 124; influence of, 4, 5, 24, 48, 56, 68, 78, 79, 86, 103, 166, 171, 186, 199, 213, 225, 250 (*See* also under indiviudal artists); leads trio with Roosevelt Sykes and Son Joe, 72; male partners and, 110; marriages, 24, 45; moves to Adelaide Street, 83; obituaries for, 86; physical appearance, 61, 63, 110; jewelry, 62, 63, 71; plays at folk festival, 73; plays at Walls, 76; plays diverse instruments, 29; plays for King Biscuit Time, 78; plays for white audiences, 65; plays standing up, 74; poverty in last years, 79, 80, 84; prostitution and, 127; pseudonyms, 14, 25, 36, 38; recorded output of, 86; recording contracts, 243; reputation as guitarist and blues artists, 3, 4, 22, 53, 71, 86; song writing and, 48, 50, 52, 224; street singing and, 20, 59; teaches Brewer Phillips, 79; tobacco and, 38; traveling and, 20, 22, 39, 59, 61, 73, 211, 214; violence and, 15, 68, 69, 70, 71; violent clubs and, 77; wages of, 242, 243; wins *Blues Unlimited* Readers' Poll, 3, 87; wins W. C. Handy Awards, 3
Memphis Minnie, compared to, Aretha Franklin, 79; Bessie Smith, 3, 71; Eugene Debs, 131; male guitarists, 10, 58, 59, 92, 95, 231; Walt Whitman, 131

ists, 10, 58, 59, 92, 95, 231; Walt Whitman, 131

Memphis Minnie, early career, joins traveling show, 15, 62; leads trio in Lake Cormorant, 22; partnership with Willie Brown, 21, 24

Memphis Minnie, records for: Bluebird, 38; Checker, 67; Decca, 35; JOB, 67; Okeh (1933) 235; Regal, 66; Vocalion, 103

Memphis Minnie, repertoire, 148; lists of songs, 65; popular songs, 22, 65; postwar, 66, 67; rural imagery in, 15, 141, 201, 204; weakness of certain late songs, 50

Memphis Minnie and Daisy Johnson, letter in *Blues Unlimited*, 85

Memphis Minnie and Joe McCoy; and National guitars, 30, 243; duets by, 28, 140; early sessions in Chicago, 27; first recording session, 24, 103; influence of others on, 245; marriage ends, 36; reputation, 30

Memphis Minnie-Jitis Blues, 29, 147-148; (lyrics), 146

Memphis rehearsal hall, 77

Memphis Slim, 4, 19, 24; accompanies Memphis Minnie, 53; on Lester Melrose, 37; on Minnie's success, 243; on street singing , 20, 60; on the death of Joe McCoy, 37

Memphis Willie B (Willie Borum), 20

Mendelssohn, Fred, 66

Meningitis Blues, 29, 147

Midnight Special, 26, 30

Milk Cow Blues (Kokomo Arnold), 38, 204, 205

Millroth, Thomas, on Minnie's reputation, 86

Mills and grinding, 186

Mimicry, 110, 174

Miniaturization, 110, 111, 113, 206

Minnie Minnie Bumble Bee, 32

Minnie the Mermaid (torch song), 25

Minnie the Moocher (Cab Calloway), 25

"Missing Women, on the Voodoo Trail to Jazz" (Cavin, Susan), 152

Mississippi Sheiks, 23, 217, 220

Moaning the Blues, 36, 167; (lyrics), 165

Montgomery, Little Brother, 54; accompanies Memphis Minnie, 67

Moody, Peter, 87

Moonshine (lyrics), 118

Morand, Herb, 24

Mortality rates in Harlem, 145

Moss, Buddy, wages of, 242

Mother Fuyer (Dirty Red), 149

Mr. Crump (W. C. Handy), 18-19

Mr. Tango Blues, 66, 209, 246

Muddy Waters, 16, 59, 66, 74, 103, 175, 247; as urban stylist, 8, 74; influence of Memphis Minnie on, 4, 48, 68, 186; on Minnie's temper, 68; on Tampa Red and Lester Melrose, 41

Mulcahy, Jim, 18

Music, as locus of subversion, 116

Musicians, functions of, 115, 116

My Butcher Man, 191, 234, 235; (lyrics), 235

My Mamma Was a Sailor (Julius Daniels), 175

My Strange Man (lyric), 166

My Washwoman's Gone, 32

Myers, Louis, 11

Names and naming, power of, 173

National guitars, 30, 31, 80, 243

Negation, meaning of, 135

Negro, An Anthology (Nancy Cunard), 97

Nelson, Arnett, 45; accompanies Memphis Minnie, 44

New Bumble Bee, 103, 106, 108; (lyrics), 108

New Dirty Dozen, 31, 94, 129, 140, 213; (lyrics), 170

New Highway 51 (Tommy McClennan), 222

New Orleans, image of, 155-156

Night Watchman Blues, 50

Nighthawk, Robert. *See* Robert Lee McCoy.

Nixon, Hammie, 127

North Memphis Blues, 32, 191, 251; (lyrics), 197

North Memphis Cafe, 197
Norvo, Red, 66
Nothing In Rambling, 48, 174, 216; (lyrics), 215

Oh Believe Me (Believe Me), 65
Oliver, Paul, on Minnie's reputation, 86
On the Sunny Side of the Street (popular song), 66
101 Highway (Jimmy McCracklin), 222
Oppenheim, Meret, 83
Opposition, as radical negating principle, 97, 153, 238
Oster, Harry, 201
Out in the Cold, 218, 221; (lyrics), 219
Outdoor Blues, 218; (lyrics), 218
"Ozymandias" (Percy Bysshe Shelley), 231

Panama Club, 18
Paper of Pins (traditional song), 180
Paranoiac-critical method, 94, 95, 168
Parker, Barber, 47
Parks, Rosa, 228
Passis, Monroe, as Minnie's manager, 66
Patton, Charlie, 16, 208, 221; record sales, 246; wages of, 242
Penrose, Valentine, 229
Perls, Nick, on Peetie Wheatstraw and blues of the 1930s, 42
Perryman, Rufus, 171
Peters, Nancy Joyce, 163
Petrillo, James, instigates recording ban, 49
Petway, Robert, influence of Memphis Minnie on, 166
Phelps, Norman, influence of Memphis Minnie on, 250
Phillips, Brewer, 60; on Big Bill and Memphis Minnie, 70; on folk festival, 73; on Memphis rehearsal hall, 78; on Minnie and Son Joe's marriage, 46, 80; on Minnie as mentor, 79; on Minnie as song writer, 52; on Minnie's meningitis, 147; on Minnie's physical appearance, 62; on Minnie's tobacco chewing and snuff dipping, 38; on paucity of pop material in Minnie's repertoire, 65; on pawning Minnie's guitars, 80; on playing standing up, 74; on Roosevelt Sykes and Memphis Minnie, 72; on Sonny Boy Williamson and Memphis Minnie, 70; on violent clubs, 77
Phillips, Esther, 99
Phonograph records, 245-248
Physicians, 144, 146; authority of, 151; discrimination practiced by, 144
Please Set a Date, 48
Plymouth Rock Blues, 15, 30, 94, 141, 148, 191; (lyrics), 139
Poet, as listener, 167; role of, 93, 94
Poetry, as living experience, 96; as interpretive principle, 112
PONY (Prostitutes of New York), 128
Poor and Wandering Woman, 214
Postwar blues, advent of, 66; as evidence of new poetic need, 75
Powell, Eugene, on dreams and blues, 222
Prisoner of Love (Billy Ekstine), 66
Promise True and Grand (Bukka White), 29
Prostitutes and prostitution, 124, 128, 129, 130
Pryor, Snooky, 53, 67; as urban stylist, 43
Pseudonyms, 172, 173, 209
PUMA (Prostitutes Union of Massachusetts), 128

Queen Bee (John Lee Hooker), 103

Rahon, Alice, 33
Railroad Bill (traditional song), 130
Rainey, Ma, 7, 99, 244; compared to Memphis Minnie, 3, 86; death of, 174
Rats, unconscious meaning of, 160
Ray, Harmon, 37
Reachin' Pete, 38; (lyrics), 117
Red beans and rice, as evocative of "down home", 155
Reinhardt, Django, 44
Remember Me, 117
Rider, meanings of, 137

Rimbaud, 94

Ringling Brothers. *See* Memphis Minnie, early career.

Rockin' Dopsie, influence of Memphis Minnie on, 48

Rogers, Jimmy, 37, 47, 54, 66; accompanies Memphis Minnie, 67; as urban stylist, 74; influence of Memphis Minnie on, 68, 71; on "Squirrel", 38; on blues contests, 59; on Minnie's physical appearance, 63; on Minnie's recording sessions, 72; on Minnie's temper, 69

Rolling Stones, influence of Memphis Minnie on, 103

Rooster, meaning of, 138

Rosemont, Franklin, 233

Rosemont, Penelope, 101, 239

Rosetta Records, 99

Rowdy Old Soul, 26

Running and Dodging Blues, 45

Russell, Tommie Lee, 11

Sad Letter Blues (Muddy Waters), 175

Sail On, Little Girl, Sail On (Bumble Bee Slim), 22

Sane, Dan, 19, 245

Save Me Some (Jed Davenport), 28

Scat singing, 135, 188

Scruggs, Irene, 241

Sellers, Brother John, on Big Bill and Memphis Minnie, 70; on Memphis Minnie's Blue Monday parties, 56; on Minnie's reputation, 71; on Studs Terkel and Memphis Minnie, 61

Selling My Pork Chops, 39, 191

Set Down Gal (Kokomo Arnold), 155

Seven Sisters, 156

Sewing machine, image of, in blues, 171

Shade, Will, on character of Beale Street, 17

Shake Mattie, 32

Shaw, Robert, 11

She Put Me Outdoors, 184

She Wouldn't Give Me None, 28, 177, 183, 184, 213

Shelley, Percy Bysshe, 231

Shines, Johnny, 37, 67, 113; influence of Memphis Minnie on, 4, 24; on juke joints, 244; on Minnie and Kansas Joe, 24; on Minnie as a youth, 63; on Minnie's drinking, 68; on Minnie's gambling, 45; on Minnie's temper, 15, 69; on National guitars, 30, 244; records *Bumble Bee,* 103

Shout the Boogie, 52

Sidran, Ben, 254

Signifying, 169, 172

Silence, meaning of, 135

Simone, Nina, 99

Sin and a Shame Blues, 46

Sitting on Top of the World (Mississippi Sheiks), 32

Skeeter Blues (Mae Glover), 104

Smith, Bessie, 7, 99, 126, 244, 246; compared to Memphis Minnie, 3, 71, 86; wages of, 10, 242

Smith, J. B., 113

Smith, J. T. "Funny Paper", 113, 156

Smith, Mamie, 9

Smith, Whispering, influence of Memphis Minnie on, 48

Snakes, meaning of, 237, 238

Socket Blues (lyrics), 240

Soft Winds (Benny Goodman, Lionel Hampton), 66

Soo Cow Soo, 191

Sortier, Amanda, 37

Sousoulas, George, 197

Southern cities, racial demographics of, 17

Southern clubs, Palace (Memphis), 76; Red Light (Millington), 77

Southern, Eileen, 87

Special Stream Line (Bukka White), 202

Speckled Red. *See* Rufus Perryman.

Spies, August, 133

Spirituals, as veiled messages of revolt, 137

Spivey, Victoria, 87

Spottswood, Richard, 63

Squat It, 36

"Squirrel" (unidentified pseudonym), 21, 38

St. James Infirmary (traditional song), 25

St. Louis Blues (W. C. Handy), 18

St. Louis Jimmy, 4, 41, 61, 67

Stack O Lee (traditional song), 130

Stackhouse, Houston, influence of Memphis Minnie on, 250

Standing up, as postwar style, 74

Stinging Snake Blues, 27, 234, 235; (lyrics), 237

Stockyard Blues (Floyd Jones), 75

Stokes, Frank, 19, 245

Stranger Blues (traditional blues), 166

Street musicians, as subversive, 116, 187

Street singing, 59, 60, 217

Sunnyland Slim, 4, 24, 27, 44, 53, 54, 66, 67, 70; accompanies Memphis Minnie, 72; on Minnie as song writer, 52; on Minnie's travels, 39

Surrealism, 189, 228, 233; and African social tradition, 96; and blues, 97, 167, 168, 197; as focus for study, 92, 96; importance of streets and alleys in, 123

Sweningsen, Charles, sees Minnie perform, 73

Sykes, Roosevelt, 41, 44, 69, 70, 73, 77; accompanies Memphis Minnie, 54, 72

Sylla, Cheikh Tidiane, on surrealism and African social tradition, 96

Sylvester and His Mule Blues, 15, 35, 253; (lyrics), 252

Take This Hammer (traditional song), 75

Talking blues, 201

Tampa Red, 4, 27, 41, 54, 57, 77, 86; rehearsal hall at house of, 41

Taub, Debra, 177

Taylor, Eddie, 20

Taylor, Hound Dog, on Memphis Minnie, 4

Taylor, Koko, 3

Tears on My Pillow, 50, 167, 229, 243

Temple, Johnny, 243

10 Below Zero (Bobo Jenkins), 221

Terkel, Studs, memorial show for Big Bill Broonzy, 76; on Memphis Minnie, 86

Terrible Operation Blues (Georgia Tom and Jane Lucas), 148

Terry, Sonny, 73, 247

That Will Be Alright, 25, 211

That's Your Yas Yas Yas, 32

Theatre Owner's Booking Association (TOBA), 19

Thomas, Elvie, 11

Thomas, James "Son", on dreams and creativity, 222

Thomas, Rufus, 72, 80

Thornton, Big Mama, influence of Memphis Minnie on, 48, 87

Three Times Seven, 50

Titon, Jeff, on Minnie's reputation, 86

Tonight I Smile with You, 50, 52

Trains, meaning of, 210

Transmutation, 93

Travel, as mental activity and status symbol, 208

Travel blues, meaning in, 213

Tricks Ain't Walking No More, 32, 128; (lyrics), 124

Trost, Dolfi, 233

Trouble in Mind (Richard M. Jones), 57

Tudor, Dean and Nancy, on Minnie's reputation, 86

Turpentine Blues (Will Weldon), 20

Tzara, Tristan, 112

Union. *See* Chicago Federation of Musicians, under Memphis Minnie; and Petrillo, James.

Up the Country Blues (Sippie Wallace), 161

Vinson, Mose, accompanies Memphis Minnie, 40

Vinson, Walter, 23

Vocalion, and field recording, 27; history of, 26; sexist labeling of Minnie and Joe's records, 31

Voodoo, 97, 154, 157, 203, 238; and the use of poisons, 157; as matriarchal, 152; compared to poetry, 153

Walker, James, 72, 77, 78, 79

Walker, Joe Louis, on buying blues records, 247

Walker, Sam, influence of Memphis Minnie on, 186

Walker, T-Bone, 44, compared to Memphis Minnie, 3

Walking and Crying Blues, 233

Wallace, Sippie, 161

Waller, Fats, 173

Walton, Wade, 139; visits Minnie, 84

Wants Cake When I'm Hungry (lyrics), 196

Warren, Baby Boy, 4, 197

Washboard Sam, 4, 37, 41, 66; as Melrose artist, 42

Washerwomen's Association of Atlanta, 241

Wasn't It Sad About Lemon (Walter and Byrd), 48

Watt, James, on blues contests, 59; on Memphis Minnie, 11; on Memphis Minnie's showmanship, 15

WDIA, 78

Weary Woman's Blues, 38

Weaver, Sylvester, wages of, 241-242

Weldon, Casey Bill, 39

What Fault You Find of Me?, 28, 183; (lyrics), 178

What's the Matter with the Mill?, 15, 31, 32, 68, 140, 184, 188, 191; (lyrics), 184

What's the Matter with the Mill? (Charlie Burse, The Heartfixers, Bob Wills), 186, 187

Wheatstraw, Peetie, 27, 77, 86, 127, influence of on 1930s sound, 42

When My Dreamboat Comes Home (popular song), 66

When My Man Comes Home, 52

When the Levee Breaks, 22, 25

When the Sun Goes Down, Part 2, 39

Where Is My Good Man?, 135

Whistling, 202, 203

White Citizens Council, 144

White, Washington ("Bukka White"), 29, 84; on Memphis Minnie, 4, 87; sings "talking blues," 202; wages of, 242

Whitman, Walt, 131

Whittaker, Pee Wee, accompanies Memphis Minnie, 20

Why Don't You Do Right? (Harlem Hamfats), 37

Wiggins, James "Boodle It," influence of Memphis Minnie on, 213

Wiggins, Phil, on buying blues records, 247

Wild woman, image of, 183

Wild Women Don't Have the Blues (Ida Cox), 183

Wiley, Geeshie, 11

Wilkins, Joe Willie, accompanies Memphis Minnie, 78

Wilkins, Robert, 19, 245

Williams, Big Joe, 41, 77, 222, influence of Memphis Minnie on, 250

Williams, Clarence, 242

Williams, Fred, 47

Williams, J. Mayo, 26; as Minnie's manager, 66

Williamson, Sonny Boy (John Lee Williamson), 41, 50, 60, 70; influence on Little Walter and Snooky Pryor, 43

Williamson, Sonny Boy (Rice Miller), 254; accompanies Memphis Minnie, 78; plays for King Biscuit Time, 78

Willie the Weeper (torch song), 25

Wills, Bob, influence of Memphis Minnie on, 4, 187, 199

Witch, compared to blueswoman, 153

Witchcraft, 152, 154

WLOK, 80

Women, as mourners, 227; as symbolic of the repressed, 238

Women as listeners to blues records, 247

Women Prostitutes of Lyon Speak to the People, 128

Women's Suffrage Movement, 203

Woolf, Virginia, 228

Work, as non-musical activity, 254

World of Trouble, 67, 218; (lyrics), 220

Yellow Bee (Bertha Lee), 103

Yellow Dog Blues (W. C. Handy), 18

You Can't Give It Away, 35, 140, 172, 188; (lyrics), 129
You Dirty Mistreater, 32
You Don't See Into the Blues Like Me (Lonnie Johnson), 251
You Gonna Look Like a Monkey (Smokey Hogg), 172
You Got To Move (You Ain't Got To Move), 35, 36

You One Black Rat (Eddie Kirkland), 78
You Ought To Move Out of Town (Jed Davenport), 28
You Stole My Cake, 31, 140, 184, 191, 235
You Wrecked My Happy Home, 38